DANGEROUS PURSUITS
MEDIUMSHIP, MIND, AND MUSIC

STEPHEN E. BRAUDE

ANOMALIST BOOKS
*San Antonio * Charlottesville*

Chapter 1, which appeared in the *ASPR Newsletter* 28, No. 1 (1993): 8-11, has been expanded substantially for this book.

Chapters 2 and 3 are revised versions of reports that originally appeared in the *Journal of Scientific Exploration* (JSE): vol. 28 (2) (2014): 285-343 and vol. 30 (1) (2016): 27-55.

Chapter 4 appeared first in the *JSE*: vol. 31 (3) (2017): 435-356.

Chapter 5 is loosely based on a book review that originally appeared in the *Journal of the Society for Psychical Research* vol. 53 (1985): 40-46.

Chapter 6 is based on material from my book *The Limits of Influence: Psychokinesis and the Philosophy of Science*, Revised Edition. Lanham, MD: University Press of America, 1997, but that material has been considerably revised and expanded.

Chapter 7 originally appeared in A.J. Rock (Ed.), *The Survival Hypothesis: Essays on Mediumship* Jefferson, NC: McFarland, 2014: 21-39.

Chapter 8 is a slightly revised version of the essay that appeared in *JSE*: vol. 23 (2009): 195-210.

Chapter 9 is a substantially expanded version of an essay that appeared in *JSE*: vol. 12 (1998): 141-150

Chapter 10 is a considerably revised and expanded version of an essay that appeared in *Transactions of the Charles S. Peirce Society* vol. 34 (1998): 199-220

Chapter 11 is a moderately revised version of an essay that appeared in my book *First Person Plural: Multiple Personality and the Philosophy of Mind* (Rev. ed.). Lanham, MD: Rowman & Littlefield, 1995

Chapter 12 is an expanded and otherwise tweaked version of a paper that appeared originally in *International Jazz Archives Journal* vol. 1, No. 2 (1994): 4-13.

For information about the publisher, go to AnomalistBooks.com, or write to:
Anomalist Books, 5150 Broadway #108, San Antonio, TX 78209

In memory of Jon Braude

Table of Contents

Preface

Probably every author knows that refining a manuscript is a process that can continue indefinitely unless it's halted by a spasm of sanity, At least *published* authors know this. They know that at some point they must say "enough" and send their creations out into the world, to be either savored, reviled, or ignored. That's both the joy and the anguish of deadlines. Now I don't know how often published authors later, and with a fresh perspective, get the opportunity for a do-over—for yet another chance to express themselves more clearly or elegantly, or to make other changes that have come to seem mandatory, such as adding, excluding, or moving chunks of text. I had that good fortune several years ago,* and now I have it again, this time collecting different material which I believe deserves continued or expanded exposure, and which I again hope I've succeeded in improving, not only in substance and style, but also in accessibility.

The title of this collection, *Dangerous Pursuits*, is a wry allusion to my obstacle-strewn career path over the past several decades—to the vindictive hostility, ridicule, and condescension I've encountered (both inside and outside the academy) for my decision to look carefully at the data and theoretical issues of parapsychology. I've discussed elsewhere how that career decision affected me professionally, and I needn't review the details again here. I'll just note that pursuing the paranormal in an academic environment is not for the timid, no matter how responsibly and carefully it's conducted. And it certainly won't put one on a fast track to professional success or prominence—that is, unless one becomes a vocal skeptic (or debunker). *That's* a career move much more likely to enhance one's celebrity. I should also add that I was fortunate (not smart) enough to make my fateful career choice *after* earning tenure. That allowed me to see clearly how the privilege of tenure can at least sometimes work as intended. Granted, some people abuse that privilege and treat it as an invitation to indolence. But for those interested in pursuing controversial areas of inquiry, tenure really can provide a precious (though still limited) measure

---

* Braude, S.E. (2014). *Crimes of Reason: On Mind, Nature & the Paranormal.* Lanham, MD: Rowman & Littlefield.

of academic freedom.

So as far as my academic audience is concerned, I'm confident that intrepid senior faculty can inspect these essays with impunity. Of course, I also hope they'll be read and enjoyed by untenured junior faculty and beleaguered students, although those two groups should perhaps read the book only in the privacy of their bunkers. I feel especially sorry for students who too often suffer at the hands of dogmatic mentors for naively expressing an interest in the paranormal, expecting their intellectual curiosity to be respected rather than derided and punished. Untenured faculty should simply know to keep their academically-incorrect interests to themselves until they've successfully demonstrated their competence in mainstream scholarly activities.

And of course, I also hope this book will interest those fortunate enough to have avoided the nastiness of university politics. To that end I've tweaked the prose of all the essays to make them somewhat more informal and accessible, and more similar in style and tone than they were before. Furthermore, although the individual essays are self-contained (as they were originally), now they often connect with and reinforce each other in a way that wouldn't have been discernible in their previous and widely scattered incarnations. Moreover, much of my newly-added material helps to fortify those connections between the essays.

Now although I've crafted most of the chapters to be accessible (and hopefully of interest) to the general public, a few chapters will perhaps be of greatest interest to more veteran or advanced readers already somewhat drenched in the minutiae of the relevant data and issues. But even there, I've tried to explain, for the benefit of a wider readership, why the minutiae matter. In any case, it shouldn't be surprising that here, as in many areas of life, the devil is in the details.

The essays that follow represent many of my post-tenure research interests. But their main focus is the topic of mediumship—both mental and physical. Of course, that topic overlaps several other major themes in parapsychology— perhaps most conspicuously, the evidence for postmortem survival and the unsettling question of the limits of paranormal influence. Most of the essays in this book either address those issues at length or at least touch on them briefly. In other respects, however, the chapters are fairly diverse. There are contemporary case investigations, historical essays, conceptual and terminological clarifications, philosophical speculations, and more. And the chapters are pretty evenly balanced between those that are largely empirical and those that are more theoretical.

Chapter 1, "The Fear of Psi," introduces a theme that appears again in several other chapters—namely, the disquieting (if not terrifying) ramifications of positing the existence of paranormal (psi) phenomena, and how those implications might have profoundly influenced both the resistance to psi research and also the manner in which psi phenomena manifest in life.

The next four chapters deal with the topic of physical mediumship. Chapters 2 and 3 are reports of my hands-on studies, between 2010 and 2015, of the prominent physical medium Kai Mügge and his Felix Experimental Group (FEG). This was work that yielded some tantalizing, and often quite compelling, evidence of macro-PK (psychokinetic influence on observable objects), but also revelations of at least occasional cheating, which of course complicates the assessment of the case as a whole. Nevertheless, I believe there's a residue of phenomena from the FEG that can't reasonably be attributed to conjuring or malobservation.

Chapter 4 is a slightly revised survey of the career and phenomena of the Brazilian spiritist Carlos Mirabelli, arguably the most astounding physical medium of all time. Mirabelli's case is also marred by some clear cheating and otherwise suspicious phenomena. But the best-controlled accounts are astonishing, and also very difficult to dismiss. So this chapter might serve as a particularly good test of one's boggle threshold.

Chapter 5, "A Case Study in Shoddy Skepticism," is loosely based on my highly critical review of Trevor Hall's 1984 book, *The Enigma of Daniel Home*. I include it in this collection for several reasons: first, because I raise the subject of Home's mediumship, approvingly, in many of the other essays; second, because contrary to what Hall alleges, Home's phenomena are often very well documented—in fact, some of the best-documented in the history of psi research; and third, because Hall's intellectually corrupt appraisal of the case could easily mislead unwary readers. So, since people continue to read and cite Hall's book, I consider it important to expose and clarify his dishonest rhetorical strategies and to warn others that the book is merely a piece of dialectical sludge. And along the way, the chapter provides additional impressive examples of Home's reported mediumistic accomplishments.

The next three chapters are largely theoretical essays about mediumship (both mental and physical) and also the extent or limits of paranormal influence. Chapter 6, "Reflections on Super Psi," is an examination of the claim that some parapsychological evidence, and even some seemingly humdrum features of daily life, might be best explained by appealing to a degree or kind of psychic functioning that's substantially more impressive or extreme than what we apparently find in the lab. The essay tries to clarify the super-psi hypothesis, and it also takes a critical look at familiar but flawed objections to positing extreme manifestations of psi.

Chapter 7, "Making Sense of Mental Mediumship," is a somewhat revised and expanded survey of the main issues involved in assessing the evidence for postmortem survival. It focuses in particular on the seemingly intractable problem of deciding between the survivalist and living-agent psi interpretations of the data. And it also addresses the issue of the extent to which metaphysical presuppositions should be allowed to bias our appraisal of the evidence.

Chapter 8, "Can the Deceased Have a Perceptual Point of View?," deals with a peculiar feature of mental mediumship—namely, that ostensibly discarnate communicators often respond appropriately to and correctly describe what's currently going on in the physical world. But since *by hypothesis* those communicators have no physical body to provide a perceptual point of view, survivalists need to explain how postmortem awareness and knowledge of the current physical world can occur without an organism that experiences the world and represents it accurately enough to ground veridical postmortem reports. I argue that the best answer to that question may ironically weaken the case for survival.

Chapter 9, "A Grumpy Guide to Parapsychology's Terminological Blunders," examines some modern attempts to replace a familiar—but allegedly politically or professionally toxic—parapsychological vocabulary with terms the psi-squeamish might be less likely to consider signs of voodoo science. I argue that these efforts are massively confused and inadequate, and also (as if that weren't enough) unsophisticated empirically. This chapter includes discussion of an issue about which many have expressed concern—namely, whether telepathy poses a threat to mental privacy.

I hope that Chapter 10, "A Peircing Examination of the Paranormal," is not one that only a philosopher could love. I wrote a distant ancestor of it for a relatively small set of professional philosophers, but I wrote this extensive revision to be friendlier and more pertinent to the general reader. The chapter surveys the previously unexplored and intriguing parapsychological writings of a towering intellect, Charles Sanders Peirce, the founder of American Pragmatism. Although Peirce wasn't as active in psi research or theorizing as his better-known colleague William James, he was an exceptionally important figure in philosophy, science, mathematics and logic, and no mere parapsychological dilettante. And he had much of interest to say about various types of parapsychological evidence. So although there's plenty of material here for those already interested in Peirce, there's also an opportunity for newcomers to this genius to become acquainted with a very interesting mind.

Chapter 11, "Multiple Personality and the Structure of the Self," deals with a flawed principle that undergirds some familiar theorizing about both dissociative phenomena and the occasionally peculiar results of brain bisection. I call it the *Principle of Compositional Reversibility*, and it asserts (very roughly) that splitting of the personality (or self) into parts reveals an underlying pre-dissociative structure of the self that made those post-dissociative divisions possible. In its strongest form this CR-principle claims that dissociation *reverses* earlier processes leading to pre-dissociative functional organization or unity. I examine the problems with this position and argue that it commits what I call the *Humpty Dumpty Fallacy*. I then consider the more modest ways in which dissociation sheds light on the nature of the self.

The final Chapter, "The Language of Jazz Improvisation," is clearly the outlier in this collection. I encourage you to think of it as a light dessert after a relatively heavy meal. As some readers probably know, I've had an existence and identity parallel to my life as an academic—namely, as a jazz pianist. Granted, it's something of a stretch to consider that side of my life a dangerous pursuit (at least if you ignore several of the venues in which I've performed). But it certainly didn't offer the job security I enjoyed in my tenured academic post. By contrast, my musical gigs were jobs I could easily be fired from. Not that this happened…at least not often. But the possibility of losing the gig always hung over the members of the band, like the equally disconcerting and insulting feeling that we were sometimes little more than sonic wallpaper for many of the patrons.

Anyway, I include this piece because, frankly, I still believe it's worthwhile, and besides, there should always be room for dessert. Nathan Davis, an outstanding saxophonist and the original editor of the *International Jazz Archives Journal*, invited me to write it for one of the publication's inaugural issues. I'd like to think the essay merits wider exposure. I know it addresses an issue that many jazz audiences have confronted. Hopefully, that issue will also interest the somewhat different audience for this book. In fact, for this incarnation of my essay, I've added a section on a possible parapsychological dimension to the topic.

Finally, I'd like to thank Patrick Huyghe, of Anomalist Books, for supporting my decision to prepare this do-over, for his discerning and thorough editorial guidance with my revisions and additions, and more generally for his support of my work over the years. I'm also very happy to share the blame for this project.

1. The Fear of Psi

Humble Beginnings

The year was 1968, and I was in graduate school, working toward my Ph.D. in philosophy. I had no interest in parapsychology at the time, and to the extent I had any solid philosophical views at all, I fancied myself to be a kind of hardnosed materialist. That wasn't because of any careful, sustained thought I'd given to the subject (although of course I knew some of the relevant literature). It was mostly just a bit of semicritical intellectual posturing, something which I felt suited the person I believed I ought to be, probably (I'm ashamed to admit) because it's what my mentors urged that I ought to be.

At any rate, it was a slow afternoon in Northampton, Massachusetts (as most afternoons in Northampton were apt to be), and two close friends stopped by my house, just to hang out. Since we'd already seen the one movie in town and could think of nothing else to do, my friends suggested that we hold a séance (they considered it to be a game called "table-up"). They said they'd done this several times before and that when it worked it was great fun. Although I was somewhat underwhelmed at the proposal and suspicious of their prediction that the table would move without normal assistance, I went along with it and accepted my friends as instructors in the game of table-up. We used a small folding table that I owned and placed our fingers lightly upon its surface, concentrating silently on the command (and sometimes muttering softly), "table-up!" For about 20 minutes, nothing happened. Then to my astonishment, for the next three hours the table tilted and nodded in response to questions, spelling out answers according to a naively cumbersome code my friends had recommended: nodding once for the letter *A*, twice for *B*, and so on. The three of us were blissfully unaware that veteran spiritists used a better method: asking yes/no questions and having a table nod (or rap) once for "yes" and twice for "no."

Despite our naïve methodology, we apparently contacted three different entities, only one of which provided information it seemed possible to confirm. That communicator claimed to be someone named Horace T. Jecum (the spelling may well have been botched in the process of implementing our awkward code), and he claimed to have built the house where I was living (a classic

1

and quite old New England-style home, built some time toward the end of the eighteenth century). Compared to the assertions made by the earlier "communicators" (especially the one claiming implausibly to be the mythical River Styx), I figured that this apparent piece of information should be easy enough to confirm; all I had to do was to check the records at City Hall. Unfortunately, it turned out that my house was so old that it antedated the city records. So I never found out who built the house, much less whether the person's name was anything like that of Horace T. Jecum. I also recall trying unsuccessfully to discover whether someone with a name like Horace T. Jecum had lived in or near the area. But I'm certain that my additional inquiries (such as they were) were no more than perfunctory. I made no intensive effort to pursue the matter further and seriously challenge my philosophical complacency. I ended my inquiry at that point.

Of course, quite apart from the information allegedly conveyed by means of table tilting, there remained the peculiar fact *that* the table tilted for three hours. I doubt that I could describe the event so as to quell all skeptical concerns. However, I will say that I'm personally convinced that my friends weren't playing a trick on me. It was my table—not a prop; it was daylight; we were not under the influence of either legal or illicit substances; I knew my friends well, and they weren't given to practical jokes; the phenomena occurred for a long time, allowing ample opportunity for inspection; I'm convinced that nothing but our fingers touched the table and that they rested lightly on its surface; and finally, even when one of my friends left the table to go to another room, the table continued to tilt and spell out answers to questions, rising *under* the fingers of the two remaining sitters. And it did that even when we were standing beside the table, quite obviously not lifting it with our knees.

So I was plenty impressed by the phenomena but nevertheless happy enough to postpone dealing with it philosophically until I'd taken care of some grubby practical concerns—in particular, earning my Ph.D., landing a job, publishing some respectable mainstream philosophy, and then getting tenure (I may be crazy, but I'm not stupid). Because I knew that my mentors and colleagues would, for the most part, adopt a supercilious and condescending attitude toward an interest in psychic stuff, I simply put the whole matter on the back burner for about eight years—actually, putting it out of mind—until (as a tenured professor) I had what I naively thought would be the academic freedom to pursue whatever philosophical research I wanted.[1]

2

An Unknown Fear

Now, although the physical phenomenon of table tilting is undoubtedly interesting, what intrigues me just as much about that episode in my life is my immediate visceral reaction to what I observed. Not only did I experience alternating blasts of skepticism, puzzlement, and curiosity, but the table movements scared the hell out of me. That's undoubtedly one reason I didn't pursue the Horace T. Jecum incident more thoroughly. But why should I have felt such an intense fear? I didn't understand my reaction at the time (although, characteristically, I was at no loss for inadequate hypotheses). Now, however, I think I might have a clue as to what was going on, and if I'm right, it helps explain certain outstanding peculiar features of both the evidence for, and the literature about, PK, as well as some distinctive behaviors of both skeptics and partisans of psi research.

It's tempting to account for my reaction by appealing simply to the fear of the unknown. But that won't get us very far. There are lots of unknown things that don't scare us at all. So what was it, *specifically*, that frightened me? Of course, on the surface at least, it appeared that something other than the three people in the room caused the table to move. So perhaps I was afraid of the possibility of discarnate agency. But why should that have been frightening? Granted, I might have recognized that the table movements were *ostensibly* produced by a discarnate agent, but that doesn't mean I took that option seriously. Although I'm hardly certain of this, I may well have been too blindly and thoroughly entrenched in my few philosophical conceits for the possibility of discarnate influence ever to have been a live option in my mind, even unconsciously. In any case (and more important), since that time there have been other contexts in which I've genuinely suspended my customary philosophical prejudices—I've actually gotten quite good at this--and allowed myself to entertain seriously the possibility that discarnate surviving personalities were influencing events around me. For example, I did that often during the several years I spent getting to know the healer Olga Worrall. But at no time did I ever experience fear in connection with the phenomena I observed.

I recognize, of course, that the very possibility of postmortem agency raises the specter of hostility and revenge from beyond the grave, just as a matter of principle. If we can influence the world at all after our bodily death, clearly that influence can be either positive or negative. Nevertheless, my guess is that the potential threat of discarnate influence is simply not as deeply intimidating as another possibility—namely, that one or more of those present in the room psychokinetically—and unconsciously—caused the table to move. Although

I'm sure I didn't clearly grasp this point at the time (that is, in the informed way I now recognize it, after many years of thinking about the issues and their implications), I'm also certain that I wasn't entirely oblivious to it. After all, I may not have given any serious thought in those days to parapsychology, but it's not as though I was totally ignorant of the *concept* of psychokinesis.

Still, why should *that* have been frightening? What's so scary about PK among the living? In some of my other works and elsewhere in the literature, interested readers can find more or less elaborate answers to that question.[2] For now, however, an abbreviated tease will have to do. The crucial point, I think, is this. It takes almost no conceptual leap to connect the possibility of innocuous psychokinetic object movements with other, far more unsettling, applications of PK. Whether we acknowledge it consciously or not, if we can make a pencil, cigarette, or table move, even just a little bit, by means of PK, and if (as many believe) we can heal a person simply through our intention to do so, then in principle you'd think we should be able to do such things as cause auto accidents, heart attacks, or merely annoying pains and tickles in another person. It's a very small step conceptually from the former to the latter.

Moreover, given our current (and considerable) state of our ignorance concerning psychic functioning, we're simply in no position to suppose that occurrences of psi must always be of small or moderate scale. In fact, we have no idea at all just how refined or large-scale psi might be. But quite apart from that issue, there's no reason to think that car or airplane crashes, heart attacks, and so forth, require more (or more refined) PK than that required for small object movements. Clearly, events of small magnitude can have extensive consequences. For example, a car crash (say) could be caused, in principle, by a well-placed small-scale psychic nudge (such as a ruptured fuel line). Thus, there seems no escaping the conclusion that if PK can be triggered by unconscious intentions, then we might be responsible for a range of events (in particular, accidents and other calamities) for which most of us would prefer merely to be innocent bystanders. Moreover, we'd all be potential victims of psychically triggered events (intentional or otherwise) whose sources we couldn't conclusively identify and whose limitations we couldn't assess.

And many, quite reasonably, find that to be genuinely scary. That's because it forces us to entertain seriously a world view which most of us associate, usually condescendingly, only with socalled primitive societies. It's a magical picture of reality according to which people can interfere with others' lives in all sorts of ways we'd prefer to be impossible. Of course, some of these interactions might be beneficial; but what scares us, I believe, is the threat of psychic snooping, telepathic influence, and potent malevolent uses of PK (such as the "evil eye" and hexing). Granted, there are places in the world where beliefs of that sort are quite common and are treated as a matter of course. But this picture of reality doesn't sit very well in most developed countries.

In fact, over several decades of public lectures, I've had many opportunities to see how much distress I cause when I simply raise the issue with my audiences. Significantly, that reaction has been especially intense at various New Age conventions where attendees focus exclusively on the potential benefits of psychic influence, apparently refusing to acknowledge the obvious point that no power can be used only for the good. I must confess, I've found it mischievously satisfying on those occasions to play the role of spokesperson for the Dark Side. With gratifying regularity, I've sent some in my audience home in tears.

Another kind of revealing episode is the reception I received when I spoke to my university's physics department on my work in parapsychology. I had a good-sized audience of faculty and grad students, and I assumed that because I'd been invited to speak, they actually wanted to know what I was up to. But about two minutes into my talk I mentioned that I studied various ostensible manifestations of PK (including my table-up experience). And that unleashed a torrent of outrage from several faculty who went through the all too familiar routine of insisting that it could only be fraud, that there was no credible evidence from the lab or elsewhere, and so on. Of course, I'd seen this dance many times. I knew these professors were just posturing and bluffing, feigning knowledge of the evidence, and it would have been easy to expose them—if I'd only had the chance. But I was simply prevented from going on with my presentation. Various faculty continued to vie for their turn to condemn me—for example, by noting stupidly how the Amazing Randi had shown once and for all that apparent PK was a fraud.

Of course, what's so striking about the behavior of these faculty members is that their reaction was wildly disproportionate to my supposed offense, not only in the intensity of their response, but also in their willingness to pretend to speak authoritatively on a matter about which they knew (and knew they knew!) almost nothing, and in the ease with which they resorted to lame or sleazy dialectical tactics (such as generalizing from the weakest cases) whose flaws they'd clearly identify and protest if they'd been the targets of the attacks themselves.

Interestingly, one distinguished member of the department, from China, came to my defense and pointed out that there'd been some respectable and relevant work in his homeland on chi gong. Moreover, several of the grad students came up to me afterwards and apologized for the behavior of their mentors. They expressed their regrets at being prevented from hearing my presentation, and they assured me they were interested and asked for advice on what to read. So the event wasn't without moments of gratification.

I should also note that psi researchers aren't the only ones singled out for fear-based ignorant and irrational scorn, targeted for what in fact should be seen as a laudable expression of intellectual curiosity. Students also pay a price. I hear this frequently from young audience members at invited talks and in unsolicited letters and emails. In fact, many of my own students have told me that their mentors (usually, in the psychology department) threatened them with reprisals, or at least lavished on them the sort of ridicule I've often encountered, simply because they declared their intention to take my seminar in philosophy and parapsychology. However, most of those students merely wanted the opportunity to study the material and make up their own minds about it. I know this; I taught them and saw how critical and curious they could be, and how most didn't enter the class with their minds made up one way or the other about what was going on. Their behavior was much more commendable than that of their mentors.

Interestingly, it's not just parapsychological outsiders who exhibit the fear of psi. Most (or at least many) parapsychologists nowadays will concede that the fear exists even within their ranks. In fact, even if they don't admit it openly or display it flagrantly, parapsychologists have more subtle ways of betraying that fear. As psychiatrist and psi researcher Jule Eisenbud persuasively argued, one way laboratory psi researchers exhibit the fear is by means of seemingly innocent or careless mistakes, oversights, and omissions that undermine an experiment.[3] Eisenbud viewed these missteps as analogous to apparently innocent slips of the tongue, bits of behavior that reveal thoughts and feelings of which the speaker may not be consciously aware.

But perhaps an even more interesting manifestation of the fear of psi is a widespread kind of "methodological piety," in which researchers exhibit "… endless pseudoscientific fussiness and obsessional piddling, which, as often as not, results in never getting anything done unless under conditions that virtually strangulate the emergence of anything faintly resembling a psi occurrence."[4] To put it another way, some researchers manage to make experiments so complicated and artificial that they snuff out all manifestations of psi except, apparently, enough to be significant at the .05 level (that is, only marginally significant according to the standard prevailing in the behavioral sciences).

That's still sufficient to merit publishing a paper, and it helps researchers to feel successful and to justify their work within the field generally. But it's not enough to seriously challenge a possibly deeper wish that psi simply doesn't occur.

Varieties of Denial

But what's arguably more interesting still is the reaction of parapsychologists—or, rather, lack of reaction—to the infrequent studies of hypnosis at a distance. Distant influence over others' thoughts has been reported anecdotally since ancient times. And in modern times there have been some very respectable studies of the phenomenon.[5] But, due no doubt to the frightening implications of telepathic mind-control, psi researchers have pursued a rigorous hands-off policy. In fact, parapsychologists have typically pursued other much less potentially significant lines of research instead. And they've certainly made no effort to replicate the studies—something they do sedulously for less interesting phenomena.[6]

Another (and related) striking manifestation of the fear of psi is the way that fear apparently shaped the course of parapsychology around the turn of the twentieth century. Skeptics often like to sneer that dramatic paranormal physical phenomena, such as full table levitations and materializations, seem to have disappeared from the parapsychological scene. The main reason, they often charge, is that modern technology has simply made it too difficult to get away with the fraud that was more easily perpetrated in the late nineteenth and early twentieth centuries, and that this why most physical mediums today refuse to submit to serious controls. But even though that position is often promulgated as an obvious piece of received wisdom, a moment's reflection reveals it to be clearly defective—if not simply foolish. Often, it demonstrates such a grossly superficial command of the data and issues that one can only wonder why proponents of this view would risk embarrassment by flaunting their ignorance in print.

Without going into the whole matter here,[7] we should note, first, that the skeptic's appeal to modern technology is double-edged. Turn-of-the-century technological primitiveness affected not only the means for detecting fraud, but also the means for producing it. Similarly, today's advanced technology has made possible a range of both fraudulent practices and snooping devices that couldn't have been employed during the heyday of Spiritualism. Just as there were no small electrical devices (such as miniature video cameras) in the late 1800s capable of catching fraudulent mediums in the act, there were also no similar devices capable of producing the largescale phenomena under controlled conditions for which we have good evidence. Forget about those phenomena explainable, in principle, by means of sleight of hand and diversion techniques. Skeptics often like to focus on those cases, but they're relatively unimportant, if not totally irrelevant to a proper assessment of the evidence for observable PK. What really matters is that there's a substantial residue of phenomena produced under conditions in which no accomplice or device could have been concealed, some of which even today's technology can't produce. Consider, for example, the late nineteenth-century medium D.D. Home's materialized hands. They were warm, mobile, and solid enough to carry objects around; sitters could poke a hole in them which would then "heal;" and (unlike stuffed gloves) rather than being retracted into a hiding place in the medium's clothing, they would dissolve in sitters' grasp.

One of my favorite examples concerns Home's accordion phenomena. Many observers reported that Home was able to make accordions play either untouched or when held at the end away from the keys. In fact, sometimes the accordions were said to play melodies on request. Now, Home preferred to have the accordion do its thing under the séance table, because he said the "power" was strongest there. Obviously, that could easily be regarded as suspicious. But to a more generous or openminded investigator, it might simply indicate Home's sincere and idiosyncratic beliefs about the workings of psi. The renowned scientist William Crookes fell into that latter category, although he also realized why others might, quite reasonably, be concerned about phenomena that the medium preferred to produce under the table. So instead of taking a glibly dismissive attitude toward Home's avowed beliefs, Crookes devised a way to test Home's accordion phenomena while still allowing him to remain more or less within his apparent comfort zone.

First, Crookes bought a new accordion for the occasion; clearly, then it wasn't Home's own instrument, nor one he had an opportunity to tamper with beforehand. Second, Crookes picked Home up at his apartment and watched him change clothes. That allowed him to determine that Home wasn't concealing a device capable of producing the phenomena (although because this was in the early 1870s, it's unclear what such a device could have been). Crookes then took Home to his house, where he'd built a special cage for the accordion, constructed out of wood and wire. The cage fit under Crookes' dining room table, and there was only enough space above it for Home to reach in and hold the accordion at the end away from the keys. There was not enough room for Home to reach down further and manipulate the instrument and its keyboard.

Nine observers were present, all of them members of the Royal Society. One of them was stationed on each side of Home, to make sure his feet remained in his boots, and another went under the table with a lamp in order to observe the accordion closely. Under those conditions, observers reported that the accordion expanded and contracted, that the keys were depressed, and that sounds came from the instrument. Crookes then instructed Home to remove his hand from the cage and place both hands on the table, at which point Crookes ran an electric current through the cage. However, the untouched accordion still flopped about inside it.[8]

I consider this to be one of the most important experiments in the history of parapsychology. No one has succeeded—or even tried—duplicating this phenomenon under conditions similar to those imposed on Home—and for good reason.

So if skeptics don't simply ignore Crookes's accordion test, how do Home-detractors deal with it? Consider the strategy adopted by parapsychologist, magician, and historian Peter Lamont.[9] Lamont's book on Home purports to provide a lengthy, detailed, and relatively agnostic examination of Home's career and the evidence for his phenomena. Still, Lamont manages to avoid presenting the accordion test as a compelling and pivotal piece of evidence. He does this by describing the test only very cursorily, omitting relevant details, and getting others wrong. And then he barely discusses the matter thereafter.

For example, Lamont fails to mention that Crookes went to Home's apartment and watched him change clothes. And he gives an inaccurate description of the material out of which Crookes's cage was constructed. Lamont also claims that Home removed the accordion from the cage, when in fact it was his hand that he removed (which of course makes the event much more impressive). And nine witnesses were present for the test, not four, as Lamont claims. Equally disappointing, when Lamont suggests various (frequently highly implausible) ways in which Home might have faked the materialization of warm, mobile, fleshy spirit hands that ended at the wrist, he conveniently ignores aspects of the accounts that are likely to be most problematical for the debunker. These include reports that although the spirit hands had been solid enough to transport objects around the room and for sitters to shake hands with them, they then melted or dissolved in sitters' grasp. I don't believe even present-day technology can duplicate that phenomenon.

In any case, I find it especially interesting that Lamont omits and misrepresents some details of Crookes's accordion experiment and its setup, especially since he purports to write with an historian's obsessive care and respect for details. These might appear to be relatively innocent oversights or bits of carelessness. But why would they occur in connection with what is surely one of the most important tests in Home's career (arguably *the* most important)? To me, it gives the appearance of avoidance behavior, of not wanting to look squarely at the material that matters most. Perhaps, in fact, it's a not-too-subtle example of the easily avoidable errors and misjudgments, noted by Eisenbud, that often indicate resistance to and fear of psi. Significantly, as in other (and more overtly tawdry) criticisms of Home (such as the Trevor Hall book described in Chapter 5), Lamont spends a disproportionate amount of time discussing poorly documented reports, including Home's alleged levitation out the window of Ashley House.

Nevertheless, the fact remains (as skeptics like to note), we no longer see such things as Home's accordion and other phenomena. But if we can't explain that fact by appealing to the advent of modern technology (or to a greater degree of gullibility around the turn of the century), what sense can we make of it? I want to suggest that the fear of psi has probably played a major role.

To see this, we should note first that the dramatic PK occurring around the turn of the twentieth-century took place within the context of the Spiritualist movement, which was enormously popular at the time, and which gave rise to the widespread practice of holding séances around a table for the purpose of contacting deceased friends and relatives. Furthermore, the great mediums of that era were all sincere spiritists. That is, they believed that they were merely facilitating phenomena produced by discarnate spirits; they didn't believe they actually produced the phenomena themselves. But that means that those individuals were off the hook psychologically no matter what happened. For example, if nothing (or only boring phenomena) occurred, the medium could always attribute the failures to an inept communicator or to a "bad connection" between this world and the spirit world. But more important, when impressive phenomena did occur, mediums didn't have to fear the extent of their own powers. They didn't have to worry about what psychokinetic havoc they might wreak (consciously or unconsciously) outside the safe confines of the séance room.

As time went on, more and more people, both in and out of the field of psychical research, took seriously the possibility that physical mediums might in fact be PK agents and therefore the actual cause of phenomena attributed by others to surviving spirits. And even when the mediums and other spiritists resisted this belief, the fact remains that the belief was increasingly "in the air" and difficult to ignore as growing numbers of secular researchers began to investigate the phenomena for themselves. But this can only have had a chilling effect on the psychology of mediumship generally. Mediums knew that even some sympathetic investigators considered them to be causes of—and not simply vessels for—paranormal physical phenomena. So they now had a concern that quite possibly had never entered their minds before—namely, that they might have powers they couldn't control and that conceivably could do great harm.

It's not surprising, then, to find that Eusapia Palladino's impressive phenomena in the 1890s and first decade of the twentieth century were less impressive than those of Home twenty years earlier.[10] And it's even less surprising to find that many of the mediumistic "superstars" in the next several decades of the twentieth century had increasingly less intimidating repertoires of phenomena. For example, by the time we come to Rudi Schneider in the 1920s and 30s, the most sensational phenomena tended merely to be medium-sized object movements. And more recently, alleged PK superstars such as Nina Kulagina and Felicia Parise produced even smaller-scale phenomena.[11]

Moreover, it's interesting to note how PK superstars in the latter half of the twentieth century seemed to *suffer* greatly when producing their phenomena. Their spiritistic predecessors typically went into a trance or at least into a state of passive receptivity, and occasionally they were tired afterwards. But more modern PK stars have more thoroughly accepted their role as the originator of their physical manifestations, and they seem quite clearly to be making a conscious effort to achieve those results. But of course, since they acknowledge their own role in the production of the phenomena, it's not surprising that they should have to work so hard (say) to make a cigarette or pill bottle move a millimeter or an inch. In fact, consider how convenient effortful PK is psychologically—that is, from the psychic's point of view. If PK subjects feel it's necessary to expend a great deal of energy to produce only a small effect, then (in a careless line of thought characteristic of much self deception) it can easily seem to them as if their life or health would be endangered by trying to produce a phenomenon worth worrying about.

Bad Reasoning and Bad Behavior

I can't let the topic of the fear of psi drop without noting again another of its apparent and (to me at least) striking manifestations, one that's as common today as it was during the heyday of spiritualism. I'm referring to what I described earlier, concerning my attempted presentation to the University of

Maryland Baltimore County physics department. It continues to amaze me how carelessly and unscrupulously otherwise smart and honest people argue against the existence of psi generally and its more dramatic manifestations in particular. There are, of course, careful, courageous, and reflective critics of the field. But too often critics resort easily to lines of argument they'd be quick to detect as dishonest or indefensible in other contexts—for example, if those arguments had been used against *them*. In fact, it's almost as if a veil of idiocy suddenly descends on those who are otherwise penetrating and intelligent. In my view, it's unlikely that parapsychological skeptics would resort so easily to *ad hominem* and straw man arguments in most other contexts. But that's precisely what dominates large chunks of the skeptical literature.

In the case of *ad hominem* arguments, we find career parapsychological skeptic Trevor Hall spending a considerable portion of his small book on D.D. Home trying to establish the medium's vanity (relying in part on testimony from someone whose lies about Home had been well-established) and worrying equally irrelevantly about whether Home had an affair with one of his benefactors. And we find the skeptical writer Ruth Brandon speculating on the possibility that Home might have been homosexual. (I'll have much more to say about Hall's book in Chapter 5.)[12] And as for straw man arguments (that is, generalizing from the weakest cases), quite often one finds skeptics arguing, say, that the case of Home should be ignored because the medium's small-scale phenomena might be mimicked by sleight of hand, or because the most poorly documented bits of evidence (such as Home's alleged levitation out the window at Ashley House) are weak. Now are we supposed to believe that, all of a sudden, these critics don't understand that the most carefully documented pieces of evidence, and the phenomena most difficult to explain away, are the ones that count? In the case of Home, what really matters is that Home often produced large-scale phenomena, on the spur of the moment, in locations never before visited, with objects supplied by sitters, in good light, and with ample opportunity to observe the phenomena closely while they were in progress. It's also important to note that Home did this for nearly twenty-five years without once being detected in trickery. (Naturally, there were allegations of fraud, but they were all second or third hand, and none were substantiated.)

It's obvious that many skeptics are intelligent people, and I suggest that it's highly unlikely that these shabby criticisms of the parapsychological evidence are simply the sorts of occasional and more or less random attacks of stupidity that all persons experience sometimes. Indeed, if that's all the criticisms were, then presumably those lapses wouldn't occur so exclusively and so transparently in connection with parapsychology. It's much more plausible that many skeptics are simply in a kind of conceptual panic, that in the grip of this panic their reason and integrity go by the wayside, and that their fear of psi is little different from what I felt back in 1968.

2. Investigations of the Felix Experimental Group

Kai Mügge hails from Hanau, Germany. The most consistent and persistent (of several) stories about Kai's early years is that, after witnessing large-scale poltergeist events in the home of a friend when he was 11 years old, Kai became interested in physical mediumship and formed the first of several sitter groups when he was 15.

In 2005 Kai, at the age of 37, organized a circle for physical mediumship named The Felix Experimental Group (FEG). The FEG began without any group member functioning as a medium, and the dominant (and perhaps the only) phenomena occurring during those sessions were table movements. However, Kai eventually became the group's medium, and around that time the group began reporting many of the classic phenomena of physical mediumship, including object levitations, raps and moving lights around the séance room, movement of objects at a distance from the medium, apports, and the production of ectoplasm. Kai now earns a living from his mediumship. But apparently his professional background was in marketing and sales, and we know that he also worked as a documentary filmmaker, producing three films about heroin use in Frankfurt.

I first learned about Kai and the FEG early in 2008, from Jochen Söderling (pseudonym), the cardiologist who eventually became its circle leader. Presumably because of Jochen, and also my reputation (such as it was) as a reasonably knowledgeable proponent of the best macro-PK cases, I soon thereafter found myself included among the email recipients of FEG updates. But as far as I can now reconstruct, my first direct contact with Kai occurred in the fall of 2009, when we arranged for the first of a series of get-acquainted Skype video calls. By that time, I'd already been planning with my Austrian friend and colleague, Peter Mulacz, to apply for funding to visit the FEG, and our email discussions had begun with Jochen to make that visit happen.

At the end of March, 2010, Peter and I were able to travel to Hanau for an introductory visit with FEG members, and we were treated to one cabinet sitting and one table séance, all under casual controls. Prior to our visit, we discussed with both Kai and Jochen the importance of studying and documenting the Felix Circle phenomena under good conditions of control. Both Kai and Jochen expressed their desire to do the same, and indeed, their apparent concern with carefully documenting the phenomena seemed consistent with their obvious appreciation and knowledge of the mediumistic literature.

At the same time, however, both Kai and Jochen were eager for us to see, in the most impressive forms possible, the dramatic kinds of phenomena they had obtained during their sittings. Based on their own experience and also their knowledge of the literature, they said they were concerned that controls (including the use of two hi-definition infrared camcorders we'd purchased) would inhibit (if not snuff out) the manifestations they wanted to share with us. They were also concerned, based again on their own experience with previous visitors to the group, that the delicate group dynamics would inevitably be altered merely by having strangers—especially vigilant and critical ones—sit in. And they were concerned that those dynamics might easily be seriously upset if controls were imposed too early. We understood and respected this position. In fact, we felt it was supported by the entire history of mediumistic investigations, as well as oft-cited and relatively recent studies of the psychodynamics of PK sitter groups.[1]

Accordingly, we agreed that the essential first step to a thorough and proper study of the Felix Group phenomena would be (a) to socialize with the group members (or at least as many of them as we could meet prior to the first séance), and (b) see for ourselves what a typical séance is like. We said we hoped we could gradually introduce and tighten controls, and both Kai and Jochen said they wanted this as well. But they cautioned that this might reduce the magnitude of the phenomena and possibly eliminate them altogether. Kai also said that the speed with which we'd be able to introduce controls was not entirely up to the group members. It was also dictated by Kai's control personality, who ostensibly possessed him during cabinet sittings, and who identified himself as the late parapsychologist Hans Bender, hereafter simply HB. The HB persona claimed to be aided in these matters by a team of postmortem assistants, identified merely as the "Chemists."

During our introductory cabinet séance, the group experienced loud, abundant, and rapid knocking sounds around the walls and ceiling of the room, as well as anomalous object movements of various sorts. The latter included a floating paper "trumpet" with a luminescent strip brought within inches of each sitter's face. Later, during brief periods of red light alternating with periods of darkness, we saw an ostensibly materialized hand and arm hanging from the medium's mouth, and then a moving, large, and not especially lifelike hand moving on the medium's left shoulder while the medium's own hands remained visible and motionless in front of him. At the table séance, we were able to use our infrared camcorders for part of the time, and we recorded quite vigorous movements of the table. When the cameras were turned off, we experienced what seemed to be a complete table levitation.

Because most of the phenomena occurred in darkness with no apparent controls, neither Peter nor I could attest to their legitimacy. But we agreed that a controlled follow-up investigation was warranted, and Kai and Jochen concurred. The exigencies of my retirement from the university and subsequent move from Maryland delayed my next visit until August 2012.[2] This time I participated in two table séances and one cabinet sitting, assisted on two of those occasions by documentary filmmaker Robert Narholz (who was highlighting the FEG for his forthcoming film, *Finding PK*). By this time both Robert and I had been embraced as friendly and trustworthy observers by the FEG, and we were optimistic that we'd be able to impose reasonable controls that nevertheless respected the idiosyncratic psychology of the medium.

But before proceeding with my account of subsequent séances with the FEG, one crucial matter must be addressed. Because the circle leader, Jochen, prefers (wisely, I'd say) to remain anonymous in order not to jeopardize his reputation as a cardiologist, and because Jochen can too easily and glibly become a target for suspicion so long as nothing is known about him, I believe I should say something about my experiences with and impressions of him as a person.

The objective facts about Jochen, so far as they don't reveal his identity, are these. As I now write this, Jochen is in his 40s. He's a distinguished cardiac surgeon and medical researcher who is widely published and who presents original research at major medical conferences throughout Europe and also in the US. He's affiliated with several hospitals and works at one of the world's most distinguished research centers in Germany.

I was first introduced to Jochen in January 2007. He wrote me an email saying he'd read and very much liked my book *Immortal Remains*,[3] and he was eager to engage me in philosophical discussions about the implications of survival data. Very soon, this turned into a protracted dialogue about memory trace theory, psychophysical reductionism generally, and the viability and significance of the various sorts of anti-mechanistic arguments I've advanced over the years in my papers and books. It became clear very quickly that Jochen was a voracious reader and a very thoughtful and intelligent person. In short order he read nearly everything I'd ever written, and also began a careful study of the parapsychological literature and the work of other philosophers of science and mind. I could easily understand how Jochen had risen to prominence as a research scientist so early in his life. He clearly understood the philosophically and other technically difficult works he read, and his questions were invariably probing and sophisticated. And it seemed as though he never slept.

Soon after our discussions began, Jochen brought up the topic of macro-PK and the sorts of dramatic cases I covered in *The Limits of Influence.*[4] He'd already devoured that book as well as much of the primary source material and many important secondary works. So we were able to engage immediately in detailed, penetrating, and wide-ranging discussions about the possibility of fraud in the strongest cases of physical mediumship, as well as in cases documented with less thoroughness and rigor than those of (say) D.D. Home, Eusapia Palladino, and Rudi Schneider, three great and painstakingly investigated mediums during the mid-nineteenth and early twentieth centuries..

I met Jochen face-to-face for the first time in February 2008. I was speaking at a conference in Dortmund, Germany, and Jochen traveled to see me. He grilled me as usual about the difficulties of reconciling my anti-mechanistic arguments with the prevailing assumptions of medical science specifically and the physical sciences generally. Jochen also informed me that he'd recently joined a PK sitter group near Frankfurt. He told me he'd seen some impressive phenomena, and he was clearly wrestling with the issue of how best to explain them. In the months that followed, I received many email inquiries from Jochen about the scope and adequacy of the skeptical arguments he'd been reading (with his customary appetite), and we also reviewed some of the better-documented physical mediumship cases from the heyday of Spiritualism. It was obvious that Jochen was conflicted about the phenomena (he used to write me that they really "kicked my brain") and that he was determined to be as thorough and fair as possible in evaluating them. I'm convinced that Jochen applied his usual scholarly standards to his study of the FEG phenomena, and now, after many years of immersing himself first-hand in the phenomena and continuing to study both the primary and secondary literature, I'd easily rate Jochen as being one of the most informed people on the planet with respect to the history of macro-PK and the relevant issues concerning the possibility of fraud. Moreover, since he began his involvement with the FEG, Jochen has also reached out to many other psi researchers, and I'm confident that they would confirm my impression of him as extremely bright, conscientious, knowledgeable, and thorough.

Hanau, Germany, Summer 2012

Kai's (and the HB persona's) views about the nature of mediumship and the conditions conducive to its demonstration have been profoundly shaped by Kai's familiarity with the literature on the subject. Because he claims he's not as natural or prodigious a mediumistic talent as Home, Palladino, and some others (indeed, he said he had spent many years working diligently to develop his abilities), he claims he's more likely than these virtuosi to be subject to various constraints—in particular, the negative influence of unsympathetic observers and the inhibiting effects of infrared and other light sources.

So although Kai understood and agreed with me about the advisability of infrared recording, he was pessimistic that HB would allow it. Nevertheless, he was very open to other controls, including a strip search and my intrusive hands-on control of him during the cabinet séance, even though he felt that these measures would at least somewhat diminish the magnitude of the effects. He understood the reasonable point that it was better to document modest phenomena under good conditions of control than dramatic phenomena under poor conditions.

Since the time of my original visit to the FEG, there had been a notable addition to the regular sitters of the FEG—Kai's wife Julia. The two met in 2011 and married in May 2012. During the period covered by this report, Julia gradually assumed a more prominent role in the séances, including sharing circle leader responsibilities with Jochen. On the occasions when both were present, she operated the red light, connected to a rheostat, which is used to illuminate Kai or the room. During cabinet sittings, she typically sat to Kai's right, sometimes controlling him but invariably operating the red lamp according to instructions dictated by HB. In these circumstances, Jochen still performed the duty of circle leader, and he also took charge of operating the CD player, needed for providing inspirational and energy-inducing music into the proceedings.

I'll now describe in detail the three sittings conducted during this visit to Hanau. In the absence of blow-by-blow video, the details are obviously crucial, because they help convey both the flavor of the occasions and the difficulties involved in documenting them.

TABLE SÉANCE 08-22-2012
ATTENDEES (in the order of seating, clockwise)
Kai Mügge (medium)
Martine (a neighbor and regular sitter)
Steffy Wolpert (Kai's sister-in-law and regular sitter)
Stephen Braude
Robert Narholz (filmmaker, musician)
Jochen S. (circle leader, chef de music)
Elke Mügge (mother of medium)

As is usually the case in Hanau, the séance was conducted in the cellar/ bomb shelter of the Mügge house, and it began around 8 pm. Also as usual (during this period), it was divided into two phases: the first in total darkness, and the second under the occasional illumination of the small red lamp (controlled this time by Steffy). At its brightest, the sitters and their hands were clearly visible, and even at a lower setting one could discern those details after adjusting to the light.

Beforehand, Kai expressed his preference for eschewing video recording, preferring (he said) to work on building a good dynamic with Robert and me for the next séance or two, and hopefully for increasing the chance of getting the dramatic levitations reported on other occasions (when, reportedly, the table levitated very high and for long periods). Although I was naturally disappointed at being denied the opportunity to video the proceedings, I didn't find Kai's request unreasonable, and so I accepted his preference, especially since there was still the prospect of using video in a subsequent sitting. I didn't realize at the time that Kai would frequently prohibit video recording at the last minute.

The table used was a dark, circular plastic table 35.5 inches in diameter. Before the séance began, I tried lifting the table myself in order to simulate a levitation. I found that, even though the table was quite light, this was difficult to do, and that it was possible only by extending my arms a considerable distance under the table top. But even then, I couldn't reproduce the sort of smooth rise I'd experienced on my previous trip to Hanau, and it was extremely difficult to prevent the table from tilting to one side. I was also unable to raise it level off the ground by hooking my thumbs under the table top or by placing my foot under a table leg. Jochen and others have also reported being unable to simulate a table levitation by hooking the thumbs under the table top. Thus, so long as all fingers are visible on the table, and so long as at least all but one of the sitters' feet are visible under the table, it seems unlikely that fraud best explains a levitation of at least several seconds duration and in which the table top remains parallel to the ground—at least in the absence of some apparatus (such as pins in the table top) that prior inspection of the room and table failed to uncover, and certainly in the absence of any evidence suggesting that Kai at some time studied the art of conjuring.[5] (As I will reveal, evidence did eventually surface showing that Kai had learned some magic.)

The sitting began with an invocation by Kai to the spirits to grace us with their healing power and with demonstrations of their power and presence through the movement of the table. To the accompaniment of some shamanic chanting music, the table began to move within a few minutes, often quite vigorously.

Because the aim of the sitting was to get some clear levitations, and since the mere movements themselves are considerably less interesting if not documented on video, I'll discuss just the levitations.

There were five levitations in all, the first two in total darkness and the others in varying degrees of red light. We were all seated during these phenomena. Robert and I had agreed to divide the observational controls; he would look above the table and I would look beneath it. The most interesting levitation was the third, which occurred in red light sufficient to see all hands on the table and which was notable for the manner in which it rose. Although in all five levitations, the table seemed to float upward (as opposed to being pushed), the table on this occasion rose relatively slowly and quite gently, about 18 inches at most, and (like the other levitations) remained aloft for 2 to 3 seconds. I could see most feet under the table. Neither Robert nor I noted specifically whether Kai's or other sitters' thumbs were visible above the table. However, although visible thumbs would have made the phenomena even more impressive, for the reasons mentioned previously it's unclear how serious that omission is.

So this table sitting can be ranked as intriguing, but no more than that. If the levitations were genuine, then the smooth rise of levitation no. 3 is perhaps the most interesting feature of the observed events, and it connects obviously to similarly smooth object movements reported in the most scrupulously documented poltergeist and physical mediumship cases.

CABINET SÉANCE 08-24-2012
ATTENDEES (in the order of seating, clockwise [double checked by Robert Narholz with the official seating chart])
Kai Mügge (medium)
Stephen Braude (control of medium's left leg and arm)
Renate (from Bavaria. This was her sixth cabinet séance with FEG. She is a spiritualist and a great believer in Kai's powers.)
Jochen S. (circle leader, chef de music)
Vanessa (originally from Mexico City, now Berlin; this was her first séance of any kind)
Robert Narholz
Elke Mügge (mother of medium)
Torsten (first time FEG sitter. He claims an angel appeared to him while drowning and is convinced of the existence of God and the afterlife/spirits based on his "personal experiences and evidence.")
Martine (a neighbor and regular sitter)
Jens (first time FEG sitter)
Ute (seasoned FEG sitter, but no regular)
Julia M. (medium's wife, control of medium's right leg and arm, light operator)

I arrived first at the Mügge house, shortly before 6 pm, and after a few minutes chatting upstairs with Kai's parents, I went to the cellar to inspect the premises. Jochen and Robert arrived about five minutes later, and Jochen then walked me through the inspection again, making sure I looked at all parts of the séance room and adjacent areas. Jochen was very insistent about this, wanting to satisfy himself that I didn't miss something that might come back to haunt me later.

Jochen then began to prepare the séance room by arranging the chairs and PK target objects, and sealing off light sources around windows with black tape. Robert meanwhile began setting up cameras in case we were later given permission to do video recording. The PK target objects, placed at the far end of the circle away from the cabinet, were (as usual) a small conga drum, and atop that a tambourine and maracas, alternating with a luminescent plaque or balls, or a handkerchief.[6]

As usual, Kai placed a strip of black tape on the floor in front of the cabinet. He says the tape marks the near boundary of the PK field which he believes emanates from him. But according to Kai, the main reason he uses the tape is that, once he emerges from the cabinet, it helps him keep a good distance in the dark from the object movements and other physical phenomena occurring at the far end of the circle. Kai also realizes that this would help deflect facile charges from critics that the phenomena are caused by Kai moving out into the room. It's easy to feel the tape in the darkness with one's shoe, and since I'd arranged to sit immediately to Kai's left while controlling him, I could place my foot in that area to make sure Kai's leg didn't move beyond it. Moreover, the distance from the tape to the drum and target objects was approximately 49.5 inches, considerably greater than Kai's reach.

The other sitters began to arrive around 7:30 pm and assembled in the Mügge's dining room around a large dining table. Kai arrived soon thereafter, already apparently in a somewhat distracted or light trance state, but still able to communicate normally. He'd also begun to sweat profusely and was drinking large quantities of black iced tea. After the sitters briefly introduced themselves (and because there were several first-time sitters), Kai provided a lengthy introduction of at least 45 minutes about the nature of the controls that would be imposed on the medium, and also the various rules of procedure (e.g., keeping legs and arms close to one's body, not grabbing the "entities" when touched). Kai claims he's been injured (sometimes bleeding) back in the cabinet when this last condition has been breached.

Shortly before 9 pm Kai retreated upstairs to deepen his trance state. Then while the guests remained in the dining room, Julia and I returned to the cellar to check it out once again—this time in darkness illuminated by Julia's flashlight. The explanation for the darkness was that the light bulbs had been removed from their sockets (it's a standard FEG precaution). Moreover, Julia and Jochen insisted on this re-inspection of the premises, for the obvious and sensible reason that the room had been left unattended since my earlier examination. I asked Julia to shine the light on all parts of the séance room, including the cabinet and the curtained-off adjacent space next to the séance area where Kai's computing equipment is set up. I was satisfied that all was in order.

The sitters were asked to leave all watches and cellphones outside the séance room. Then Julia admitted the guests, one by one, into the séance room after checking them with a metal detector. I was scanned as well. (I later learned that for some reason, Robert was *not* scanned; he just walked in and finalized the camera arrangements.) At this time the red light in the séance room was on, and some additional light entered from the hallway. Then, while Robert remained in the room to re-check the cameras and ascertain that nothing suspicious occurred, Jochen and I went upstairs to strip-search the medium.

We found Kai dressed only in his underpants (briefs) and evidently considerably further into his trance state (though still conscious of his surroundings). Kai cooperatively allowed us to see under the folds in his belly and inside
his underwear. We didn't conduct a full cavity search, but it was clear that no
contrivance or mass of cloth or other material was concealed externally. Jochen
then provided Kai with a fresh set of clothes, which I inspected before Kai
dressed.

Moreover, as I watched, Kai also drank the remaining liquid in a large,
transparent plastic bottle of black tea (he typically drinks large quantities of
liquid before cabinet sittings to avoid dehydration from the heavy perspiration that usually follows). The point of this was twofold. First, in order to
help deflect the skeptical charge that he regurgitates ectoplasm, Kai wanted to
drink something that could stain a white or light-colored material. Granted,
blueberry syrup (which the medium Eva C. had swallowed prior to producing
ostensibly materialized forms) would be a more effective means of accom-
plishing that goal, but it wouldn't be as effective in combating dehydration.
Second, Kai wanted to empty this bottle and not take it with him to the
cellar. Some have suggested that Kai, who often carries the bottle with him,
used it to conceal something that later helps him fraudulently to produce his
phenomena. Neither Kai nor I have yet been told exactly how that would be
accomplished, and so that skeptical objection is currently toothless. But Kai
wanted the point to be moot for this séance.

Jochen and I then walked Kai down to the cellar. Kai walked in front
of me, with his hands raised in full sight the entire time so that I could be
sure that he wasn't grabbing some accessory on the way downstairs. En route
downstairs, Kai asked Jochen to go back and bring him a towel that he'd forgotten (to be used for his perspiration). I remained with Kai (his arms raised),
and Jochen handed me the towel for my inspection before passing it on to Kai.
We then proceeded to the cellar.

The séance began around 9:30 pm and lasted for 3 hours 15 minutes.
The room was completely dark, and despite the loud music playing from the
CD player, we could hear Kai clearly as he began his "holotropic breathing,"
a heavy panting and moaning that could easily be mistaken for the sounds
of sexual activity. Ordinarily, this happens only at the beginning of a cabinet
séance, but this breathing recurred throughout the evening's activities, as if the
medium needed to re-enter the state from which he was involuntarily slipping.
Kai later confirmed that it's unusual for him to moan and breathe heavily
throughout the séance. He attributed this partly to the lack of energy being

contributed by some of the first-time sitters.

As far as I'm concerned, Kai's continued heavy breathing and moaning only made it easier to affirm that throughout the entire séance, Kai was sitting in the area of the cabinet and not moving out into the room. Because the physical controls, which I will describe, were not continuous, this additional and continuous audio control was especially welcome.

After about 15 minutes, HB began to speak through Kai, first in German, but then, at Julia's request, in English. The HB voice is rather coarse and sounds like a partial groan. HB apologized for his lack of command of English and claimed that he was drawing on Kai's knowledge of English (which is considerable). So communication in English with HB was at no time problematic.

HB then exchanged greetings with all the sitters. He explained that the medium would periodically be controlled by the sitters at his sides (at his command) and that at other times he would ask the sitters to form a chain or "circuit" by holding hands. Since the chain terminated with me on one side and Julia on the other, she and I were asked to hold the sitter's hand next to us with both our hands. Jochen was permitted one free hand to manipulate the CD player, but the adjacent sitter not holding one of his hands would instead place a hand on Jochen's shoulder. Thus, assuming the honesty of the sitters, one could ascertain that the sitters were in their chairs and not doing something suspicious or in violation of the rules of procedure. Moreover, at those times I could still ascertain that the medium remained in his place by the cabinet because my right leg and foot still touched his left leg and foot, and because the medium's heavy breathing and talking were still clearly audible from that location.

As usual, the first physical phenomena were rapping and scratching noises on the walls or ceiling. Some of the sounds occurred directly behind me, even though my chair was two or three inches at most from the wood-paneled wall.[7] Moreover, the sounds were clear and bright, with a wider spectrum of frequencies (especially high frequencies) than the more muffled sounds we'd expect if someone were producing them through the 16-inch-thick concrete wall between the wood paneling and the wine cellar outside the séance room. I'd been warned that, in my position next to the cabinet (and behind the area where Kai says the PK field penetrates), I'd experience fewer physical phenomena than the others, and presumably fewer such phenomena than I experienced on my previous visit. That turned out to be the case, but I felt it was a reasonable tradeoff for being able to control the medium and for being maximally close to the ectoplasm I hoped would appear later.

The raps and other physical phenomena were not as abundant as I'd experienced previously. But it's clear nevertheless that they often came from positions that could not have been produced at all (or without detection) by the medium or a sitter—for example, from the wall several inches behind my head. The raps also moved quickly around the ceiling and wall and often switched locations more rapidly than one person would have been able to move in the dark (especially without detection). During all this, I clearly heard the medium breathing heavily from his position by the cabinet.

Soon, sitters reported being touched, but their reports were no more informative than simple exclamations of having been touched. It would have been more helpful had they described what the touches felt like. Again, I could clearly hear breathing in the cabinet over the music and conversation.

Next, some sitters reported seeing a light or lights in the room. Robert says he felt as if he had a personal light that spent several minutes in front of him, sometimes between his knees, and sometimes within eight inches of his face. During the first minute or so when these first reports were occurring, I saw nothing, but then I saw a small bright yellow-white light toward the ceiling and slightly to my left and in front of me. It was about the size of a small LED, but unlike an LED of comparable brightness, nothing (not even dust) was illuminated in front of it. So it does not seem to have been a light *beam*. Soon the light began to move, and move rapidly, around the room, above and (on the wall) behind the sitters, around the ceiling, and at one point even resting on or near the floor, near to where some sitter's feet would have been (and at that point it was very clear that the light was illuminating nothing in its immediate vicinity).

The next phenomena occurred at the location of the drum, the top of which was covered by maracas and bells. Although I heard nothing from these objects, others reported hearing minor scratchings and sounds of movements in the vicinity, and some of the items on the drum were knocked over. But these events were too faint and distant from my location to make any impression on me.

HB then ordered Julia to prepare three luminescent ping-pong-sized balls I'd purchased two years earlier for the group. She charged them with a small flashlight and then positioned the balls on a square black plate, which she placed on top of the drum. According to sitters nearby, after Julia returned to her seat and extinguished the flashlight, the black plate rattled and the balls were knocked over. After the balls were placed back onto the plate, the plate rotated slightly. HB asked if anyone saw a structure blocking the light from the balls (presumably the entity or entities manipulating the objects). Some say they did, but others not. I did see small black and brief obstructions of the light from the balls. Suddenly, one of the three balls rose quickly (or jumped) and fell to the ground.

Between the occurrences of the different physical phenomena, HB would pause, ostensibly to store up and concentrate energy for the next manifestation, and on two occasions to deliver messages from "communicators" to specific sitters. (These were non-evidential and not impressive enough to merit attention here.) While the physical phenomena occurred, I controlled the medium, and I sometimes controlled Julia as well. During the phenomena I was aware at all times of the medium sitting next to me and to my right (the phenomena thus occurred to my left and sometimes behind me). I was always in contact with the medium's left foot and usually with part of his left leg, and during the phenomena I usually held at least his left hand—and sometimes felt his right hand beneath that of Julia (when I controlled her as well).

More precisely, the controls worked as follows. I sat to the medium's left, only a few inches away. My right hand held his left hand and rested on his left leg, which I also touched with my right leg (and my left foot was in front of his left foot). When prompted by HB, I also reached across the medium's lap and my left hand grabbed one or both of Julia's hands in such a way that my left forearm rested on Kai's right leg. This meant that my body effectively blocked the medium's body in such a way that I could easily tell if he was trying (say) to reach out into the room. I could also be sure that he didn't move from his spot during the phenomena, many of which took place at least 50 inches from him.

Significantly, and despite his considerable physical separation from the PK target area, the medium's body often twitched during or immediately prior to the occurrence of phenomena. Moreover, he would often squeeze my hand just prior to or during the phenomena occurring out into the room. This synchronization between a medium's muscle movements and phenomena at a distance has frequently been reported in the better cases.[8] I should also mention (though it should be obvious) that there's a distinct tactile difference between Kai's massive and fleshy (and sweaty) hands and the considerably more petite and dry hands of Julia. So it was easy to confirm during the periods of double control that I held Julia in her place and that neither she nor the medium had moved out into the experimental area in order to produce the phenomena.

As far as the moving light is concerned, I know some have suggested that it might have been produced surreptitiously by someone waving the little LED flashlight that Julia used to rearrange the objects on or near the drum located 49 inches away from the black tape on the floor. However, I believe that this was not the case during this séance because that flashlight was placed inaccessibly under my chair. I'm also reasonably confident that neither Julia nor anyone else using a different mini-flashlight produced the light movements above and to the right of my head. There was no room to maneuver to the right of my chair, and I blocked access from the front and left. So because the light above me and to my right arrived there in a straight path from my left, if someone were carrying a flashlight to produce the effect, that person would have needed to travel along a path obstructed by my body, which was leaning slightly forward and whose legs were still in contact with the medium. So I believe I would have detected by bodily contact someone standing near enough to me to be able to move the light sufficiently far to my right.

Now I can't rule out the possibility of a conspiratorial sitter breaking the chain of hands and using an extended fiber-optic device to create that light and move it undetected to my right. But there's no reason to think that the mandatory conspiracy occurred, or that the broken chain of hands would have gone undetected. I'll comment further in the next section about problems with the skeptical appeal to one or more conspirators.

After the light phenomena and the second and final communication delivered through HB, HB announced that the energy was rather weak, partly because of some of the new sitters (HB had complained earlier both that someone had extended a limb too far into the "field" and that some sitters were not singing loudly and contributing enough energy to the proceedings), and partly because of the unfamiliarity of having me control him. Since, under the circumstances, he felt he could not provide a full menu of the usual physical manifestations and also produce ectoplasm, he asked which we'd rather see. Ectoplasm was the unanimous choice.

So HB retreated back into the cabinet, ostensibly to build up energy, and he asked Julia to let in some fresh air from the darkened hallway outside the séance room (it had indeed become very stuffy). After about 10 minutes, the ectoplasm portion of the evening began.

Jochen and Robert asked repeatedly if we had permission to video record, and HB apparently conversed with the Chemists on the matter. Eventually, he conveyed the news that no video would be permitted. That's especially disappointing in light of the phenomena that followed. Moreover, last-minute decisions to prohibit or seriously restrict video recording turned out to be rather common in my experience with the FEG. Granted, Kai's explanation that these matters are all governed by HB and the Chemists should be considered with an open mind, but in the wake of subsequent evidence for at least occasional FEG fraud, that pattern of refusals can only arouse additional suspicion.

HB directed Julia and me several times to draw back the curtains of the cabinet, and he instructed Julia as to the appropriate rheostat setting of the red lamp. After each display in red light, HB would retreat back into the cabinet and close the curtains while Julia extinguished the lamp and we waited for the next instruction to pull back the curtains and turn on the red light again.

In the first display of ectoplasm, the red light revealed the medium pulling a substantial quantity of material from his mouth, allowing it to fall into a heap onto the floor, between his legs but slightly in front of him and outside the cabinet. The material looked like very fine cloth, somewhat translucent and perhaps resembling tulle, muslin, or cheesecloth. I was approximately 3 feet from the material and could see it reasonably well. I estimate that the mass resting on the floor was roughly rectangular: 12-16" L x 6-8" W x 4-5" H. The medium retreated to the cabinet after this.

When, at HB's cue, Julia and I reopened the curtains, we saw the mass still on the floor. HB said he wanted us to see how it embodies energy within itself, and indeed the mass seemed to be flexing throughout, as if it was breathing and animated from beneath. We observed this for 20-30 seconds before the medium (whose hands were inside the cabinet during all this) retreated again behind the curtains.

The next two viewing periods followed the same format and revealed roughly the same thing. In each case, the "breathing" mass served as a base for a gradually developing "arm," about 1.5-2" in diameter, topped with a hand-like appendage having distinguishable (but not clearly separated) fingers. (I didn't recall whether the hand was already visible in a rudimentary form when the light was turned on, or whether it actually appeared from within the mass. But I do recall that the "arm" grew and rose gradually out of the mass.) The fingers remained in a curved, not fully extended position, as if the hand was prepared to grip something. This made it look somewhat like the head of a cobra, as the appendage turned back and forth left and right. The first time this happened, the appendage rose to a height of about 5 or 6 inches. The second time it rose higher, perhaps 12 inches or more, and it seemed to wave as it turned left and right.

The next time we opened the cabinet, we saw an already formed long protrusion or narrow (handless) column coming from the mass, rising to a height of 3 or 4 feet, looking like a semi-transparent tube. The medium's left hand passed slightly back and forth across the top, as if to show that nothing was pulling the protrusion up from above. I can't say what Kai's right hand was doing during this time.

The next display was supposed to show how the ectoplasm can cover the medium and return some of the energy to his organism. This time we saw the material looking like a fine netting covering the medium's legs and part of his torso as if it was a partial cocoon. After this and once the medium was again behind the cabinet curtains, HB said that, because the medium had lost so much water in the hot séance room and during the strain of the long séance, we wouldn't be able to see the ectoplasm retreat into the medium's body. So he quickly thereafter ended the session.

The sitters then filed out of the room, leaving Julia and me alone with Kai, who took at least 10 minutes to regain his senses. The red lamp was turned on, and I could see in and around the cabinet; nothing suspicious was visible. Julia also showed me the bucket traditionally kept near the medium in case (as I was told sometimes happens) he has to vomit when emerging from trance. Nothing was in the bucket except for a damp towel previously used to cool the medium and which I'd inspected earlier as well. Kai took his time smoking a cigarette, and then slowly walked ahead of me with Julia, upstairs. I was the last person in the séance room.

Reflections on the Phenomena

Now, what about possible skeptical concerns? No doubt some will wonder about the periods of darkness between viewings of the ectoplasm in red light. However, since I strip-searched Kai, examined the fresh clothing and towel we gave him, and examined the cabinet and room both before and immediately after the sitting, it would be hasty to rush to skeptical judgment. Certainly, it's not inherently suspicious, and there could easily be other reasons besides deception for the several retreats behind the curtain. HB claimed that it was to "re-charge"—that is, to build up his waning energy for the next demonstration. He described his need to retreat occasionally behind the curtain as being like a fish that could exist for short periods out of water, but which then needed to return to the water before re-surfacing. That may or may not be a fair account of what's actually necessary for the phenomena to occur non-fraudulently. And if it is a fair account, it could either be because (a) it's a generally accurate description of how the world works (that is, what it takes to produce spiritistic phenomena), quite apart from what the medium believes or what the medium's psychic abilities are, or (b) because it's how the world works for mediums not as prodigious as Home, Rudi Schneider, and some others, or (c) because Kai (or HB) believes that's how the world works and so that's how it works in his case at least.

Some have suggested that the medium used a very fine thread or hair to manipulate the ectoplasmic mass on the floor. This dialectical maneuver seemingly takes a cue from Frank Podmore's unconvincing attempts to explain the phenomena of D.D. Home.[9] Let's call this skeptical proposal the *Puppeteer Hypothesis*, and although I can't rule it out, it seems problematical, for the following reasons. The mass was outside the cabinet and the medium remained inside, behind the ectoplasm. Admittedly, I wasn't looking at the medium's hands while concentrating on the ectoplasm, and so I can't say that the medium wasn't manipulating difficult-to-detect magicians' strings strung over the hoop to which the cabinet curtains were attached. Michael Nahm (in his accompanying report[10]) advanced substantive reasons for considering this option seriously, at least for some ectoplasmic manifestations. However, the breathing (or flexing) seemed to be animated from within the mass, and the mass was expanding (and seemingly flexing) from several different points along its surface, suggesting that several strings would presumably have been necessary. And as for the ectoplasmic hand, I question whether any thread(s) could explain how it gradually took shape, grew and partially opened, and became more determinately hand-like. Then, as the hand turned left and right and back and forth, I believe that too would have required puppet-like hairs manipulated from above or from within the cabinet. Thus, if Kai was a mere puppeteer, I believe he would have needed quite a few threads, which he expertly manipulated from his place within the cabinet. These would have allowed him to move the surface of the ectoplasmic mass on the floor at different points, separately raise an ectoplasmic arm and hand, separately open and change the shape of the hand, and then also move it left and right. I can't say this is impossible, but it begins to look as though the degree of conjuring required would be quite sophisticated.

Furthermore, I did see Kai's left hand pass over the long, handless protrusion emerging from the mass, and which thus didn't seem to have a string attached to its top. Moreover, since I was with Kai from the time he was strip-searched, and because I detected no strings on him (much less a more conspicuous device), any strings he might have used would presumably have been concealed within the cabinet (perhaps, as Nahm suggests, behind the strips of black tape affixed to the inside of the curtain, ostensibly to enhance the opaqueness of the cabinet), or perhaps hidden in his rectum or gut—something I again can't rule out (and which I'll discuss again in connection with the later Austrian séances).

I imagine some will also raise concerns about Jochen's free hand during the earlier (PK) portion of the séance. I concede it's not ideal, but several considerations lessen its significance. For one thing, Jochen was still connected by one hand to an adjacent sitter (either Vanessa or Renate), and so unless his neighbors failed to report it or colluded with him, he couldn't have been free to produce phenomena outside the range of his free arm—for example, the light to my right or the raps above my head. Another is that similar phenomena have been reported at séances that Jochen didn't attend. So the determined skeptic would have to develop some version of a conspiracy counter-explanation, involving a team of widely dispersed assistants helping Kai no matter where he holds a successful séance. That's always a sign of skeptical desperation in my view.

But perhaps most important is the significant fact that the medium twitched immediately prior to or simultaneously with the production of the phenomena. I felt him squeeze my hand tightly and press both his hand and leg against my leg, as if he was straining to expel the phenomena from his body. And on some of these occasions I held Julia's hand as well. The phenomena thus seem directly connected to what was going on in the medium. But given my intrusive controls it seems unlikely that Kai was surreptitiously manipulating the objects at the far end of the circle. Of course, some might wonder if Kai had an accomplice among the sitters. But that conjecture faces a major obstacle: How would some conspirator elsewhere in the room have felt those physiological cues to know when to produce the object movements fraudulently? Neither Jochen nor any other non-controlling sitter had perceptual access to Kai's hand-squeezing and muscle tension.

There's one more issue, having to do with Julia, or perhaps with me. And it concerns the following incident. Several times during the object movement part of the séance, we noticed light entering from outside the séance room through small cracks in the séance room door and a door just outside that. We thought that maybe Kai's brother or sister-in-law (who live on the floor above the cellar), or a friend of theirs, might have entered the cellar—although Jochen and Kai assure me this never happens, because these people all know to stay clear of the cellar when Kai has guests for a séance. The third time this happened—but *after* the object movements described above had already occurred--Jochen asked Julia if she could go upstairs to ask the people not to come downstairs again. Jochen didn't want to do this himself, because his role as circle leader is to monitor the interaction between HB and the sitters (and control the music). Julia then asked HB for permission to leave, and it was granted. She left the room for 50 seconds (the audio recording of the proceedings shows that she left from 1.16.25 to 1.17.15). She then returned and reported that no one had at any time entered the cellar area. Jochen (and later Kai, when he learned about this and confirmed with his family that no one had come downstairs) are convinced that the turning on of the lights was paranormal.

Now I didn't realize Julia had left the room. I thought she remained in the entrance way to the séance room and simply peered into that space. My confusion was probably due to the fact that the conversation between Jochen, Julia and HB happened quickly and in German. In any event, I didn't follow Julia out of the room to confirm that she brought nothing back with her that might have assisted the subsequent production of ectoplasm, and I blame myself for not pursuing her in order to be able to report that she did nothing suspicious in her absence. Nevertheless, although this was an unfortunate lapse in control (indeed, I'm assured it's an unprecedented occurrence for anyone to leave the room in the middle of a séance—unless it's someone who fainted and who doesn't then return—which I was told happens occasionally but rarely), I believe it's far from fatal, for the following reasons.

First, when Julia left the room after the séance had ended, I saw nothing suspicious on her person, and I'd remind the reader that I saw no props in or around the cabinet. Moreover, as is the case with the object movements, Kai began producing ectoplasm long before he met Julia. More precisely, Kai and Julia met in March, 2011. But Kai had been holding cabinet sittings with ectoplasm since the summer, 2009. So once again I suggest that we be careful not to point a suspicious finger at Julia if it commits one (as it would seem to here) to a more general conspiracy theory of Kai's mediumship.

Besides, if Julia had retrieved some contraption when she exited the room, when would she have used it? I often controlled both her and the medium during the object movements and lights. So it seems clear that she wasn't an accomplice for *those* phenomena. And neither she nor the medium were positioned above the ectoplasm—that is, in a position to be the hypothesized puppeteer. Moreover, if Julia smuggled in a device to animate the ectoplasm, where was it, what kind of device could it be, and how would it have been concealed in my post-séance inspection around the cabinet? No simple and easily concealable device could have produced a breathing mass on the floor that gradually sprouted an animated hand. If a critic believes otherwise, it's the critic's responsibility to specify what such a device is. And obviously, the mere (and arguably remote) possibility of fraud is no reason to discount the phenomena. The more pertinent issue is: was there any indication or reason for thinking fraud was *actual* and not simply possible? A priori conviction in the impossibility of the phenomena counts for nothing and would be the cheapest form of glib criticism. Furthermore, it's worth noting again that Kai has conducted successful cabinet sittings that *neither* Julia nor Jochen attended, and that recourse to a larger conspiracy of confederates is a desperate skeptical gambit.

So this séance was clearly a major advance over my 2010 cabinet séance with the FEG. I commended Kai for allowing me not only to control him directly, but also to conduct a strip search, and to observe him after the séance (i.e., in conditions I'm quite sure most self-respecting persons would feel to be particularly vulnerable or unattractive). And while I've noted various respects in which the controls could have been better still, I saw no reason not to be encouraged by the results. Kai seemed pleased as well. He indicated he'd be happy for Robert and me to make a return visit and that he would very much like to include hi-res video recording of the ectoplasm. As it turned out, and as I describe below, before a year had passed we were indeed able to improve upon the controls in the Hanau séances and obtain video footage of the ectoplasm.

I should add that the events of the cabinet sitting convinced me that for any follow-up séances we needed to reduce the number of sitters, especially first-timers. I was quite disappointed that so many attended the cabinet séance, since for months I'd been discussing with both Kai and Jochen my preference for working only with a bare minimum. I sympathized with Kai's interest and willingness to include more sitters. For one thing, he was inundated with requests from potential attendees, to the extent that he abandoned his previous work as a videographer. And for another, he seemed to take energy from the enthusiasm of the sitters, and the more the merrier. As it happened, Kai did screen the first-time participants ahead of time, both before meeting them, and while he interacted with them prior to the séance (he always had the last-minute option of denying them the opportunity to participate). He felt they were acceptable, but that turned out to be wrong in one or two instances.

I should also add that I don't consider it intrinsically suspicious either that Kai charges for his time and the apparent physical stress of cabinet sittings, or that séances and trance workshops have become his primary) source of income. Kai has a right to be paid for his time, and in fact we provided him with an honorarium drawn from the research funding I'd received. Still, the issue is complicated. Granted, Kai enjoys the undoubtedly seductive attention and adulation of sitters and workshop participants who take him to be a guru, and granted, the work is very steady, presumably more so than his video work. But Kai told me that, at least during this period, he charged far less than mediums (such as David Thompson) who don't allow serious control. In fact, Kai told me that his fees barely managed to defray his travel expenses. However, I must note that Kai's mediumistic success allowed him to move from an exceedingly modest flat into a much larger and more elegant flat, which he and Julia decorated lavishly. So either Kai charged fees that did much more than barely cover travel costs, or he raised his fees considerably soon after my visit. So although there's an unpleasant aroma about this, I'd still insist that Kai is entitled to make a living off his skills if there's a market for it. That's completely clear in the event that Kai's mediumistic abilities are thoroughly genuine. But I'd argue that it's clear enough even if Kai's abilities are only sporadically genuine. But that's a debate for another time.

TABLE SÉANCE 08-25-2012
ATTENDEES (in the order of seating, clockwise)
Kai Mügge (medium)
Elke Mügge (mother of medium)
Jochen S. (circle leader, light operator)
Stephen Braude
Julia Mügge (medium's wife, music operator)

This session was held on the spur of the moment. Robert had left Germany, and the attendees had gathered in Elke's dining room for snacks, convivial conversation, and discussion of the previous day's cabinet séance. I believe we were all tired from lack of sleep. The séance had ended in the early morning hours, and Kai evidently hadn't slept at all—as (I was told) is often the case after a cabinet séance. But everyone seemed relaxed and in good humor. So despite the general level of fatigue, we decided to try a table sitting, and Kai was eager to try infrared video recording.

I hurriedly set up my IR camcorder on a tripod, and I tried to find a location where the view would show as much of the table as possible. I aimed the camcorder between the initial positions of Kai and Julia. I couldn't foresee that Kai would find his chair very uncomfortable and that, while shifting his body (in the dark) to feel better, moved to the right and blocked considerably more of the view.

Apparently, my camcorder battery had been more depleted than I realized, and the camera shut off after 30 minutes. But during that time, we had two small table levitations. The smallest lasted about one second, and the table rose only a couple of inches. The other levitation lasted nearly 3 seconds and the table rose to a height of approximately 8 inches. Although Kai's body blocked much of the table, the video shows clearly that the table top was level and parallel to the floor. One can't tell from the video whether Elke (totally out of view) lifted the table normally, but it's highly unlikely. First, I'm confident that deception of this sort would be totally out of character. And second, Jochen and I can attest to how difficult it was to raise Kai's table smoothly by oneself, and we're much stronger than Elke. Moreover, one of Jochen's arms is visible, and the position of his body is incompatible with his reaching his unseen hand far enough under the table. That's also the case with Kai, who moved his right arm up and down above the table, imitating the levitation technique of Eusapia Palladino.

Clearly, the video of this levitation is not evidential. Nevertheless, granting the integrity of the sitters in this friendly and very relaxed sitting, it's arguably a valuable document of a full table levitation. (One can view it online at https://tinyurl.com/wdr7726.)

After the camcorder battery failed, Kai requested red light. From that point on, we enjoyed no more table levitations, although the table occasionally moved quite vigorously, often to the rhythm of the music. Kai soon began to remark that he was feeling some twitching in his left arm, which I learned later is often a precursor to an apport. But at the time, I didn't realize that this might have connected to a request Kai made a little while earlier in the dark, for the "spirits" to present me with a gift.

At one point, Kai was standing next to the table. I could see all the sitters, and I could see that they all held hands in a chain. Suddenly we heard the sound of something dropping onto the table. A quick search on the floor revealed a small metal statue of the Indian goddess of wisdom, Saraswati, in the familiar pose in which she's often represented, and which is also tattooed onto Julia's arm.

Because this séance was very spur of the moment, I made no careful inspection of the room prior to the beginning of the séance, and I conducted no search of Kai's body or clothes. Also, I can't be certain of what might have happened in the dark prior to turning on the red light. But when the apport appeared, all sitters were visibly joining hands around the table and Kai was talking normally (suggesting that the statue was not hidden in his mouth). Besides, the apport fell loudly onto the table, as if it had been propelled—rather than released—there. If the object had been hidden in Kai's mouth (clearly visible in the red light) or on his body, he would presumably have needed to make some sort of spitting, blowing, or other detectable motion to expel it so forcibly. And if the apport had been concealed externally and somehow positioned ahead of time to fall onto the table, presumably some kind of time-release mechanism would be required. I can state confidently that I saw nothing on the ceiling or elsewhere when the lights were turned on.

Austria, May 2013

In order to tighten the séance conditions both significantly and relatively painlessly (psychologically) for Kai, Robert and I arranged for the next sittings to be held at Robert's large private farmhouse outside Salzburg. We also arranged for a small and very compatible group of sitters, all of whom Kai liked, all of whom were experienced with the FEG, and all of whom could be lodged comfortably in the farmhouse and kept under casual surveillance. In our more grandiose moments, Robert and I fancied that this investigation would be a contemporary analogue of the well-known and successful experiments with Eusapia Palladino, conducted on Richet's private island.[11]

Robert and I were aided in these investigations by Michael Nahm, a biologist and psi researcher, whom I've mentioned earlier, and who was quite experienced with the FEG, both as a sitter and a controller.[12] We were very grateful for his expertise, suggestions, and his help in making Kai feel comfortable and among friends.

PARTICIPANTS:
Kai Mügge (medium)
Julia Mügge (medium's wife, music or light operator)
Jochen S. (circle leader, light operator)
Anna S. (Jochen's wife)
Michael Nahm (biologist, parapsychologist)
Stephen Braude
Robert Narholz (co-investigator, homeowner)

The séance room was a large space in Robert's farmhouse occasionally used as a spare bedroom. Its wooden floor was divided into two roomy areas by a pair of steps. Robert removed all the furniture except for six folding chairs (with cushions placed on top), a more substantial wooden chair for Kai, two small wooden tables (one for the red lamp and the other for the CD player), and a plastic séance table 33.5" in diameter. The upper portion of the room had some built-in shelves with nothing on them. But otherwise the room was quite bare. The curtained windows could be locked top and bottom from the inside, and then interior shutters could also be locked from top and bottom. Except for brief periods during the setup of the séance room in which we wanted additional light or fresh air, the windows were locked at all times. They were also covered in black paper to prevent outside light from entering the room, and indeed, the room was completely dark when the door was closed and lights turned off.

Robert and I also installed padlocks on the séance room door, both inside and out. The room was kept locked when not in use; I had sole possession of the key, and no one knew where I kept it when it wasn't on my person. When sittings were in session, the room was locked from the inside. The locks are not heavy duty, but they and the interior and exterior door latches are quite noisy. So if someone tried to enter the room during a séance, it would be obvious.

For the cabinet sitting, Kai and Julia brought their own assembly, consisting of dark black curtains which they attached to a jumbo hula hoop. The hula hoop was originally broken down into several pieces, each of which I examined carefully before the pieces were attached together. The curtains had strips of black tape attached in many places to the interior, to enhance the opaqueness of the not-quite-opaque, thin material. Robert, Michael, and I inspected all the materials (including those black strips) closely, and for the purpose of verification Robert made a close-up video recording of the objects and the inspection process itself.

The other objects brought by Kai and Julia were PK target objects to be used in both table and cabinet sessions—for example, luminescent white balls, a luminescent plaque, and the usual paper "trumpet" with a luminescent strip attached around the large opening. They also traveled with a small flashlight for charging the luminescent strips. We inspected all these objects as well, but as it turned out (and to our surprise), they played no role in our sittings—except for the flashlight, which we used occasionally to manually change settings of the red lamp controls in an otherwise dark room, and which was used in a table séance to permit a view inside Kai's mouth prior to an apport.

TABLE SÉANCE 05-11-2013

The séance began after dinner at 7:40 and lasted 1:37. Sitters (clockwise): Kai, Stephen, Anna, Robert, Julia, Michael, Jochen. Sitters emptied their pockets and removed all rings and watches to forestall the objection that a familiar conjuring trick involving pins placed on the table was used to raise the table. (I was unable to remove my wedding ring.) The lamp was placed on Julia's right side, between her and Robert.

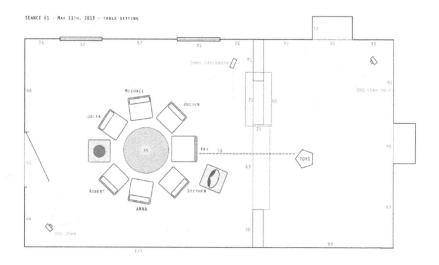

SEANCE #1 · MAY 11TH, 2013 · TABLE SITTING

The door remained locked until sitters entered around 7:30. Various "inspirational objects" were placed in the rear of the room near the window or on the shelves. These included the samples of gold-colored foil from my case of Katie, the Gold Leaf Lady[13] which I had shown for the first time to Kai and the others (except Robert) several hours prior to the sitting. But not even Robert knew prior to late afternoon that day that I had the foil with me. Jochen thought that Kai might be sufficiently intrigued by the foil samples to use them subconsciously as a basis for an apport (the kind of thing that he's noticed on many previous occasions). So when Kai finally entered the room, several minutes before we began, Jochen drew his attention to the foil samples, and also to the copy of an obscure Hungarian book on physical (apport) mediumship that Michael was in the process of translating (Elemèr Pap's *Toward New Horizons*).

The red lamp was on a small table by Julia's side and was controlled by a rheostat. The light was turned off as the séance began and turned on at Kai's request at several points during the séance. Kai also instructed Julia as to the brightness of the illumination.

Kai requested that I control him from his left side and that Jochen control him from his right. Julia expressed considerable eagerness for controls. She even said she preferred that Jochen *not* be seated next to Kai, because he was more likely to be considered by some as suspect than either Robert or Michael. But Kai clearly felt comfortable with Jochen by his side and overrode Julia's request. In any case, Julia asked repeatedly during the sitting for her neighbors Robert and Michael to ensure that she was well controlled.

Although we had several cameras set up to record the proceedings, Kai evidently felt some anxiety about the new locale and the pressure to come up with good results, and so he requested that we begin with all cameras off and that we turn them on only when strong phenomena started to occur.

After some table movements, we had a total of four table levitations. At the beginning of the séance, Kai insisted that Jochen and I be in good contact with and control of his hands and feet—at least until we had some good table levitations under tight controls and then could be more casual. So Jochen's left knee touched Kai's right leg and his left foot rested on Kai's right foot. His left hand rested atop Kai's left hand. My controls on Kai's left side were the mirror image of Jochen's. These controls were in place for levitations 1, 2 and 4. For levitation 3, my right foot and leg only touched the left foot and leg of Kai. But I could feel Kai's foot clearly though the thin slippers I was wearing.

The levitations lasted between 2 and 8 seconds, and each time the table rose smoothly, approximately two feet off the ground. It was clear to all sitters that the table surface was always in a horizontal position during the levitations. Before levitation 4, Jochen and Michael felt a breeze, despite the windows all being closed. Then Julia said she felt it, and then Robert added that he felt it on his left side.

There were two apports during the séance, especially interesting given that they occurred in sufficient red light to view Kai and the area above the table clearly.

Apport #1: Kai stood up and asked Jochen and me to hold his hands. He then asked Julia to shine the flashlight on his mouth. We could clearly see Kai sticking out his tongue and wiggling it, and at one point a 1.75 "-long, 3/8 "-thick crystal (Figure 2) dropped, loudly and apparently forcibly, onto the table. Probably because Kai had called our attention to his mouth (for the purpose of misdirection?), most sitters had the impression that the apport emerged from that vicinity. However, the appearance of the object was too sudden for me to say where, exactly, it came from. Nevertheless, although we didn't search Kai ahead of time, it's questionable whether Kai had previously concealed the object on his person and at some point in the darkness transferred it to his mouth. For one thing, Kai didn't spit or blow the object out of his mouth; his tongue was sticking out when the crystal appeared. So if the object had been concealed in Kai's mouth, it's unclear how it could have been ejected orally with enough force to land loudly on the table. It also seems unlikely that Kai regurgitated the object. We had finished a large meal less than an hour prior to the séance, and I can't imagine how Kai could have regurgitated that one object with no stomach contents from dinner. I can't affirm that Kai didn't propel the object onto the table with one of his hands, although that seems quite unlikely. Jochen and I held Kai's hands, and I believe the light shining onto Kai's face from the flashlight would have revealed any such action.

Apport #2: Kai started to shake and grabbed my and Jochen's hands. Then, with Jochen holding Kai's bare forearm (as usual, he was wearing a short-sleeve T-shirt) and feeling over and under Kai's right hand, we clearly saw, under red light, Kai extend his right arm and spread the fingers of his hand. I was holding Kai's left hand at the time. Jochen had been controlling Kai's right hand and arm for several minutes. The apport suddenly dropped forcibly and loudly from the vicinity of Kai's extended right hand and bounced off the table onto the small table with the red lamp next to Julia. In his notes written later in the evening, Robert described this event as follows: "[Kai] stretched out his right hand, which I could see clearly, and Jochen grasped it, touched it and checked it all over, and we all joined hands, standing up, and then, BANG, something landed on the table."

Kai was apparently inspired by Katie's golden foil and the Pap book. Prior to the apport's appearance, he said he or the Chemists were extracting copper either from the foil or from somewhere else. And indeed, the apport was a slightly reddish copper nugget, about ¾" square. It may also be relevant that Kai and Michael earlier in the day had been discussing a mid-twentieth-century psychic with the surname Messing, which in German means "brass." The foil appearing on Katie's body has been determined to be brass.

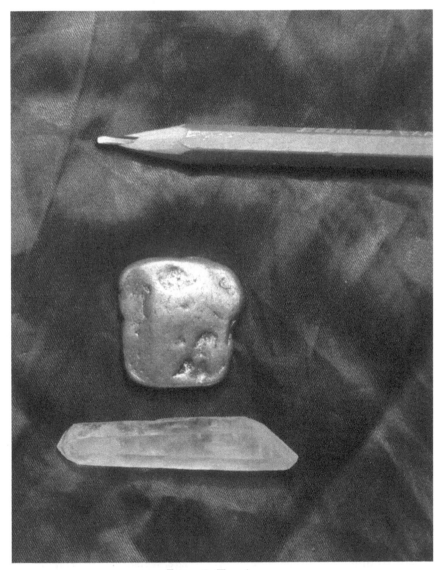

Figure 2. Two Apports

For the final 25 minutes of the séance, we turned on the cameras, but no phenomena occurred during that period. In retrospect it's difficult to say whether the running cameras inhibited the phenomena or whether Kai was simply tired by then. Indeed, it seemed that the session exhausted Kai. He was dehydrated from having no water or (his favorite) iced tea to replenish what he lost through perspiration, and toward the end of the session he apparently lapsed into a state of stupefaction, barely able to speak. At that point he wanted merely to pause the session for a short time, but Julia decided there was no point in continuing. So the session ended.

Synchronistic postscript: Because we held a second exhausting table séance the next day, the day after that, May 13, was designated a day of rest for Kai, who spent the time quietly at the farmhouse sleeping and making travel arrangements for future séances. So Jochen, Julia, Anna and Michael toured Salzburg (an hour's drive away), and as they passed a shop selling gemstones and crystals, Michael saw in the window a large copper nugget, looking very much like a larger version of the apport we'd received two days before. The shopkeeper informed Michael that this is the form in which copper is mined, and that this particular nugget came from Michigan. Inside the shop were more copper nuggets. It's also worth emphasizing that on the day of the séance, it was I who first mentioned copper to Kai and the group, when Kai asked what the composition of Katie's brass foil was. Before that, neither brass nor copper had been topics of conversation.

At first, Kai seemed quite despondent about this turn of events, saying he felt it diminished the significance of the apport. He said that although he'd never before held a piece of copper, he felt that because such objects were easily obtainable, it would lead some to suggest he'd hidden the nugget on his person prior to the apportation. In fact, Kai said that he didn't know that copper came in the form of such nuggets (indeed, none of us knew that). He said he'd believed that the apported object was highly unusual, if not one of a kind, and that his mental images prior to the apport suggested to him that he was forming an object from bits of copper taken partly from Katie's foil samples. So for that reason and because Kai said he felt he had to work especially hard to produce the apport, he was disappointed to discover that his object wasn't something of high strangeness, novel in shape or constitution.

Although I could understand how he felt, I was unable to share Kai's apparent disappointment with this turn of events. (I'll comment later on the evidentiality of the apports.) For now, though, it's sufficient to remember that Kai's arm was bare, his hand fully visible and fingers spread when the apport fell from the vicinity of his hand.

TABLE SÉANCE 05-12-2013

The séance began after dinner at 8 pm and lasted 1:55. Sitters were arranged as before, with a large gap between Julia (and the red lamp) and Robert, to allow for a clear video camera view under table. Michael, Robert, and I carefully checked the table underneath beforehand, and the process was documented on video. Sitters again removed all rings and watches. I wore no shoes, which allowed a more sensitive method of controlling Kai's left foot. The sitters were vigilant throughout to remain in touch with their neighbors' hands and legs. In fact, because Julia was too far from Robert for normal control, she proposed placing both her knees against Michael's right leg. She did this throughout the séance, and while her left hand was in contact with Michael's right hand, her right hand remained on the lamp switch (which is why we were able to capture the levitations under illumination).

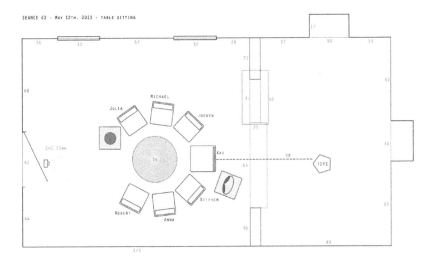

Prior to this sitting, Kai had received indications from the Chemists that they wanted to have one, but only one, video camera turned on for the séance, placed in the most optimal position for a clear view of the proceedings. Naturally, Robert and I were disappointed once again. For obvious reasons, we had hoped to use more cameras under red light or (even better) under infrared illumination, which in Hanau had worked nicely, but which Kai, HB, or the Chemists continued (I must say, unconvincingly) to resist. Nevertheless, our results on this occasion were promising (if still imperfect), and left Robert and me feeling cautiously optimistic about improving them further in the future.

Figure 4—Farmhouse séance room

For the first 70 minutes at least, there were no phenomena apart from some table sliding and occasional shudders suggesting an incipient levitation. After that, we had two strong levitations with one weak levitation between them. The strong levitations lasted between 2-3 seconds each, with the table rising between 1.5 and 2.5 feet. When the strong levitations began, Kai instructed Julia to turn on the red light. That allowed us to see and video record the first levitation as it began its descent. And it permitted a good view of the second strong levitation almost from the beginning of its ascent. The video was recorded with a very high ISO (12,800) and slowish 1/13 sec exposure (on an f1.8 lens wide open), but it was sufficient to capture most of the movement clearly and smoothly. The original image is faint, but after tweaking with image enhancement, Kai's feet and those of most others are clearly visible on the floor, and the sitters' hands are clearly visible on the table top. One can also see my right hand touching Kai's left hand and my right foot touching his left foot. The enhanced video segment (Figure 5) is grainy but more than adequate. It's perhaps the best video to date of a full table levitation.[14]

*Figure 5: The table as it begins the ascent (top) to its
zenith (middle), and returns to the floor (bottom).
Notice that Kai's feet clearly remain planted on the floor.*

Kai again seemed exhausted by the end of the séance. Julia reported that they've never gone two hours without a break (usually they take a break after about 45 minutes). Kai immediately went for a short nap afterwards, which Julia also claims Kai never does. It was clear to us all that, despite our efforts to make this meeting as cordial and easygoing as possible, Kai felt considerable pressure to obtain good video documentation of his phenomena. From a sympathetic point of view (rather than the more sinister one encouraged by subsequent revelations), it's feasible that Kai felt more intimidated by having a battery of video cameras trained on him than in having just one aimed in his direction. And it's probable that he wanted to work under conditions as close as possible to those he finds successful at his séances for the general public—in particular, darkness most of the time and red light occasionally.

Discussion among the sitters after the séance revealed that most had felt under some pressure to obtain good video documentation, and that after more than an hour had passed with no results, they'd begun to give up and assumed the session would produce nothing of interest. (I know I started to ponder how best to counter Kai's disappointment.) But I estimate that's about the time we started to see table levitations. Assuming the genuineness of the phenomena, this seems intriguingly like a release-of-effort phenomenon, and it suggests (what should have been clear anyway) that success in these matters doesn't depend solely on Kai.

CABINET SÉANCE 05-14-2013

The séance room was carefully searched before and during setup of the cabinet, with video recording of most of the action. And of course, the room and windows were kept locked at all times except during setup and preliminary testing of the video cameras in low light, during which either or both Robert and I were in the room. An overturned bucket (replacing the usual conga drum as a repository for target PK objects) was provided by Robert and secured on the floor by tape on one side, 53 inches from the strip placed in front of the cabinet. Robert, Michael, and I placed pencils (provided by Robert) underneath the strip so that Kai could easily feel with his shoes where it is and thereby not pass beyond it. The reason for securing the bucket to the floor on only one side was to allow it to be lifted to ensure that nothing had been surreptitiously placed beneath it.

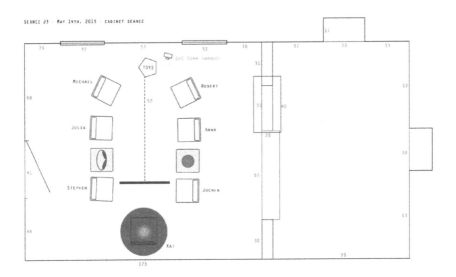

Robert, Michael, and I examined the entire room and its contents after setup was completed and then again a few minutes before the séance commenced. This inspection included a careful search of the cabinet, curtain, and curtain seam, and the process was documented on video. We also examined the black cloths used to cover the PK-target objects with their luminescent strips. These luminescent objects would ordinarily be charged and then set aside for the anticipated object-movement portion of the séance, but kept stashed away and covered near the red lamp to preserve the darkness of the room.

The room was locked at all times except immediately prior to a séance (to allow sitters entrance to the room) and during séance preparation. Whenever the room was open, an investigator was always present—usually either (or both) Robert or me, and briefly Michael as he swept the floor and installed his temperature gauge (which yielded no information of interest—the room temperature was basically constant throughout).[15] Robert had one of his fisheye lens miniature GoPro video cameras running as sitters were searched and entered the séance room. He also videoed my walking downstairs with Kai after the strip search. His other GoPro camera was stationed in my bedroom upstairs, which was located directly above the séance room. This would have allowed us to determine whether knocks heard on the ceiling during the séance were caused by an accomplice in my room. In any case, the house was locked, certainly making it difficult (though not impossible) for someone to enter while the rest of us were locked inside the séance room.

Kai spent about 30 minutes, starting around 7:30, reviewing issues and procedures of the séance. He reminded us that although our goal for the evening was to document ectoplasm on video, HB and the Chemists had their own agenda and concerns. Moreover, he (Kai) was in no position to challenge them, since he could only receive communications and not respond, much less interrogate his communicators. So he warned us that the communicators might protest our plan to have Jochen operate the red lamp and control Kai from the medium's right side (rather than have Julia as controller from the right, which has been the usual practice for more than a year now). I was to be the controller on the medium's left side, and there was no question that this would be acceptable.

After the review session, Kai went upstairs to begin his trance, a process that I gather can include meditation, lots of liquids, and at least sometimes the ingestion of psychotropic drugs. During this time, Robert instructed Julia as to the optimal red-light settings for video, and then Robert and I made a final review inspection of the séance room, which we again documented on video. As expected, the room and its contents hadn't been altered and we found nothing suspicious. Then Jochen and I went upstairs to conduct a strip search of Kai, who awaited us dressed only in his underpants and socks. I looked inside his underpants, checked his socks, examined the folds in his belly, looked inside his simple athletic shoes (no removable heel), and determined easily that he was concealing no device or stash of material that could be produced as ectoplasm. Jochen and I also carefully inspected the clothing (sweat pants and T-shirt) that Kai would wear for the séance, and they too concealed nothing. Before leaving the room, Kai took a large drink from his latest bottle of iced tea, as usual to help forestall the dehydration he experiences during his heavy perspiration in the cabinet (and during an ordinary day, for that matter). The iced tea again was black tea, which would presumably stain any material regurgitated by Kai. However, although the tea is dark, it's not opaque, and one can clearly see if objects are concealed in the bottle. As a further precaution, Robert supplied two water bottles and another iced tea bottle for the séance room, which he videoed me inspecting as we completed our final search of the séance room. Nothing suspicious or out of the ordinary was contained in the sealed bottles, and no one could object that the bottles were props that Kai introduced into the room.

After the strip search, Jochen led Kai downstairs to the séance room, and

Kai again kept his arms raised with hands in full view as I followed the pair downstairs. Robert videoed this transit. I unlocked the séance room and led Kai inside. At that point (after Kai seated himself in the cabinet), we allowed the other sitters to enter as Robert and I patted down the male sitters to make sure they introduced no props into the room. Anna independently did a strip search of Julia. After this, I locked the séance room from the inside. The house had already been locked by Michael (and the key hidden, even from Robert), and a GoPro camcorder was placed in a far corner of my bedroom upstairs, with a full view of the door and the entire room.

The séance then began around 8:40 pm, and Kai went through his usual "holotropic" breathing fairly quickly. Once HB had announced himself and greeted the sitters, he noted that he understood the purpose of this gathering, and so he said he would skip the usual object-movement portion of the séance and concentrate just on the production and viewing of ectoplasm. He claimed that making target objects move at the far end of the circle would expend valuable energy, which he preferred to collect and store in order to document the medium extruding ectoplasm.

HB then insisted, as a precondition for the evening's program and to ensure that Kai's interests are protected, that we grant Kai the right to determine whether any videos collected from the séance are made public. Neither Robert nor I had any problem with that request.

HB then asked to see which levels of red light were necessary for adequate documentation. After that, the medium retreated behind the curtains again to build up energy. While that was going on, most sitters reported seeing lights from within or around the cabinet, rather than traveling around the room (as is often the case during Kai's cabinet sessions). For example, I saw a bright yellow-white light inside the bottom front of the cabinet, and several of us saw a greenish faint glow from the top of the cabinet. So if the light was produced normally, it remains to be explained what device produced it and how it escaped detection during the strip searches and cabinet examinations both before and after the séance. If instead the light had been produced outside the cabinet, it would have been very difficult for the medium to have reached that location. Nevertheless, Jochen reported that he saw a smallish rectangular light on his side of the cabinet, clearly outside the curtains and very close to his face.

HB asked me to describe my strip search of Kai in detail, and then he asked whether under the circumstances Kai could have concealed anything that produced those lights. I replied modestly that I'd found nothing that would account for the lights. Granted, I didn't perform a full cavity search, and so I can't guarantee that Kai had no light-emitting devices concealed (say) in his rectum. And although I'd taken some steps to rule out the regurgitation hypothesis, I can't say conclusively that Kai hadn't brought up a light from his gut (and then re-swallowed it or placed it in his rectum). But if that mere conjecture is the best skeptics can do to explain the phenomena, then they need to do more in order to undermine the case for the paranormality of the lights. After all, as I noted earlier, we have decent evidence that, during ob-ject-movement portions of cabinet séances, lights and other phenomena occur at a distance from the medium while he's under full bodily control—that is, under conditions in which it's irrelevant to appeal to previously concealed light sources operated by the medium's body.

Moreover, in fairness to Kai, we should acknowledge that in agreeing to a strip search, careful control of his limbs during phenomena produced out of his reach, and some video documentation, Kai has submitted to what we might consider an important first level of convincing controls. Nevertheless, we should also note that he hasn't yet submitted to full cavity searches or oth-er controls (e.g., wearing sealed boxing gloves or one-piece suits) that would more conclusively rule out the suggestion that he hid fake ectoplasm or other accessories in his rectum.

I should also add that it's not facile skepticism to wonder if Kai used his rectum as a hiding place. On the contrary, there are two good reasons for taking the rectum-hypothesis seriously in Kai's case. The first is that drug mules often use the rectum as hiding place, and this is something Kai certainly knows from his immersion as a documentary filmmaker in the Frankfurt drug scene. And perhaps more important, it's not unprecedented for physical medi-ums to stash material in their rectums. Probably the most notorious such case is that of the Hungarian medium Ladislaus Laszlo (mentioned by Nahm in his 2014 report).

The case of Laszlo is relevant here for another reason. In addition to hid-ing objects in his rectum, Laszlo conducted cabinet sittings in a way that fa-cilitated cheating, and Kai's cabinet séances suffer from the identical lack of control. As Eric Dingwall observed about "the enormous importance of the hand-control" in the case of Laszlo, "…if the hands are held then the arrange-ment of the products [e.g., ectoplasm] becomes a matter of some difficulty. Laszlo's hands were sometimes held and sometimes not. *Often the hands were free behind the curtains between the appearance of different phenomena.*"[16]

Similarly, many sitters during Kai's cabinet séances have observed that Kai spends considerable time behind closed curtains before and between phenomena, that in many cases they hear noises coming from the cabinet, and that those noises could easily be interpreted as Kai retrieving "products" from previously unexamined or undetected locations. We should keep these matters in mind when considering the phenomena that follow.

So, returning to the events of the séance: During the period, early on, of singing and "energy-gathering," I and some others thought we heard rapping sounds from the ceiling. But there was so much noise from the music, singing, and shuffling in the cabinet, we couldn't be certain. There was also a brief period during which the cabinet curtains began to flap (I was touched on my right arm) and I and others felt breezes coming from the direction of the cabinet. HB said this was due to the Chemists concentrating the energy around the medium rather than in front of the strip on the floor outside the cabinet (as would happen during the object-movement portion of the séance).[17]

The medium then began to make choking and gurgling sounds, suggesting the imminent arrival of ectoplasm. Soon thereafter, HB instructed Jochen to turn up the red light and for Jochen and me to open the curtain. Then we clearly saw the medium pull a large quantity of ectoplasm from his mouth, which fell into a heap on the floor in front of him. The video we captured of this, although very grainy after digital enhancement, clearly shows this action, and toward the end of the sequence, when the medium's left hand was not so close to his mouth, one can clearly see that the material is issuing from the medium's mouth and not his hands or near his bare arms (Kai was, as usual, wearing a short-sleeved T-shirt). The video also reveals the thread-like nature of the material's composition during the brief period when the medium spread it with his hands. There was no odor from the material, or any evidence of the black tea or Kai's recent meal. It seems doubtful then, that the medium regurgitated the substance. Now admittedly, Kai could conceivably have regurgitated his recent meal during the period when he was alone, prior to the strip search, and then swallowed some material to be regurgitated as ectoplasm. Indeed, many yogis practice the internal-cleansing ritual of *dhauti* in which they swallow a large (3 "-wide, 4'-long) strip of cotton.[18] Nevertheless, since the ectoplasm was odor-free and showed no discoloration from the tea, I have trouble accepting that it emerged from Kai's gut or alimentary tract.

Jochen confirmed that, from his position, he could see the ectoplasm issuing from the medium's mouth. He saw Kai's left hand and fingers spread open, helping to stretch his mouth, and he could look under the hand to see that the material came from the mouth and not his hands. My view on the other side was initially blocked by Kai's left hand stretching his mouth. But he later moved that hand and used both hands to clearly pull more material from his mouth (Figure 7).

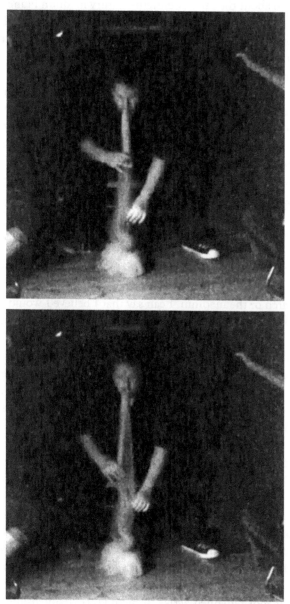

Figure 7—Extruding ectoplasm

We next had a display of ectoplasm that glowed green. The inspiration for this had apparently grown innocently out of some earlier discussions between Jochen and Kai about the early twentieth-century medium Franek Kluski having produced such a phenomenon.[19] HB asked Jochen and me three times to open the cabinet curtains, following short periods of singing and energy-gathering. The first time we saw a thin, glowing column of ectoplasm. This was followed by two more elaborate and impressive displays. In the first of these, the ectoplasm seemed to be held and stretched out by the medium's hands and rotated both back and forth, and also clockwise and counterclockwise. The next time it was held in a kind of triangular shape and brought very close to my face and then to Jochen's. I estimate that the ectoplasm was at its closest about 2 inches from my face, close enough for me to wonder whether I could be hit by it and inadvertently injure the medium (Kai usually, but unpersuasively, warned that sitters could harm him physically by touching the ectoplasm.). As the material was stretched in different directions, I could clearly see that it had a fiber (or thread)-like, structure. Although some observers of mediumistic phenomena have reported odors from ectoplasm (e.g., that of semen or ozone), I detected no odor from the material, even when it was brought so close to my face. And for those concerned about our not having performed a full cavity search of the medium, I can say that I believe I would have smelled the material had it been regurgitated (with or without remnants of Kai's recent meal) or concealed in his rectum. I should also note again that the material had no telltale discoloration, either from food or from excrement.[20]

After the display of green ectoplasm, we twice opened the curtains to view the substance on the floor in front of and between the medium's feet. HB wanted us to see how it moved and seemed to breathe. But the level of red light HB permitted was simply too dim for clear observation. At first, it was too low for anyone to see the mass clearly at all. But then HB asked for the light to be increased slightly. At that point, I bent low, about 18 inches from the mass, and could not clearly detect any movement. Perhaps that was because my head was positioned above the mass, because some others, farther back in the room and viewing the mass from the front, reported seeing a slight movement on its right side. The video of this seems to confirm that report. It shows a brief, small movement toward the end of the clip. Moreover, it also seems clear that the movement wasn't caused by the medium's foot because his left foot (the one closest to the movement) was visible and flat on the ground, while his right foot remained active, sometimes partially visible and audible. Indeed, it's standard procedure for the medium's right foot to tap loudly in order to indicate when to open and close the curtains.

The final ectoplasm display was of Kai completely covered by a "netting" of material from his head to the floor. This "cocoon" is typically created when Kai takes the ectoplasm (either still on the floor or already within his hands), stretches it, and covers himself with it. Allegedly, this re-energizes the organism, although on this occasion it was followed by Kai's premature awakening from trance and thus to the official closing of the séance. A very faint image of the cocoon was captured on video. It revealed that the cocoon was wrapped around Kai and clearly connected to the mass of ectoplasm on the floor. It showed Kai moving the material with his hands, but it was not clear enough to confirm sitters' impression that the ectoplasm seemed to be of one seamless piece. That impression, if correct, is interesting because the previous, glowing ectoplasm was spread and torn and revealed gaps between parts of the material. So it's an open question whether the cocoon was new material or whether it was a repaired version of the previous material.

The medium's emergence from trance happened behind the closed curtain. So we were unable to observe what happened to the netting we'd just seen covering him. But as I'll note again, subsequent observation of both the cabinet and Kai immediately after the séance revealed no hidden netting, and no remnants or moisture on the floor.

It's also worth mentioning that during the darkened portions of the séance, the sitters' hands were accounted for. Jochen had one hand on the curtain (ready to open it at a moment's notice) and the other on the lamp controls (ready to turn it on at a moment's notice). I had my right hand by the curtain and my left hand holding Julia's right hand atop the CD player. All other sitters had hands joined. Jochen and I needed to be ready with our hands next to the curtain, awaiting the stomping sound of the medium's foot, signaling us to either open or close the curtains.

After I unlocked the door, the sitters filed out of the séance room. I remained behind to examine the room and cabinet, and to observe Kai recover from the trance. He appeared as if he needed to vomit into the bucket kept at his side for that purpose, but I observed afterwards that the bucket contained nothing but some moisture (presumably from spit) and two mostly dry (and odorless) paper towels Kai used to dab his mouth and face.

In the meantime, at Kai's urging, Jochen conducted another strip search and reported to me that nothing suspicious was found on Kai's person or in his clothes.

The entire time of the séance was approximately 1:40.

TABLE SÉANCE 05-16-2013

Sitters were arranged as in the previous table séances. Kai was concerned from the beginning that there would be no phenomena because he was tired from the previous three séances, and because in nearly nine years of mediumship he'd never been able to have more than three successful séances in one week. But inspired by our earlier results, and intrigued by what he'd seen of Robert's GoPro cameras, he was eager to try a table séance with Robert's conventional video camera positioned as before, supplemented by a GoPro attached to my chest.

Julia's right hand throughout rested on the red-light control (awaiting Kai's instructions to turn it on, but sometimes turning the light on under her own volition), and occasional periods of illumination revealed that sitters' fingers were lightly touching the table top, hanging down (as it were) with palms raised.

By comparison to the earlier table sittings, this séance was, indeed, disappointing. The table slid and rotated dramatically on the wooden floor and partially levitated (usually in darkness) a few times. Turning on the red light tended to snuff out or decrease the table movement, even when the sitters closed their eyes (just in case the inhibiting factor was, not the light itself or our knowledge that it was on, but rather the sitters' perception of it).

During a short break after nearly an hour of this activity, we decided to place rug under the séance table. This would prevent the table from sliding along the floor, and Kai suggested that it would force the energy to concentrate instead on raising the table. Under these conditions the table shuddered dramatically and seemed to make efforts to rise up. We also had three brief partial levitations, captured in part on video. Still, we couldn't rule out the possibility that one or more sitters could consciously or unconsciously simulate the table's movement on carpet under these conditions.

After Kai unsuccessfully challenged the spirits with an ultimatum to end the séance if they didn't produce better results, the session was brought to a close.

Perhaps surprisingly, this negative séance may in fact be a positive result. If, as some magicians like to allege, it's so easy to raise a levitated table with one's hands or just one's thumbs, Kai had ample opportunities in both darkness and dim red light to make it happen. Granted, Kai could have been feigning exhaustion—that can't be ruled out in principle. But it seems more likely to me that if Kai were simply a fraudulent medium, he would have availed himself of the opportunity afforded by darkness to impress us further, rather than go through what would have been the fruitless charade of placing the rug under the table and presenting the spirits with an ultimatum.

Comments on the Austrian Sittings

The video of the table levitation is certainly interesting, but it would be more convincing if Kai's thumbs were visible above the table. Of course, even if it's true that it takes only two thumbs and a little bit of practice to raise a light four-legged table quite smoothly, the fact that a table levitation can be simulated by trickery doesn't establish that it can *only* be produced by trickery. Nevertheless, since neither Jochen nor I (seated to Kai's sides and controlling him) can attest to having controlled Kai's thumbs, subsequent attempts at recording the phenomena clearly need to be conducted under better illumination, with more cameras, and with more sensitive cameras (which we've since obtained), or of course while clearly holding Kai's entire hand in ours. Regrettably, as long as FEG séances require Kai and others to be in contact with the table, the evidence for the genuineness of the levitations will never be as compelling as those from stronger cases of physical mediumship—for example, the Palladino levitations from the 1908 Naples sittings, which often occurred out of Eusapia Palladino's reach.[21]

The apports must be rated as less evidential still, simply because Kai wasn't searched prior to the séance and because in these cases it's especially difficult to rule out masterfully applied sleight of hand. However, both apports occurred in decent red light, good enough to see Kai's extended arm, hand, and fingers clearly, and also (in the case of the crystal) while a flashlight was shone directly into Kai's mouth.[22] The copper apport remains intriguing though, in view of the fact that it seems to have been produced as a typical Kai reaction to something that had recently commanded his attention and fascinated him. I'd shown him Katie's foil only a few hours earlier, and he presumably had no opportunity during that interval, while still at the farmhouse, to come up with a nugget of copper. None of the rest of us had ever before seen a copper nugget, and it's likely that Kai was truthful in saying that he too had never seen one. This apport was the first such object ever to appear in an FEG sitting; FEG apports are routinely collected by Kai in a display case back in Hanau; and they're also reported on the FEG's blog. Had there been previous copper nugget apports, the event would not have been kept secret. And perhaps most important, it seems highly unlikely that Kai would have traveled to Austria armed in advance with a copper nugget, the significance—indeed, the whole point—of which turned out to be tied closely to an event that he couldn't have predicted.

Moreover, as I noted previously, Kai's bare right arm and fingers were fully visible when the apport appeared, and Jochen had been visibly feeling up and down that arm while I controlled Kai's left hand and foot. Furthermore, the audio recording of this event documents dramatically how loudly that apport struck the table, as if it had been forcibly propelled there and bounced off the table. But if that action had been initiated by Kai's right hand, I believe it would have been seen clearly by all the sitters. And there was certainly no contraption in the room that could have produced that effect. Now, I must note that I've seen an apport drop from magician Jeff McBride's bare arms.[23] However, I didn't observe or examine his hands on this occasion, whereas Kai's exposed hand, fingers, and arm were fully visible while Jochen ran his own hand up and down the arm. Moreover, Jeff's apport was dropped softly, as if it was released; it wasn't propelled forcibly as Kai's apport was. I believe it's correct to say that a conjuror would need some kind of overtly visible movement to make the apparently apported object move so vigorously under the conditions obtaining at our séance. But we observed no such movement.

The ectoplasmic manifestations, although produced under decent conditions of control (in stark contrast to those allowed with any other current physical medium), were likewise produced under conditions that can and should be tightened further. As I've noted, it's not easy to defend the skeptical suggestion that Kai hid the ectoplasm at some point either in his rectum or his gut. And that suggestion seems even more implausible when we recall that Kai would have needed to swallow or conceal inside him not simply the mass of ectoplasm (including the hand, arm, and column seen in Hanau) but also any devices he used to produce lights and other phenomena occurring during the cabinet séance but not discovered in the cabinet or séance room when the sitting was over. Still, given the current suspicion legitimately attaching to some of Kai's phenomena, more needs to be done to rule out those options.

Moreover, after learning of Nahm's conjecture that Kai manipulated the mass on the floor by means of strings pulled by his hands while behind his body, I viewed our video footage again of the moving mass on the floor. Although the video is very dark and outlines of Kai's arms are extremely dim, it's nevertheless obvious that Kai's hands are indeed behind him, apparently hidden. Kai's arms are partially visible, also placed behind him, and they seem to be moving, although that might be an artifact of the digital noise. In any case, why should Kai's hands be behind him during this display? If Kai had been doing nothing to manually manipulate the ectoplasmic mass, his hands could have rested on his knees, where they would have been visible in the red light.

There may be an innocent explanation for this, but under the circumstances it can only fuel suspicion.

Moreover, certain regular features of a Kai cabinet sitting are probably doomed to arouse suspicions in some people—including, of course, darkness, the cabinet itself, and the alleged need to retreat behind the curtain. Many would also point suspiciously to the loud singing requested by HB, which could be interpreted as providing covering noise for furtive actions within the cabinet. Kai (or HB) maintains that this helps concentrate energy within the cabinet and for all we know that might be the case. So I believe we must acknowledge and respect this common feature of a spiritist belief system and work around it as much as possible. And indeed, the resourceful experimenter still has many control options available, at least in principle.

It's also unfortunate, and perhaps needlessly suspicious, that the disappearance of the ectoplasm occurred out of sight, in the cabinet. Still, it's not obvious that the ectoplasm's disappearance must be attributed to conjuring. I found nothing suspicious, and certainly no trace of the material, in the cabinet when the séance ended, and Jochen found nothing when he strip-searched Kai afterward. Granted, we can't positively rule out that the material found a temporary home in one of Kai's orifices (fore or aft). But (in addition to problems noted above in sustaining that conjecture) various additional proposed controls should help rule that out.

I should note that I've seen Jeff McBride pull a mass of paper "ectoplasm" out of his mouth (something which can be compressed initially to a very small size and placed in the mouth),[24] which, after he collected it, he then made vanish with a clap of his hands. I've learned that there are devices that magicians can conceal in their sleeves that can rapidly retract the expelled material. Of course, I didn't strip search Jeff in advance or examine his clothing (or even just the roomy sleeves of his kimono) prior to his demonstration. But it's highly unlikely that Kai, who as usual was wearing a short-sleeved T-shirt, had any such accessories at his disposal and which escaped notice in the strip search and inspection of his clothing and the cabinet. As magician and psi researcher Loyd Auerbach wrote me after viewing my slides from the videos and studying an earlier account of these events, "The problem is disposal of the material afterward. [It's] one thing to hide a compressed packet, quite another to get rid of or re-compress the material."[25]

Kai seemed quite encouraged by the results of these sittings, and he at least seemed eager to introduce more cameras and better light into the proceedings. He was well aware, and often proudly informed others, that he's the only physical medium currently consenting to any respectable controls. He was also aware that good video documentation of his phenomena could secure for him a significant place in parapsychological history. Furthermore, if Kai's discomfort with video recording is what it seemed to be, rather than a ploy to avoid exposure, it's reasonable to think he could gradually come to feel more comfortable with multiple cameras pointed in his direction, just as people repeatedly interviewed on camera gradually adjust to the presence of cameras and eventually stop noticing them. That's why I left Austria feeling hopeful that future séances would yield even better results.

Revelations and Concerns

Of course, now the picture is murkier than it was in Austria. In his 2014 report that accompanied mine, Michael Nahm presented a compelling, though still largely circumstantial, case for regarding some of Kai's phenomena as fraudulent. As Nahm recounts, and complicating matters further, Kai eventually confirmed that he purchased, from a Halloween supply store, both luminous (green) and non-luminous cobweb material resembling at least some of the material displayed as ectoplasm in FEG cabinet sittings. Kai even sent me a video he'd made, but never posted online, in which he attempted to demonstrate how different that material was from the ectoplasm from his séances. And in emails to me, Kai claimed that he bought the material to evaluate suspicions he'd heard in 2012 about his having used Halloween-type cobweb to simulate ectoplasm. But after making the videos and assuring himself that there was no resemblance, he decided not to go public with this because (he said) so many people experience the entire mediumistic act as genuine (implying, to me at any rate, that some of the mediumistic act is *not* genuine), that he didn't want to raise suspicions needlessly about a single allegation concerning material that didn't resemble his ectoplasm.

However, Kai's communications on this matter only raised additional questions and concerns, and one doesn't have to be a rabid skeptic to figure them out. First, I'll concede that the non-luminous ectoplasm I've seen didn't look like the material shown in Kai's video. The non-luminous ectoplasm I observed, especially the fine netting covering Kai like a cocoon, looks more like a fine cloth than the more clearly synthetic and stringy material of the cobweb in Kai's private video. But the luminous cobweb Kai manipulated in his video looks very much like the glowing green ectoplasm I saw in Austria.

Moreover, Nahm also purchased some Halloween cobweb and informed me that there are different kinds and qualities of cobweb, and that the material he bought, right out of the bag, looks different from, and more condensed than, what Kai displayed in his video. It may be, as Nahm suggested, that Kai's material had already been manipulated and stretched thin.

Second, Kai claimed he learned about suspicions concerning the cobweb in 2012, and he seems to say that he produced his video clip at that time. But I know that Kai purchased cobweb in late 2013, and that he purchased non-luminous material in an amount—one kilogram—considerably greater than what would be needed (say) just to satisfy his curiosity about what the material looked and felt like and how it behaved (the material *is* available from that vendor in a 500 g size).

Third, one can only wonder how Kai was able to evaluate the similarity between the Halloween cobweb and the material produced while he's ostensibly in trance. Kai always claims he must ask, when he comes out of trance, what happened during the séance because (he says) his awareness of the world around him is replaced entirely by HB. But then if Kai is genuinely in the kind of trance he reports, he's not actually aware of what the ectoplasm looks or feels like. So if Kai is telling the truth about that, then he can only know what the ectoplasmic material is like from underexposed or blurry still photos or videos. But in that case, one would think that sitters can speak more authoritatively about the resemblance than Kai can.

Finally (and perhaps most important), even if Kai's reason for withholding information about the cobweb from his followers is defensible (and I'm not sure it is), he has no such reason for withholding it from his investigators, especially those with whom he ostensibly had open and honest communication. Nevertheless, when Nahm asked Kai whether he'd ever seen or heard of the fake cobweb, Kai said he hadn't.[26] Kai told me about his purchase and testing of the material only in May 2014—after he learned that I and my colleagues had been alerted about the matter. The news of Kai's purchases also was a revelation and disappointment to Jochen, who is much closer to Kai than either Nahm or myself.

Moreover, to make matters worse, based on communications I've had with both Kai and Jochen, I would say it's now indisputable that on some occasions Kai used something at least similar to a magician's device called the D'Lite Flight to produce a moving light while pretending to be in trance. Why am I so confident of this? During a Skype conversation with Jochen, I asked him directly whether Kai had confessed to using a device to produce the moving light that Nahm was preparing to describe for his 2014 report. Apparently, the directness of my question took Jochen by surprise, and he hesitated for some time, evidently struggling to figure out what to say. The reason for that seemed obvious. If Kai had never confessed to having cheated, Jochen could easily have said so; there would have been nothing to hide. So I inferred that Kai had made some sort of admission and sworn Jochen to secrecy. Because Jochen believed (and still believes) that *some* of Kai's phenomena are genuine, I know he didn't want to jeopardize his relationship with Kai and thereby lose his opportunity to study those phenomena. And because Jochen is an honorable man, my question put him in the unenviable position of having to lie to one friend to keep a promise made to another. So, faced with conflicting moral obligations, Jochen was commendably unsure what to do. At any rate, in his startled hesitation, he didn't directly violate any confidence, and I didn't force the matter.

However, I then confirmed my understanding of what had happened in a Skype video conversation with Kai. I told Kai why, on the basis of my talk with Jochen, I now knew that he'd cheated and only feigned being in trance on some occasions. Now if Kai had felt that my accusation was unwarranted, he could *and should* have challenged my inference. But he offered no protest, and in fact he couldn't even look at me through most of our talk. Instead, he apologized many times and made some general and not altogether clear comments about the differences between public sittings and séances conducted for scientific scrutiny. Indeed, in subsequent emails Kai repeatedly took pains to distinguish his public demonstrations from the sessions conducted under my supervision. It's difficult not to see that as a tacit admission that at least some phenomena at the public séances may be faked. At any rate, although my Skype conversation didn't elicit an explicit confession, I consider Kai's response to my challenge to be functionally equivalent to one.

However, it's important not to get carried away with skeptical enthusiasm. I should also note that most of the moving-light phenomena I've observed were quite different from those that can be produced by the D'Lite Flight or similar devices. Indeed, during my 2010 trip to Hanau, in the portion of the table sitting recorded with high resolution IR video, I observed a bright light hovering between my legs. I was seated several sitters away from Kai, near the far end of the table from his position, and although the IR video would clearly have revealed the deployment of a device or any suspicious movements on Kai's part, nothing in the video arouses concern.

In general, none of the light phenomena I've observed—with the possible exception of the lights within the cabinet in Austria—resemble effects that could be produced by something like the D'Lite Flight. That's at least consistent with Kai's repeated assertion that those phenomena occurred only during a relatively short period of his mediumship. Of course, a more sinister interpretation of this is that Kai abandoned that trick when others started to express their suspicions about the light phenomena, and from what I can gather those opinions were indeed expressed around that time.

Besides, Nahm has challenged Kai's claim that the suspicious light phenomena occurred only briefly in 2011. In any case, as Nahm also noted, some features of Kai's ectoplasm (including the ectoplasmic "arm" and "hand") captured in still photos, also arouse suspicion. And it may be significant that, although I observed the hand/arm phenomena in Hanau, they were not part of the more scrupulously controlled Austrian séances. It wouldn't be unreasonable to suggest that under the conditions of control in Austria, which included a more thorough inspection of the cabinet than the one I'd conducted in Hanau as well as much better control of the séance room, Kai was unable to introduce whatever strings or contraptions he might have used on other occasions to manipulate the mass of ectoplasm between his feet.

Nahm proposed in his 2014 report that Kai should dispense with the bucket he brings to the cabinet. In that connection, we might now reasonably raise a few concerns about the bucket. The original explanation I heard for the bucket was that Kai occasionally needs to vomit after the cabinet sitting is over. However, it's easy to generate a sinister interpretation of this as well. For one thing, I'm not aware of any *recent* occasions (or any in the past several years) in which Kai has actually vomited into the bucket (and I'd welcome evidence to the contrary). But then a skeptic could sensibly propose that in the early days of Kai's fraudulent ectoplasm, he hadn't yet really mastered the process of swallowing the material after extracting it from its former hiding place (such as his rectum), and so occasionally and quite understandably he'd gag and vomit after trying to ingest it. Furthermore, the skeptic could propose that after Kai mastered the art of swallowing the ectoplasm, he would have private time, soon enough after the séance, to bring it back up and dispose of it. For example, in Austria, Kai would have needed to keep the material in his gut only long enough to come gradually out of his "trance," and then for Jochen to conduct his post-séance strip search. That interval would be no more than 10 minutes, well within the time limits recommended for dhauti practitioners. I hasten to add that I'm not prepared yet to endorse these skeptical suggestions, but in the present circumstances they don't seem quite as outlandish as they might otherwise.

In any case, I have to say that my experiences with the FEG have been less overtly suspicious than those on which Nahm's more thoroughly negative appraisal relies, though (as we've seen) various, and possibly innocent, incidents or features of those séances can now justifiably be treated with more suspicion than before. In fact, it may well be the case that in Austria the tighter controls forced Kai to rely only on what he could genuinely produce, and perhaps that's why Kai's Austrian phenomena were fewer and less spectacular, and why nothing of much interest occurred in Kai's fourth séance. But I should also add that I've had fewer sittings than Nahm with the FEG, and so (the critic could argue) fewer opportunities for Kai to successfully execute a trick.

Nevertheless, even in Nahm's view, some of Kai's phenomena are not so easily dismissed as fraudulent, and both Nahm and I agree that some of the best evidence for macro-PK comes from cases of mixed mediumship (the well-known Palladino case is perhaps the best example, but perhaps also the case of Carlos Mirabelli, described in Chapter 4). So the challenge now is to determine to what extent there's a residue of untarnished and more convincing FEG phenomena, and of course whether any of the phenomena produced under my supervision continue to survive scrutiny.

One problem, of course, is that Kai remains wary of working in the light, although he's grudgingly (but only occasionally) permitted very low illumination, and even then only for relatively brief periods of time. And, despite our success during my second Hanau visit in capturing a table levitation with an infrared camcorder, Kai (or HB) has since refused requests to permit additional infrared video. This inevitably troubles even open-minded observers, especially since the red lamp used for the séances generates at least as much IR energy as the tiny beam from my IR camcorder.

Moreover, if Kai used the D'Lite Flight (or something similar), then we have to entertain seriously that his knowledge of magic tricks extends beyond that single device. It seems highly unlikely that Kai simply discovered that one trick and nothing else. Indeed, we have to consider that at some point Kai conducted a search for magic devices, either on his own or by consulting someone knowledgeable. As Robert Narholz said in an email to me, "The intricacies of finding, acquiring and learning modern magic tricks surely require more directed effort and premeditation than, say, Eusapia's leg pushing up the leg of the table. It would be unreasonable to assume that Kai would (a) direct his efforts to one single gimmick only, or (b) that while researching that gimmick he wouldn't come across a lot of other "suggestions."[27]

All of this further erodes the confidence we can place in Kai's cabinet phenomena, and perhaps all of his phenomena. But again, that loss of confidence can be neutralized if Kai successfully submits to more stringent (and not necessarily heroic) controls. For what it's worth, in the months following the Austrian sessions, Kai continued to claim that he was ready to conduct further tests with me, and he once again agreed to tighter controls.

Another problem is that, even if we ignore the case for fraud presented by Nahm and also Kai's oblique confirmation of the faked light phenomena, we can easily see why many would reasonably suspect Kai of resorting occasionally to trickery. First, Kai gives séances (actually, *public demonstrations*) with considerable frequency, and he seldom has a failure or negative séance in which no (or almost no) phenomena occur. That's quite remarkable, especially for a medium who claims to be less prodigious than the greatest past mediums, all of whom had many negative séances. D. D. Home even lost his powers for an entire year. Moreover, on Kai's travels (throughout Europe, coast-to-coast US, and several times to Australia), he's often been quite exhausted, both from the rigors of traveling, his customary lack of sleep, and also from the intensity and apparent physical strain of the séances themselves. We saw, in our final Austrian séance, how an exhausted Kai was unable to mediate even a modest table levitation. But of course, it's one thing to have a largely negative séance (after three successful sessions) for experienced investigators, none of whom would find a negative séance a cause for alarm or suspicion. And it's another thing to disappoint paying customers who expect to see miracles.[28]

It may well be, as Jochen once suggested to me, that most (if not all) the great mediums were "mixed" mediums—that is, combining genuine with fraudulent phenomena. After all, from a business perspective a medium's occasional recourse to fraud isn't difficult to understand. That naturally complicates the process of establishing the authenticity of the strongest phenomena. But as long as those phenomena are thoroughly controlled, as they have been in other, and more impressive, cases from the history of physical mediumship, the challenge is manageable, and a medium's lapses don't automatically discredit the best-documented and controlled phenomena. Again, the case of Eusapia Palladino perhaps illustrates this most dramatically. So it seems that the general strategy for evaluating a case of mediumship remains the same whether it appears to be an instance of mixed or "pure" mediumship. In all cases, *the phenomena that matter are the ones most difficult to explain away.*

Besides, as common sense (or at least a course in elementary logic) dictates, the inference "Some of Kai's phenomena are fraudulent → all of Kai's phenomena are fraudulent" is invalid, just like the analogous inference "Some money is counterfeit → all money is counterfeit."

At any rate, my view du jour is that the most impressive of Kai's phenomena are the table levitations and the object movements occurring at a distance under four-limb control of the medium. Nothing uncovered so far about Kai's deceptions justifies discounting those manifestations. So at this point, the resolute skeptic wanting to impugn everything Kai has produced can only fall back on general, though admittedly reasonable, doubts about Kai's character. But nothing of interest follows from that about Kai's best-controlled and documented phenomena. Indeed, as I've noted, the history of (mixed) physical mediumship illustrates the point clearly.

The apports will remain of marginal value at best as long as Kai isn't subjected to the sorts of controls required in connection with the ectoplasm.[29] Similarly, the manifestations of ectoplasm, the most dramatic of Kai's phenomena, still need to be better-controlled. I've suggested to Kai several easy steps we could take for our next Austrian sessions to strengthen the case for the genuineness of the ectoplasm. First, we could supply our own cabinet. Kai readily (actually enthusiastically) agreed to this, because (a) it's one less thing to carry on his travels, and (b) it's obviously not an issue for him—indeed, he's often had his hosts in other countries supply the cabinet. Second, we could sew Kai into a one-piece jumpsuit in order to counter the suggestion that he's retrieved ectoplasm hidden in his rectum. There's already a precedent for this, both in the cases of Eva C. and in connection with the thoughtography of Ted Serios.[30] Kai has agreed to this control as well.

Alternatively, or additionally, we could adopt the clever procedure used in the case of Charles Bailey[31] and seal Kai's hands in boxing gloves prior to the séance. That would help counter any number of skeptical suggestions about Kai's ability to retrieve and manipulate ectoplasm and other devices for producing physical phenomena. However, Kai's reaction to that suggestion was notably cooler than to the proposal about a one-piece suit; one can only wonder why. And of course, we could have Kai drink blueberry juice or syrup just before the séance to help counter the regurgitation hypothesis. Kai knows about the application of these controls in cases he already admires, and so we can only hope he (or HB) will allow them later. Time will tell. If (despite his earlier assurances) Kai fails to submit to these tighter conditions, it will only raise more doubts, even among those with open minds. And in that case, if we hold further sessions in Austria, it might be more productive and illuminating to concentrate on the object movements under four-limb control and the table levitations under better illumination.

In a development following our sessions in Austria, Kai has finally allowed sitters to touch his ectoplasm. Now if we could do that, it might allow us not only to feel whether the ectoplasm resembles fake ectoplasm or other materials available from magic or Halloween stores, but also to capture some small portion of the material which we could subject to analysis. Prior to this, Kai (or HB) had refused to allow sitters to touch the ectoplasm on the standard spiritist grounds that doing so could harm the medium.

In fact, Kai has claimed that he sometimes bled and felt great pain when sitters touched the ectoplasm. But that prohibition against touching is clearly unconvincing. After all, the ectoplasm falls from the medium's mouth onto the floor, and to my knowledge that contact never caused pain or harmed the medium. Moreover, Kai himself stretches and otherwise manhandles the ectoplasm with no sign of personal discomfort, much less injury. In any case, perhaps the most impressive thing Kai could do to establish the genuineness of the ectoplasm would be to allow us to view and document the disappearance of the ectoplasmic "cocoon" and its alleged re-absorption into Kai's body, which we're told sometimes happens nearly instantaneously.

I understand the (often instinctive) suspicious reaction many have when reading accounts of mediumistic séances conducted under low illumination or in total darkness. Likewise, I understand the retrospective negative or skeptical reactions investigators experience when they reflect back on what previously seemed like convincing demonstrations.[32] Indeed, I've had those reactions myself on many occasions. However, I believe we must remain open to the possibility that both light and attention, and indeed the medium's beliefs and fears (rational or otherwise), can inhibit genuinely paranormal physical phenomena. The entire history of physical mediumship suggests as much, as do more recent experiments in table-tipping.[33]

In fact, we need to bear in mind that, at our current and considerable level of parapsychological ignorance, we should be especially circumspect in making assumptions about the conditions favorable or unfavorable to the production of phenomena, or about the forms in which the phenomena should manifest. Feilding addressed the point nicely, in connection with Eusapia Palladino's séance preferences.

... I cannot explain why she wished to do these things, any more than I can explain many other items in her procedure, such as why she should wish to have a table, or why she should require a curtain at all. I find, in talking with friends, that when I mention the curtain, they inevitably say, "Ah, a curtain! Why a curtain? What a suspicious fact!" I agree that it may be suspicious, but it is not necessarily so. It is suspicious when used by a materializing medium who goes behind it, and, when a "spirit" comes out, refuses to allow spectators to ascertain whether he is himself still there. But in Eusapia's case, where she sits outside it, I cannot see that, given certain obvious precautions, it is necessarily suspicious. She says it helps to "concentrate the force." Perhaps it does. I do not know what the "force" is, nor what it requires to "concentrate" it. Nor does anyone else. To a person ignorant of photography it is possible that the use by the photographer of a black cloth over his head would be suspicious. In dealing with an unknown force one can only judge empirically of the utility of certain conditions. That the curtain does have some bearing on the phenomena is clear. Eusapia appears to be en rapport with something within. And she constantly seems to experience the necessity of establishing this rapport by momentary contact with the curtain or by enveloping the table or part of herself in its folds. We never perceived, however, that the phenomena which followed this action had any normal relation to it whatever.[34]

I also remind and encourage readers and investigators to heed the advice of Oliver Lodge, who counseled researchers to

... have the common sense to treat [the medium], not as a scientific person engaged in a demonstration, but as a delicate piece of apparatus wherewith they themselves are making an investigation. She is an instrument whose ways and idiosyncracies must be learnt, and to a certain extent humoured, just as one studies and humours the ways of some much less delicate piece of physical apparatus turned out by a skilled instrument-maker.[35]

In my view, then, since it still seems premature to discount all FEG phenomena as fraudulent, I believe we should try to keep an open mind, first about whether Kai has any paranormal abilities at all, and second, if Kai does have some PK or mediumistic ability, then about his expressed beliefs concerning the conditions that either enhance or inhibit his phenomena. As far as the latter issue is concerned, it would take nearly transcendental hubris to claim that we know significantly more about these matters now than Fielding knew more than a century ago. Still, in the current and justified atmosphere of suspicion, we should nevertheless hold Kai to a higher level of evidentiality than he's so far attained, closer to that enforced in other, better-controlled, cases of mixed mediumship. So, for now, it wouldn't surprise me if, after the smoke clears from investigating the extent of Kai's deceptions, it turns out that (as he originally claimed) he really is just a modestly endowed psychic subject, and that the familiar and understandable frailties of greed and arrogance, and the lure of fame and adulation, led him to his present predicament.

Moreover, as I mentioned previously, resourceful experimenters can find ways to circumvent several (if not most) of the obstacles Kai has routinely placed in the way of optimal controls. I believe we've already succeeded to some extent in doing that. But we clearly need to go further, and I've noted some obvious and relatively painless next steps we could take to improve the quality of documentation. It seems clear that if Kai wants to salvage or re-habilitate his reputation outside the somewhat incestuous circle of uncritical spiritists who've been financing his current and very comfortable lifestyle, he must now voluntarily submit to—and succeed under—many test conditions he's so far resisted. In fact, he at least has to *try*. So long as Kai continues to resist better conditions of illumination and observation, especially those in which other carefully investigated mediums have succeeded, his mediumship will be tainted and remain an easy object of skeptical suspicion, even if some of his phenomena remain hard to doubt.

Of course, there will always be skeptics, no matter how many precautions are taken. So, practically speaking, investigators may simply have to ac-knowledge a law of diminishing returns in applying controls. Besides, it would hardly be surprising if at some point (given human psychology), continually tightening controls simply snuffs out the phenomena. And how readily that occurs will undoubtedly vary from one subject to the next, just as our inhibi-tion-thresholds vary widely in many familiar life contexts. I believe that's one reason why laboratory phenomena are so modest compared with phenomena in natural settings, if the phenomena can be duplicated at all in the lab. As I've argued elsewhere,[36] since we really are nowhere close to knowing what psi's natural history is (i.e. its function or purpose—if any—in real-life settings), for all we know it may be similar in crucial respects to familiar phenomena or abilities (e.g., sexual performance, athletic skills) that can only be evaluated in their natural contexts, not in the straitjacketed conditions required for formal experiments.

3. A Follow-Up Investigation of the Felix Circle

Two years later, in October 2015, I supervised a new series of séances in Hanau, Germany, with Kai Mügge. Undaunted by the revelations about Kai's cheating and the continuing difficulty of imposing adequate controls, I wanted to try to obtain better documentation of Kai's table levitations than my team was able to achieve in Austria in 2013.[1] In the process, my collaborators and I witnessed some interesting phenomena that are difficult to explain away normally given the control conditions imposed at the time. These include object movements beyond the reach of the sitters, a very strange "exploding" sound from the séance table, and some extended levitations in which the table seemed to sway or swim in mid-air. But what may be most interesting about this series of séances is the way the phenomena reflect the complex and tortured underlying psychodynamics of the occasion. Indeed, what readers need to know about the FEG phenomena has as much to do with personalities involved as with the phenomena themselves.

In the previous chapter, I noted why at least some of Kai's phenomena were quite compelling and why I was reasonably confident that certain ones were genuine. I found Kai's table levitations to be especially noteworthy, and on two occasions I'd been able to make video recordings of the event—one in infrared light, and the other in light from an incandescent red lamp. Unfortunately, both videos were problematical. In the former, Kai inadvertently (in the darkness) blocked much of the view of the table, so that one of his hands was not visible; the other hand was waving up and down, imitating Eusapia Palladino's practice of encouraging a table to rise. In the latter, although hands and feet are visible, it's not clear in the dim light where Kai's thumbs were. I've noted why I doubted the skeptical suggestion that Kai could have produced an apparent levitation with his thumbs, in a table he had no opportunity to rig, and in which the table's movements had the sensory characteristics of being weightless and buoyant (rather than forced upwards). Nevertheless, it seemed worthwhile to try to obtain better quality video of Kai's table levitations, and I contacted Kai to coordinate an additional series of séances.

But from the beginning, this series proved to be a struggle to arrange, and the difficulties came as no surprise. For one thing, when Michael Nahm and I published our 2014 reports on the FEG,[2] we already knew that Kai had cheated on at least one occasion (not supervised by me) by using a light-emitting device similar to a magician's trick called the D'Lite Flight. That device employs a diode at the end of a very thin wire attached usually to the user's thumb, which can make it appear as if points of light are moving around in the vicinity of the magician. In 2011, regular Felix Circle investigator Jochen S. (pseudonym) took two series of photographs, (remarkably, in retrospect) at Kai's request, from séances in Koblenz. From the start, the reddish lights shown on those photos looked suspicious to Jochen and quite unlike the more convincing lights he'd seen at a distance from the medium. After Jochen shared the photos with Nahm in 2014, Nahm noticed that they revealed how the movement of Kai's thumb corresponded to the movement of these lights, just as they would if Kai had been using a device like the D'Lite Flight. Thereafter, Jochen also revealed to us that he had discovered a light-emitting device in Kai's travel bag after one of the Koblenz séances. Furthermore, he told us that after he confronted Kai with the combined evidence of his discovery in 2011 of Kai's light-emitting device and Nahm's discovery about the photos in 2014, Kai apologetically admitted to using the device and to having concealed it on the shelves behind his curtained "cabinet" during the séances in Koblenz. (For more details, including Jochen's first-hand account of this sequence of events, see the Appendix of this chapter.)

The publicity generated by Nahm's and my papers, and subsequent internet discussion by Nahm and others of additional possible instances of fraud, initially led Kai to flatly refuse my proposal to obtain better video documentation of table levitations than we'd recorded in Austria. I told Kai that neither Nahm nor I had been able to explain away, credibly, certain of the manifestations observed in the Austrian series of séances,[3] and that if Kai wanted to demonstrate that he was more than a mere fraud, the best course would be to document even more clearly those phenomena that are most easily captured on video and most resistant to glib skeptical dismissals. I argued that his table levitations should be the focus of a follow-up series of séances.

Kai was apparently unmoved by my arguments, and his resistance was supported by his wife and members of his family, all of whom argued that he only had more to lose from further work with those determined to study him only under conditions acceptable to scientists. During those few occasions when Kai seemed amenable to trying some further tests, he nevertheless maintained that he couldn't return to the Austrian farmhouse of my videographer, Robert Narholz. I'd considered that location nearly ideal because it could be controlled easily and wasn't otherwise accessible to Kai. But Kai claimed he'd been terribly uncomfortable there under conditions of constant scrutiny and the pressure to produce good phenomena. Moreover, because Kai claimed that the location was now further tainted by Michael Nahm's transformation from a friendly investigator to one of his most vocal and fierce critics, returning to the farmhouse was, Kai said, out of the question.[4]

I then figured that if any further work with Kai was to occur, it would have to be in more congenial surroundings—presumably, his home base in Hanau, Germany. I also recognized that we'd probably have to work in the usual Hanau venue for Kai's séances: the bomb-shelter basement in Kai's parents' house. Although I realized this would inevitably raise red flags for critics, I figured that we could minimize concerns fairly readily. After all, we intended only to study the most easily documented of Kai's phenomena—table levitations. Our limited goal was to obtain even clearer video recording of the levitations than we got in Austria, figuring that if these could be even more firmly established as genuine, then Kai's most ardent and shallow critics would have to abandon the claim that Kai is nothing but a cheat, and that this might open the door to more reasoned and calm appraisals of Kai's mediumship as a whole. Moreover, since Kai had recently cleared out his curtained off computer/media nook from the bomb shelter location, the séance room itself was quite bare and would be very easy to search and declare free of suspicious devices. And besides, if we had good video from multiple angles of the levitations, it should be obvious that no tricks were employed. I did try, unsuccessfully, to secure an alternate location for these table séances. But (not surprisingly) Hanau hotels were opposed to the idea of having late night singing and séance-frivolity occurring in one of their conference rooms.

Fortunately, Kai seemed open to the idea of holding further table séances in Hanau, although his wife, Julia, and family members still tried to discourage him. Even though we had to wait two and a half years before holding our follow-up tests in Hanau, in October, 2015, I should note that those delays were not due to Kai. On at least two occasions, Kai and I settled on a period when he had an opening in his very busy schedule, but it was difficult to get other key members of my team to break free at those times. The main hold-out on those occasions was former circle leader Jochen. Although Julia had assumed regular duty now as circle leader, Kai still considered Jochen to be a crucial component in the mix—someone he not only trusted and liked, but also someone whose scientific credentials both Kai and I recognized were impeccable. Quite understandably, Jochen's schedule was even busier than Kai's. He divided his professional time between research at a world-famous scientific institute and his cardiological clinical work at a hospital. Moreover, he was scrupulous in devoting as much time as possible to his wife and children.

As the time for our tests approached, the entire enterprise fell under a cloud of attacks on both Kai and Jochen. The attacks on Kai were the usual critical assaults, including recent criticism from Peter Mulacz and Michael Nahm in the Society for Psychical Research's magazine, *Paranormal Review.*[5] The attacks on Jochen included charges that he was an accomplice in Kai's fraud and (in a direct effort to undermine his professional career) threats to reveal Jochen's real identity and contact his employer about Jochen's allegedly "unscientific" FEG activities. And just shortly before the trip was to take place, Jochen's identity was indeed revealed in an online blog written by a former, embittered, FEG member. So just as the travel to Europe was about to begin, both Kai and Jochen were deeply shaken and wary about our plans to hold séances as scheduled.

My main collaborator, as in the Austrian 2013 investigations, was filmmaker Robert Narholz, who is preparing a documentary tentatively called *Finding PK.* Since Nahm had no inclination to associate with Kai again after he learning of Kai's repeated cheating, and since Nahm was now persona non grata at the Felix Circle anyway, we replaced him with someone Kai liked and trusted, and whom Robert and I also could trust—noted journalist Leslie Kean, perhaps best-known to readers as the author of an outstanding survey of evidence for UFOs, and more recently a critically-acclaimed book on postmortem survival.[6] During her research on mediumship and postmortem survival, Leslie had attended several of Kai's séances in the US and other physical mediumship circles in the UK, and was quite familiar at this point with the history of the subject and the current state of physical mediumship. Because she'd become a seasoned and critical observer, Robert and I were certain that her presence would be a great asset.

Boots on the Ground

Leslie and I arrived in Hanau on September 30; Robert's arrival was scheduled for October 3. Leslie and I had hoped to devote the first few days in Hanau to recovering from jet lag and trying to establish a positive and friendly working relationship with Kai and Julia. I hadn't seen Kai (except via Skype) since our 2013 Austrian sessions, and although those Skype sessions had mostly been friendly (including the one where I confronted Kai about his cheating), I was eager to have some time, before testing, to re-establish the in-person warmth we'd previously enjoyed. Unlike some, I didn't regard what I knew for certain about Kai's cheating to be an inevitable impediment to cordiality or even to friendship.

So Leslie and I spent some time, soon after arrival, with Kai, Julia, and Jochen at Kai's new, and quite comfortable modern apartment. Kai showed us various rare books from his impressive collection of works on physical medi-umship, and then the five of us went to dinner. It was clear that Jochen and Kai were both very anxious—Kai because he was afraid of failure and how that would be interpreted by critics and others, and Jochen because of the recent internet exposure of his real identity and the blogger's unauthorized (and illegal) use of Jochen's photos of Kai apparently employing a device like the magician's D'Lite Flight. Jochen also informed us that his wife was firmly opposed to Jochen being identified, even under his usual pseudonym. At the time they were both quite afraid of further efforts by the blogger to harm Jo-chen professionally.

I did my best to diminish Kai's concerns. I reminded him that our goal was simply to do a more thorough job of documenting the table levitations, and that Robert, Leslie, and I all understood that—especially under the pre-vailing tensions—there was no disgrace in getting no, or only disappointing, results. So I assured Kai I wouldn't be writing a damning critical report about our meeting if he simply tried, but failed, to get the results we'd aimed for. And Leslie and I assured him further that we were confident that something of value would happen, and that we had no doubt that we'd get some good table levitations. The main thing, I quite clearly reminded Kai, was that he shouldn't do anything foolish. I believe Kai understood precisely what I meant by that.

Kai informed us soon after our arrival that he'd be able to participate in only four séances. That came as a surprise. Robert and I had been under the impression that Kai's cabinet séances took more out of him than table séances, due to the physical toll of Kai's "holotropic" breathing and the apparently physically demanding process of producing ectoplasm. So we were hopeful that we could hold more than four sessions, and at least a few on consecutive days to maximize our opportunities for good documentation. After all, we held table séances on consecutive days during our Austrian sessions with Kai in 2013. So we figured we'd spend our first few days in Hanau just hanging out cordially and holding casual séances, and then when Robert arrived we'd begin to hold well-controlled sessions. But Kai now explained that he needed one day's rest between séances.

I expected Kai's reason for this requirement to be that the stress of the occasion made each table séance more exhausting than it would be under more usual, and informal, circumstances. Instead, Kai's justification was that table levitations are *more* exhausting than cabinet sittings because in the former he feels more conscious responsibility and stress than when he's in a trance during cabinet sittings, at which times his waking consciousness and its sources of stress are allegedly switched off. So curiously and to our surprise, Kai was claiming that a cabinet sitting is one of his few opportunities to sleep. Now, if Kai's waking consciousness is really and fully switched off during a cabinet séance (a matter deserving further scrutiny, and which Michael Nahm claims is simply false[7]) that might indeed reduce one kind of stress. But considering Kai's pronounced sweating and physical exhaustion after cabinet sittings, I doubt in any case that table séances overall take more out of Kai than cabinet séances.

In fact, I suspect that Kai's reluctance to hold more séances may have had a more mundane explanation than the one he provided. I consider it more likely that Kai was simply anxious and ambivalent about the entire investigation, and that as a result he was sleeping even less than usual and was worried that stress and fatigue would lead to poor results in the table séances. I think Kai hoped to get as much rest and relaxation as possible between the séances, anticipating that each occasion would be difficult for him. And as it happened, Kai reported throughout our visit that he was indeed sleeping poorly, and even less than usual.

Because Robert would be able to join us only from October 3 until the 9th, and although Jochen had family obligations, Leslie and I decided that we should hold a séance without them on the 2nd, just to get Kai warmed up and at least somewhat adjusted to the presence of experimenters generally and us in particular. Kai agreed this was a good idea.

So an informal séance #1 was held on the evening of October 2, in darkness, lasting about an hour. Sitters (clockwise) were Kai, Elke (Kai's mother), Leslie, me, and Julia (operating the CD player and red light). The table was Kai's usual plastic garden table, 33.5 inches in diameter and 28 inches high. (See Fig. 1) Before we began, Kai asked Leslie and me, individually, to discern how hard it was to lift the table when other sitters' hands were resting atop it. We both agreed we couldn't make the table rise either smoothly or with its top horizontal (much less both together). And any movements we could produce resulted in table movements that felt obviously different from the way ostensibly genuine levitations feel—namely, slow, buoyant, and weightless and not as if pushed. I've found that when others try manually to move the table upwards, the table feels as if it's being forced upwards, whereas levitated tables seem to float.

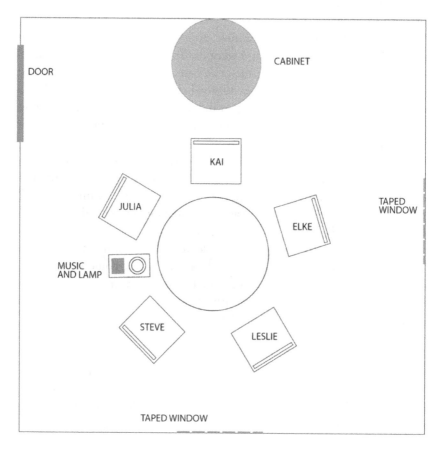

Fig. 1. Configuration of séance room for séance 1.

In addition to the levitations we would experience, several other interesting events occurred. For example, a few lights were visible at various points around the room, some of them observed collectively. In fact, Leslie, Julia, and Elke each reported seeing lights around the cabinet at the other end of the room and presumably out of Kai's reach. For those, Kai's position at the table was easy to judge by his loud singing. Moreover, we all heard a few strong raps on the wall, far away from the sitters, whose locations, again, were easily discerned by their singing. And (perhaps most interesting) the bell hanging from the ceiling behind my head rang loudly. The bell was located behind me; I was seated across from Kai, and I'm certain that no sitter was within reach of that bell. In fact, the bell was closest to me, and I couldn't reach it from a sitting position.

We also had four table levitations, none lower than 1.5 feet from the ground; the shortest lasting about 4 seconds. The final two were the most impressive. For the third levitation, the table rose at least 2 feet, remained there for about 5 seconds, started to descend slowly but remained several inches off the ground, and then slowly rose again to a height of about 2 feet, remained there for several seconds, and then descended rapidly, hitting the laminate flooring with a plastic thud.

In the fourth levitation, the table rose at least 2.5 feet, and after being aloft for several seconds, it began to sway, dipping first to my left, then to my right, and back and forth a few more times, almost as if it was "swimming" to the rhythm of the music. When that was done, the table descended rapidly. The whole event probably lasted at least 15 seconds.

Kai, as usual, was dressed in a short sleeve T-shirt. Clearly, there were no hidden contraptions up his sleeve—that is, something he could extend under the table in cover of darkness to make the table rise or "swim." In fact, as usual when we greet each other, we did so with an extended and warm hug. So there was at least a hug body check, and I felt nothing under Kai's shirt.

Formal Séances

The second séance, the first formal session, was held on Oct. 4, the day after Robert arrived. We set up two cameras, but Kai was clearly nervous about their presence. For one thing, he claimed (as he often does) that the phenomena like to hide and that attempts to capture them will likely either reduce them or snuff them out altogether. Robert and I assured Kai, as we had done many times before, that it was better to record modest phenomena under good conditions than florid phenomena under poor conditions. Kai said he understood, and I'm quite sure he did. But Kai was also concerned that the cameras might be turned on accidentally or surreptitiously, as had happened with Peter Mulacz's infrared camcorder during our initial investigation. So, to calm Kai down, Robert covered the cameras with a black cloth and kept the cameras turned off. Our plan was that if good phenomena occurred and Kai was prepared to experiment, we'd turn the cameras on later, and in the meantime simply accept the fact that Kai needed to get accustomed to the presence of low-light sensitive cameras. We didn't like the fact that this left us only two more opportunities to get the video footage we'd hoped for. And Kai had already conceded that the longer we waited to get such footage, the more pressure he'd feel at the later séances. Still, Kai wasn't ready to begin with cameras turned on and uncovered.

So, after dining with Kai and Julia, my colleagues and I needed about an hour to clear the room. We removed Kai's standard black cloth "cabinet," which routinely hangs toward the back of the room, and other pieces of unnecessary furniture. The chair that had been in the cabinet (the standard resting place of focus objects like a tambourine) remained, and a large circular drum (diameter approximately 18 inches) was placed against the chair legs, leaning somewhat precariously. (see Fig. 2)

Fig. 2. Circular drum (and other "focus" objects) arrangement for séance 2.

Robert, Leslie and I checked the room thoroughly. We unlocked and removed the tape from the various windows, and determined that there was nothing behind them but Styrofoam, and certainly no hidden devices. Robert and I also toured the various nearby rooms of the basement, confirming there was no access from those rooms to the séance area. Robert made video recordings of these tours as well as my inspection of the séance room. We also inspected the séance table, looking carefully underneath. There was certainly no hidden contraption or anything else suspicious. Finally, I locked the door leading upstairs to the rest of the house, and we also locked the door leading to the laundry room.

Elke was disappointed to learn that I wanted to exclude her from this séance because I wanted to keep sitters to a minimum. Kai was disappointed as well, though he shouldn't have been surprised, and he was wary of our desire to remove the cabinet curtain from the room, claiming that its presence helped concentrate the energy. I promised to bring it back if we got no results, in the belief that video documentation could show conclusively that no previously hidden contraption capable of levitating the table emerged from the cabinet.

Sitters clockwise from Kai were Leslie, Robert, Jochen, me, and Julia (who, as usual, operated the CD player and red light).

The séance was in two parts. The first was rather unimpressive; Kai had tired during the hour's wait to set up the room, and his initial enthusiasm and energy seemed to have abated somewhat. Still, we had three full levitations in darkness, preceded by fewer than the usual amount of table movements—the table just started to rise without the customary strong preamble. The levitations ranged from 3 to 6 seconds, and from 6 inches to 12 or 15 inches. After the levitations Kai had Julia immediately turn up the red light to show that Julia and Leslie were controlling Kai's hands and resting their feet on his feet. Of course, that doesn't tell us where those limbs were immediately prior to the turning on of the light, but Leslie was controlling Kai the entire time and was able to state that Kai's left hand and foot hadn't moved under her right hand and foot.

After the break there were two strong levitations and more vigorous table movements than we enjoyed in the earlier part of the séance. On two occasions the table rocked quite violently to my left and right, each time lifting two legs high off the ground and then returning to the ground with great force and a loud plastic thud against the laminate floor. The last of these table-leg-banging events seemed to signal the end of the evening's session; at least that's how Kai understood it.

For the fourth levitation, the table slowly rose as high as 24 inches, the whole event lasting perhaps 10 seconds. It occurred in stages, initially rising about half that distance and then—when I thought the event had reached its peak—rising the rest of the way. Levitation number five was another "swimming" table event, with the table rising again about 2.5 feet high, dipping back and forth several times over the course of 10-15 seconds.

At one point I saw a bright red light in the vicinity of Julia's lap. I asked her whether she had turned on a light and she said no.[8] Other sitters reported seeing a few lights. We also heard a strong knocking sound, which some thought came from behind me but which I thought came from the wall on my left (well beyond Julia's reach, judging by the location of her voice).

By far the most outstanding non-levitation event was a loud whack from the drum leaning against the chair with the focus objects. The chair was out of Kai's reach, and besides, Leslie confirmed that she'd been touching Kai's left leg and hand (the side closest to the drum). When the séance was over Leslie hit the drum moderately with her hand, to see how the sound compared with what we'd heard. The resulting sound was clearly not as loud as it had been earlier, and Leslie's relatively modest pressure on the drum knocked it from its precarious upright position. Undoubtedly, a more forceful, normally produced sound would easily have moved the drum from its position. I should add that the drum (before Leslie struck it) was positioned as it had been before the séance began. I suppose skeptics could argue that since Kai wasn't searched beforehand, he might have concealed some device on his person that could have banged the drum. But Kai was wearing a short-sleeve T-shirt as usual, his nearest hand and leg were controlled by Leslie (his other hand and leg were ostensibly controlled by Julia), and if the drum had been forcibly hit—in the dark—by an ordinary object capable of producing such a loud sound, why wasn't the drum knocked over or moved from its original position?

We can't also state with certainty that Kai didn't smuggle in some device, undetected in my hug body check, that could be used to raise the table. But that supposition seems both implausible and also inadequate for explaining the types of levitations we observed. First, at least one hand and leg were controlled by Leslie (and the other by Julia). And even so, the swaying (or swimming) table would be particularly difficult to produce under the prevailing conditions.

Interestingly, Robert impressed us before the séance began by demonstrating that he could raise the table fairly smoothly with his hands, as long as he could grip one table leg between his own legs. But there's no reason to think

Kai did this. For me the tactile and kinesthetic experience of Robert's lifting the table was conspicuously different from that of Kai's ostensibly genuine levitations. As I've noted on other occasions, the manually raised table didn't feel weightless or buoyant as it moved upward. Furthermore, when the presumably genuine levitations took place, we know that Kai's legs were spread apart (this was confirmed immediately following the levitations, when Julia turned up the red lamp to illuminate hand and foot controls). I suppose Kai might have braced two table legs with his own spread knees and supported the table in that manner, but Leslie (and presumably Julia) nevertheless controlled Kai's hands and feet, and in any case Kai couldn't have made the table sway under those conditions. Leslie also confirmed that Kai didn't have any sticky substance (like resin) on his palms that could have been used to raise the table when she controlled his hand by placing her hand on top of his (with his palm faced down on the table).

Furthermore, Robert tried a little experiment of his own. While the table was aloft, he pressed down on his side of the table to see whether it would dip there, as it presumably would if it was being raised manually by Kai from his position across from Robert. He reasoned that if Kai had been lifting the table with his hands from his side of the table, one would think that the table would yield relatively easily to Robert's applied pressure at the opposite side. But the table resisted, as if the "force" raising it was applied uniformly, or from the center of the table.

One of the persistent criticisms (especially from Peter Mulacz) is that Kai is uncooperative and that he (rather than the experimenters) specifies the séance conditions. That was clearly not the case this evening. Granted, Kai didn't let us do whatever we wanted, but we didn't expect to do everything we wanted. We recognized that Kai was already anxious, and we knew from the start that we'd probably need to tighten séance conditions gradually. In that light, I think it's fair to say that Kai was quite cooperative. As I noted (and as we expected), he was unhappy about not having Elke or the cabinet present in the room, and he also lamented the removal of many carefully arranged accessories for his normal séances. But he understood what was at stake, and his concern seemed genuinely only to be that the phenomena would be less strong under our imposed conditions—not that no phenomena would occur.

The only conditions Kai actually required were darkness and the covering of the cameras. The former is a common séance condition and no big deal, and we compensated for it to some extent with hand and leg controls. The latter request was completely unnecessary, since we weren't attempting then to record the proceedings. Instead, we were interested primarily in getting Kai more comfortable with rather Spartan séance conditions, enhanced scrutiny, and the presence (but not the activation) of cameras. In my view, Kai was needlessly paranoid about the latter condition, insisting that we cover the cameras with a black cloth, so that they wouldn't surreptitiously or accidentally record the proceedings. However, I understood that this had to do with Kai's experiences with Peter Mulacz, who had lied to him[9] and violated séance protocols. So I urged Kai to overcome his fear and reminded him that I'd always been honest and respectful of him and had never violated any agreements. In any case, Kai's heightened wariness, justified or not, was a notable element throughout this investigation, and it undoubtedly was an impediment to success.

I also attach little significance to the fact that Kai resisted turning on the cameras during this séance. The next two séances made clear that Kai was willing, after this period of adjustment, to permit the running of more cameras and more sensitive cameras than we'd had in Austria, and also that he was also willing to have the red light turned on—not just after the levitations began (which is what occurred in Austria), but while waiting for the phenomena to occur.

In an email to me Kai offered various reasons for what he perceived as his disappointing results in séance 2. One was his concern over the access and rights to whatever video footage we obtained, a matter which he thought had not yet been settled with Robert (although Robert and I thought the matter had been clarified). Another was the concern over hidden filming, a fear Kai placed fully on the shoulders of Peter Mulacz.

But apparently the main issue was that Kai said he was caught up in Jochen's extreme distress over, first, the disgruntled blogger's threats to reveal Jochen's identity, and second (and more important) Jochen's concern that the blogger had accused him of covering up Kai's fraud, and then threatened to make that claim to Jochen's employer. Jochen naturally feared that this allegation, even if false, might be enough to undermine his pending professorship.

Of course, the only reason this was even an issue for Jochen is that he had felt implied pressure from his friendship with Kai not to reveal the truth about Kai's cheating with the D'Lite Flight-type device Jochen had discovered in Kai's travel bag. That put Jochen in the compromising position of having to lie to me or others in order to protect what Kai revealed in confidence to him. From the start, Kai should have confessed to the fraud, explained why he fell from grace, apologized, and moved on. Instead, Kai's dishonesty on this matter (and probably other matters) continued unabated. Ever since Michael

Nahm's and my previous accounts appeared, Kai has had many opportunities to admit that he cheated with the D'Lite-type device, but he's consistently denied it. Moreover, when Robert interviewed Kai for his documentary, after our series was completed, Robert asked directly if Kai had ever used a device like the D'Lite Flight, and Kai again denied it.

Fig. 3 shows the arrangement of the séance table for séances 3 and 4.

The third séance was held on October 6. The results were disappointing but not entirely unanticipated. Robert set up two video cameras: a low-light Bosch Dinion Starlight HD surveillance camera viewed the table top and showed sitters' hands, and a hacked Panasonic Lumix GH2 captured the view under the table. We planned only on illumination from the red light next to the CD player. Despite Kai's lack of communication during the day, he apparently had been working himself into a positive mental state and seemed ready (and maybe even eager) to get results. We'd agreed to have the cameras running all the while, uncovered, and Kai seemed at least cognitively (if not emotionally) to be at peace with having the cameras record nothing so long as the room was dark. To help him get into and remain in a positive frame of mind, we allowed Elke to join us again, despite the fact that as a family member she's a natural target of suspicion, and also despite the fact that the extra body around the table only increased the difficulty of obtaining a good camera angle on the proceedings. We dealt with the former issue by having

Elke controlled by Jochen initially and (after a break) by Leslie. The latter issue was solved by normal hard work in setting up the cameras.

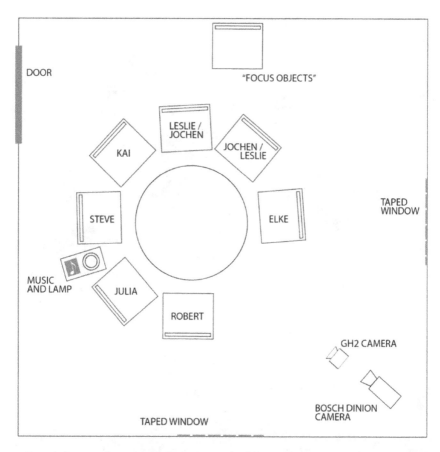

DOOR

"FOCUS OBJECTS"

LESLIE / JOCHEN

JOCHEN / LESLIE

KAI

TAPED WINDOW

STEVE

ELKE

MUSIC AND LAMP

JULIA

ROBERT

GH2 CAMERA

BOSCH DINION CAMERA

TAPED WINDOW

Fig. 4 shows a diagram of the room and table arrangement for those sittings.

Sitters clockwise from Kai were Leslie, Jochen (they switched position after the break), Elke, Robert, Julia, and me. Both Julia and Kai cooperated fully throughout the séance. Julia offered no resistance to being moved away from Kai and seated on the opposite side of the light and CD player, and she insisted throughout on placing her hands during the séance on the hands or arms of her adjacent sitters (Robert and me). Kai likewise remained in contact with me throughout—his right leg touching my left leg (and often his knee pressing firmly onto my leg), and his right hand either next to or atop my left hand, or else on my shoulder. Leslie informed me that Kai did the same (on his left) for her, in the first half of the séance.

Fig. 5 shows the clarity obtained with the Bosch camera, and it also shows Kai (center) with his hands on the shoulders of adjacent sitters, something he did often during the séance.

Fig. 6 shows a synchronized split view with the two cameras.

The table began to shudder even before we had officially started the séance—simply when we started placing our hands on the table. So it appeared that we were poised for serious action. However, although we got some vigorous and dramatic table tilting (the table even fell over on its side on two occasions), we got no levitations, and the phenomena pretty much dwindled after about 15 minutes. During some of the table tilting, the table remained quite still in a tilted position—on one occasion for about 10 seconds, and on another, about 14 seconds before falling over. Video shows how little contact

Kai had with the table on those occasions(Figs. 7 and 8). At one point we took a 5-minute break, hoping to have a return to dramatic table movements, but the second half of the séance was largely uneventful. Kai repeatedly addressed the "spirit control" as if it was an entity (other than himself) that feared the presence of the camera. Over and over he shouted "the cameras don't record in the dark." Of course, one has to wonder if Kai was reminding himself of this.

I think it's fair to say that Kai's willingness to work with cameras exceeded what he allowed in Austria, where we had to wrestle with him to use even one camera. Here, in the second séance, he allowed them to be set up in the room, ostensibly ready to use if the spirit control agreed, even though their presence worried him. In the third séance, Kai arrived seemingly at peace with (and possibly almost enthusiastic about) the idea of having two cameras running all the while. Now the sinister interpretation of this would be that, since the sessions were held in the usual bomb shelter location rather than a neutral location as in Austria, Kai had ample time to rig the location. On the other hand, we looked over the location very carefully before each séance, and we found no device on Kai or in the basement that could have produced the most dramatic table movements or the drum thwack.

Fig. 7. Split view of extreme table tilt. The table remained in this position for 10 seconds before moving further in the same direction and then falling over.

Fig. 8. Split view from 8 seconds after that in Fig. 7. The video makes clear that Robert's right hand is actually off the table (not pushing it).

The fourth séance was held of October 8. This was our final séance. Leslie, Robert, and I arrived at 7 pm, again searched the séance room and surrounding rooms carefully, and again determined that there was no possibility of an accomplice entering the séance room or any concealed apparatus for raising tables. Then, to give some encouragement to Kai, we added the cabinet back into the séance room, at its usual place next to one of the walls (and we searched the cabinet carefully). Robert also added a GoPro4 action camera to the two cameras used in the previous séance. Once everyone appeared, I locked the doors leading to the outside, as usual, and kept possession of the removable key leading from the basement to the front door. Jochen, Kai, and Julia appeared in the basement around 8 pm. Jochen was agitated by a discouraging talk with Michael Nahm earlier in the day, concerning Jochen's role in the sittings and the allegation of his being a co-conspirator in Kai's fraud. But I urged Jochen to try to hide his feelings, so as not to pollute what we'd hoped would be Kai's positive state of mind. Overall, I'd say that Jochen did this fairly effectively. Still, he was feeling overwhelmed and undoubtedly somewhat distracted by the recent assaults on his character and the threats by the disgruntled blogger to harm him professionally. So I don't think we can rule out that Kai was sensitive enough to pick up on some of this.

It was hard to gauge Kai's state of mind when he arrived. He seemed positive, but subdued and low energy—ostensibly from lack of sleep, but no doubt also from increased anxiety and lack of confidence. He kept singing to himself prior to our sitting around the table (and even as we sat around the table), as though he was making an effort not to think about his worries over obtaining good video during the evening. And although the séance had some intriguing moments, it can't be rated as a success, and Kai struck me once again as being relatively low in energy and enthusiasm throughout the proceedings.

Sitters clockwise from Kai: Leslie, Jochen, Elke, Robert, Julia, and me. Apart from one table levitation and a mysterious exploding sound from the table toward the end of our session perhaps the most interesting features of the session were psychodynamic. The session began, as before, with strong movements, but nothing special emerged from them. Even after a break, it still seemed as if we were likely to have an uneventful séance; the few table movements we felt were slight. Now I knew that psi researcher Kenneth Batcheldor had found that a light-hearted atmosphere during séances could counter psi-resistant states of mind and lead to good results.[10] So I suggested in the spirit of Batcheldorian frivolity that we concentrate less on making the table do something dramatic and simply redirect our attention elsewhere. So I suggested whimsically that we talk about the weather. Almost immediately, the table responded with more vigorous movements, as if it was glad for the relief from such unrelenting earnestness. And that led Robert, Leslie, and Jochen to join me in making jokes or comments about different kind of weather, shouting out what kind of weather we should discuss: thunder, lightning, floods, monsoons, hail, and so on. While we did that, the table continued to respond strongly. But Kai seemed unable or unwilling to enter into the spirit of the moment. Instead, he kept invoking the spirit control to make the table move. (I also think neither Julia or Elke participated in the frivolity; I could hear my neighbor Julia continuing to sing softly to the music.) Then, continuing in this frivolous vein, I suggested we tell jokes, and I rattled off a few jokes. Again, the table seemed to like the playful atmosphere. In fact, our one brief levitation, lasting about 3 seconds and rising about a foot, occurred during this period. But although Kai laughed at the jokes, he never really joined in or supported the effort to be less serious and less focused on success.

Why was that? One plausible hypothesis is that Kai, who is invested both psychologically and financially in his role as a promoter of spiritism, felt and disliked the fact that success under these Batcheldorian conditions of distraction implied that his own role (or that of the spirits) was not as crucial as he'd like to think. And that might have been exacerbated by Robert's chiming in approvingly when I noted that this seemed to confirm Batcheldor's views. Or, perhaps Kai was simply too anxious to succeed. After all, a blank séance would undoubtedly have encouraged some to argue that Kai could only produce phenomena fraudulently and under conditions of his own choosing.

Often, during the séance, the table's movements were short and jerky, but strangely forceful, as though the table movements had great energy behind them but not enough or the right kind to break the table free from its location, or even result in the more usual circular movements and banging of legs against the ground. Then, toward the end of the evening, during another period of relative calm from the table, there came an exceptionally sharp and loud sound, and shock wave, seemingly from inside the table, like a kind of explosion but with a very short envelope (that is, attack and decay). The event apparently startled and frightened us all. I'm quite certain Kai played no role in this. My left leg was touching his right leg (indeed, the two of us were crammed into very close contact to allow for a good camera view of the table), and my left arm was in contact with Kai's right elbow and forearm. Leslie reports similar contact with Kai's left side. Then, as we felt along the table to see what might have happened to it, I noticed that the round center piece (which could be removed for an umbrella to be inserted) had been raised upwards. (Fig. 9) I tried to push it back down and found that it fit very tightly and could be returned to its original position only with difficulty. I then tried pushing it back up from underneath, and that too required several attempts and some effort. I also confirmed, from photos taken before the séance, that the center piece had been flush with the table top prior to the séance. Our instinctive impression of this event was that the table, which had been moving fitfully and continually all evening but which had levitated only once, and briefly at that, had built up a great deal of energy that needed to be released somehow. The sound and shock wave, indeed, seemed to issue directly from within the table, as if some force had exploded there and that the release of energy and vibration within the table pushed the center piece upwards.

Fig. 9. Raised center portion of séance table. Pushed up after the séance for illustration.

I should add that Julia's left hand, all the while, was on my right hand, and that Jochen was in contact with Elke. Leslie reports that although she was sitting close to Jochen and had occasional physical contact, she was not controlling him. Now, for those who think (stupidly in my opinion) that Jochen is a co-conspirator and can't be trusted, I should add that to manually move that center piece upwards required a kind of push from below that, even if it could be accomplished quickly in one rapid movement (contrary to what I experienced when trying to move it), would not have made the kind of sharp explosive sound we heard. It would presumably also have required a kind of lucky pinpoint precision of attack that's very difficult (if not impossible) to execute in the dark. Similarly, that explosive and very loud sound would not be produced merely from a forceful thwack on the underside of the table, or a bang administered to the top of the table. Simply forcefully hitting the table abruptly, either from above or below, would have produced a much different kind of sound, a thinner and characteristic timbre of striking a plastic object, not the sharp, explosive blast we heard. Also, a blow from below would have forced the table upwards. But the table was still when the sound occurred, and the only movement of the table during the explosion was its sudden, intense, and brief vibration, not a movement upwards. And all this happened within the table top, not in the table's legs, and not in the contact between the table's legs and the laminate floor. In any case, the table legs are covered with a soft material to facilitate sliding around the floor; the legs hitting the floor simply could not have made a sharp sound.

This event was clearly reminiscent of the famous exploding sound from Freud's bookcase when he and Jung were arguing. Many interpret that event as a symbolic (and I'd say psychokinetically mediated)[11] representation of the intense clash between the two men. Similarly, no doubt there was a great deal of tension in the séance room—certainly on Kai's part, however much it might have been veiled by Kai's rather unconvincing and low-energy displays of optimism and enthusiasm. In fact, Kai frequently expressed dissatisfaction and frustration with the spirit control for not providing more impressive phenomena. Jochen, too, was tense over the threats to his professional advancement from the disgruntled blogger, and no doubt all sitters were at least somewhat anxious simply because this was our last chance for success.

One final comment about the exploding sound. It wouldn't be surprising if séance raps exhibit anomalous characteristics similar to those paranormal researcher Barrie Colvin found in recordings he made of poltergeist raps, and which he has analyzed in considerable detail.[12] We haven't yet had the opportunity to see if we can separate out the exploding sound from the background music and conversation. However, when or if that effort succeeds, Robert and I will pursue the matter.

Weltschmerz and fragile psyches

At this point in the history of psi research it's inexcusably naïve to think that the experimenter's state of mind (or personality) is irrelevant to the outcome of an experiment. Experimenters aren't simply passive observers, and experimenter effects of various kinds are well-known in the behavioral sciences generally.[13] My remarks so far on the psychodynamics of this October 2015 series have focused primarily on Kai's and Jochen's state of mind. But the attitudes of Robert, Leslie, and myself were undoubtedly a crucial ingredient as well, and they deserve additional comments.

When Robert, Michael Nahm, and I carried out our 2013 Austrian tests with Kai, we were optimistic about the prospects for success and reasonably confident in Kai as a trustworthy collaborator who understood and shared our goals of documenting his phenomena under the best controls possible. But a great deal happened, and happened quickly. First, compelling evidence surfaced of Kai's cheating on some previous occasions, and that naturally cast a long shadow over the Austrian investigations. Then, because Kai responded very badly to these revelations and the doubts that arose in their wake, distrust and hostility among various formerly cordial collaborators became a more prominent part of the emotional background.

It was some time before things calmed down to a point where it was feasible to discuss holding further tests. Even so, it was no longer possible to recapture the earlier state of optimism and enthusiasm. And although Kai realized that the purpose of the proposed new investigation was to demonstrate more clearly than before that at least some of his phenomena were indisputably genuine, negotiations for arranging the new tests were often tense and required revisiting many of the painful exchanges, charges, and counter-charges of the previous months. Robert, Leslie, and I spent a great deal of time trying to assure Kai that we weren't out to sabotage him á la Mulacz, denounce him in the way he felt Nahm had been doing, or simply put him in a position where he could only look worse for trying to cooperate with us. So as the time approached for our visit to Hanau, I think it's fair to say that Robert and I were somewhat fatigued from the effort of trying to make Kai feel more secure and positive, and that we were not very positive ourselves about the prospects of improving on the documentation achieved in the 2013 Austrian sessions. We (and also Leslie) were genuine in our expressions of confidence that we'd get some good table levitations—and indeed, we got some very interesting and impressive ones. But we were also candid with Kai concerning our uncertainty—which Kai shared—about improving on the Austrian table levitation video. We all knew that the psychological environment for the occasion was badly polluted—if only because of the attacks on Kai and Jochen, never mind how the investigators themselves felt about it. That's why we took pains to assure Kai that failure to improve on our earlier results wouldn't necessarily look bad for him and require publishing a critical report.

So even though my team expected to have tables levitate for us, the fact remains that we weren't nearly as excited and optimistic as my Austrian team had been two years earlier. Indeed, thanks to the convincing revelations about Kai's cheating in séances not supervised by me, our confidence in Kai and his mediumship had inevitably been eroded, and we were less inclined to put a positive or sympathetic spin on actions or statements that were at least superficially suspicious (for example, Kai's explanation of why he could hold a séance only every other day). Undoubtedly, we wondered whether we were wasting our time and money on this investigation.

Now Kai is both very intelligent and also very sensitive. Of course, he was aware of much of this, and of course that residue of mutual under-the-surface mistrust, pessimism, and lack of enthusiasm would likely have a stifling effect on the proceedings. But then we must concede that the somewhat disappointing results of this series of séances needn't reflect negatively on Kai. We were investigating the phenomena in his repertoire that are most likely to be genuine (and which I continue to believe are genuine). But there's no reason to think that Kai can produce them easily no matter how psychologically repressive the situation might be. And it's doubtful—or at least an open question—whether we can ever return to something close to the state of grace needed to obtain further convincing documentation of Kai's phenomena generally or table levitations specifically.

So what can we conclude? Although we didn't meet our original goal of improving on the video documentation from Austria, we obtained phenomena that, under the conditions of the séance, remain difficult to dismiss. These include the "swimming" levitated table, the ringing of the bell behind and above my head while Julia's and Kai's locations (determined by touch and voice) were clearly far away, the loud bang on the drum (out of reach for both Kai and the other sitters), and the explosion from the table in the final séance. These events, in my view, reinforce the conclusion reached in my initial report—namely, that despite the cloud of suspicion generated by confirmed cheating in the past, some of Kai's phenomena seem quite clearly to be genuine.

I also believe it should be noted again how cooperative (even if unhappy) Kai was about some of the test conditions, how anxious he was over success, and how sensitive he was to the various stresses both he and Jochen felt from recent attacks. It's also worth reiterating that in both our 2013 Austrian sessions and the 2015 séances in Hanau, Kai has been willing to conduct table séances under conditions he dislikes, including a few that even some of the least controversial mediums agreed were probably unfavorable to the phenomena. After all, there are still many unknowns about what makes mediums tick and why or when various situations suppress or facilitate the phenomena. Furthermore, these sessions reinforce what most veteran investigators of mediums know already—namely, that navigating the psychodynamics of mediumistic investigations is a complex and often tricky business, and that taking such matters seriously is the only way to advance beyond mere proof of the phenomena to an understanding of why they occur (or fail to occur) and why they take certain forms rather than others. They may also lend support to the view that the medium's beliefs or general state of mind—and also that of the sitters—may be more of an impediment to success than the tightness of the controls.

Appendix: *Kai and the D'Lite Type Device*

As I've explained, Jochen was at the center of the discovery of Kai's cheating. He took the photos that revealed Kai's use of a magic trick, and it was he who found the device in Kai's travel bag and eventually revealed what he knew to Nahm and me. As a result, Jochen naturally came under some scrutiny himself. In fact, he was subjected to a great deal of unfair criticism. So for the record, and for the sake of Jochen's reputation, several things need to be made clear.

First, soon after Nahm's and my JSE papers appeared, Jochen reported what he knew to various investigators, including both Nahm and me. Although he was initially in an understandable quandary about how to handle Kai's confession, Jochen was neither complicit in the fraud nor determined to keep the matter a secret. He also sent Nahm his sequences of suspicious photos from the Koblenz séances, which Nahm then (and with Jochen's permission) forwarded to me. However, because he didn't want to be cut off from Kai's inner circle and still hoped to observe and investigate the séance phenomena he still believed might be genuine, Jochen withheld his discovery of Kai's cheating from some of Kai's key sponsors and advocates. I firmly believe that Jochen's choice here was defensible, even if ultimately counter-productive. Moreover, he felt that since I'd explained convincingly in my earlier report why I knew Kai had used the D'Lite-type device, the truth was out there (at least for the world at large, if not for Kai's uncritical believers). So although Jochen planned eventually to go on record publicly about what he knew, there was no present urgency to do anything more. The only question for him was a matter of timing: when to finally brace himself for the predictable backlash from Kai for providing explicit testimony.

But that testimony deserves to see the light of day. Because I had wanted to be absolutely certain about the way the relevant events unfolded, on Oct. 22, 2015 Jochen sent me the following statement describing what occurred.

The first time I saw the flashing red spirit light phenomenon I felt uncomfortable with it and immediately considered it to be suspicious. This "spirit light" looked very different from those I had witnessed during several previous séances around the table, rather than at cabinet sittings. At Kai's table séances, the shape, brightness and local appearance of the lights vary considerably, and they also seem to be both elusive and (perhaps most important) outside Kai's radius of action. In comparison to these, the "spirit light" in Koblenz with its red flashing appearance looked like an electrically driven one controlled by Kai within the cabinet. My skeptical concerns were further substantiated after I took a series of photos of Kai and the moving red light.

So I decided to look into Kai's travel bag after a séance in Koblenz. I expected to find a device in case the "spirit light" was mechanically produced. And indeed I found a boxed device with a light-emitting diode at the end of a very thin wire attached to a fake thumb. I was totally shocked and rushed out of Kai's room. The next day I searched the Internet and found a magician's prop, which is commercially available for everyone and which looks very similar to the gimmick I detected. It is called the D'Lite Flight (https://www.youtube.com/watch?v=tZfnjSbbU2g).

Unfortunately, I didn't take a photo of the device in the travel bag. But I confronted Kai with what I had discovered, and he denied ever using such a trick.

Nevertheless, I tried to find out myself whether this gimmick could explain the suspicious-looking flashing red light effect which I saw at the end of the cabinet séance. As I wanted to find out how it could have been naturally done, I looked for the wire, the "thumb," or the LED light during later séances, but I could not detect anything. The red light re-appeared only once or twice again (as far as I remember) in my presence, this time under very poor conditions of observation. Thus I was not able to figure out whether and how Kai might have fraudulently produced it. I also took a closer look at the series of photos I had taken, but I didn't see anything clearly demonstrating the use of the prop, like the wire, despite the fact that the red light effect still looked very suspicious. I realize in retrospect that it was my mistake that I didn't notice Kai's thumb movements and also that I didn't enhance the photo series. Fortunately, I later sent the series to Michael Nahm, who instantly noticed in the unedited photo series how the movement of the light corresponded to the movement of Kai's thumb. [This was revealed even more clearly after Nahm enhanced the photos—SB.]

After Nahm showed me that Kai's thumb was indeed moving on these photo series in accordance with the movements of the red light, I confronted Kai again, asking him whether he used the D'Lite-type device and insisting that he tell me the truth because of compelling evidence of fraud. This time he admitted he had indeed used the device I found in his travel bag, and he said several times that he'd made a mistake in doing so. He also told me that he'd hidden the device on the shelves behind the cabinet, which he could reach from within its curtains. He apologized to me for having done this, and I felt pressured by him not to mention it to anyone.

While my second FEG report was in preparation, I felt that the right thing to do would be to inform Kai about the impending appearance of Jochen's statement. Jochen and I had no wish to harm Kai personally, and indeed, we both not only forgave him but still believed that some of his phenomena merited further study. My goal in informing Kai was to give him fair warning, and to encourage him to do the right thing, demonstrate some integrity, admit his mistake, and apologize. I told him that in the past, his efforts to try to defend himself against charges of fraud had only made him look less credible. I suggested instead that he follow the lead of many other public figures who've been caught in some kind of scandal by displaying some openness and contrition, and thereby presenting themselves sympathetically to the world. I reminded him that mediums (like all of us) are human and have frailties, fears, lapses of judgment, and other weaknesses, and I suggested that his own errors could be forgiven if only he'd admit them, accept responsibility for his mistakes, and pledge to do better in the future. After all, and in sharp contrast to

Kai, Eusapia Palladino candidly admitted that she'd cheat if given the chance, and investigators simply went with it and tried not to give her the chance! Of course, Eusapia (unlike Kai) didn't adopt the posture of a guru and proclaim herself to be a messenger of great spiritistic truths. Perhaps that's why Kai has not sought forgiveness or redemption. Despite many opportunities to come clean, he's consistently and dishonestly proclaimed his innocence.

Unfortunately, after telling me—in very carefully chosen words—that he simply couldn't admit he'd cheated (which, I remind you, is not at all the same thing as denying that he cheated), Kai contacted Jochen, and from what Jochen later told me about that conversation, I gathered that Kai had badgered and bullied—or otherwise tried to manipulate—him to retract his statement, in part by making him feel guilty about destroying his long friendly relationship with Kai and Kai's family. Apparently in his conversation with Jochen, and certainly during my Skype session with Kai in which I told him about Jochen's impending statement in the *Journal of Scientific Exploration*, Kai was clearly concerned solely with saving his own hide. He expressed no concern for the way Jochen had suffered from keeping largely silent about the D'Lite-type device. Reprehensibly, Kai even told me that Jochen had no legitimate reason to feel any pressure from the attacks on his character or professional life.

The emotional strain from all this was temporarily too much for Jochen to bear, and he said that he needed to cut himself off from all things FEG-related. So from late October 2015 until February 2016 I had no contact at all with Jochen. I can report now that Jochen has voluntarily broken the silence, to let me know that he understands and accepts my obligation to present the facts he'd previously revealed only to a select few. I should add that I'm also happy to do what I can to set the record straight about Jochen and to help remove whatever cloud of suspicion might hang over him in the minds of some who follow the adventures of the FEG.

As for Kai, I suppose some will wonder whether he's simply a good medium who will cheat, or has cheated, on occasion (either out of necessity or convenience), or whether his character is more thoroughly corrupt. If the former, then like Eusapia, Kai should be manageable in case investigators want to study the FEG phenomena further. But what about the latter option? Granted, because of Kai's disregard of, and apparent manipulation and bullying of Jochen, some may want to impugn Kai's character generally. But of course, there's no reason to think that good psychics can't have character flaws, or (like most people) behave badly and strike back when feeling threatened. My own view is that no matter what one's opinion may be of Kai's personality or behavior, the fact remains that he can produce impressive phenomena that are often difficult to attribute to fraud, and he's shown that he can be cooperative, at least so long as he feels it's in his interest. Accordingly, I'm not prepared to recommend a hands-off policy, Indeed, I'd gladly work with Kai again.

I realize, of course, that Kai's enthusiasm for working again with me may be, let's say, more muted. For some time after the revelations of his cheating and my publication of Jochen's statement, Kai portrayed me as someone who wanted to ruin his career. However, Kai and I are in a better place these days. I never stopped reaching out to him in a friendly manner, and eventually Kai requested that we (figuratively) "smoke a peace pipe." As a result, our few communications have been cordial. In any case, as Kai knows, I've been one of his staunchest defenders in the face of serious and sometimes well-founded charges against him. For example, I wrote a stinging rebuke of former collaborator Peter Mulacz's irrelevant and irresponsible article on the FEG.[14]

In fact, as I've made quite clear in everything I've written about Kai since the revelations about his cheating came to light, I don't consider the fact of Kai's having cheated earlier, in séances I didn't supervise, to be of much significance. True, it forces us to focus more on the extent of Kai's cheating, and that remains a valid concern. Since Kai learned and used at least one magic trick, we have no choice but to consider how many others he might have in his repertoire (and use with impunity in darkness). But of course, any competent investigator of physical mediums needs to focus on the possibility of fraud anyway, if only to deflect the inevitable and distracting glib criticisms from those who want simply to debunk the phenomena no matter what. At any rate, in addition to the intriguing events reported in this chapter, I continue to maintain that Kai has produced some results *under my supervision* that have not been satisfactorily explained away, and which are not tarnished by what Kai did with the D'Lite-type device. That's been my position all along, and I still await an adequate normal explanation of Kai's object movements across the room when he's under competent four-limb control (e.g., as described in my last chapter, which also included some control of Julia).

So I do hope that I can have another shot at documenting Kai's table levitations—and other phenomena. But the psychological background and conditions of observation would have to be considerably better than they were this time in Hanau.[15]

4. The Mediumship of Carlos Mirabelli

As remarkable as at least some of Kai's psychic powers appeared to be, they pale in comparison to those of the Brazilian medium Carmine (Carlos) Mirabelli (1889-1951).[1] His case is one of the most tantalizing and frustrating in the history of psychical research. To see why it's tantalizing, consider how his story has been introduced in two modern surveys of the case. The generally skeptical parapsychologist Eric Dingwall wrote: "I propose discussing a case in which the most extraordinary occurrences are recorded, so extraordinary indeed that there is nothing like them in the whole range of psychical literature."[2] Similarly, psi researcher Guy Playfair wrote:

> If everything they say about Carmine Mirabelli is true, he was without doubt the most spectacular physical effects medium in history…Mirabelli was surely the medium to end all mediums. You name it, and he is said to have done it; automatic writing in over thirty languages living or dead, speaking in numerous foreign tongues, materializing objects and people, transporting anything from a bunch of flowers to large pieces of furniture (including levitation of himself even when strapped to a chair), producing impressions of spirit hands in trays of flour or wax inside locked drawers, dematerializing anything in sight, himself included.[3]

Furthermore, Mirabelli reportedly produced full-form materializations in bright daylight, and these were often recognized as deceased relatives, acquaintances, or well-known public figures by those attending the séance. Sitters would watch them form; attending physicians would carefully examine them for up to 30 minutes and report ordinary bodily functions; photographs of the figures would be taken (for example, Fig. 1); and then they would slowly dissolve or fade before everyone's eyes. Moreover, Mirabelli reportedly materialized animals as well.[4]

Fig. 1. Dr. Carlos de Castro (right) seems alarmed at finding the deceased poet Giuseppe Parini between himself and the entranced Mirabelli.

Unfortunately, however, the case of Mirabelli never received the full scrutiny and documentation accorded D.D. Home, Eusapia Palladino, and some others. In part, this may be due to the prevailing antipathy toward physical mediumship among prominent members of the Society for Psychical Research (SPR) at the time.[5] That antipathy had arguably reached a zenith over the earlier mediumship of Eusapia Palladino.[6] Moreover—and undoubtedly contributing to the problem—there's some evidence of fraud in Mirabelli's case, most notably a doctored photograph of the medium apparently levitating.[7]

Nevertheless, Mirabelli's phenomena were witnessed by many, often under conditions apparently sufficient to rule out fraud, and they were often described in great detail. But most of those accounts were written in Portuguese, and for that reason they may have been either ignored or unfairly discounted by Anglo-American and European researchers.[8]

Beginnings
Mirabelli was born to Italian parents in 1889, and Playfair writes that "...like many sons of immigrants he never quite mastered either his ancestors' or his adopted country's language. He learned some English and possibly also some German, but certainly became no skilled linguist."[9]

Mirabelli's history with psychokinesis seems to have begun in his early 20s, with some poltergeist-like outbreaks while he was employed at a shoe store. Legend has it that shoe boxes would fly off the shelves and sometimes follow the fleeing Mirabelli into the street. As a result, many concluded (foolishly) that Mirabelli was insane, and before long he was committed to an asylum. However, the psychiatrists in charge apparently had other ideas, and rather than putting Mirabelli into a straitjacket, they ran some tests and found that he could move objects at a distance. Their conclusion was that although Mirabelli wasn't normal, he also wasn't insane. In their opinion, the phenomena occurring in Mirabelli's vicinity were "the result of the radiation of nervous forces that we all have, but that Mr Mirabelli has in extraordinary excess."[10] So after a stay of only 19 days, Mirabelli was released.

Mirabelli's mediumistic career began at this point and very quickly flourished. In response to a rapidly proliferating array of astounding reports, local newspapers began taking sides in the case, some (not surprisingly) accusing Mirabelli of outright fraud and others taking a more sympathetic view of the matter. But, of course, accusations of fraud come with the territory, and Mirabelli had many credible supporters. Indeed, as Dingwall observed, Mirabelli's "…friends and supporters included many from the best strata of S. Paulo society. Engineers, chemists, mathematicians, medical men, politicians, members of the various Faculties of Universities—all testified in his favour and recounted the marvels that they had witnessed in his presence."[11]

Because Mirabelli's feats were so astonishing, eventually a 20-person committee was established to adjudicate the case. The committee concluded that a more formal investigation should be conducted by people well-qualified to determine the authenticity of Mirabelli's phenomena. And that investigation was carried out by the Cesar Lombroso Academy of Psychical Studies, founded in 1919 for this purpose. However, according to the SPR's Theodore Besterman, that Academy consisted only of Mirabelli and his wife, and thus Mirabelli was merely investigating himself.[12] But as we'll see later, Besterman may not be an entirely reliable reporter in this case. At any rate, the Academy's report was published in 1926, and it was that report which brought Mirabelli to the attention of researchers in the northern hemisphere.

Dingwall emphasized one very important feature of Mirabelli's manifestations, which he cautioned might well be "forgotten by those who try to belittle the claims of Mirabelli,"[13] and which in fact were apparently forgotten later by Besterman.[14] That important feature is that "…the greater part of the phenomena observed with Mirabelli were investigated in *broad daylight*, even the materializations, telekinesis and levitations. When evening sittings were held these were undertaken in a room *illuminated by powerful electric light*."[15]

I should note that Mirabelli also practiced healing in addition to the physical phenomena already noted. Moreover, his automatisms extended beyond writing to painting and musical performances. According to Playfair,

> ...he could paint in a number of different styles, produce portraits of dead people which were identified by surviving relatives (fifty paintings of his were once exhibited in Amsterdam), and also conjure musical phenomena out of thin air. Witnesses recall having heard ethereal concerts in his presence, ranging from snatches of opera to military fanfares, while the musically untrained Mirabelli (who was untrained in practically everything else as well, come to that), would sing lengthy arias in a number of languages, often while doing something else at the same time, like writing or painting.[16]

The phenomena observed during the Academy's investigation were divided into three categories: (1) automatic writing in 28 different languages including some dialects, as well as three dead languages (Latin, Chaldaic, and Hieroglyphic); (2) spoken mediumship in 26 languages including seven dialects; and (3) physical phenomena including "levitation and invisible transportation of objects: the dematerialization of organic and inorganic bodies: luminous appearances and a variety of rapping and other sounds: touches: digital and other impressions upon soft substances, and finally the materialization of complete human beings with perfect anatomical features."[17]

Mirabelli's linguistic productions on "a wide range of subjects from medicine, law, sociology, to astronomy, musical science and literature"[18] are remarkable because, as Playfair noted, "All witnesses I have interviewed agree without hesitation that Mirabelli could not even speak either of his own languages (Italian and Portuguese) correctly."[19]

The automatic writing was also remarkable for its diversity, quantity, and speed. According to Dingwall,

> we find [mediumistic control] Johann Huss impressing Mirabelli to write a treatise of 9 pages on "the independence of Checho-slovakia" in 20 minutes; Flammarion inspiring him to write about the inhabited planets, 14 pages in 19 minutes, in French; Muri Ka Ksi leading him to treat the Russian-Japanese war in Japanese, in 12 minutes to the extent of 5 pages; Moses is his control for a four page dissertation entitled "The Slandering" (die Verleumdung), written in Hebrew;

Harun el Raschid makes him write 15 pages in Syrian: "Allah and his Prophets," which required 22 minutes and thus down the list, his most extensive work mentioned being 40 pages written in Italian about "Loving your Neighbor" in 90 minutes, and the most odd feature mentioned is an untranslateable [sic] writing of three pages in hieroglyphics which took 32 minutes.[20]

Altogether the Academy reported 392 sittings. They were held at 22 different locations, the majority of them (349) in the facilities of the Academy Of these 392 sittings, 189 were for spoken mediumship (apparently all positive), 93 for automatic writing (of which 8 were negative), and 110 for physical phenomena (47 of which were negative). So 63 sessions were positive for physical phenomena. And of those, 40 were held in broad daylight and 23 at evening or at night, but in bright artificial light. Moreover, in those sessions Mirabelli was clearly visible to witnesses, often sitting tied up in his chair, and in rooms searched before and after. Nevertheless, witnesses reported many occurrences that would seem to be impossible to produce fraudulently under those conditions.

For example, an armchair, with Mirabelli seated in it and his legs under control, rose two meters above the floor, remained aloft for two minutes, and then descended 2.5 meters away from its original place.

On another occasion, a skull rose into the air and began accumulating bones until it became a complete skeleton. Observers handled the skeleton for a while until it began to fade away, leaving the skull floating in the air. Soon thereafter, the skull fell onto the table. Mirabelli was bound throughout the event, which lasted 22 minutes in bright daylight. One of the sitters confessed later that when the skull initially rose into the air, he had mentally asked whether the rest of the skeleton would appear.

The Academy's report also cites a materialization occurring in a room of about 1000 square meters, with stone walls and locked doors. Three knocks were heard, and then a child's voice called "Papa." One of the investigators said that he recognized the voice of his recently deceased daughter, and then a materialization began to take shape. It was of a young girl wearing (according to the investigator) the dress in which she'd been buried. The weeping investigator embraced the phantom, and a doctor who was there felt her pulse while the figure answered questions "tonelessly but sensibly."[21] The investigators photographed the figure and eventually published it in their report. After that the phantom floated into the air and then, 30 minutes later, dematerialized.

All 10 investigators testified to what had occurred.

Another materialization with Mirabelli as the medium is so astounding that Dingwall's description deserves to be quoted in its entirety.

> Phenomena began by an odor of roses which filled the room, and after a few minutes a vague cloudy appearance was remarked forming over an arm-chair. All eyes were rivetted upon this manifestation and the sitters observed the cloud becoming thicker and forming little puffs of cloudy vapour. Then the cloud seemed to divide and move towards the sitters floating over them and condensing while at the same time it revolved and shone with a yellowish golden sheen. Then a part divided and from the opening was seen to emerge the smiling form of the prelate, Bishop Camargo Barros, who had been drowned in a shipwreck. He was wearing his biretta and insignia of office and when he descended to earth he was minutely examined by a medical man. His respiration was verified and the saliva in his mouth examined: even the inner rumblings of the stomach were duly heard and noted. Other sitters also examined the figure and fully satisfied themselves that they were not the victims of illusion or disordered imagination. The Bishop then addressed them and told them to watch carefully the mode of his disappearance. The phantom then approached the medium who was lying in his chair in a deep trance, and bent over him. Suddenly the body of the phantom appeared to be convulsed in a strange manner and then began to shrink and seemingly to wither away. The medium, controlled by the sitters on either side, then began to snore loudly and break into a cold sweat, whilst the apparition continued to draw together until it was apparently absorbed and finally disappeared. Then again the room was pervaded by the sweet odor of roses.[22]

Yet another Mirabelli materialization report is likewise worth noting.

> During the course of a sitting a bell which was on the table rose ringing into the air. The medium awoke from his trance and told those present to look at the figure of an old man enveloped in a white mantle. While he was speaking there was suddenly a loud noise and to the amazement of the sitters they found amongst them an old man as described by the medium. Two of the sitters recognized the phantom

as that of a physician recently deceased and photographs were taken while the form was examined for some fifteen minutes by two medical men who stated that it appeared to be a normal human being. After the examination was completed the figure was seen dissolving away from the feet upwards until only the upper part of the body remained floating in the air. One of the medical men who had examined the figure rushed forward exclaiming "But this is too much!" and seized the half of the body floating in front of him. Uttering a cry he sank unconscious to the ground, while what was left of the phantom disappeared instantly. The sitting was closed and the doctor carried from the room and restoratives applied. When he recovered he told the sitters that what he felt was a spongy, flaccid mass of substance and that then he experienced some kind of a shock and fell to the ground.[23]

At another sitting conducted in good light, Mirabelli, tied to his chair with bonds sealed, disappeared from the séance room and was found later in another room, "though the seals put on his bonds were intact, as were the seals on all the doors and windows of the séance room."[24] Moreover, the bonds remained in the room from which Mirabelli disappeared. They simply fell to the floor after Mirabelli disappeared.

Perhaps the most famous of Mirabelli's disappearances was his apparent spontaneous transportation from São Paulo's Luz train station to São Vicente, about 50 miles away. According to witnesses, he simply vanished from the platform, where he'd been standing among friends. After about 15 minutes, those concerned friends got through by telephone to the home where they'd all been heading and were told that Mirabelli had been there for the past 15 minutes.[25]

Not surprisingly, Mirabelli was a polarizing figure for Brazilian spiritism, especially because he was somewhat flamboyant and self-aggrandizing, and perhaps especially because he accepted substantial fees for his services. It's worth noting, then, that some of the testimony in Mirabelli's favor was provided by witnesses predisposed against the medium. Perhaps the most important account is that of Carlos Imbassahy, a highly respected figure in the orthodox Brazilian spiritist community, and the author of the 528-page *O Espiritismo à Luz dos Fatos* (*Spiritism in the Light of Facts*), a history of psi phenomena.[26] Imbassahy was clearly not an admirer of Mirabelli. He considered the medium to be "either a vulgar fraud, a skilful [sic] conjuror, or at most a medium who had got mixed up in the wrong company, both incarnate and discarnate."[27]

Imbassahy was at home one day with a businessman friend, Daniel de Brito, when another friend arrived along with Mirabelli. Imbassahy reports that there was nobody he was less eager to see than Mirabelli. Characteristically, the medium made himself comfortable and started speaking in "detestable Italian mixed with Portuguese and Spanish words,"[28] purportedly from Cesare Lombroso. After that, he turned to de Brito and "proceeded to give the startled businessman an account of his life from the cradle onwards. Brito had never met him before, and was not a well-known figure himself, but the medium seemed to know all there was to know about him. Imbassahy was reluctantly impressed."[29]

Then, when Mirabelli learned that someone in Imbassahy's house was ill, he asked for some bottles of water, which a maid promptly brought and placed on a table four or five meters away from the medium. Mirabelli would often "magnetize" water as part of a ritual for his many efforts at mediumistic healing. The four men joined hands to form a "current"; light in the room was provided by two 100-watt bulbs; only the maid touched the bottles; Mirabelli had no time to prepare a trick; and his hands were held during the phenomena that followed. Imbassahy reports: "Immediately, in full view of us all, one of the bottles rose half way up the height of the others, and hit them with full force for five or ten seconds, before returning to its place. We thought they must have been cracked. This was clearly seen and heard, with no shadow of hesitation. People in the next room also heard it, and the patient became extremely alarmed!"[30] Imbassahy reluctantly concluded that Mirabelli had genuine mediumistic gifts, although he continued to disapprove of him personally.

When Playfair visited Brazil in 1973, he interviewed Mirabelli's son Regene, "a businessman and accomplished amateur hypnotist with a keen interest in the scientific rather than the spiritual side of psychical research."[31] Playfair recorded some of Regene's fascinating recollections.

> I was sitting on the arm of a heavy renaissance-style sofa. Father liked me to stroke his hair, and I was doing this when the sofa simply began to move, with both of us sitting on it. Then I clearly saw the shadow of a figure on the floor in front of us; there was sunlight coming through a heavy glass window beside the sofa. Then the door of the cupboard across the room opened and a quill pen came out and was shot into the wooden floor like an arrow.[32]

That incident sent Regene rushing from the room in terror, screaming for his mother. But,

> Out in the hallway there was a heavy brass cuspidor that had fallen over, blocking the passage. We heard loud bangs and crashes coming from a room beyond, and when I rushed in, there was Mother lying on the floor with every piece of the furniture in the room on top of her. She wasn't hurt because "they" had the consideration to place a thick mattress over her first![33]

On another occasion Regene and the rest of the family joined a dozen friends for a session to help a bedridden invalid in another room. Regene reports:

> Father told us all to form a current, and he said not to worry about any phenomena that might happen. I was sitting about two meters from a table where there were three bottles of water, corked. This was to be "fluidized" and used to treat the sick man. We all sat there, and suddenly the bottles rose into the air, about thirty centimeters, and we heard three clinks as each struck the other. Then the bottles slowly began to turn over in mid-air, and stayed like that, upside down for a moment or two. I could see them very clearly, and the water inside them seemed to have gone solid, for it stayed in position, with a gap just under the cork. Then all the bottles fell hard onto the table and rolled about, although they did not break.[34]

It's also worth mentioning that investigators often closely monitored Mirabelli's physical condition during his various manifestations. Dingwall summarized their observations.

> [Mirabelli's] temperature, it was found, varied from 36.2 to 40.2: the pulse rate from 48 to 155; and the respiration was extremely various, sometimes being fast and stertorous and at others short and almost imperceptible. At times the body became rigid with cold sweats and abundant salivation was remarked, whilst occasionally there was general muscular contraction with tremors, glassy eyes and contracted pupils.[35]

European and American Investigations

Eventually, news about Mirabelli began to spread more widely beyond the borders of Brazil, and at that point veteran American and European researchers began taking an active interest in the case. In August 1928, philosopher and SPR president (1926-27) Hans Driesch sat with Mirabelli and later wrote a letter recounting his experiences.[36]

Driesch was clearly unimpressed with the linguistic productions he observed. Mirabelli spoke Italian (in which Driesch was fluent) as if the medium's father were speaking through him. But Driesch wrote: "There was not the slightest idea of a 'trance' and I believe the whole affair was *not at all* genuine, but a comedy."[37] Later, Mirabelli seemed to speak Estonian to a young Estonian girl he had brought with him, but Driesch could not believe that the girl's father was really speaking through the medium. He assumed instead that Mirabelli had probably learned some Estonian.

However, Driesch was somewhat more sympathetic regarding Mirabelli's physical phenomena. As the company entered the hostess's dressing room, "Mirabelli cried and said some prayers and then, suddenly, a small vase on one of the tables began to move and finally fell down. I could not observe any sort of mechanical arrangement such as a wire or string or otherwise."[38]

Driesch was highly suspicious of several apports that occurred on this occasion, especially since Mirabelli wore a large overcoat "with enormous pockets."[39] But there was more. For example, Driesch, Mirabelli, and their hostess stood on a veranda whose windows were closed, and other members of the company stood inside the adjacent drawing room. Mirabelli began to pray for a sign, and then the open folding doors between the veranda and drawing room slowly closed. "This was seen at the same time by the persons in the drawing room and those on the veranda. It was rather impressive, and no mechanical arrangements could be found."[40] But Driesch added, cautiously, "Mirabelli had been in Pritze's villa already about an hour before we arrived, alone with Frau Pritze. He *may* have made some arrangement before we came—I do not say that he did."[41]

In January, 1934, SPR member May Walker had sittings with Mirabelli and published a short and favorable report soon after.[42] For the first sitting,

> There were four phenomena in all, witnessed in good white light sufficient to see each person clearly and also all the objects in the room. My camera, with which I had just taken a photograph of the medium was lying on a long wooden table at some distance from

where we were standing, holding Mirabelli's hands. It began to move about on the table and jumped on to the floor. A small fan laid on my upturned palms, began to wriggle about as if alive, then falling off. In this case, Mirabelli's fingers were near my hands, but not touching them and it almost seemed as if some magnetism issued from his fingers, causing the fan to move.

My hat, a large straw one, turned completely round on the table and three tall glass bottles filled with water all shook together. Later one of them fell over on its side. There was an interval of some minutes between each phenomenon.[43]

The second sitting took place in a private garden, "owing to the fact that so many things in the house had been broken by psychic means."[44] It was held in the evening, "well lit by electric lamps,"[45] and most of the phenomena were apports, which Walker found moderately persuasive. However, she wisely preferred indoor phenomena, and the next evening her wish was granted.

The third sitting began with some object movements and an apport, the authenticity of which Walker was not prepared to endorse. But, she said,

Of the last phenomena, however, I had no doubts. All of us adjourned to the back room, where, on a table against the far wall, were about a dozen large wine bottles filled with water.

We formed a chain in a semi-circle at the other side of the room, Mirabelli being at one end of it, but a considerable distance from the table. He asked for a sign that the water had been magnetized—which I understand he thinks is done by his father, who has passed over.

Immediately came the jingling together of the bottles;—then a loud noise which shook them still more, as if some one has rapped on the table. After a slight pause, one bottle fell over on its side.[46]

Regrettably, Walker doesn't indicate why she was certain that Mirabelli hadn't prepared the bottles somehow in advance. In any case, she concluded that Mirabelli had presented her with "the best telekinesis I have ever seen."[47]

Later the same year (in August), the SPR's Theodore Besterman visited Mirabelli. By this time Besterman had already established himself as critically cautious but open-minded with regard to at least moderate-scale demonstrations of physical mediumship. He's perhaps best-known for his oft-cited study of slate-writing, which showed that under certain (rather poor) séance conditions and for certain kinds of small-scale ostensibly paranormal phenomena, subjects can make observational errors and sometimes report events that never occurred.[48] But Besterman was also prepared to endorse the carefully obtained evidence for the early 20th-century PK star Rudi Schneider's ability to deflect an infrared beam at a distance.[49]

However, when it came to Mirabelli, it seems that something simply rubbed Besterman the wrong way, right from the start. It may be that he was predisposed to distrust Mirabelli because four years earlier he'd skeptically reviewed the published accounts that were available at the time.[50] At any rate, during Besterman's visit to Brazil, Eurico de Goes, "one of Brazil's first serious psychical researchers,"[51] took minutes of the several sessions (at least five) that Besterman attended. According to those minutes,

> ...flowers materialized, bottles on a table jumped around, one even hopping onto the floor, a picture left the wall to float in mid-air and land abruptly on someone's head, a chair slid along the floor for about ten feet, the front-door key drifted out of its lock, and Mirabelli came up with a learned written discourse in French, writing nearly 1800 words in 53 minutes.[52]

Initially at least, Besterman seemed to be impressed. At least that's how he presented himself to his Brazilian hosts. De Goes quoted him in English as having written that "Mr Mirabelli's phenomena [are] of the greatest interest... Many of them were unique of their kind."[53] Notice that this quote doesn't endorse the phenomena as authentic, and it doesn't contradict his earlier skeptical review of the published accounts of Mirabelli. So it's not really surprising that by the time Besterman wrote his 1934 report for the *Journal of the Society for Psychical Research*, he showed little if any enthusiasm for what he'd observed in Brazil. Indeed, in his often sarcastic and condescending report he accused Mirabelli of fraud and provided some examples of phenomena he believed to have been faked.

Significantly, in Besterman's sessions, Mirabelli didn't allow the sorts of controls reported in some of the most striking cases mentioned previously— for example, binding Mirabelli to an armchair and sealing the bonds. Besterman reported that it was clear he was allowed to be no more than a spectator, and he remarked, "No sort of control was at any time exercised, suggested or asked for by any sitter other than myself, and then without success."[54] Séances were held in the evening, with illumination varying from complete darkness to bright electric light from seven or eight uncovered bulbs.

The largest group of phenomena witnessed by Besterman were apports, which Besterman claimed "were undoubtedly all faked"[55] and facilitated by obvious methods of distraction and occasionally by darkness as well. Besterman also reported moving bottles of "magnetized" water, similar to what Walker had reported months earlier. However, in Besterman's case, the phenomenon occurred in darkness. Not surprisingly, Besterman conjectured that Mirabelli looped a black thread around the moved bottle (rather than attaching it to the bottle) so that it could be easily retrieved.

After briefly mentioning and dismissing some other minor physical phenomena, Besterman then reported two other examples in detail. The first does, indeed, seem to have been a simple conjuring trick, as Besterman noted. Besterman described the performance as follows:

[Mirabelli] went into another room accompanied by [one of the sitters], there, we were told, held the coin in his open palm, with the sitter's open palm over it. The coin then vanished, Mirabelli returned to the room in which we were sitting, and asked me where I wanted the coin re-materialised. I elected for my own pocket and in a moment or two Mirabelli announced that the coin had been precipitated into my breast-pocket; there I duly found it. This performance was repeated with each of the male sitters present, with success, except that on one occasion I ventured correctly to forecast to my neighbour where the coin would be found. It must be noted that at no time during the progress of this phenomenon did Mirabelli approach within three yards of the main body of sitters.[56]

As Besterman correctly observed,

The way this trick was done was simple in the extreme. At a given moment, before the lecture, Mirabelli asked the male sitters one by one into an adjoining room, where he examined them "magnetically," making passes over them, etc. While doing so he slipped a coin into the pocket of each "patient." The vanishing of the coin is of course elementary palming, and the rest is obvious. All that is required is unlimited impudence and a sufficient number of similar coins. What first aroused my suspicion was this: when asked to examine the 1869 coin I *did* examine it and made a mental note of its characteristics.

When I found the coin in my breast-pocket I immediately saw, from minute characteristic marks, that it was not the same one, and the rest was then obvious. Again, every coin was found in an outside breast-pocket except X's, who had his materialised into his hip pocket, and X had been the only 'patient' who had been asked to take his jacket off, as I happened by chance to notice.[57]

Besterman claimed that only one phenomenon during his sittings was "really impressive." This was the turning of a blackboard placed on the top of a bottle, occurring in bright light sufficient for filming the event, and with the medium and sitters holding their hands over the board. This occurred twice, and Besterman was unable to duplicate the effect by blowing on the board. He was also certain that no threads were used. He wrote:

> I am still puzzled by this phenomenon; taking into account the good light, the fact that Mirabelli performs the phenomenon completely surrounded by standing "sitters," who seem to have complete liberty of movement, and the fact that he expressed no objection whatever to the filming, although I strongly emphasised the fact that the camera and the film were very special ones and would show every detail, the fact that Mirabelli allowed me on each occasion to arrange the *mise en scène* and did not precipitate himself on the board as it fell, the fact that the room, the table, and the bottle were all different, though the board was the same, all these circumstances make the hypothesis of threads practically impossible, while any other fraudulent method is difficult to conceive.[58]

Besterman's report elicited a sharply critical response from Dingwall,[59] claiming that Besterman was merely "bringing back stories of silly tricks."[60] His remarks criticized not only Besterman's negative appraisal of Mirabelli, but his positive views as well, and are worth excerpting.

> Mr Besterman has come to a surprising conclusion. He thinks that there is a *prima facie* case that Mirabelli may possess some paranormal "faculty," and this is based on the fact he was unable to detect the *modus operandi* of a revolving blackboard effect. Apart from the fact that there was no reason why he should have been able to understand it, are we expected to believe...that because...[Mr Besterman]

could not and cannot discover how certain conjuring tricks are done there is a *prima facie* case for the successful performers possessing "paranormal" faculties? It is this that makes psychical research ridiculous, and rightly so.

In my account of Mirabelli, which was printed in 1930 by the A.S.P.R., I described certain phenomena and named the parties who were said to have been present...Did Mr Besterman interview any one of these persons? Did he talk to any of the sitters who are recorded as being present at the alleged materializations of Bishop Barros, Prof. Ferreira, or Dr de Souza's daughter? To say that their testimony "is of relatively little value" is beside the point. It is as valuable as that of Mr Besterman, since what they record is quite as striking as anything with D. D. Home. Do these witnesses exist? Were they present at these sittings? Were they lying or are they made to record phenomena which never took place at all? Or must we admit that certain "*events took place which were described by those who witnessed them in the terms we have read*"? What were those events?" I wrote these words in 1930. No answer has been attempted. Yet in 1934, at heavy cost to the S.P.R., Mr Besterman goes to South America ostensibly to inquire into what he terms Mirabelli's "astounding feats" and comes back with tales of revolving objects which puzzled him.

The problem of Mirabelli is the same as that of Home. In the latter case the witnesses are dead and cannot now be interviewed: in the former case they are living and can be seen and cross-examined. Signed statements by Dr G. de Souza, Dr Moura or Dr Mendonça describing in their own words what they saw on certain occasions as recorded in *0 Medium Mirabelli* would be worth far more than stories of revolving blackboards and jumping cameras which puzzled observers who would be equally puzzled by 90% of conjuring tricks performed by even moderately skilled artistes.[61]

To this, Besterman responded simply that Dingwall's criticisms called "for little comment."[62] But Dingwall was justified in complaining that Besterman made no effort to follow-up on the most intriguing eyewitness reports of dramatic phenomena under good controls. Fortunately, but much later, Playfair was able to interview some of the surviving sitters at Mirabelli's séances, and that information informs his detailed account.[63] Playfair also generously concedes: "it must be said that little useful research can be done in two or three weeks in Brazil even today, and even when one speaks Portuguese, as I do and he did not."[64]

So readers should keep in mind that Besterman claimed never to have observed the most dramatic phenomena on which Mirabelli's fame largely rests, and it should be mentioned again that he never observed the medium submitting to the seemingly good controls so often reported by others during those events. This is somewhat reminiscent of a feature of the case of Eusapia Palladino, whose most impressive phenomena often occurred under the most stringent controls,[65] and who had few if any reservations about cheating when conditions were looser, or when she disliked her investigators, or when she was lazy, or when the "force" was weak.[66]

However, as Playfair noted, Besterman may indeed have witnessed something more spectacular and less amenable to charges of chicanery. He may have intentionally failed to report an apparently impressive materialization. This was evidently not a full-figure materialization, but rather "radiations…on a corner of the table."[67] Playfair reports:

> At the very first meeting, according to the minutes [of the séances], Mirabelli announced that he could see an entity named Zabelle, whom he described in detail. Besterman said he had known a lady of that name in London who was now dead, and when he asked for a sign of her presence, bottles began to jump around on a table, one of them even falling on to the floor at his request. Besterman mentions the bottles, but not the mysterious Zabelle.
>
> At the second meeting, Zabelle again dropped in and became visible enough for Dr Thadeu de Medeiros to take a photograph of her. This is reproduced in de Goes's book, and is one of the more credible materialization photographs I have seen…According to the minutes, which de Goes reports Besterman as having signed, Zabelle performed a number of feats to prove her presence.
>
> In the minutes of the third meeting, we are told that Besterman examined the photograph of Zabelle and declared that there was a strong resemblance to the lady he had known. The face on the photograph is extremely clear, more so than in most pictures of this kind.[68] (See Fig. 2.)

Fig. 2. Apparent materialization of Zabelle.

Besterman's failure to mention these incidents is certainly surprising. De Goes's minutes claim that at the first of the three meetings "Besterman…confessed that he had never seen anything so interesting."[69] Playfair correctly observes,

It is surprising that Besterman makes no mention of this episode. It is clear from his lengthy published report that he was anxious to miss no opportunity to discredit Mirabelli's powers, and if the Zabelle story were untrue, here was an excellent opportunity to do so.

If, on the other hand, it was true, then Besterman is guilty of suppressing strong evidence in favour of the medium.[70]

The Phantom Ladder
However, if one wants to find evidence of Mirabelli cheating in connection with his more spectacular manifestations, one need only consider the famous (or at least notorious) photograph of Mirabelli allegedly levitating (see Figs. 3a & b). This photo was published outside of Brazil for the first time in the first (1975) edition of Playfair's *The Flying Cow*. And in that book Playfair noted that he was unable to authenticate the photo, and that it might be faked.

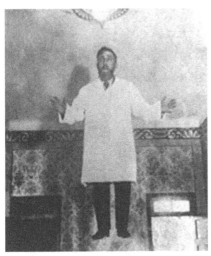 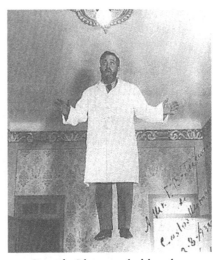

Fig. 3a. Mirabelli apparently levitating.   *Fig. 3b. Phantom ladder photo inscribed to Besterman.*

Confirmation came in 1990, when American researcher Gordon Stein found an original print of the photo in the SPR archives in the Cambridge University Library, showing clearly that the image had been retouched to re-move the ladder upon which Mirabelli was standing. It's unclear whether the original negative had been retouched, or whether a print was manipulated and then re-photographed. But in any case, the damning evidence is clear (see Fig. 4), and Stein was undoubtedly justified in claiming that Mirabelli "knowingly passed off a fraudulent photo of himself as genuine."[71] Curiously, Mirabelli had signed the print and inscribed it "To Mr Theodore Besterman." And equally curiously, Besterman—clearly no fan of Mirabelli—failed to seize the opportunity to mention the obvious fraud in his report. At any rate, Playfair was quick to publish a paper discussing the discovered fraud, and he updated the account of Mirabelli in a later edition of his book.[72]

Fig. 4. The signs of retouching the photo to hide the ladder.

Summing Up

Obviously, the case of Mirabelli must be regarded, *at best*, as one of so-called "mixed mediumship"—that is, combining fraudulent with genuine phenomena. Equally obviously, and as the case of Palladino illustrates clearly, one

---

* I found this image in an online search. Evidently it was taken from a BBC program covering the case of Mirabelli, but apart from that I don't know its origin. I should mention that I have a print of the ostensible levitation, and I've seen many others. In all of those, the retouching is not so obvious. Nevertheless, all the prints I've seen show a noticeable difference in clarity between the wallpaper behind Mirabelli's torso and that behind his feet. This can be seen in Figs. 3a and 3b.

can't plausibly argue that a person who cheats once will cheat all the time. Indeed, there can be obvious (and perhaps even defensible) reasons for a medium cheating occasionally. In fact, an irony of the Palladino case is that her willingness to cheat when allowed set the stage for the most convincing and stringently controlled séances in her career—the 1908 Naples sittings.[73]

But assuming that Mirabelli wasn't fully, exclusively, and honorably devoted to promoting spiritism, what might his reasons have been to cheat? The most obvious candidates would be money and fame. Now (as I observed in the case of Kai Mügge) there's nothing inherently scandalous in someone psychically gifted wanting to make mediumship a primary source of income. However, perhaps there's more to the story than that. By all accounts, Mirabelli was not averse to liberal self-promotion; Playfair describes him as flamboyant and vain. He also claims that Mirabelli "was a big spender, who would think nothing of buying ten suits or a dozen pairs of shoes at a time, only to give most of them away."[74] Clearly, that's a lifestyle that somehow needs to be funded.

Besterman's spin on Mirabelli's fiscal profile is somewhat less neutral or forgiving. He wrote:

> Though he is anxious not to be considered as a professional, in fact he is. Directly or indirectly Mirabelli demands and obtains (as I know only too well) substantial fees, far more substantial, indeed, than any ever asked of me before when attending sittings on a medium's own premises. The procedure is this: Mirabelli founds or causes to be founded an institute, for which he works, on the premises of which he lives, and to which sitters make payment. It was in this way that the Academia de Estudos Psychicos "Cesar Lombroso" was founded at Sao Paulo in September 1919; and Mirabelli's move to Rio de Janeiro led to the foundation there, in November 1933, of the Institute Psiquico Brasileiro.[75]

So if we're to assume that Mirabelli was nothing but a cheat, and that he cheated not only to live comfortably, but to live lavishly as well, how do we account for the reports of his most compelling manifestations, and his materializations in particular? Skeptics might initially appeal to the usual suspects: malobservation, naivete, and collusion among witnesses. But that would seem to require an implausibly large number of gullible, incompetent, or corrupt people, whose otherwise primary disqualification as witnesses is that they weren't fortunate enough to be SPR insiders. Mirabelli's manifestations were observed by more than 500 people (more than 100 of them foreigners), often supported by photographs, and the phenomena were typically produced in bright light and often under decent controls.

Nevertheless, Besterman condescendingly impugned the competence of the many witnesses who testified to Mirabelli's most dramatic manifestations. He wrote:

> ...their testimony is of relatively little value. These gentlemen have in most cases had no experience with mediums other than Mirabelli, and they have no notion of the conditions under which psychical research should be conducted. Their testimony, in short, has such value as can be given to evidence put forward by inexperienced and more or less casual visitors, concerning events over which they have no control.[76]

However, it's Besterman whose claims appear to be worthless. For one thing, many of Mirabelli's impressive and well-documented phenomena evidently did in fact occur under good controls, including bright light, sealed binding of the medium to his chair, and holding a materialized phantom as it melted in the observer's grasp. Moreover, in many cases knowing how to control or properly observe such large-scale manifestations, often in locations at which Mirabelli had no opportunity to prepare a trick, doesn't require a rich prior history of mediumistic investigation. Besides, the phenomena continued for many years. One would think that at least some of Mirabelli's regular investigators learned from experience how best to control the medium and accordingly became more careful and shrewder with time. Revealingly, Besterman admitted in a footnote to the previous quoted passage that his judgment was based, not on any attempt to meet with and query those whose reports he was impugning, but rather on his very limited experiences with Mirabelli, which were not controlled.

At least Besterman didn't resort to the famously lame hypotheses of collective hypnosis or collective hallucination. I've dealt in detail elsewhere with these latch-ditch maneuvers,[77] and so I'll just mention a few salient points here. First, regarding hypnosis: there simply is no evidence that the appropriate kind of mass hypnosis has ever occurred—that is, inducing people to issue the same or concordant observational reports in conditions widely recognized as being unfavorable to hypnosis, and (even more important) despite the well-known and great variability in human hypnotic susceptibility. Actually, if a medium could, through suggestion, get different people, of different degrees of hypnotizability, simultaneously to experience and report the same phenomena, and also to do this under conditions unfavorable to suggestion, that ability would arguably be as paranormal as what it's supposed to explain away. In fact, it looks suspiciously like telepathic influence.

The second hypothesis, of collective hallucination, is simply ridiculous. It can't even remotely account for Mirabelli's continued success under good conditions, and often for many years. Since Mirabelli's witnesses weren't engaged in something like mushroom rituals, there would have to be a lot of spontaneous hallucinating going on, over decades, remarkably resulting in people having the same or similar non-veridical experiences. Besides, the hallucination hypothesis fails to account for the causal relevance of Mirabelli's presence. If the medium had nothing to do with witnesses' allegedly false observational reports, why were they hallucinating in the first place? But if Mirabelli was responsible, then (since he presumably wasn't dispensing hallucinogens) it looks like this hypothesis is really just one of collective hypnosis, the inadequacy of which I've just noted.

But can the materializations at least be explained away satisfactorily by positing an array of confederates posing as the deceased? Dingwall disposed of that conjecture:

> I will even grant the possibility of wholesale confederacy and assume (for the sake of argument) that the materializations are confederates of the medium or of the sitters. But confederates are human beings and human beings do not usually rise into the air, dissolve into pieces and float about in clouds of vapor. Confederates do not lose half their bodies, feel like flaccid sponges and give violent shocks to people who try to seize them.[78]

It's also worth noting that Mirabelli's reported phenomena aren't particularly outlandish when compared to lesser materialization phenomena for which there exists good evidence.[79] Some are simply more complete, complex, or virtuosic. Besides, in the absence of any kind of credible scale for determining degrees of strangeness, and in view of the abundance of decent evidence for partial materializations (including evidence from the cases of Home and Palladino), it would be prudent to heed Richet's warning that

> ...it is as difficult to understand the materialization of a living hand, warm, articulated, and mobile, or even of a single finger, as to under-

stand the materialization of an entire personality which comes and goes, speaks, and moves the veil that covers him.[80]

The fact remains that many of Mirabelli's apparently well-attested and decently controlled manifestations resist easy—or any—plausible skeptical dismissal. Certainly, Besterman's exposure of, and conjectures about, conjuring tricks under no controls fails to address the challenge posed by the much more spectacular and controlled physical phenomena reported in Mirabelli's case. So although Mirabelli's manifestations are perhaps not as well-established as, say, the best of D.D. Home, Eusapia Palladino, Franek Kluski, and others, good reasons remain for taking the case seriously, and perhaps for regarding it as indicating just how dramatic PK phenomena can be.[81]

5. A Case Study in Shoddy Skepticism

The Man in Question

The late nineteenth century medium Daniel Dunglas (or D.D.) Home was arguably the greatest physical medium of all time. Granted, some of Mirabelli's materialization phenomena (if genuine) may surpass those of Home—although it's unclear on what plausible scale of impressiveness we could make such measurements.[1] But Home is certainly a gold-medal contender in several areas—perhaps most notably in novelty and diversity of large-scale phenomena, and perhaps even the number of well-attested reports.

Home's mediumistic career lasted almost 25 years, and during that time he was never detected in fraud, despite very careful conditions imposed by some of his investigators. Moreover, Home often produced phenomena in séances held at the spur of the moment, in good light, and in locations he'd never visited before. So unless one posits, desperately and implausibly, a team of accomplices over the years, not one of whom ever seized the spotlight to spill the beans on their boss, it's obvious in those cases that Home had no opportunity to make the sorts of preparations needed to arrange large-scale effects in advance. That makes it especially intriguing and impressive to read, for example, that as Home entered a location for the first time, the large bookcase at the other end of the room started moving toward him. In general, the objects moved during those séances (tables, bookcases, pianos, and personal items belonging to sitters) were not props Home carried from place to place, or things to which he had access prior to the séance.

Of course, some claimed that Home cheated; that just comes with the territory. But those very few allegations were second or third hand, and none have ever been substantiated. In fact, it seems as if the allegations were merely unhinged skeptical cries of outrage that the phenomena couldn't possibly have been genuine.

Besides, another reason the case of Home is so difficult to discount is that Home had an enormous repertoire of impressive phenomena. So if skeptics hope to explain the case away, they must account for an unusually wide range of effects, many of which happened in quick succession (and sometimes even simultaneously)–again, often under conditions in which the effects could easily have been detected as tricks. Home's phenomena included the movement and complete levitation of large objects, including tables (sometimes with several people on top) and pianos. Objects could also become heavier or lighter on command; William Crookes tested this phenomenon instrumentally. But before that, it was customary for objects (such as tables) to become too heavy to lift or tilt, or simply more difficult to move than before. Home could also handle hot coals and transfer incombustibility to other persons and objects. And in his presence, there were also so-called earthquake effects, in which the entire room and its contents would rock or tremble. His séances might also feature supple, solid, warm, and mobile materialized hands, of different sizes, shapes, and colors, that ended at the wrist, would carry objects, shake hands with the sitters, and then dissolve or melt in their grasp. And this is just a partial list.

In general, critics have handled this case very poorly, and as I noted in Chapter 1, no skeptic or magician has succeeded in duplicating Home's accordion phenomena under even loose conditions, much less under conditions as stringent as those imposed by Crookes. You can be certain that if a Home-critic had pulled that off, we'd know about it, especially if the feat was accomplished—or even just reported—by a publicity-hound like James "The Amazing" Randi.[2] The more typical and insidious skeptical approach to Home is exemplified in an absolutely terrible book written by Trevor Hall and published in 1984: *The Enigma of Daniel Home.*[3] Its subtitle is "Medium or Fraud?" and beneath that the dust jacket reads "The mystery of Britain's most famous spiritualist unraveled." However, nothing of the sort occurs. Instead, Hall's book is little more than a profusion of hearsay, innuendo, irrelevant detail, and fallacious arguments. And sadly, the book is cited to this day and hailed as a penetrating exposé.

Because Hall's book is so often mentioned approvingly as an authoritative demolition of Home,[4] and because Hall's specious rhetorical tactics are either long-standing disreputable skeptical ploys or else novel strategies that others have subsequently duplicated, I want to examine salient details of his efforts to cast doubt on Home's mediumistic credentials. Some of those details may be idiosyncratic to Hall, but there's value in getting clear both on Hall's general strategies and also the falsehoods he perpetuates about Home's life and career. Intellectually lazy or dishonest critics follow Hall's lead too often and too easily, and newcomers to the field may be easily misled by Hall's apparent command of irrelevant detail. So I believe it's important to set the record straight on Hall's shabby arguments and travesties of historical research. The case of Home deserves better than what Hall (and those in his wake) have given us.

The Grubby Details

I realize that Hall's book may seem impressive to those who are unfamiliar with the case of Home, and who might accordingly be dazzled by the profusion of details and citations, and therefore the apparent breadth and depth of his scholarship. What they won't know is that Hall completely ignores evidence tending to undermine his unfavorable appraisal of the case, and that his mastery of the material is confined largely to irrelevant detail. In fact, Hall's book is simply one in a long line of works about parapsychology in general, and physical phenomena in particular, whose persuasiveness rests entirely on certain traditional questionable tactics. Hall's favorites, evidently, are first, to generate suspicion about Home's character in order to cast doubt on the genuineness of his phenomena; and second, to focus only on the weakest cases, while ignoring those in which the evidence is strongest and in which consideration of Home's personality or character is clearly irrelevant. Both ploys commit elementary fallacies of reasoning taught in probably every beginning class in logic or critical thinking.

For example, Hall spends a surprising amount of time (the book's first two chapters) trying to establish Home's vanity. His principal concern there is to demonstrate that Home added his middle name "Dunglas" and claimed falsely to be a descendant of the Earls of Home. Now first of all, the suspicion about Home's name, and the allegation of vanity, are old issues, dating back to the beginning of Home's career. But most important, they're also clearly irrelevant to the question of whether Home's phenomena were genuine.

Nevertheless, it's interesting to note the suspicious manner in which Hall tries to execute this criticism of Home. First, he wants to establish that Home invented an aristocratic background to ensure social success, as if that could be a damning indictment of Home's mediumistic prowess. Moreover, one of Hall's pivotal pieces of evidence is a remark from Scottish physicist Sir David Brewster,[5] who made other statements about Home that we know without doubt to have been lies. Nevertheless, Hall suggests, on the incredibly weak basis of Brewster's scientific credentials, that Brewster was a reliable witness. He conveniently fails to mention how Brewster's daughter unwittingly exposed her father's dishonesty on the subject of Home. Even more remarkably, Hall fails to mention this while citing the source—the daughter's book—in which Brewster's deceptions were conclusively revealed![6]

The story of Brewster and Home is interesting on several levels. Among other things, it illustrates something regrettably (and perhaps surprisingly) common—namely, how prominent but unscrupulous scientists can abuse, not only their influence as public figures, but also the power and prestige of their positions within the scientific community. It also illustrates clearly how Hall conveniently ignores facts obviously pertinent to his discussion when those facts would be detrimental to his case.

In 1855, Brewster attended two of Home's séances, first (at the invitation of Lord Brougham) in the home of William Cox and then at the home of John and Emma Rymer. After the Cox séance, Home wrote to a friend in the United States, claiming that Brewster and the others had admitted their inability to explain his physical phenomena by any normal means. Thereafter, the letter was published in some U.S. newspapers, and before long the story of the Cox séance traveled back to London, where Home's letter was reprinted in the *Morning Advertiser*. Evidently this embarrassed Brewster because he then wrote to the *Advertiser*, denying that he'd found the phenomena inexplicable and charging, "I saw enough to satisfy myself that they could all be produced by human hands and feet, and to prove that some of them, at least, had such an origin."[7]

But Brewster's letter rankled those who'd attended the séances with him, and that led to an intense exchange in the *Advertiser*.[8] Cox wrote and reminded Brewster that he'd remarked at the time, "This upsets the philosophy of fifty years." Brewster also alleged that he hadn't been permitted to look under the table. Cox denied this, as did T.A. Trollope, who had attended the Rymer séance. Trollope pointed out that Home and John Rymer had actually encouraged Brewster to look under the table, which Brewster did, and that while he looked under the table, the table moved apparently without Home's agency. Trollope also noted that Brewster admitted to having seen the movement. Nevertheless, Brewster maintained his skeptical stance, although he modified it, revealingly, writing, "Rather than believe that spirits made the noise, I *will conjecture* that the raps were produced by Mr. Home's toes...and rather than believe that spirits raised the table, I *will conjecture* that it was done by the agency of Mr. Home's feet."[9]

It wasn't until 1869, a year after Brewster's death, that the controversy was settled and Brewster's dishonesty revealed. Brewster's daughter published in that year *The Home Life of Sir David Brewster* (no pun intended), in which she unwittingly included the account of the séances her father composed at the time. Of the Cox séance he wrote,

[Lord Brougham] invited me to accompany him in order to assist in finding out the trick. We four sat down at a moderately-sized table, the structure of which we were invited to examine. In a short time the table shuddered, and a tremulous motion ran up all our arms; at our bidding these motions ceased, and returned. The most unaccountable rappings were produced in various parts of the table; and the table actually rose from the ground when no hand was upon it. A larger table was produced, and exhibited similar movements.

...a small hand-bell was then laid down with its mouth on the carpet, and, after lying for some time, it actually rang when nothing could have touched it. The bell was then placed on the other side, still upon the carpet, and it came over to me and placed itself in my hand. It did the same to Lord Brougham.

These were the principal experiments; we could give no explanation of them, and could not conjecture how they could be produced by any kind of mechanism.[10]

After these revelations, the *Spectator* remarked, lamely, "The hero of science does not acquit himself as we could wish or expect."

So much for integrity of Hall's key witness on the subject of Home's allegedly suspicious vanity. In any case, the topic of Home's character is a blatant red herring. Even if Home did invent a middle name and an aristocratic background for himself, and even if he was fickle and opportunistic, he may still have produced genuine phenomena. In fact, parapsychological history since the days of Home has confirmed over and over that neither sainthood nor a mere absence of character weaknesses are prerequisites for possessing psi ability, or probably any other ability for that matter.

It's a striking omission for Hall to ignore Brewster's documented dishonesty when it came to Home. But Hall's book has many convenient omissions. As with the Brewster case, the most interesting are those in which Hall refers to incidents in Home's career as if they bolster his skeptical appraisal of Home, but then omits details about those same incidents—often well-known details—that actually strengthen the case for Home. To take another interesting example, Hall refers to a frequently-mentioned séance at the Springfield, Massachusetts house of Rufus Elmer, but he completely ignores the fascinating, persuasive, and oft-cited written account of phenomena observed on that occasion.[11]

To appreciate how convenient (and reprehensible) that omission is, it's worth looking at the report from the Elmer house sitting. Home was temporarily residing at the Elmers, and during January 1852 they were visited by an ostensibly skeptical investigating committee whose members included poet William Cullen Bryant and a young engineer and economist, David A. Wells, who eventually became quite famous for his writings on science and economics. After several sittings, all the committee members signed a statement about what they experienced during one sitting in particular. This document may not be the strongest piece of evidence from Home's career, but it's far from negligible. It also resembles, both in the magnitude of the reported phenomena and the types of controls allowed, many other accounts of Home's mediumship.

The undersigned...bear testimony to the occurrence of the following facts, which we severally witnessed at the house of Rufus Elmer, in Springfield...

1. The table was moved in every possible direction, and with great force, when we could not perceive any cause of motion.

2. It (the table) was forced against each one of us so powerfully as to move us from our positions—together with the chairs we occupied—in all, several feet.

3. Mr. Wells and Mr. Edwards took hold of the table in such a manner as to exert their strength to the best advantage, but found the invisible power, exercised in an opposite direction, to be quite equal to their utmost efforts.

4. In two instances, at least, while the hands of all the members of the circle were placed on the top of the table—and while no visible power was employed to raise the table, or otherwise move it from its position—it was seen to rise clear of the floor, and to float in the atmosphere for several seconds, as if sustained by some denser medium than air.

5. Mr. Wells seated himself on the table, which was rocked for some time with great violence, and at length, it poised itself on the two legs, and remained in this position for some thirty seconds, when no other person was in contact with it.

6. Three persons, Messrs. Wells, Bliss and Edwards assumed positions on the table at the same time, and while thus seated, the table was moved in various directions.

7. Occasionally we were made conscious of the occurrence of a powerful shock, which produced a vibratory motion of the floor of the apartment in which we were seated—it seemed like the motion occasioned by distant thunder or the firing of ordnance far away—causing the table, chairs, and other inanimate objects, and all of us to tremble in such a manner that the effects were both seen and felt.[12]

8. In the whole exhibition, which was far more diversified than the foregoing specification would indicate, we were constrained to admit that there was an almost constant manifestation of some intelligence which seemed, at least, to be independent of the circle.

9. In conclusion, we may observe, that Mr. D.D. Home, frequently urged us to hold his hands and feet. During these occurrences the room was well lighted, the lamp was frequently placed on and under the table, and every possible opportunity was afforded us for the closest inspection, and we admit this one emphatic declaration: *We know that we were not imposed upon nor deceived.*

Wm. Bryant
B.K. Bliss
Wm. Edwards
David A. Wells

The problem here isn't simply that Hall ignores this major aspect of an incident to which he refers. Rather, and as with many other skeptical discussions of Home's career, nothing in Hall's book comes even close to debunking reports of similarly impressive large-scale phenomena, likewise produced under decent conditions of observation and control. And there are many such reports, all of which Hall sedulously avoids. Moreover, it's important to keep in mind when reading accounts of phenomena that might initially seem to be caused by Home exerting an undetected effort of his own, that Home suffered from consumption for much of his life and was probably not strong enough to produce the effects by normal physical means. In fact, it's likely that some of the phenomena in this account couldn't be physically and surreptitiously produced by a normally healthy person.

Hall tries a different kind of impotent skeptical maneuver in a chapter devoted solely to what was sometimes called Home's "mystery of iniquity." Hall counters fellow skeptic Eric Dingwall's suggestion that the mystery concerned Home's homosexuality, and he offers in its place allegations concerning Home's failure to pay for a fur coat. The triviality of this discussion is really quite breathtaking. Quite apart from the fact that the chapter amounts to little more than a compilation of gossip about a famous nineteenth-century figure, the speculations about Home's moral failings are once again irrelevant to the question of whether his phenomena were genuine.

We find another, all too common, anti-Home strategy in one of the surprisingly few chapters purporting to review Home's phenomena. Hall suggests that Home's success can be attributed to a combination of conjuring and the power of suggestion. Once again, the uninformed are likely to find the discussion impressive because Hall discusses some well-known studies by Theodore Besterman and some other prominent SPR members concerning several ways in which experimenters fooled sitters in bogus seances.[13] However, he fails to mention the equally well-known fact that their phenomena and séance conditions differed in significant ways from the best of those reported in connection with Home. Besterman et al showed—as if it could really have been sensibly doubted—that under poor conditions of observation and control, and for certain small-scale apparently paranormal phenomena (for example, slate writing), sitters can err in their observations and report events that never occurred.

So how could those experiments be relevant to a fair appraisal of the case of Home? As I've noted, Home often produced very large-scale phenomena, on the spur of the moment, in locations never before visited, with objects supplied by the sitters, in good light, and with opportunity to examine the phenomena closely while in progress. Hall also fails to explain how Home might have been able to practice his alleged conjuring and suggestion under those conditions *for nearly 25 years without being detected in trickery* (Hall does mention two—and only two—alleged exposures; I'll comment on them in a moment). And of course, he says nothing about the very best pieces of evidence, such as Crookes's accordion-in-a-cage test and his equally ingenious spring-balance experiments for testing Home's ability to change an object's weight.[14] Instead, Hall cites reports of how other mediums of the period cheated. But he offers no evidence that Home may have been guilty of the same tricks.

Had Hall wanted to give the case of Home a genuinely scholarly and fair appraisal, he would have mentioned and responded to the arsenal of familiar arguments designed to show that deception and suggestion *can't* account for many of Home's phenomena. At the very least he could have cited the well-known paper by Count Perovsky-Petrovo-Solovovo (hardly one of the more credulous members of the early Society for Psychical Research), dismissing the hypothesis of suggestion.[15] What Hall gives us instead is a version of the tired argument from human bias, claiming that Home successfully manipulated sitters' already credulous beliefs in occult phenomena. Of course, the argument from human bias is double-edged. If biases in favor of psi phenomena may lead one to mis-report or make an error in observation, so may biases *against* psi phenomena. (In fact, negative biases seem to explain the regrettable behavior of David Brewster—not to mention Hall's own mishandling of the evidence.) There's simply no excuse for perpetuating the old myth that only the biases of "believers" undermine claims regarding the paranormal. The defects of that position are so well-known that it's intellectually irresponsible for Hall to dismiss testimony favorable to Home by invoking human bias, and then to make no effort to counter the familiar and obvious arguments against that strategy.[16]

The accusations of fraud cited by Hall ("considered" would be too strong a term) are those of a Messr. Morio (the so-called Barthez exposure) and barrister Frederick Merrifield. Quite apart from the fact that Hall was apparently unable to dredge up more than two mere allegations concerning nearly a quarter-century's worth of mediumship, he makes no mention of psi historian George Zorab's examinations of both sets of allegations.[17] Zorab's more detailed and penetrating discussion demonstrates that the cases are far more complex than Hall suggests, and that there are good reasons for thinking that Home was guilty of no fraud at all. Furthermore, although Hall cites Perovsky-Petrovo-Solovovo's paper as his source for the Morio accusation, he conveniently fails to mention Solovovo's reluctant conclusion that Morio's evidence seems only to have been second- or third-hand, and that the "chief witness on the negative side was undoubtedly strongly prejudiced against Home, as he himself admits."[18] Nevertheless, Hall will undoubtedly mislead many readers simply by virtue of including that citation in the text. It creates the false impression that his examination of the evidence was scholarly and thorough. And although in fact there's no good, *first-hand* evidence that Home was ever guilty of fraud, Hall's discussion will probably deceive many readers into thinking that damaging testimony was suppressed.

Perhaps even worse, Hall argues that Home should be considered a fraud in virtue of his association with the medium Frank Herne. Hall writes, "It seems to me axiomatic that the honesty of a medium may be judged by his or her associates." Of course, this is an elementary association fallacy that beginning students in critical thinking classes learn to identify early on. And it's easy to demonstrate the flaws in this particular version of it, even if we grant Hall his assumption that Herne was a total fraud. I don't pretend to know whether that assumption is defensible; like many mediums, Herne may have been a partial fraud. Moreover, considering the shabbiness of Hall's examination of Home, we can hardly accept his assessment of Herne as a given.

But let's assume, just for the sake of argument, that Herne had no genuine mediumistic powers. Even so, and quite obviously, whether or not Home's association with Herne was suspicious depends on the nature of and reason(s) for the association. Some associations (even intimate associations) with dishonest persons confer no guilt whatsoever; in fact, they might be quite innocent. (Consider, for example, the familiar character, immortalized in fiction and film, of the unwitting spouse of a bigamist, brutal assassin, or anti-government spy.) But Hall tells us virtually nothing about the nature of Home's relationship with Herne. In fact, he mentions only that the men attended one séance together and that Home apparently promised to give another séance with Herne. Now first of all, that constitutes no evidence that the two mediums had any relationship worth mentioning. But in any case, prominent spiritualists of the day were likely to have known one another and to have met at séances, independently of their varying degrees of competence and honesty, or their differing motives. In fact, it was probably inevitable that Home would know the other prominent contemporary mediums; it would have been in his interest to do so whether or not he or they were frauds.

To support Hall's charge, one must first show that Home *knew* Herne to be a fraud, and then demonstrate that the two were in collusion. But Hall does nothing of the kind. Nor does he evaluate competing (and possibly more reasonable) accounts of the relationship between Home and Herne. For example, Home's interest in Herne (even in Herne's dishonesty) could have been part of an interest in protecting the image of Spiritualism, or (more cynically) in preserving his own pre-eminence among mediums. After all, Home often insisted that other mediums shouldn't be trusted. Hall's analysis here, as elsewhere, is intolerably superficial.

This is not the only instance in which Hall conveniently skims the surface of personalities and relationships that could make a real difference to his attempted debunking of Home. A particularly interesting example is when Hall addresses the notorious affair between Home and Jane Lyon. Mrs. Lyon was an elderly and wealthy widow who offered to adopt the adult Home, and who also offered him financial security if he'd agree to the adoption and also change his surname to Home-Lyon. Remarkably, Home accepted those terms, and in 1866 he formally took the revised surname. Accordingly, and against the advice of her solicitor, Mrs. Lyon deposited 24,000 pounds (an enormous sum in those days) in Home's bank account and prepared a will that would perpetuate Home's wealth. She insisted, against the protests of others, that she hadn't been influenced by any ostensible spirit communications conveyed by Home. In fact, and as if to emphasize her trust in her adopted son, she wrote to her solicitor,

> My Dear Mr. Wilkinson—On the occasion of my adopted son taking the name of Lyon, I wish to give him a little surprise. I intend to add six thousand pounds to the twenty-four I have already given him, making a sum total of thirty thousand.[19]

Later, however, Mrs. Lyon changed her mind and sued Home in order to regain all her money.

Now this isn't the place to consider all the sordid (but fascinating) aspects of this interesting drama.[20] What matters here is that once again Hall avoids considering relevant detail when discussing topics that might prove unfavorable to his case. In particular (and somewhat incredibly), he makes no effort to discuss details of the interaction between Home and Mrs. Lyon. For example, he conveniently avoids discussion of events occurring during the 10 months between their initial encounter and the time Mrs. Lyon filed her affidavits against Home.

In fact, Hall makes no effort at all to examine the character of Mrs. Lyon. Regarding her testimony at the trial, he says only that it was "not impressive," thereby avoiding discussion of the grounds for thinking she committed perjury, and also ignoring the abysmal reasoning leading to the court's decision against Home. Moreover, if historian Elizabeth Jenkins' detailed account is accurate,[21] Mrs. Lyon was, as a rule, far from reliable and trustworthy; indeed, she seems to have been unstable, opportunistic, and somewhat ruthless. At the very least, her relationship with Home was undoubtedly far more complex than Hall suggests. However, on the basis of Hall's account, one would never suspect that Mrs. Lyon even had a personality.

In perhaps the most frequently cited, and also the longest, chapter of his book, Hall addresses Home's notorious alleged levitation out the window at Ashley House, during which the medium supposedly floated outside through one window and then floated back into the building via another window. Skeptics frequently focus on that incident as if it really mattered in the total evaluation of Home's phenomena. But in fact, the séance in question, which occurred entirely in the dark and with no controls, is one of the most poorly documented in the entire literature on Home. It's simply inexcusable for Hall to devote nearly one-fourth of his small book to the case and say nothing about Crookes's detailed work with Home, or about other studies conducted under better conditions and documented with greater care. Home produced nearly a quarter-century's worth of phenomena to speculate about, a great deal of that under conditions allowing for reasonable evaluation. Readers will find no discussion of that material in Hall's book.

Finally, I should mention one more example of Hall's slippery skepticism. As I noted earlier, Hall cited the work of Besterman, et al to argue that Home used a combination of suggestion and conjuring to influence sitters' reports. But Hall makes appeals to Home's alleged power of suggestion several times in his book. In some of these, he may actually be referring to hypnosis, although he never makes that clear. However, *we* can be clear about why neither suggestion nor hypnosis adequately explains away Home's overall mediumistic success. I've discussed problems with the skeptical appeal to hypnosis previously, but we can remind ourselves here of at least one crucial point. It's very well-established that people differ considerably in their degree of suggestibility and hypnotizability. That makes it almost miraculous that Home could hypnotize or otherwise psychologically manipulate a group of people so that they provide concordant nonveridical eyewitness reports, especially when—as was often the case—conditions were obviously unfavorable to such influence.

In fact, Hall generally ignores what should be an obvious guiding principle in trying to establish the reality of paranormal phenomena outside the lab—namely, that *the cases that matter are the ones most difficult to explain away*. Instead, Hall focuses on cases for which an appeal to suggestion might have some (perhaps remote) plausibility, and he discusses none of the cases for which it's manifestly inadequate. For example, Hall quotes passages from Lord Adare's *Experiences in Spiritualism*,[22] a chronicle (or diary) of mostly informal and poorly-controlled (or uncontrolled) Home séances, to support his claim that Home manipulated Adare through suggestion. The point of that exercise, clearly, was to deploy the fallacy of hasty generalization and imply that all reports of Home's phenomena might likewise be attributed to suggestion.

Besides, given the great variability of human suggestibility or hypnotizability, it's clearly a large—and unjustified—leap from the hypothesis of individual suggestion to that of group suggestion. It's also highly implausible to suppose that Home was capable of hypnotically or otherwise psychologically influencing groups of sitters for nearly 25 years without slipping up once. In fact, if Home had been able to pull that off, his alleged power of suggestion would arguably have been as paranormal as what it was intended to explain away. Actually, it would seem to be indistinguishable from telepathic influence.

Predictably, Hall fails to mention important differences between the incidents he cites and the best pieces of evidence. For example, in some of the latter Home neither moved nor spoke prior to the occurrence of phenomena, and in most of the best cases Home's relationship to the sitters was far less intimate than it was in the case of Adare, and perhaps—as some interpretations have it—less pathological as well.

Perhaps we can drive these points home by considering a few more eye-witness accounts of Home's phenomena. They're typical of many other such accounts, and it should be obvious that they pose a serious challenge to the skeptic generally, and to the hypothesis of suggestion in particular.

In 1889 W.F. Barrett and F.W.H. Myers published a review of *D.D. Home, His Life and Mission*, written by Home's second wife.[23] To their lengthy and generally favorable appraisal of the evidence, they appended a series of additional testimony, solicited on behalf of the SPR. For reasons discussed by the authors, the solicited accounts they provided are clearly above average as evidence—for example, because of independent corroborating testimony, or because the accounts were written immediately after the event, or because the phenomena occurred in locations never before visited by Home, and (in every case) because the descriptions weren't supplied by Home's wife. But as far as the phenomena reported are concerned, they're quite typical of accounts written over the entire extensive period of Home's mediumistic activity. With that in mind, consider the following.

> ...Home arrived at our house shortly before dinner. After dinner we agreed to sit in the drawing room at a square card table near the fire... In a few minutes, a cold draught of air was felt on our hands and knockings occurred...My gold bracelet was unclasped while my hands were on the table and fell upon the floor...I think I asked if the piano could be played; it stood at least 12 ft. or 14 ft. away from us. Almost at once the softest music sounded. I went up to the piano and opened it. I saw the keys depressed, but no one playing. I stood by its side

and watched it, hearing the most lovely chords; the keys seemed to be struck by some invisible hands; all this time Home was far distant from the piano. Then a faint sound was heard upon my harp [a few feet from the piano, and across the room from Home], as of the wind blowing over its strings.[24]

Another witness, a veteran of several Home séances, writes,

The séances begin by sitting round Mr. Home's table, which is rather large, as it holds 10 people sitting round it. We lay our hands flat on the table before us. After a while there is usually a trembling of the table and often a strong tremulous motion of the floor and chairs, and loud raps sound about the room and under the table. Then the table usually heaves up with a steady motion, sometimes clear off the floor, sometimes on one side to an angle of about 45 deg. Mr. Home makes a practice of asking anyone present, usually the last comer, to sit under the table to be enabled to assure his friends that no trickery was possible. I have sat so several times and heard raps about my head, some loud, some soft, and have seen the table rise from the floor and have passed my hand and arm clear through between the floor and the pedestal of the table while it was in the air. It has happened several times when we have been sitting in this way that some one of the company has been drawn back in his chair from the table, and once Mrs. Parkes, who was sitting next to me, was drawn at least a foot back and then sideways about six inches. A bell, bracelet, or pockethandkerchief, or anything taken in one hand and placed under the table is taken by the "spirit" hands, which are palpable warm fingers of various sizes and feeling, but which when attempted to be grasped always seem to dissolve in a curious manner and leave airy nothing.

Mr. Home has an accordion; it is not a mechanical one, for he left it by accident at Mrs. Parkes' house one day, and I carefully examined it. He takes this in one hand by the side of it which is furthest from the keys and places it just beneath the edge of the table. In that position I have watched it attentively as I stooped with my head and shoulders thrust under the table, and have seen the bellows begin to rise and fall, and then faint sounds to issue which, gaining in strength, at last swell out into the most beautiful spiritual airs of a strange and fantastic character. On any particular air being called for it is played, sometimes beautifully, sometimes in a very fitful uneven manner...I have several times sat next to Mr. Home when "the spirits" are playing the accordion, and he always holds one hand on the table and supports the accordion with the other. Sometimes "the spirits" remove the instrument from his hand and carry it to some other person, when the same result is the consequence. ...All these phenomena... have been done *not in the dark*, which some people say is necessary in a séance, but in bright light. I should also say that I have seen them in Mrs. Parkes' own house, where she invited Mr. Home one evening and I was present; it was the first time he had ever put foot in her house, and the tilting and rapping and music was just the same, and the table travelled along the floor, turning and pushing chairs and stools about, right up to one side and along the side of a sofa.[25]

Still another witness writes:

The incident...took place at the home of Lady Poulett...Mr. Home was there. We all saw the supper table, on which there was a quantity of glass and china full of good things, rise, I should say, to an angle of 45 deg. without anything slipping in the least, and then relapse to its normal position. There was also a socalled centretable in the room, round which we were seated—it had nothing upon it—and as we joined hands it moved and we followed it. There was Baron Reichenbach, the discoverer of paraffin, present, who laughed at us, and challenged us to move the table if we would let him get under it and hold it. He was a rather tall and powerfullybuilt man, and he got under the table and clasped it with both his arms, but it moved as before, dragging him all round the room.[26]

The Final Verdict

There are many good books on the heyday of Spiritualism; Hall's is certainly not one of them. If it has any value, it's as an unusually instructive example of dishonest parapsychological skepticism. Now I have no idea what sort of integrity others expect from historians. I do know that Herodotus is reputed to have said: "Very few things happen at the right time, and the rest don't happen at all. A conscientious historian will correct these defects." But I'm (uncharacteristically) less cynical about this. In my opinion, Hall displays an appalling disregard for the canons of historical research. Moreover, what little the reader may learn about Home and his phenomena (and it's *very* little) is irrelevant to Hall's professed aim of determining whether the phenomena were genuinely paranormal. Nevertheless, Hall and his publisher, Prometheus Books, managed to perform a minor service to psi research, perhaps most useful for newcomers to the field. They've demonstrated with unusual clarity that the enemies of serious psychical research sometimes masquerade as champions of dispassionate inquiry and metaphysical sobriety.

6. Reflections on Super Psi

The Problem and Why it Matters

Parapsychological research offers many delectable opportunities for unrestrained (and too often inept) theoretical speculation, and perhaps the most annoying is the seemingly endless debate over how extensive, refined, consistent, or controllable human psychic functioning can be. As you might expect, combatants wrangle primarily over the upper limits of what's reasonable to consider possible in Nature. So, as you might also expect, opinions vary widely on just how extreme, or super, it's acceptable to allow psi to be. That's why this is often called "the problem of super psi."

No doubt some readers—skeptics, primarily—will consider this debate to be decadently luxurious. After all, there's little point in indulging in it until we've affirmatively settled the prior question of whether there's any psi at all. Nevertheless, once that big question has been satisfactorily answered in the affirmative—and needless to say, I believe it has—this more luxurious debate is a big deal because it has implications for every nook and cranny of psi research.

The general battle lines are clear enough. Some—proponents of what we may call the *super-psi hypothesis*—claim that the best way to explain certain occurrences is to posit a degree or kind of psychic functioning that's substantially more astonishing than what's apparently revealed in the usually pale and (at best) marginally compelling statistics from quantitative psi research. Not surprisingly, others disagree, arguing that there's no justification for admitting psi of the posited magnitude or virtuosity. Remarkably, this debate over the upper limits of psychic functioning has been flourishing at least since the founding of the Society for Psychical Research in the late nineteenth century. Various subspecies of psi-conservatives continue to insist that appeals to super psi are unwarranted, and super-psi proponents continue to battle among themselves over how super psi can be.

Perhaps one reason this debate has lasted so long is that it's simply unclear what the content of the super-psi hypothesis is—that is, what it's actually proposing about the range or limits of psi. As a result, proponents and critics too often lack a clear target to debate. But perhaps more important, the problem apparently won't leave us alone. The very specter of some kind of extreme psi meets us at every turn, and it poses a recurring and nagging challenge to our unreflective boggle thresholds. It forces us to consider whether we can tolerate the idea of psi being more extensive, refined, large-scale, and unmanageable than standard experimental protocols seem to presuppose. And of course, that raises in many the fear of psi discussed in Chapter 1. The prospect of super psi suggests that ESP and PK can't be beaten into well-behaved submission by our best experimental procedures, and that psi might in fact be something science can't harness *at all*. And naturally, that raises ugly fears of responsibility over our own potentially unconscious, inadvertent, and uncontrollable psychic incursions into others' lives—or (possibly more important) their incursions into *our* lives.

Now as this book should make clear, I'm an unrepentant defender of some very dramatic parapsychological phenomena. But I have an admittedly cynical view of this topic. I consider the very concept of super psi to be defective—in fact, perhaps fatally so. Although many writers on parapsychological issues entertain the possibility of what they call super psi, and although they write as if they know what they're talking about, the evidence suggests otherwise. For one thing, it's extremely unclear which events would count as ostensible instances of super psi. And as we'll see, that's primarily because we have no defensible grounds for assigning *any* limit to psychic functioning, much less a scale that allows us to distinguish clearly different degrees of impressive psi. And that's just the beginning of the problems with the concept of super psi.

So my goal in this chapter is to pry the concept of super psi from the clammy tendrils of psi theorists and either clarify it or (if that can't be done satisfactorily) abandon the concept once and for all. I'm quite aware that this task won't be easy, because—as with the deeply unintelligible notion of a memory trace—important confusions are buried far below the surface.[1] So it's not surprising that in order to see why the concept of super psi has been so resilient (if not quite assassination-proof), we must take a very close look at some grubby particulars.

As readers may know, the topic of super psi is raised frequently and probably most often in connection with the evidence for postmortem survival. There, the challenge is to determine whether the most impressive evidence suggesting survival can be explained without positing some kind of personal postmortem persistence. And if we rule out fraud, misreporting, or malobservation as optional explanations,[2] the most recalcitrant alternative strategy is to appeal to psi among the living that merely *simulates* evidence of survival. Arguments then rage—needlessly, as I'll try to show here and in greater detail in Chapter 7—as to whether the degree of living-agent psi required for simulating evidence of survival is too extreme to be believed.

But the survival debate isn't the only arena in which the topic of super psi plays a prominent role. We find the debate also in discussions of macro-PK—especially in connection with physical mediumship and poltergeists. In those contexts, skeptics and even some parapsychologists maintain that the phenomena reported far exceed what's reasonable to consider seriously. Indeed, that's a common reaction to many of the manifestations discussed in previous chapters, such as Mirabelli's materializations and Home's large object levitations and disembodied hands.

The issue of super psi even hovers over the evidence for precognition. The problem there is that a leading strategy for explaining precognition is to invoke a form of backwards causation, or retrocausation—for example, by claiming that a precognitive awareness of a plane crash was *caused* by the *later* crash. But what if some philosophers and parapsychologists are correct in claiming that appeals to retrocausation (at least in this context) are flawed and should be rejected? In that case, one of the leading options for explaining the data is to appeal to PK or telepathic influence on the part of the precognizer—that is, to claim that the precognizer psychically and presumably unconsciously *brings about* the later, ostensibly precognized events.[3] Superficially at least—and as it turns out, only superficially—that explanatory strategy apparently requires positing a degree of psychic functioning well beyond what we elicit in the lab.

As I mentioned, many parapsychologists (and others) reject all appeals to what they vaguely call "super psi," by which they mean simply (but no less vaguely) "much more impressive than laboratory psi." And occasionally, this resistance takes forms as fascinating as the issues themselves. Sometimes the arguments are so transparently weak that one can't help but suspect that dissenters are motivated by more than mere intellectual disagreement. Indeed, it looks distinctly like a fear response. It's really quite remarkable how much passion and angry resistance can be evoked merely by sympathetically proposing some super-psi candidates—that is, phenomena at or beyond prevailing boggle thresholds. Conceptual clarity inevitably suffers under those conditions.

Nevertheless, the major objections to the possibility of much-more-impressive-than-laboratory-psi raise important and interesting issues concerning the substance of the super-psi hypothesis and its proper means of evaluation. So let's do some conceptual housecleaning. Let's examine the relevant arguments and issues in detail, to see whether we can clarify (if not demolish) the concept of super psi.

Sketch of the Hypothesis

As we'll see, there are several reasons why parapsychologists have been confused about the merits and substance of the super-psi hypothesis. Some of those confusions, undoubtedly, can be traced to the unfortunate term "super psi." After all, it's hardly clear what "super" means, and as with other normative expressions, people use it according to different evaluative scales. Obviously, what's super for one person may not be for another.

However, as much as I'd like to propose a better term for the job, I suspect that there's little to gain at this point by abandoning the expression "super psi." For one thing, by now it's very well entrenched in the parapsychological lexicon. And for another (as we'll see), certain initially plausible replacements for "super"—such as "extensive," "large-scale," "refined," and "virtuosic," at best capture only one aspect of the range of phenomena usually picked out by the term. If the expression "super psi" has any merit at all, it's that the term has many fewer syllables than the equally vague but at least more honest "much more impressive than laboratory psi."

Fortunately, some fundamental features of the concept of super psi are fairly easy to pin down. Initially, one might think that any large-scale psi effect would be an instance of super psi. But in fact, it's easy to think of counterexamples, most of which concern the transitivity of causes.[4] For example, an unimpressive or seemingly insignificant psi event might trigger a chain of causation leading to a much more outstanding effect. But if psi plays no further role following the initial unimpressive psi event, we'd probably not consider the remarkable concluding event to be a case of super psi.

The following analogy should make this clear. Suppose that I'm walking along a mountain ridge and unwittingly dislodge a small stone, and suppose that the stone falls down the mountain side, derailing a train that just happens to be passing by. If causation is transitive, then since I caused the stone to move, and since the stone's movement eventually derailed the train, we could say that *I* caused the train to derail. But of course, my role in the affair was hardly notable. The train derailment isn't something I achieved or for which I could be held culpable (or proud). All I did was to dislodge a stone, and even that was unintentional.

By contrast, suppose that I *wanted* to derail the oncoming train, and suppose that I accomplished that task by throwing a nearby stone the great distance onto the track below, at just the exact position and the exact time necessary to derail the train. Now that *would* be an achievement, and the reason it's impressive has more to do with the exquisite control of my stone-throwing than with the magnitude of the event to which it led. After all, my control over the stone's trajectory would have been impressive even if there had been no train in the vicinity. Nevertheless, my derailing the train in this way is analogous to at least one conceivable type of super psi, in which a small psi effect is cunningly or expertly calculated or coordinated to have a large-scale result. For example, suppose I cause an airplane to explode by psychokinetically igniting the fuel in its tank, or suppose I cause the death of a despised person by producing a well-placed blood clot in his brain. Or suppose I cause an apparently precognized mine collapse by psychokinetically nudging a very small section of the mine support system, which I clairvoyantly discovered to be that system's sole weak link.

On the other hand, you might think that super psi could also take the form of huge, uncontrolled psychic outbursts. For example, many would consider it to be a case of super psi if I paranormally produced a massive shock wave that collapsed the mine and surrounding mountain, even if the shock wave was an unintentional, brute psychic outburst (analogous, perhaps, to a cry of frustration), and the mine just happened to collapse as a result. Moreover, one would think that super psi might also take refined forms that have no immediate large-scale consequences. For example, suppose that I use ESP to read the erotic emails of a business competitor I want to blackmail for conducting an illicit affair. Or suppose that I use PK mischievously to delete all occurrences of the letter "m" from a document a colleague is writing, and to do this immediately after the words appear on the colleague's computer screen. If these achievements count as instances of super psi, it would presumably be in virtue of their precision and accuracy.

So let's tentatively define "super psi" (admittedly, still loosely) as "psychic functioning of a highly controlled or refined nature, or else psi of great magnitude (whether refined or not)." Obviously, that definition is still vague, and some types of frequently reported phenomena will still be difficult to classify. For example, some might question whether the object levitations and materializations reported during the heyday of Spiritualism are sufficiently large-scale or refined to count as instances of super psi. They might consider those phenomena to be impressive (instances of *dandy* psi?), but reserve the honorific term "super psi" for something even more remarkable. But as we'll see, it's not clear whether there's any plausible standard according to which a psi phenomenon is super only if it's more exceptional than levitating a large and heavy piano or materializing a warm and lifelike materialized hand—both reported in the case of D.D. Home. In any case, borderline cases are to be expected and shouldn't prevent us from dealing profitably with some intriguing and serious issues.

But before tackling objections to the super-psi hypothesis, let's briefly review the main reasons for taking seriously the central, underlying idea that psi can occur in mind-bogglingly impressive forms. This is an important initial step in understanding what a reasonable super-psi hypothesis would look like.

First, psychic functioning is probably not something that occurs only in conspicuous ways. No doubt for some at least it's an open question whether there's any such thing as *everyday* psi, or at any rate whether there's much of it. But it should be obvious that if psi phenomena occur at all, they wouldn't occur only for parapsychologists, and then only when they're on the lookout for them. After all, surprising and spontaneous occurrences of ostensible psi in real-life contexts are what drove scientists into the lab in the first place, in the arguably quixotic quest to study it under controlled conditions. Moreover, human faculties, abilities, or capacities are things that occur in degrees. Their manifestations run the gamut from the mundane to the arcane and the inconspicuous to the conspicuous. In fact, it would probably be unprecedented in the domains of human aptitudes and performance if psi functioning failed to exhibit similar variabilities.[5]

But in that case, assuming that psi occurs, it's reasonable to think that we recognize only its more striking manifestations. For one thing, instances of telepathy are likely to be noticed only between people who know and communicate with one another. Similarly, cases of apparent precognition and realtime clairvoyance are likely to command our attention only when they concern events that impress us for some reason (usually because they're crises or other sorts of unexpected or noteworthy occurrences). But we might be interacting all the time with the minds of strangers, and acquiring information by ESP of events to which we give little or no conscious attention. Presumably, similar observations apply in the case of PK; we wouldn't expect everyday PK effects to be flagrantly obvious. Object levitations don't occur under normal circumstances; so *that* sort of PK effect would undoubtedly stand out starkly. But if everyday PK is doing such things as affecting the cycle of traffic lights, foiling radar traps on the highway, stalling elevators, crashing computers, or aggravating a co-worker's arthritis, it could easily go unnoticed.

Second, no matter how counterintuitive or repugnant the super-psi hypothesis might seem, the theoretical alternatives might be even more objectionable. Consider again, but now in more detail, how we might try to explain cases of apparent precognition. Assuming we can rule out coincidence, we're left with two main explanatory options. On the one hand we have the *retrocausal* analysis, according to which the later, precognized event influences the earlier precognitive experience. For example, tomorrow's plane crash would be a causal condition of the previous day's precognitive dream. And on the other hand we have the so-called *active* analysis, which avoids a commitment to backwards causation and instead posits refined *clockwise* ESP and PK (or telepathic influence) on the part of the precognizer.[6] And that analysis likewise has two main subdivisions: First, just as an engineer might anticipate the collapse of a building after observing flaws in its blueprint or foundation, an apparent precognizer might unconsciously *infer* that the plane will crash, based on telepathically or clairvoyantly acquired *contemporaneous* information about the condition of the plane or the physical or psychological disposition of its crew. Or second, the precognizer might psychokinetically cause the plane to crash (or telepathically influence the pilot to do something fatally stupid). Now if the retrocausal analysis turns out to be deeply unacceptable (as psychoanalyst and psi researcher Jule Eisenbud and I have argued),[7] and if (as it seems) the active analysis does comparatively little violence to our received scientific or broader conceptual framework (apart from bringing psi into the picture), the active analysis appears to be the more viable alternative.

Furthermore, there's an even more abstract, and perhaps even more compelling, reason for taking super psi seriously. Given our present (and considerable) state of ignorance concerning the nature of psi, we must (at the very least) entertain the possibility of extensive or ultra-refined psi once we grant that it might assume more moderate or crude forms. For example, in the case of PK, since we still have no idea how agents affect remote physical systems, we have no grounds for assuming that PK effects are inherently limited in magnitude or refinement. Granted, there's no shortage of theoretical proposals, of varying levels of competence and sophistication, as to how psi works. Some people, after all, seem to believe that theorizing is as easy as lying. Nevertheless, there's no consensus about how even the smallest-scale PK violates or circumvents the usual constraints on influencing other physical systems. So we're in no position to set limits in advance on how far those apparent violations may go.

Actually, not only might we have to entertain the possibility of extensive psi, we might have to entertain the possibility of *unlimited* psi (at least in principle). The only way we could ever be entitled to insist that psi effects have inherent limits would be on the basis of a thoroughly developed and well-supported psi theory, one that embraces *all* the available evidence for psi (not just the laboratory evidence) and explains how or why psi functions both in and out of the lab. But at present, no decent theory forbids large-scale or mind-boggling psi (many, like observational and decision augmentation theories, have simply ignored the possibility), and no well-supported scientific theory renders any form of psi improbable.[8] So at our current level of understanding, super psi is as viable as puny psi.

In fact (as the early chapters of this book indicate), super-psi proponents can even claim a kind of empirical support. After all, the best-documented late nineteenth- and early twentieth-century evidence from physical mediumship shows that psi effects may be far more varied, elaborate, and refined than what we'd suppose from superficial interpretations of laboratory studies. But once we've accepted the reality of those mediumistic phenomena, we should be all the more reluctant to rule out the possibility of still more dramatic, refined, or wide-ranging psi effects.

Moreover, in discussions of postmortem survival—the area in which debates about super psi are most prevalent—we may not have to stretch very far conceptually at all. Most discussions of survival sooner or later consider the plausibility of explaining the data in terms of living-agent psi, and survivalists typically reject those alternatives on the grounds that they posit an unprecedented degree of psi (at least by the standard suggested superficially by lab experiments). But that's simply confused, and not just because it's foolish to extrapolate from behavior elicited under experimental straitjackets to behavior unleashed in its natural settings. For one thing, it's not at all clear that the hypothesized degree of living-agent psi must be more wide-ranging or dramatic than what's already documented in the best cases of macro-PK and remote viewing. But even more important (and as we'll see in Chapter 7),[9] *survivalists and proponents of living-agent psi apparently require comparably impressive psi achievements.*

So far we've been considering the basis for invoking much-better-than-laboratory psi in contexts where there's already prima facie evidence that something paranormal is going on. But what especially concerns psi-conservatives is the appeal to paranormal processes to explain seemingly non-paranormal everyday events. But is there really a basis for rejecting those efforts? Consider: Once we entertain—as we should—the possibility that psi might insinuate itself into everyday affairs, we can see how an appeal to covert psi might explain phenomena or regularities that would otherwise be considered mysterious or fortuitous. Pervasive and refined PK and ESP could explain why some people are healthier than others, or remarkably luckier or unluckier than others.

It could explain why some soldiers escape serious injury, despite taking repeated heroic and seemingly reckless risks on the battlefield. It might explain why some incompetent or careless motorists regularly avoid the automotive catastrophes that befall others and emerge unscathed from those that they initiate. It might even explain why some people always seem to find parking spaces.

And however distasteful the thought might be, consistent bad luck or misfortune could be an external PK analogue to psychosomatic illness. We should perhaps explore the relationship between our misfortune and our self-image (say, our degree of self-hatred), and be prepared to see people as psychically disposing or arranging events to reinforce their self-image as victimized, cursed, or unworthy individuals. Of course, an even more sinister possibility is that others are the cause of our misfortune. We should perhaps investigate the deep relationships between unlucky persons and their acquaintances and relatives—possibly even connections with strangers whose interests or agendas conflict with theirs. But on the brighter side, refined unconscious psi might undergird the careers of those who are successful in business and finance, and who seem to have a knack for speculation. It might even play a role in athletics.[10]

I must emphasize that in making these suggestions, I'm not endorsing the cavalier appeal to covert psi to explain everyday events. After all, if psi really is operating under the surface, its role is probably anything but straightforward. That's why psi is probably *not* responsible for *every* bit of luck or misfortune. That's why it might not be the reason we find a lost article of jewelry, or happen to meet "by chance" someone we needed to see, or find that our socks keep disappearing.

But now we're getting ahead of ourselves. These are the sorts of issues that have inspired the common and major objections to the super-psi hypothesis. I believe that those objections turn out upon careful inspection to be rather weak at best and egregious at worst. But nearly all raise important and interesting issues. So let's see if we can dispose of them once and for all. At the very least, this process should help us to clarify and assess the super-psi hypothesis.

The major strategies for attacking the super-psi hypothesis fall into a few major groups, which we will now consider in turn.

There's no evidence for super psi
The problem with this objection is that it rests on an indefensible assumption about what the evidence for super psi would look like. I call it the *sore thumb*

assumption. Very generally, the assumption is that if super psi occurred, we'd know it if we saw it—that is, it would stand out like a sore thumb. More specifically, the sore thumb assumption is that everyday occurrences of psi will not blend in smoothly with (or be masked by, or be indistinguishable from) the network of surrounding events of which they're a part. Instead, they'll be conspicuous or readily identifiable as instances of psi.

But clearly, the problem here concerns the possibility of sneaky or naughty psi, and so we must look again at some matters already mentioned briefly. Once we grant that psi can occur in real-life situations, we must also grant that those occurrences may go undetected. For example (and as I noted earlier), there's no reason to suppose that all instances of observable PK must be as flagrant and incongruous as table levitations or other movements of ordinarily stationary objects. Nor must occurrences of PK be preceded by some kind of overt precursor or warning (a paranormal counterpart to a flourish of trumpets). For all we know, everyday PK could blend smoothly into ordinary surrounding events. After all, there needn't be any observable difference between (say) a heart attack or a plane crash caused normally and one caused by PK. The only difference may be in their unobservable causal histories. And of course, similar observations can be made about ESP. Just as occurrences of PK might inconspicuously permeate surrounding events, our mental lives might conceal a rich vein of undetected telepathic and clairvoyant interactions, perhaps manifesting as incongruous and seemingly insignificant thoughts. And as with occurrences of PK, instances of ESP needn't announce their paranormal ancestry beforehand or in some other way flaunt their paranormal nature.

A related problem with the sore thumb assumption is that it ignores the possibly important connections between the conspicuousness of a psi event and the context of needs and interests in which it's produced. In fact, there are possible (if not likely) links between psi functioning and other organic activities that both this and the next major objection to the super-psi hypothesis overlook. In particular, they ignore the possibility that when psi plays a role in everyday life, its manifestations are linked intimately to a complex underlying nexus of desires, concerns, and idiosyncrasies of the agent's overall psychology and belief system. Again, there's no reason to assume that psychic functioning occurs only when parapsychologists are trying to induce or observe it. And there's also no reason to assume that we can judge either the role, variety, or the limits of spontaneous psi from its manifestations in experimental settings.

Actually, on its face, that second assumption seems as foolish as supposing that we can extrapolate the variety, range, or magnitude of human courage, sensuality, cruelty, or selfless generosity from their (at best) anemic or strait-jacketed manifestations in formal experiments. The situation is similar in the case of athletic abilities, whose most exquisite forms can only appear in re-al-life situations when motivations (and the stakes of winning) are especially high and when opponents are trying their hardest to win. Besides, unsolicited occurrences of ostensible psi-in-life are what drove researchers into the lab in the first place. So one would think that any psi-theoretician worthy of the title would have something to say about the possibly broad role and specific ap-plications of psi in its *natural* setting, away from the artificial constraints and contrived needs of formal experiments. Even mediumistic séances encourage displays of psi (such as materializations and object levitations) that might be quite different from its manifestations in more humdrum everyday situations. Although séances are perhaps less artificial than formal experiments, they're still highly ritualized or structured settings. Therefore, we should also be wary of taking séance-room psi to be paradigmatic of spontaneous everyday psi.

It's reasonable, therefore, to suppose that if psi plays a role in ordinary life, then (like organic capacities generally) its manifestations will range from the dramatic and conspicuous to the mundane and inconspicuous. It's also reason-able to assume that psi can be triggered either consciously or unconsciously and that its effects can range from beneficial to lethal. Those who argue that there's no evidence for super psi must, at the very least, give good reasons for believing that psi would *not* have these characteristics, and that it would ac-cordingly be discontinuous with practically every other human ability.

Furthermore, not only might everyday psi events easily escape our atten-tion, it might even be in our interest *not* to notice them. Granted, in some cultures the possibility of daily and even large-scale psi, including lethal or malevolent psi (such as hexing or the evil eye), is a familiar feature of a pre-vailing animistic world view. Members of those cultures (perhaps grudgingly) accept the possibility that human agency can be responsible for a wide range of occurrences, including those that more "civilized" people tend to attribute to impersonal causes. But within modern developed countries, such "magical" thinking is generally treated with either alarm or disdain.

I'm aware that many people accept the possibility of psychically influenc-ing normal, everyday states of affairs, at least when the effects are salutary—for example, in the realm of healing or meditating for crime reduction. But of course, no force can be used exclusively for the good. So it's both interest-ing and revealing that few of those who propose beneficial applications of psi consider equally seriously the potential for pernicious uses of the same power.

Often, they'll naively suppose that our nastier unconscious desires can be kept under wraps. Or, they'll simply ignore how the possibility of beneficial psi is logically bound up with the possibility of harmful or malevolent psi (conscious or unconscious). Arguably, then, it might be psychologically advantageous for many of us if psi were to occur covertly or at least appear to be beyond our control. In that case, we could conveniently feel like mere bystanders to events we might actually have helped shape.

Those who argue that there's no evidence for super psi are also guilty of a general methodological error, sometimes mentioned in non-parapsychological contexts. For example, in a discussion of the evidence for UFOs, astrophysicist Peter Sturrock noted the dangers of what he somewhat misleadingly calls *theory-dependent* arguments.[11] He writes:

> …if we entertain the hypothesis that the phenomena may be due to an extremely advanced civilization, we must face the possibility that many ideas that we accept as simple truths may, in a wider and more sophisticated context, not be as simple and may not even be truths.

The point applies equally to the possibility of extremely refined or large-scale psi. We mustn't reject a novel or worldview altering hypothesis on the basis of arguments or interpretations of data that *presuppose* the denial of the hypothesis. For example, despite other respects in which it's admittedly very unclear, the super-psi hypothesis undoubtedly holds that psi might be sneaky and naughty. That is, psi might be triggered unconsciously; it might be in our interest for it to work surreptitiously; and it might be used to fulfill our least admirable needs and interests. But then we can't evaluate the super-psi hypothesis by presupposing that psi will always be conspicuous and well behaved.

There's evidence against super psi

This objection actually invites us to consider the evidence, and it assumes two different forms. According to the first, the evidence *strongly suggests* that, although psi may be impressive, it has limits well below the realm of the super. And according to the second, the evidence *demonstrates* that super psi doesn't occur. Since these two variants raise different issues, let's consider them in turn

Version 1: *The evidence strongly suggests that super psi doesn't occur.* This version of the appeal to evidence has been clearly articulated by Roger Anderson:

D.D. Home made objects weighing some hundreds of pounds move and sometimes levitate, but he never made a house fly or visited a distant friend by means of that peculiar power of locomotion. Nor has any other physical medium exhibited phenomena that would lead us to suppose such feats within the realm of accomplishment...Like other human abilities, we may not be able to state *a priori* what the limits of PK may be, but it seems a safe bet on empirical grounds that they will not far exceed the virtuosic manifestations recorded with PK superstars like Home.[12]

Anderson's argument is thoughtful, and it's easy to sympathize with his intuitions. Nevertheless, his argument is flawed, for several reasons. First, it assumes unjustifiably that psi phenomena occurring within the peculiar dynamics of physical mediumship are paradigmatic of psi phenomena in radically different contexts. But as I noted earlier, we're not entitled to suppose that the best examples of mediumship indicate what non-mediums may do, or what forms psi is likely to take in situations where needs, interests, and overall belief systems of the agent(s) are different. So we can't assume that D.D. Home or Mirabelli (or any other medium) exemplify how dramatically psi might manifest *outside* a certain set of conditions appropriate to a séance or associated with mediumship generally.

The varieties of classic mediumistic phenomena may have been influenced, first, by the psychology of the medium—for example, the medium's normal capacities and interests, and of course the medium's conceptions of both psi generally and mediumship specifically and their place in nature. Home reportedly produced musical performances on untouched instruments, and those feats would have been continuous with his normal musical abilities. By contrast, Palladino, who had no normally developed musical skills, never produced more than apparently random sounds on nearby instruments. Moreover, Home had firm beliefs about the conditions favorable to the production of phenomena, and those beliefs may have influenced his success rate under those conditions. For example, he thought the "power" was strongest in dim light (and under the séance table), even though his phenomena frequently occurred in relatively bright light (and away from the table). Analogously, Palladino thought a "cabinet" facilitated the production of phenomena, and in her case perhaps it did. And perhaps more important, both Home and Palladino genuinely felt that discarnate spirits caused their phenomena. So it's not at all surprising that their mediumistic phenomena took forms appropriate to spiritistic beliefs and attempts at communicating with the dead.

Moreover, it may be that a traditional and *literal* belief in mediumship is conducive to a certain type of *conspicuous* psi occurrence. Indeed, as I observed in Chapter 1, that would help explain why physical phenomena began declining in magnitude and refinement during the early part of the twentieth century. As the Spiritualist movement waned and more and more secular investigators began studying the phenomena, an increasing number of people (including the mediums themselves) took seriously—or at least knew that others took seriously—the deeply intimidating possibility that the phenomena were caused by living agents. Many began to consider that mediums were psi *agents* rather than facilitators of (or vehicles for) postmortem influence. But that profoundly changed the psychodynamics of mediumship by raising issues of personal responsibility that don't arise for those who believe that they merely mediate the phenomena. If mediums are what they purport to be, they shouldn't have to feel responsible for the outcome of a séance, because from a spiritistic perspective both failures and successes depend primarily (if not entirely) on the skill of the ostensible communicator and the quality of the "connection" between the two worlds. But even more important, convinced mediums wouldn't have to fear either the omnipotence or the omniscience of their own thought, especially outside the safe confines and ritualized practices of the séance room.

The belief systems of the investigators might also have influenced the forms taken by mediumistic phenomena, once again most clearly in the case of physical mediumship.[13] For example, it's intriguing that W.J. Crawford, an engineer, reported displays of physical mediumship that an engineer in particular would appreciate. His greatest subject, Kathleen Goligher, exuded ectoplasm that mimicked the operation of a cantilever when levitating a table. By contrast, Richet and Schrenck-Notzing—a physiologist and a physician, respectively—observed ectoplasmic phenomena that behaved more organically than mechanically—for example, gradually taking the shape of a hand with mobile fingers.[14] It's a classic contrast, and also a pity that these investigators never experimented with each other's star subjects. It would have been an interesting exploration of experimenter influence to see what results Richet (for example) could obtain with Miss Goligher, or Crawford with Eva C.

It seems clear then, that the phenomena of physical mediumship may not be representative of PK in other contexts, where the underlying psychodynamics and hindrances to optimal psi functioning may be quite different. Nevertheless, Anderson is correct that we find no reports of houses flying (at least during periods of meteorological and geological tranquility) or people levitating over to a friend's house for a visit (although, as noted in Chapter 4, Mirabelli disappeared from a train station and a few minutes later was discovered to be 50 miles away). So we may wonder (along with Anderson), why is this? If psi functioning can assume virtually any form, isn't it reasonable to think that something like a levitated house might have been reported by now?

The answer, I suspect, is that we can't be certain what's reasonable to expect. One problem, which I discuss more fully in connection with the second version of this empirical argument, is that we're not entitled to make the inferential leap from "Event E can occur" to "Event E will (or is likely to) occur." For example, even if thoughts can kill, it doesn't follow that they will (or that it's likely they will). And in fact, phenomena that are empirically possible can always be subject to many real-life constraints.

Besides, if we're correct in assuming that real-life occurrences of psi are typically driven by our deepest genuine or perceived needs and concerns, and if we assume that it's generally in our interest for those occurrences to take forms that are culturally and psychologically appropriate (including remaining inconspicuous), we'd have to ask: In what sort of credible context would it be appropriate to make a house fly or to make oneself levitate great distances? And before answering that question glibly and quickly, I suggest keeping in mind that constraints on psychic functioning can issue not only from oneself, but also from others, just as others constrain our day-to-day activities both with their actions and their beliefs, desires, and so on.

Consider: St. Joseph of Copertino's well-attested levitations apparently covered what some would regard as considerable distances. But quite apart from the fact that any levitation would have been seen as astonishing, the form and extent of Joseph's feats were appropriate to the contexts in which they occurred. Perhaps Joseph *could* have levitated over to a neighboring monastery, but it's not clear why he would have done so. His levitations were reactions to local and fleeting inspiring events, not incidents for which long-distance levitation would have been a suitable response. If a casual remark in the garden or an introduction to the Pope was sufficient to induce a levitation, it would seem more fitting and relevant for Joseph to fly (as he reportedly did) to a nearby tree or the church altar than to take off and disappear over the horizon. Granted, observers would probably have considered the latter to be even more miraculous than Joseph's run-of-the-mill levitations. But witnesses apparently found Joseph's local flights to be miraculous enough. In fact, they might have considered a long-distance flight to have been either superfluous or meaningless, or perhaps even offensively extravagant. And that latter option may be particularly important. Joseph knew that many of his monastery colleagues found his behavior and miracles extravagant and obnoxious already—another factor to keep in mind when considering potential constraints on the flamboyance of Joseph's inspired outbursts.

But perhaps most important, Joseph's levitations seem to have been straightforward expressions of sudden ecstatic states, religiously euphoric eruptions that could be expressed easily and appropriately without recourse to long distance travel. In fact, the levitations seem merely to have been a paranormal analogue to more familiar and modest displays of religious awe or appreciation—for example, falling to one's knees, looking heavenward, and proclaiming "Praise God"—which likewise can be expressed on the spot. So if we understand Joseph's levitations, plausibly, as nothing more than an eccentric and paranormal expression of that sort of devotion, there would have been no reason for him to leave the scene, either on foot or aloft.[15]

The second problem with Anderson's argument concerns another apparently unwarranted assumption. Anderson seems to be saying that the best evidence for the existence of psi phenomena reveals a degree of psychic functioning that's still a long way from being super. He claims that it's "a safe bet on empirical grounds" that the best psi "will not *far* exceed" that of the great mediums (emphasis added). Presumably, Anderson's claim rests on a tacit standard of qualitative distance, but it's unclear what that could be.

If Anderson is concerned only with the magnitude of levitating a house as compared (say) to a table, it's true that we have no direct evidence for effects of exactly that kind. But what are we supposed to be measuring here—exactly? Many fair questions come immediately to mind, none of which have ever been addressed competently. For example: What distinguishes super levitation from humdrum levitation—the mass of the levitated object, or its size? Why, *exactly*, wouldn't the levitation of a book or table also count as super? It certainly seems more dramatic than moving a compass needle or making a matchstick move a few millimeters. Would the levitation of a heavy bowling ball count as super, but not the levitation of a cigarette? Which is more super—the levitation of a bowling ball or bar of gold, or the levitation of a large comforter covering a king-size bed?

And consider this: If all levitations occur due to a violation or suspension of the laws of gravitation—say, by means of a spacetime distortion—aren't all levitations outstanding, and for the same reason, namely, the remarkable feat of creating that kind of spacetime distortion? And in that case, doesn't the super-status of a levitation depend at least as much on the means by which it's brought about as on the size or mass of the levitated object? Moreover, according to what scale, *exactly*, does a house levitation count as significantly more super than a full-figure human materialization in bright light, with physician-certified signs of life, and which then melts into the floor? Granted, levitating houses are even less frequent—apparently there have been none at all. But what would Mirabelli have needed to do to catch up to that super-psi threshold? For all these questions, the burden of clarification falls on the shoulders of whomever makes an Anderson-like appeal to an unspecified scale of impressiveness, and that seems like a very tall order.

You might think that Anderson wanted to distinguish super from more ordinary (or dandy) psi in terms of the effect's refinement or sophistication. But then it's no longer clear why mediumistic phenomena would be substantially different from, or less impressive than, whatever it is that Anderson takes to be super by comparison. Certainly, there are no obvious criteria according to which musical performances on untouched instruments fail to count as both refined and super, and likewise for materializations either of lifelike hands or full human figures that are solid and warm to the touch and which eventually dissolve. Moreover, it's unclear why levitating a house would be considered more refined or sophisticated than those materialization phenomena. Rather, it looks more like a matter of brute psychic force.

These last concerns are reminiscent of Richet's observation concerning the varieties of materialization phenomena and the lack of a scale for comparing their significance. He wrote,

> ... it is as difficult to understand the materialization of a living hand, warm, articulated, and mobile, or even of a single finger, as to understand the materialization of an entire personality which comes and goes, speaks, and moves the veil that covers him.[16]

Version 2: *The evidence demonstrates that super psi doesn't occur.* This stronger version of the appeal to evidence seems much less convincing than the first. Its general strategy is to argue that if super psi really occurs, and especially if it plays a role in our daily affairs, then many things would be different from the way they are. For example, some argue that if large-scale lethal PK were possible, then given the enormous amount of hostility in the world (both conscious and unconscious), few people would be alive or intact today. Moreover,

> ...a monster, such as Hitler, who provoked so much ill-will, could not
> have survived for any length of time...[But] far from suffering as the
> result of being the target of so much hatred, Hitler was exceptionally
> lucky in his career and was only finally overpowered at a prodigious
> cost in lives and by a stupendous world-wide effort.[17]

Similarly, one might argue that if our thoughts can be benignly efficacious,
then most people would be happier (richer, healthier) than they are.

But this argument is exceptionally weak. As I've noted elsewhere,[18] even if
psi is theoretically unlimited in refinement or magnitude, it might be severely
curtailed in practice. For one thing, most (if not all) of our abilities or capacities are situation-sensitive; the manner or degree to which they're expressed
depends on many contextual factors. For example, our capacity for circulating
blood, digesting food, or remembering what we've read isn't constant or uni-
form over time. It varies with our mood, health, age, time of day, and so on,
and in general it can be diminished or enhanced in many ways. Even virtuosic
abilities are vulnerable to various influences. For example, the performance of
a great athlete can be impaired by injury, illness, temporary loss of confidence,
preoccupation with personal problems, great opponents, or even weak opponents having a great day. Similarly, a great comedian's ability to be witty can
be undermined, countered, or neutralized in a variety of ways and to varying
degrees. Analogously, one would think that no matter how extensive, refined,
or virtuosic psi-functioning might be, it will also be subject to actual case-by-
case limitations.

Presumably, then, hostile psi would be subject to various constraints, just
like normal forms of hostility. It would be embedded within an enormously
complex web of interactions, psi and nonpsi, overt and covert, local and global, and it would be vulnerable to equally potent interferences or checks and
balances (including psychic defenses) within that network. Analogously, we
often fail to satisfy our normal malevolent desires, despite our apparent best efforts. We can be defeated by guilt, incompetence, outside distractions and in-
terference, or adequate defenses. The difference between these all too familiar
normal cases and that of hostile psi is that in the latter, we must entertain the
possibility of an exceptionally broad range of countervailing factors, including
psychic interactions that we'll never discover. If we don't think in these terms,
we'd simply not be taking the possibility of hostile psi (or super psi generally)

seriously. In fact, we'd be committing the mistake noted by Sturrock, and in addition we'd be failing to place the operation of psi within a reasonable context of competing needs and interests.

For example, Hitler's success in surviving the paranormal influences of worldwide enmity could be explained in terms of an extensive network of competing or crisscrossing paranormal and normal causal chains. For one thing, Hitler had his admirers as well as his detractors—probably even among those who denounced him openly. And for another, Hitler presumably would have made his own contributions to the underlying network of causal influences, mounting his own defenses or undertaking evasive tactics. Furthermore, any interests, feelings, and intentions specifically relating to Hitler would have been embedded within a much larger network of equally potent interests, agendas, and so on, either irrelevant or indifferent to Hitler's welfare. But in that case, some of these additional competing influences might have neutralized attempted psychic attacks on Hitler's life. Analogously, even the world's most accomplished assassin might be thwarted, *fortuitously*, by a vast range of ongoing processes having nothing to do with his particular mission—for example, a flat tire, delayed train, lost luggage, icy roads, elevator malfunction, a migraine headache, upset stomach, or a mugger. In order to deny these possibilities, one would have to argue (implausibly) that attempts at psi influence can never be interfered with (even by other comparable psi influences) and that the psychodynamics of paranormal hostility are radically different from those of normal hostility.

Super Psi Is Preposterously Complex

Some argue that appeals to super-psi require positing a degree of psychic functioning that's simply too intricate and precise to be believed. Not only is it more complex than any psi achievement postulated by more conservative rival hypotheses, it's also antecedently implausible. For example, in order to explain precognition or the results of PK experiments with prerecorded targets in terms of clockwise psi, it may be necessary to posit an incredibly complex array of refined psi events running from earlier to later.

Consider: In order to explain the precognition of a plane crash (after ruling out coincidence), probably the default approach is to suggest a relatively straightforward (although controversially retrocausal) interaction between the later event and the earlier precognition. By contrast, a super-psi counter-explanation may require an imposing series of successful ESP (and PK) tasks—for example, learning psychically which airplane crew members' mental states, or which components of the plane, need to be affected psychokinetically in order to sabotage the flight. Similarly, whereas physicist and parapsychologist Helmut Schmidt and others have considered (retrocausal) PK on prerecorded targets to be of the same magnitude as PK on targets generated at the time of the experiment, a clockwise-psi account of successful results seems to demand an implausibly complex and well-coordinated series of psi tasks: ESP to learn the time of target generation or selection of control and test tapes, and PK of the appropriate targets at those times.[19] And in survival cases (perhaps especially in so-called "drop-in" communications), many would say that the most straightforward and compelling option is to explain the evidence in terms of a deceased communicator's needs to contact the living. Even if we can account for the data by supposing that one or more living persons unconsciously collected information from widely scattered contemporary sources, such an explanation seems both needlessly and absurdly complex.

But this general line of objection has several flaws. First (and somewhat ironically), it's not a line of reasoning that at least some parapsychologists— including Schmidt--could endorse. Following Schmidt, some would contend that the success of a psi task has little if anything to do with task complexity (for example, requiring knowledge of the target and the nature of the target system). They'd say that results depend more (or entirely) on psychological and sensory conditions at the time of the experiment (or during feedback). In fact, one reason Schmidt designed his innovative tests with prerecorded targets was that earlier experiments suggested that task complexity was irrelevant to PK success.[20]

Second, it's unclear whether this objection appeals to a defensible standard of complexity. The issue here is similar to that raised earlier concerning the magnitude of PK effects. As I noted earlier, it's reasonable to consider the most dramatic phenomena of physical mediumship as providing direct evidence of super psi—or at least something pretty close to it. But then presumably it's also reasonable to adopt an analogous position regarding phenomena-complexity. There's no obvious, credible standard according to which materializations or music from untouched instruments count as less (or significantly less) complex than the types of psi posited in super-psi accounts of precognition or PK experiments with prerecorded targets. Certainly, no one has proposed such a standard.

Third, there are at least two versions of the super-psi hypothesis, only one of which takes super psi to be a collection of controlled and monitored psi tasks. That version of the hypothesis is a variant of what some have dubbed the *cybernetic model* of PK. According to that model, PK agents acquire information by ESP concerning the system they wish to control, and then they monitor and guide their actions on that system by means of a continuing supply of ESP information (or feedback). From this viewpoint, PK is analogous to riding a bicycle or driving a car because in those activities we modify our behavior in light of feedback from the system we're controlling. Presumably, then, super cybernetic PK would be a more extreme or convoluted version of that sort of activity, requiring the agent either to control and monitor an extremely complex system, or else (as in tests with prerecorded targets) to complete an imposing series of well-coordinated cybernetic tasks (possibly on several different occasions).

But one could also treat super psi as something that's relatively or completely indifferent to task complexity. According to this *magic wand* hypothesis, the most relevant causal influence in producing psi effects is the subject's *need*, and there may be no underlying process of any significance to study or describe.[21] Perhaps psi of that sort would be analogous to effects sometimes reported in connection with biofeedback, hypnosis, and healing.[22] For example, subjects have learned through biofeedback to fire a single muscle cell in the arm (and no surrounding cells), and researchers have successfully treated children's warts by painting them with what the children believed was a magic dye. In these cases, there's no need or reason to suppose that subjects monitor and selectively control intervening and underlying bodily processes. In fact, the subjects usually have no idea what those underlying processes might be.

The Super-Psi Hypothesis Is Unfalsifiable

Apparently, this objection at least has the virtue of being true because it seems that we can never *prove* or *demonstrate* that super psi *didn't* occur, no matter what the evidence turns out to be. If super psi can be inconspicuous and pervasive, if it can be triggered by unconscious needs and desires, and if we can't specify limits to its degree of magnitude or refinement, then we can't, strictly speaking, falsify hypotheses positing its operation.

Some might consider this to be a peculiar concession, but in fact an analogous situation arises whenever we posit the operation of any degree or magnitude of psi, either in or out of the lab. The so-called *source of psi problem* is that we can't be certain, even in seemingly innocent lab experiments, exactly whose psi was responsible for (or contributed to) the obtained results, and so we can't conclusively rule out various obvious or arcane interpretations of those results. For example, ostensibly double-blind ESP tests can, in fact, be blind only for normal forms of information acquisition, not for rogue psi. Therefore, results can always be explained in terms of experimenter or onlooker ESP of targets and telepathic or PK meddling with the official subject or with recording devices. And in PK experiments we likewise can't determine conclusively exactly who contributed to the obtained result, and whether contributions were made by the official subject, or by one or more of the experimenters, or by an onlooker, or by a hostile skeptic at another location, or by an apparently disinterested person living on a Tibetan mountain top. Granted, in the case of superstars like Home or Palladino, we *are* entitled to conclude that these stars play a considerable causal role in whatever phenomena occur. But we still can't determine to what extent others have contributed psychically either to the enhancement or the suppression of the results. At any rate, this is a major reason why it's worthwhile to seek out star subjects willing to work under decent controls.

In any case, the causal indeterminacy posed by the source of psi problem doesn't justify rejecting all explanations in terms of either humdrum or super psi. Even when a paranormal hypothesis is strictly unfalsifiable, we might still have good reasons to reject it. To see this, we can first distinguish two senses of "unfalsifiable." In one (strong) sense of the term, we'd say a hypothesis is unfalsifiable when it's compatible with any evidence we can muster and when (therefore) no evidence can justify preferring the hypothesis to its denial. But there's a weaker sense in which a hypothesis can be unfalsifiable. Even if the hypothesis and its denial are both compatible with the data, some evidence can reasonably be taken as rendering the hypothesis less plausible than its denial.

For example, I've often argued that a plausible living-agent psi (LAP) explanation of survival evidence can be unfalsifiable in the weaker sense. That is, evidence *can* be relevant to whether or not we accept *or reject* it. Even if both survival and LAP explanations are compatible with the data, our choice between them can be based on our assessment of *how well* the competing hypotheses handle the evidence. More specifically, it would be based on (a) whatever information we could gather concerning the needs, interests, idiosyncrasies, and so on of relevant individuals, (b) assumptions about the relevance of that information, and also (c) a set of higher-level assumptions about explanatory simplicity, systematicity, predictive fecundity, and conceptual cost.

I believe that my analysis of the Sharada case of apparent reincarnation with responsive xenoglossy[23] makes this clear. This is a very interesting case. The subject, a Marathi-speaking woman named Uttara, began to have apparent memories of an earlier life when she was in her thirties. These memories occurred during dramatic changes in Uttara's personality, at which time she fluently spoke a language (a somewhat archaic form of Bengali) which she apparently neither spoke nor understood in her normal state, and which she apparently never had an opportunity to learn.

Now the main point of my analysis was to show how apparent evidence of survival can be handled by a living-agent psi hypothesis with real empirical credentials, even though both the LAP and survival hypotheses were compatible with the totality of available (and foreseeable) evidence. I argued that the LAP hypothesis gained in plausibility relative to various discoveries about the needs, interests, history, and behavior of the principal figures in the case. However, had no such needs, interests, and so on turned up after careful and thorough psychological probing, that would indeed have counted against LAP and in favor of survival. Nevertheless, it remains true that all the available evidence was compatible both with positing the operations of a reincarnated mind and with positing motivated psi among one or more living persons. And the rival hypotheses can also always be tweaked to accommodate whatever future revelations emerge about the case. The challenge then, as always, will be to judge—or guess, really—which contestant accords more neatly both with our aesthetic instincts concerning explanatory simplicity and with many (usually very abstract) background assumptions, which themselves don't enjoy absolute certainty.

I've also argued that if we found a survival case at or close to an imagined theoretical ideal, it would be irrational not to prefer the survivalist explanation over LAP (See Chapter 7 for an example).[24] Even so, a suitably strong LAP alternative would still be compatible with the evidence. That's why no evidence for survival will be conclusive in the way many would prefer. But mere compatibility with the data is not what's at issue.

It's also important to emphasize how, when we compare rival hypotheses in survival cases, what counts as reasonable or rationally satisfying is always somewhat conjectural. It depends critically on subtle details of the subjects' histories and psychological background, the cultural and more local social milieu in which the relevant behaviors occur, and (perhaps most important but also the most debatable) the many abstract and high-level theoretical assumptions against which any inquiry takes place. But these aren't barriers to making sensible or reliable conjectures. They're merely obstacles to attaining absolute certainty, which many would say is an unrealistic goal to begin with—on a par (as William James noted) with the perfectly wise man and the absolutely complete experience.

Besides, notice that we live comfortably with a similar degree of uncertainty all the time—in fact, nearly every time we speculate about the mental lives of ourselves and others. Consider the hypotheses "Sally is angry with me" and "Sally is not angry with me." In many real-life situations, there may be no way to decide conclusively between them. For example, even if Sally *claims* not to be angry, one can always interpret that remark as (say) a sign of Sally's reluctance to admit anger, or a sign of self-deception or lack or self-awareness. Similarly, in many cases there's no way to distinguish evidence suggesting the absence of anger from evidence suggesting veiled anger.

Nevertheless, some people are much better than others at selecting among these sorts of rival hypotheses, and accordingly they make less of a shamble of their lives than those who are more explanatorily challenged. In fact, our psychological survival depends on our ability to weigh weakly falsifiable rival hypotheses about others' mental states. It's by means of that evaluative process that we *reliably* determine whom to confide in, how to speak to other people (for example, which issues to avoid, what "tone" to take), whom we can rely on in times of stress, or trust with an intimacy, and so on. And clearly, the ability to do this requires a mastery of a certain kind of theoretical activity: generating hypotheses about people's intentions, desires, needs, interests, capacities, and so on. And even though these hypotheses are weakly unfalsifiable, some are highly justifiable on pragmatic grounds, and others are not. That's demonstrated by the way the former successfully guide our dealings with other people, and the latter do not.

The situation seems much the same when we evaluate any proposed non-survivalist super-psi explanation. For example, even if a car crash caused by sneaky psi is indistinguishable from one caused normally, we could still have reason—although never a conclusive reason—for choosing one explanation over the other. As with many conspiracy theories, we might have to string together a cumbersome and convoluted array of facts to support the sneaky-psi alternative, but in principle it could be done. We'd have to find plausible links to the needs and interests of the presumed aggressor and tell a reasonable story about (say) conflicts between that person and the driver of the car. We could also look for revealing patterns in the data (say, accidents befalling other people the presumed aggressor doesn't like). Of course, in most cases, we'll have too little information to know whether the super-psi explanation is a live option rather than a mere possibility in logical space. But in those cases where we *can* make educated guesses, our decisions will rest on the kinds of pragmatic criteria I mentioned earlier. We're looking for the story that makes the most sense systematically and which appeals to our instincts about explanatory simplicity. And although the process is undoubtedly more fallible and uncertain than we'd wish, it's essentially the procedure we follow any time we explain human behavior.

Of course, the uncertainty of hypothesizing about super psi is generally greater than the uncertainty of our everyday conjectures about others' mental states. There may not even be many psi-regularities, or they may be far less conspicuous than ordinary psychological regularities. Or perhaps very few of our psi efforts successfully negotiate the complex underlying network of competing interests and interactions in which all such attempts would be embedded. Nevertheless, in all those situations the information needed to choose one hypothesis over another requires a certain amount of digging below the empirical surface. In the super-psi case, the process will of course be more daunting, and in many situations we'll simply have to conclude that we don't know what to say. But that's not unprecedented, or a reliable sign that we're entertaining hypotheses that are empirically defective. Often enough in acceptable everyday attempts to explain human behavior, we're likewise unsure what to say.

Living with Super Psi
Let's consider, finally, what sort of utility, if any, we can anticipate from a judicious reliance on super-psi hypotheses. Even if we grant all the obvious obstacles to determining whether psi was operating in a given case, we can still speculate about how it might manifest. That is, we can consider whether there are certain kinds of events or regularities in particular which the appeal to unusually extensive, refined, or successful psi might help explain.

For example (as I noted earlier), some people seem to be remarkably lucky or unlucky. Now undoubtedly many cases of exceptional luck or misfortune can be explained easily by reference to familiar processes. But other cases seem to have no obvious explanation, especially when streaks of luck or misfortune continue for a while. Similarly, some people seem consistently to have a knack for making highly speculative business or investment decisions, whereas others seem regularly to fail at this activity. Some (but not others) seem repeatedly to operate within a surrounding maelstrom of chaos or disaster, and of these some always seem to be victims, while others seem always to escape unharmed. Why are these sorts of regularities sometimes strikingly long-term? Why is it that the lives of certain people are regularly filled with annoyances and difficulties, apparently not of their own making, while those of others are relatively trouble-free in the same respects? Why do some people repeatedly have difficulties with the postal service, mail-order companies, bank computers or personnel, or automobiles, appliances, or other purchases (including items noted for their reliability), while others seem never to have any such problems?

I'm not suggesting that there are simple answers, or any answers, to these questions, and I certainly don't recommend that we take it for granted that psi is operating in these interesting cases. After all, streaks of good or bad luck might still be fortuitous, or explainable in normal terms once we've drilled below the psychological surface. But if psi functioning does operate in the world on a day-to-day basis, we might reasonably expect it to manifest in these ways, even if it doesn't do so consistently or often. And in that case, it might be worthwhile to carry out depth-psychological studies of lucky and unlucky people. We could look for connections between their good or bad fortune and such things as their self-image, hidden agendas, and relations with others. Of course, no definite conclusions about the presence of psi will emerge from such studies. But occasionally a psi hypothesis might be particularly enlightening or suggestive in the way it systematizes an otherwise motley array of previously unconnected occurrences, or in the way it makes sense out of otherwise seemingly paradoxical features of a person's life.

Another possible stage of operation for everyday psi is the scientific laboratory, however paradoxical that might seem. In fact, a disturbing aspect of acknowledging the possibility of even modest psi in life is that psi might also contaminate ordinary and otherwise apparently clean experiments in science. After all, we have no reason to think that PK on machines or quantum processes operates only in the context of parapsychology experiments. Similarly, it would be foolish to suppose that the only machines susceptible to PK are those designed to test for PK. So for all we know, PK might play a role in the everyday gathering of scientific data. That's especially plausible when we consider the possibility (if not the likelihood) of experimenter-psi, and also the fact that in conventional areas of science, a great many scientists jointly expect or hope for specific results.

In fact, orthodox scientists are at least as motivated as parapsychologists to get their desired results. And because they're not engaged in parapsychological experimentation and are probably not thinking about psi (or seriously entertaining its possibility), they probably don't suffer from the inhibiting fear of psi that arguably keeps results in parapsychology at relatively non-threatening levels of significance. Indeed, it wouldn't be surprising if the resistance of some scientists to parapsychology stems (in part, at least) from the unacknowledged fear that unchecked and uncontrollable psi could cast a shadow of doubt over centuries of accepted scientific results.

So let's suppose that psi might have influenced experimental outcomes throughout the history of normal science. Although there's probably no way to demonstrate that this occurred, it might still be possible to lend confirmatory weight to the supposition. For example, the following intriguing line of inquiry might be fruitful, given enough time and patience. Suppose our scientific theories evolve in such a way that what were formerly considered to be crucial experiments are now seen as comparatively peripheral. Or suppose that technological advances reveal that earlier crucial experimental results were crude and misleading. Suppose, in other words, that we come to view formerly important experiments as relatively unimportant or flawed, so that their results no longer matter for scientific theory. If this reassessment of earlier experiments became widely accepted, we could then conduct those experiments as they'd been conducted initially (for example, making measurements by the techniques now regarded as inadequate), to see if they yield the same results as before. If the current results are more consistent with prevailing scientific beliefs than with those that prevailed when the tests were originally conducted (for example, if the crude methods of measurement yield the distinctly different sorts of results we'd now expect), that might suggest that the results have all along been at least skewed by experimenter expectation and possible psi influence.

At any rate, we needn't focus only on the bleak or troublesome side of psi. Presumably, if psi can do harm or mischief, it can also do good. For example, even if there's little hope of attaining conscious control of psi, we might be able to improve or maintain our health and fortune by cultivating the appropriate goals, attitudes, and feelings. Perhaps we can't be the ultimate masters of our destiny, and perhaps we're as generally incompetent, unwilling, or self-defeating when it comes to using psi for our benefit as we are in the case of our other capacities. Nevertheless, we might be far from impotent, much less pawns or helpless victims of larger karmic or impersonal forces whose inexorable tendencies and direction we're powerless to divert. Although psi might not make us gods, we might be more powerful than we realize.

But with that power, of course, comes responsibility for the things it can achieve. And responsibility for our actions is something most people assume only grudgingly and many others fear. Accordingly, one would think that the greater the power of psi, the more we have to fear, and the more we'll resist either using psi or acknowledging its existence. Indeed, the fear of assuming responsibility for large-scale (or any) psi might be one major reason why its manifestations are rarely conspicuous. As I've noted, covert psi would perpetuate the useful illusion that we're merely spectators rather than agents in the calamities that surround us.

Moreover, the fear of responsibility might even be a serious constraint on the use of psi under the surface. It might be one of the countervailing circumstances I mentioned earlier. We often curb our normal aggressive tendencies in order to avoid responsibility for the actions they would produce. Similarly, the burden of responsibility might inhibit us, not simply from using psi conspicuously, but from using it at all. Perhaps (as I suggested in Chapter 1), it contributed to the reduction in quantity and quality of PK phenomena with the decline of the Spiritualist movement, and today the fear might express itself in the chance results or small-scale effects obtained in parapsychology experiments. In fact, since parapsychologists are as likely as others to suffer the fear of psi, one would expect progress in parapsychology to be made by those who possess, not just the requisite intelligence and perceptivity, but also a hefty and profound dose of moral courage.

Final Thoughts

I began this chapter hoping to clarify and evaluate what's meant by affirming the reality of super psi. But I believe we've seen that, while there may be good reasons for taking seriously the possibility of mind-bogglingly remarkable forms of psi, we're still no closer to knowing what super psi is—that is, beyond knowing that it's apparently much more impressive than laboratory psi. When (or rather if) we ever figure out in detail how psi operates in daily life outside the lab, we might have justification for assigning psi some upper limit of impressiveness. But that won't provide relief from the ineliminable normativity of the term "super" and the difficulty or impossibility of devising a generally acceptable scale of impressiveness for the phenomena that do or can occur.

So although I believe we can say confidently that psi sometimes takes forms that challenge our boggle thresholds, I see no reason to suppose there's really some natural phenomenon picked out by the term "super psi." What we know, and what sensible people have known all along, is that psi phenomena can occur in many forms and in varying and sometimes dramatic degrees of impressiveness, like talent or intelligence. Unfortunately, the term "super psi" will probably pollute the parapsychological lexicon for a while longer, fostering the illusion that there's some specifiable thing in Nature to which it refers, and sadly I see no way of rendering the expression idiot-proof. On the contrary, we might as well wait for the inevitable better idiot to come along who'll propose a second worthless category—something like super-duper psi.

7. Making Sense of
Mental Mediumship

It's one thing merely to ponder whether we survive bodily death and dissolution, and it's another to consider specifically and very carefully whether there is (or can be) *scientifically compelling evidence* for, or an otherwise rational basis for belief in, the survival of bodily death. Many people have enviably firm beliefs, pro or con, about the mere possibility of survival, but that certitude usually betrays a limited command of the evidence and theoretical issues. However, even the well-informed can all too easily overestimate or underestimate the case for survival. In fact, it can be difficult enough merely to remain objective about the subject and to keep biases and hopes from clouding one's judgment. Nevertheless, when people examine the issues and data very closely and comprehensively, they usually conclude that the topic of postmortem survival is dauntingly complex, and they often find it frustratingly difficult to reach a confident conclusion one way or the other about what the evidence shows.

Of course, a major problem is that the evidence is difficult to interpret. As in any scientific inquiry, what might appear to be a straightforward empirical matter conceals an array of thorny philosophical issues. That shouldn't be surprising; there's no such thing as a purely empirical inquiry. Every science rests on numerous abstract presuppositions, metaphysical and methodological, and too often we lose sight of what those presuppositions are. In fact, even our most mundane beliefs and our seemingly most innocent statements are inextricably linked to many deep and normally unexamined assumptions. Fortunately, in daily life we don't usually need to consider, evaluate, or even understand those assumptions in order to determine whether our statements or beliefs are true. For example, when I assert, "The table is brown," I accept certain widely shared presuppositions about (say) the nature of observation generally, color perception in particular, and the stability of physical objects and their properties over time.[1] It's only when we're engaged in philosophical analysis, or when actual problems emerge in communicating with others, that we're likely to recognize some of our tacit assumptions and appreciate the role they play in determining what we actually mean and think. Perhaps more important, it's only in these problematical contexts that we're likely to realize how vague, ambiguous, and assumption-laden our statements really are. Ordinarily, these abstract assumptions are invisible simply because they're ubiquitous. But without them, inquiry can't even *begin*.

So it shouldn't be surprising that when we evaluate the evidence suggesting postmortem survival, we must look carefully at the meaning of central concepts and the assumptions on which they rest. We must also confront venerable underlying problems about scientific explanation, the criteria for weighing rival hypotheses, and the nature and justification of empirical knowledge generally. These are familiar and challenging issues in philosophy, and the topic of survival throws them into unusually sharp relief.[2] Moreover, as we'll see later when we consider our explanatory options for cases suggesting survival, there are many more difficult questions to address before we can know what to say about the evidence. For example, we'll need to consider: What do we mean by calling some information *obscure*? Are we entitled to impose any limits at all on the range of psychic functioning among the living? To what extent is practice essential for manifesting a skill? And: How do we know what's reasonable to assume about the deceased's presumed desire or ability to communicate? And those issues are just the tip of the iceberg.

The Problem of Identity

The topic of survival also connects intimately to ancient and persistent questions about the nature of identity generally and personal identity in particular. When mediums appear to channel information from, or dramatically impersonate, our deceased friends or relatives, or when children seem to display the memories, traits, and abilities of deceased strangers in cases of ostensible reincarnation, it's at least tempting to claim that the deceased have somehow survived the death and dissolution of their bodies. However, many philosophers wonder whether we can use the concepts *identity* or *person* intelligibly when we talk about postmortem survival. For example, if we believe (as many do) that our personhood and personal identity are intimately and essentially tied to our physical embodiment, then we might wonder whether *anything deserving to be called Stephen Braude* could survive my bodily death.

This is undoubtedly an interesting and challenging question, and it's why many believe that we need to solve the long-standing philosophical problem of personal identity before we can decide whether there's compelling evidence of postmortem survival. It seems to me, however, that this ancient problem is overrated as an impediment to deciding whether someone has survived bodily death. Since my view on this matter flies in the face of what many consider to be received wisdom, a few additional words are in order.[3]

In important respects, how we handle ostensible survival evidence parallels what's obviously true about the way we deal with *ante*mortem identity. Every day we make decisions, successfully and with no trouble at all, about the persistence of personal identity, and we manage to do this without the benefit (or more likely, the hindrance) of philosophical training. For example, we identify spouses, children, friends, and co-workers as being the same individuals we met at our previous encounters. And most do this without having anything of interest or substance to say either about the abstract concept of personal identity or the empirical basis for our successful everyday judgments about identity. Obviously, then, we don't need a metaphysical or scientific grasp of the nature of identity simply to make correct identifications.

In fact, only a relatively small number of philosophers have a command of the metaphysics of identity, and they don't come close to a consensus on the issues. Moreover, probably any of several different metaphysical theories will be compatible with our everyday, pre-analytic judgments of personal identity. If a metaphysical theory plays any *useful* role at all, it might merely be to show how we could theoretically ground our generally and conspicuously successful practice of identifying persons. Furthermore (and despite a glut of TV shows, movies, and books about forensic science), most people know little or nothing about the medical, biological, or psychological criteria for determining bodily or psychological continuity. But despite all that, our strategies for identifying others generally work just fine, and probably they've remained stable for millennia. At the same time, however, our prevailing philosophies and scientific background theories have changed profoundly. Apparently, then, we haven't been prevented, either by our ignorance, theoretical naivete, or shifting conceptual trends, from making successful judgments about identity.

So how do we manage this? The process is ultimately pragmatic; philosophical or scientific theorizing comes later in the order of things. Indeed, as I noted earlier, scientific reasoning itself rests on a bed of controversial and (at best) pragmatically warranted philosophical positions. If you need to be convinced of this, just take a quick survey of the vast literature on whether (or in what respect) induction is a legitimate form of inference. Now granted, scientifically justifying an empirical hypothesis (such as the survival hypothesis) differs from our everyday practices in a number of respects. But the difference is one of degree and not of kind. Scientific reasoning and justification have distinctively high empirical standards and proceed very carefully and systematically. But as far as the survival hypothesis is concerned, both scientific justification and everyday reasoning are subject to our inevitable reliance on concepts whose theoretical analysis, clarification, and warrant remain up for grabs, and whose practical deployment needn't be systematic.

Consider: The survival hypothesis inescapably relies on the concept of a *person*. What's at issue is whether a person, or personal consciousness, can in some sense survive bodily death and dissolution. Thus, our interest in post-mortem survival concerns something more interesting and intimate than the scenario envisioned by some Eastern religions and New-Age pundits: a kind of merging with the infinite, or being-in-general (a grand soup of consciousness). Although that might count as a form of *life after death,* it's certainly not the *survival of death* that people have anticipated, feared, or desired for centuries. Merging with the infinite would be a condition that obliterates whatever is distinctive about us, both physically and psychologically. But people who wonder about personal postmortem survival wonder about such things as whether *they* will be able to reunite with and continue to enjoy the company of their deceased relatives, communicate with (and maybe harass) the still-living members of their families, remember things that happened to them while physically embodied, retain some of their distinctive character traits and interests, or enjoy a postmortem existence in which they simply get their hair back. In general, they wonder whether *they* will continue to exist in some form or another after bodily death. And they wonder whether that future individual bears something like the same relationship to their present self that their present self bears to their physically and psychologically remote infant self. As a result, these cases present the epistemological challenge of deciding whether they provide evidence for the postmortem persistence of a specific individual. And they present the metaphysical challenge of explaining how such persistence is possible and what such continuity consists in.

However, most of us have, at best, only a very fuzzy notion of what identity is, or what a *person* is, and that's equally true of those who try scientifically or philosophically to assess the survival hypothesis. In fact, to the extent we even have *a* (single) concept of personhood or personal identity, it's as loose and elastic as most of our concepts. But ordinarily it serves us very well; we have little if any trouble deciding who's who. Although some have trouble distinguishing identical twins, and although we sometimes mistake a person for someone else, those problems are uncommon, and usually they're quickly resolved. In fact, that's about as difficult as it gets for everyday identifications.

Fortunately, we seldom deal with drastic or sudden changes in a person; physical or psychological changes in those we know are usually subtle or at least gradual. And few of us are forced to deal with really rare or exotic puzzles over a person's identity. Ordinarily, we needn't worry about whether our acquaintances are being skillfully impersonated; we seldom receive phone calls or other communiques from people we thought had died; and most of us never contend with identity puzzles generated by cases of DID (dissociative identity disorder—formerly, multiple personality disorder).

Moreover, when we make identifications in daily life, we rely generally on both physical and psychological continuity, and under optimal conditions we can identify people with respect to continuity of both sorts. In many cases, though, we have less to go on. We might interact verbally with someone via telephone, text, or email, but not see the person's body. We might see a person but observe no psychologically significant behavior. And even if we believe all along that a person's psychological properties supervene on the bodily,[4] in making identity judgments we weigh psychological and physical continuity differently in different cases, relying sometimes on only one of them.

As you might imagine, philosophers like to concoct various sci-fi or theological scenarios to challenge our general strategies for judging identity. Allegedly, these exercises sharpen our thinking about identity. But if any cases help at all in that respect, real-life cases do it as well—among them, cases of DID and cases suggesting postmortem survival. Curiously, though, none of these real or imagined extreme cases threatens to undermine our *ordinary* concepts of a person or personal identity. Presumably, that's because there's no reason to think that an adequate concept should handle every conceivable case it might be thought to cover, no matter how exotic. Our ordinary concepts tend to be just fine for ordinary cases. The weird cases are ones we can't resolve—and shouldn't even expect to resolve—without an uncommonly reflective decision on the matter. In fact, I see no reason for insisting that every puzzling case has a solution, much less a preferred or privileged solution. The really recalcitrant and unusual cases may simply need to be handled on a case-by-case basis, as current situations help dictate, and without any uniformly applicable guiding principle to help us along the way. At any rate, the ostensibly postmortem cases strike us as particularly vexing because they apparently undercut both our familiar reliance on bodily continuity as well as common assumptions about how psychological properties depend on physical states of affairs. But let's put that apparent predicament into perspective and consider just how big a predicament it really is.

First, we need to keep in mind the cultural variability in the concept of a person, which might help combat our tendency to assume smugly that there's something privileged about our common presuppositions about personhood. At the very least, these differences highlight dramatically how familiar concepts may conceal a rich vein of underlying—and by no means certain—metaphysics. For example, although for many of us the presumption of one-person/one-body is our default presumption (at least outside the context of, say, a spouse or friend with DID), that's not the case in other cultures. For instance, the Ndembu, the Ashanti, and the Bushmen of the Kalahari have interesting and unusual approaches to what they perceive as the conceptually problematic birth of twins, triplets, and so on.[5]

Moreover, in our culture, our rough-and-ready ordinary concept of a person is largely *normative* (what Locke termed a "forensic" concept). When we use the term "person" in everyday life, we're not picking out a *natural kind*—that is, either some a priori specifiable piece of ontological furniture or at least something whose nature scientific inquiry will decide (for example, something that inevitably links persons to the biological species *Homo sapiens).*[6] Our ordinary concept of a person (such as it is) concerns things we value about ourselves and each other, and it rests on various presuppositions about the ways people should be treated. In our culture at least, we typically regard persons as (among other things) entities who have (or could have) an inner life relevantly similar to our own, who have various rights and perhaps obligations, and who deserve our respect, consideration, and so on. And we accept the normativity of this conception of personhood irrespective of our views (if any) about how persons might (or must) be configured biologically or otherwise—for example, whether fetuses, dolphins, computers, brains in a vat, alternate personalities, or disembodied spirits, could be persons. Interestingly, an Argentinian judge seemed recently to be thinking along those lines and ruled that a certain orangutan should be considered a non-human person, entitled therefore to some of the legal rights accorded human beings.[7] Similarly, I'd argue (along with philosopher Anthony Quinton)[8] that what we value most about persons are their psychological traits and that this is why we're often content to make identity judgments (even in exotic cases such as DID and apparent postmortem survival) solely on the basis of psychological continuity.

As philosopher C. J. Ducasse (1961) once noted, a typical mediumistic scenario resembles in critical respects a more familiar (or at least less exotic) situation, one in which identity judgments *need to be* made without relying on evidence of bodily continuity. Suppose I received a phone call over a noisy connection from an individual purporting to be my friend George, who I thought had died in a plane crash. Although I can't establish the speaker's identity by confirming his bodily continuity to the George I knew, and although the noisy phone line sometimes makes it difficult to hear what the speaker is saying, nevertheless my conversation can provide a solid practical basis for concluding that George is really speaking to me. The speaker could demonstrate that he had certain memories that no one but George should have, and he could exhibit characteristically George-like personality traits, verbal mannerisms, as well as idiosyncratic motives and interests. Whether or not the persistence of these traits satisfies some metaphysician's criteria of identity, they often suffice for real-life cases. In fact, you can be sure that if the relatives or friends speaking on the phone to the George-claimant were metaphysicians, they'd handle the situation the same way—with no philosophical reservations whatsoever.

Of course, in survival cases we actually have evidence *against* bodily continuity. Nevertheless (as we've seen), we must grant that we routinely make identity judgments satisfactorily (and with a clear conscience philosophically) on the basis of psychological continuity alone, even if we suspect or believe strongly that the psychological supervenes on the physical. And (as I noted earlier) we must also grant that we typically make these judgments in the face of considerable philosophical and scientific ignorance (or at least uncertainty) about what (if anything) might constitute identity. That should be enough to seriously challenge the claim that we can't acceptably make identity judgments in cases suggesting postmortem survival when we don't know how to explain survival in the apparent absence of bodily continuity. So let's consider briefly how, in a state of comparative metaphysical or scientific innocence, we'd assess apparently good evidence for postmortem survival, under conditions where we can confidently assert the absence of bodily continuity. Presumably (and as we'll see), what we'd want to say depends largely on the same thing that concerns us most deeply in everyday cases: *how we value persons.*

Explanatory Options
Consider, then, how this would work in practice.[9] Generally speaking, a case suggests postmortem survival because (a) some living person demonstrates knowledge or abilities closely (if not uniquely) associated with a deceased person, and (b) we have good reason to believe that this knowledge wasn't obtained, or the abilities developed, through ordinary means. For example, suppose that a medium purportedly channels information from my late Uncle

Harry. And suppose that she provides information—for example, the location of a secret will—that no living person besides Harry ever knew (at least by normal means). And suppose that, although the medium never met my uncle, she takes on various of his characteristics, such as his quirky interests and perspective on politics, his distinctive laugh and caustic sense of humor, and his idiosyncratic syntax and inflection. And suppose the medium also demonstrates Uncle Harry's ability to speak Yiddish, even though she never studied (or better, was never exposed) to that language.

However, before we can accept even such an impressive case as indicating postmortem survival, we have to rule out a number of counter-hypotheses, some more obvious and easier to eliminate than others. First, we need to consider what I call the *Usual Suspects*: fraud, the closely related misreporting and malobservation, and cryptomnesia or hidden memories. For some cases, these are clearly viable options, but for others they are not. That's one reason the topic of postmortem survival is so interesting: the best cases easily deflect counter-explanation in terms of the Usual Suspects.

However, the Usual Suspects are merely the first wave of skeptical counter-explanations, and they posit nothing more than relatively normal (or possibly abnormal) processes as alternatives to postmortem survival. By contrast, a second wave of relatively exotic counter-explanations is more refractory, and the explanations fall into two classes. The first class posits clearly abnormal or rare processes, such as dissociative pathologies, rare mnemonic gifts, extreme or unprecedented forms of savantism, or equally rare latent creative capacities. I've called this class of counter-explanations *The Unusual Suspects,* and although they too seem to be ruled out in the very best cases, advocates of the survival hypothesis (hereafter, *survivalists*) have, in general, done a poor job of countering them.[10]

And that's not surprising; this type of skepticism can't be dismissed easily. For example, it's significant that prodigies and other gifted people manifest various abilities without having first to undergo a period of practice. It's equally significant that savants display abilities that we wouldn't expect, given their equally dramatic cognitive and physical deficits. Some calculating savants, for instance, can factor any number presented to them, even though they can't add the change in their pocket. Similarly, a well-known musical savant was spastic until he sat down to play the piano. Clearly, these cases must be considered when evaluating a medium suddenly manifesting an ability associated with an ostensibly deceased person. They pose a clear challenge to those who argue that the anomalous ability persuasively indicates survival when the medium never spent time practicing and developing it, and when the medium's previously manifested abilities seem to preclude it.

The second class of exotic counter-explanations posits something even more difficult to rule out—namely, *psychic functioning among the living*, presumably displayed in a way that simply presents the appearance of postmortem survival. This general form of anti-survivalist position is often, but unfortunately, called the *super-psi* hypothesis, and that name is unfortunate for two reasons. First, it's unclear and needlessly evaluative. Obviously, what's super for one person may not be for another, and there's no absolute or privileged standard to which we can appeal. And second, the name suggests right from the start that the degree of psi being posited is antecedently implausible. That is, many construe the use of "super" in "super-psi" as similar to its use in the phrase "super hero" rather than in "super glue." Possibly apart from a young generation of moviegoers who mistake CGI for the real thing, no one expects superheroes really to exist. By contrast, no one has a problem with the reality of super glue. We know what it means to call glue "super"; it's *really effective* glue. For these reasons I prefer to adopt philosopher Michael Sudduth's proposal to replace the name "super-psi hypothesis" with the more accurate and neutral "Living Agent Psi (LAP) hypothesis."[11]

This is not mere terminological hair-splitting; living agent psi is actually difficult (if not impossible) to rule out when it comes to apparent evidence of postmortem survival. For one thing, certain examples of ostensible mediumship seem to *demand* a living-agent psi interpretation. At their best, of course, mediums furnish detailed information for which no normal explanation will suffice, and in the cases most strongly suggesting survival, that information concerns the lives of the deceased. But sometimes mediums also provide information, to which they had no normal access, about the *present* actions, thoughts, and feelings of the living. Now although we can understand why the deceased might be said to enjoy privileged access to information about their own lives, there's no reason to think they would also have privileged access to information about current states of affairs. And since we already have plenty of evidence (from other contexts, such as remote viewing) for living-agent psi, there's no compelling reason to attribute mediumistic knowledge about the present to deceased-agent psi. After all, we don't have independent evidence, *apart from the survival cases in question*, for deceased-agent psi. But that can only make it more difficult to rule out LAP interpretations when mediums convey information about the deceased.

Moreover (and more important), if channeled information about the deceased can subsequently be verified—which (after all) is what we look for in a good case of survival—then all along it was available to the medium's ESP. Intimate facts verified by consulting someone's memories can be explained by telepathy, and facts verified by consulting physical states of affairs (e.g., the location of a hidden will) can be explained by clairvoyance. Similarly, in reincarnation cases one can appeal to ESP on the part of either the subject or relevant interested parties (such as family members), or to the paranormal influence these other parties exert (presumably telepathically or psychokinetically).

Some survivalists reject these explanatory strategies because (they say) the LAP hypothesis posits psychic functioning of an implausible degree, and more than that for which we have evidence outside of survival cases.[12] However, that survivalist line of argument is confused on two grounds: first, because there's no clear standard for evaluating the magnitude of psychic functioning, and second (and most important), because the argument overlooks a crucial (and ironic) logical entailment of the survivalist position—namely, that survivalists are committed to positing comparably impressive psi on the part of the deceased or the living, simply to explain how mediums or sitters interact with deceased communicators and how deceased communicators are aware of current physical states of affairs.

Consider how this works. Suppose a medium tells you, "Your Aunt Rose is with me, and she knows you're seriously thinking about quitting your job and becoming a circus clown." Now if that's true about you, two crucial questions arise immediately. First, how does the medium know what deceased Aunt Rose is thinking? And second, how does deceased Aunt Rose know what you're feeling? Telepathy, to put it roughly but fairly, would simply be mind-to-mind interaction unmediated by the familiar senses. And since Aunt Rose no longer has a physical body, sensory interaction with her is out of the question. So the only possible survivalist answer to these questions is that the knowledge is obtained telepathically. The only significant difference between the survivalist and LAP versions of telepathy would be that, for the former, one of the minds involved in the telepathic exchange lacks an associated physical body.

Now suppose the medium says, "Aunt Rose says she's glad you're wearing the necktie she gave you." The obvious question to ask the survivalist in this case is, "How would deceased Aunt Rose know *that*?" Since she's dead, she has no perceptual organs, and clairvoyance (to again put it roughly but fairly) would be awareness (or response to) physical states of affairs unmediated by the familiar senses. So the only possible survivalist answer to this question is that deceased Aunt Rose's awareness was an instance of clairvoyance.

So it looks like a mediumistic scenario *requires* ESP to be every bit as impressive as that posited by the LAP hypothesis. Whereas LAP posits ESP between the medium and sitter, medium and remote individual, or medium and remote object, the survivalist posits ESP between the medium and Aunt Rose, or Aunt Rose and you, or Aunt Rose and a physical state of affairs.

This is not a difficult point to grasp, and yet prominent writers on survival seem oblivious to it. Consider, for example, an intriguing recent case, concerning the manifestation of very high (and arguably grandmaster) level chess played by someone with (as far as we can tell) little or no knowledge of the game, and similar to that of a deceased Hungarian grandmaster.[13] Because I have only the most rudimentary knowledge of chess, I must defer to others for a full evaluation of the case. However, telepathic interaction between medium and sitter (or other interested parties) clearly remains a live option, no matter how little chess one knows. And in fact, non-survivalists can point to several relevant considerations. After all, the subject was playing chess with an opponent who had grandmaster skills; the idiosyncratic moves of the deceased were verifiable and therefore available through ESP to both players; and both the grandmaster opponent and others were aware of the deceased's presumed ignorance of chess strategies developed after the deceased's death (in particular, a strategy used to counter an opening variation attempted by the medium).

Nevertheless, parapsychologist Vernon Neppe[14] argues that we can rule out a living-agent psi interpretation of this case. He claims that a survivalist interpretation of the case tells a relatively straightforward causal story, positing nothing but interaction between a medium and a deceased communicator retaining at least some of his former embodied faculties. By contrast, he argues,

> ...super-ESP ... would require the repeated and active cogitation of a master chess player or players while alive, extended over a prolonged period of time with 47 different responses (47 moves in the game).[15]

This looks like a wholesome appeal to parsimony, and that's how Neppe presents it. But, in fact, it's merely a variant of the old and defective argument that an LAP interpretation presupposes an implausible degree or refinement of psychic functioning, and (in particular) *more than would be required by the survivalist*. However, contrary to what Neppe and others claim, the survival hypothesis requires virtually the same degree of psychic functioning as is posited by the living-agent alternative, and this is painfully easy to see. According to the survivalist, the persisting intelligence of the deceased communicator is causally responsible for the 47 chess moves in question. But for that to occur, the deceased would need repeated and accurate ESP (either telepathy with the medium or an onlooker, or else clairvoyance of the chess board) to know what the state of play is, and then ongoing and effective ESP (presumably telepathic influence on the medium) to convey the desired next move. Neppe's oversight here is all too common, and since the error has been noted in the literature for some time now, at this stage of the survival debate I consider it inexcusable.

Perhaps also lurking behind Neppe's discussion is another line of argument found in many survivalist interpretations of so-called "drop-in" mediumistic cases. In a good drop-in case, an uninvited communicator comes through during a séance, provides subsequently confirmed accurate information about his or her earthly life, and perhaps claims to have some important unfinished business. In the most impressive of these cases, the deceased is unknown to the sitters, and so the obvious challenge is to explain how the medium managed to acquire and convey accurate information about the deceased's life and plausible motives. Survivalists often argue that the most parsimonious strategy is to posit straightforward interactions between medium and deceased about *matters which the deceased presumably already knows*. By contrast (so the argument goes), LAP alternatives require the medium to access psychically one or more obscure sources of information, either through telepathy with still-living individuals who knew the deceased, or through clairvoyant awareness of available records of one kind or another.

However, that argument strategy seems confused over the concept of *obscure information*. Ordinarily, we understand (roughly at least) what it means to say that a piece of information is obscure. But that conception of obscurity applies only to *normal* methods of acquiring information. For example, we consider information to be obscure when it's not widely known and when it takes some work to uncover. And by saying that it takes work to uncover, I mean that the information is either outside our perceptual field or otherwise difficult to access physically (e.g., if it's behind layers of security or other barriers, or if it's remote geographically and not accessible electronically). Notice, though, that all information acquired psychically by the deceased in a mediumistic scenario, either about a living person's thoughts or about some present physical state of affairs, counts as obscure in this sense, just as it does for ESP on the part of the living. In both cases, there's no familiar *physical* access to the acquired information.

Furthermore, we don't understand how any physically or perceptually remote information might be acquired by ESP, whether it's the carefully sealed picture on the table right in front of us or an object thousands of miles away. And although it's clear on some occasions what might direct the medium to psychically look in one place rather than another——for example, the presence of a sitter with telepathically transparent interests—in other cases, we have no idea what these road signs or triggers might be. But then we simply know too little. Apart from the most psychodynamically flagrant cases (and there aren't many of those), it's merely a conceit to think we have a handle on why psi works when it does. Moreover, it's likely that psi-conducive conditions vary as much from person to person, and occasion to occasion, as do the conditions people find erotic or humorous. If so, that can only frustrate the effort to generalize about conditions favorable to psychic functioning among the living.

So as far as living agents are concerned, we're in no position to insist that normally obscure information is also psychically obscure. Indeed, good remote viewers remind us of that frequently, something survivalists should keep in mind when claiming that the mediumistic psi required for LAP explanations is antecedently implausible. Right from the start, then, it's implausible to insist that normal forms of obscurity are barriers to the operation of ESP. Besides, as we've seen, since mediumistic scenarios require the deceased to exercise ESP of some kind, insistence on the difficulty of using ESP would equally cripple the survival hypothesis. And incidentally, we're also in no position to insist that the diffuseness of information gathered from more than one source is a barrier to successful ESP. As far as we know, psychically accessing multiple sources of normally obscure information is no more imposing than accessing one.

Connected with all this is the more general issue of whether we have grounds, at our current and considerable state of ignorance, for assuming that psychic functioning has any limits at all. Even parapsychologists have boggle thresholds, and that's perfectly natural. But although they may be natural and understandable, some boggle thresholds may be rationally indefensible. For example, many people are more or less comfortable about admitting small-scale psychic happenings into their worldview—a little modest ESP here and perhaps the occasional small-scale psychokinetic random event generator nudge there. But they draw the line at anything more refined or extensive. The problem, though, is that this attitude is *not* defensible. Given that we really have no idea how *any* ESP or PK could surmount or skirt the normal constraints on information acquisition or physical influence, we're in no position to open the door to the paranormal (even as a mere thought experiment) and then decide to open it only a crack. For all we know in our current state of ignorance, super psi is as viable as puny psi. And there are several bodies of evidence—for example, evidence from physical mediumship—indicating that psi clearly occurs at a level of refinement or magnitude which, if not super, is sure as hell pretty dandy. That can only strengthen the conviction that we don't know yet how far psychic influence can go.[16]

We must also note one additional, and very important, introductory point concerning the logic of explanation. As I've mentioned, survivalists often maintain that the LAP explanation of cases compares unfavorably to that of the survivalist. And they usually support that claim, not simply by arguing that the survivalist explanation is simpler, but that it has greater explanatory power, or that it does a better job of predicting the data, than the living-agent psi alternative, or else that the LAP explanation of the data is indefensibly ad hoc. But Sudduth[17] has noted that this type of comparison of the LAP and survivalist hypotheses seems plausible only in virtue of a kind of logical sleight of hand. Survivalists like to claim that the survival hypothesis explains (or predicts) various strands of evidence. But such explanation or prediction is possible only if one makes a number of *auxiliary assumptions* about the nature and character of the afterlife. For example, in cases of mediumship we find that communications are often trite, confused, or have a dreamy quality, and that at other times they seem quite clear and coherent. We also find that only some deceased people seem to communicate, and then only for a short time. Why is that, and how do survivalists account for it (and the many other observed features of mediumship)?

On this issue, the literature on survival is too often discouragingly shabby. The problem is this. In order to explain both why the evidence from mediumship has the features we find and why it lacks certain others is to make numerous, *independently unverified* assumptions about (say) whether deceased persons would want to, or be able to, communicate with the living, the means by which that communication is achieved, and whether that communication is difficult or easy (e.g., whether there's "noise" in the "channel"). By contrast, a *simple* survival hypothesis—that is, a mere assertion that consciousness or personality can survive, *in the absence of further assumptions specifying conditions allowing the evidence to take the forms noted in the literature*—can make no specific (much less fine-grained) predictions *at all* about what the data of survival should actually look like. The same is true, obviously, about the living-agent psi hypothesis, which, in its more robust and sophisticated forms, makes numerous assumptions about (say) dissociative creativity, and the needs, interests, and motivations of the living, in order to explain why the evidence has certain characteristics rather than others.

However, as Sudduth has observed, when survivalists try to claim that the survival hypothesis explains (or predicts) the evidence *better* than the LAP hypothesis, they usually compare robust versions of LAP (laden with allegedly implausible assumptions) only to a *simple* survival hypothesis—minus the sorts of assumptions required for that hypothesis to do any explanatory work at all. The proper comparison, however, must be between *robust* survival and *robust* LAP hypotheses, where each is bulked up by assumptions that permit the prediction of the observed, fine-grained features of the data. But in that case, the empirical argument for survival may amount merely to a comparison of the auxiliary assumptions attaching to both the LAP and survivalist hypotheses. Now that's not an easy task, and a shoot-out between competing sets of auxiliary assumptions is likely to lead nowhere, at least not conclusively.

Another disreputable tactic for arguing against the LAP hypothesis—really, a form of straw-man reasoning—is in some ways the converse of the survivalist appeal to obscure information. Some seem to think that if mediumistic living agent psi actually occurred, it would work in an implausibly simple or straightforward and relatively unobstructed way. Then, when the evidence can't be explained away in terms of psychic functioning *as they erroneously construe it,* they conclude that the survival hypothesis is a better alternative. For example, clergyman and SPR member Drayton Thomas considered the possibility that Mrs. Leonard might have psychically reached out to search for appropriate information, and he claimed that this hypothesis was difficult to square with the facts—specifically that Mrs. Leonard's results varied widely from complete failures to striking successes. He wrote,

> If the medium's own activity obtained the information, it should have been more uniformly successful. There were some complete failures just where success should, on this hypothesis, have been most likely, namely in those instances where I had interviewed the applicant shortly before the sitting. Such personal intercourse showed no superiority over the cases where no interview had taken place.[18]

In a similar vein, he continued,

> ...the medium's own faculty is not the factor to which we can attribute these proxy results. If my richly stored memory yielded so little when I was sitting in the medium's presence, is it likely that the minds of distant and unknown persons would yield as much? And yet one or

two of the proxy cases have not only equalled, but have surpassed in evidential richness the majority of communications received from my own deceased acquaintances.[19]

These passages contain several errors and confusions. First, Thomas seems to confuse physical (and perhaps temporal) proximity with psychic closeness or intimacy, or at least he supposes that the two must be closely correlated. But that's no more plausible than supposing that people are most likely to succeed in telepathy experiments when their heads are touching. Moreover, Thomas seems to ignore the complex interpersonal and other contextual variables that presumably affect psychic functioning. It's no more plausible to think that a medium will automatically respond telepathically to a psychically primed sitter than it is to think that people will respond sexually just because their partner is in the mood. The history of psi research suggests strongly that psychic functioning, like most other cognitive or psychological capacities, is highly situation-sensitive, context-dependent, and susceptible to an enormous range of positive and negative influences, including mood, belief system, interpersonal relations, and even geophysical and celestial variables (such as, respectively, earth's geomagnetic field and local sidereal time).

These considerations remind us that the only respectable way for the survivalist to address the LAP hypothesis is by treating it as a *motivated* psi hypothesis—that is, to consider, *and actually try to discern*, the underlying needs and interests which might plausibly motivate living agents to psychically access information that can subsequently be verified normally. The crucial question in evaluating the LAP hypothesis in a particular case is: Whose conscious or unconscious needs or interests would be served by the appearance of evidence suggesting survival? But that question is seldom asked in the survival literature, or if it is asked, it's handled only superficially by treating the medium and relevant others as psychological stick figures. Some ostensible survival cases, in fact, do lend themselves to serious and competent psychodynamic probing, and when that happens, it's often the case that the survivalist interpretation loses all or much of its appeal.[20] More generally, the survival evidence can't be evaluated properly without taking into consideration, *in detail,* much more that we already know about human beings than is usually covered in the survival literature. Indeed, people are considerably more varied and interesting than one would ever guess from reading only the literature on survival. That's why competently addressing the survival versus LAP issue requires a decent command of the literature on hypnosis, dissociation, psychopathology generally, savants and prodigies, and second language acquisition.

Space prohibits a proper defense of that position, not to mention providing adequate examples of how superficial much of the survival literature is.[21] However, to illustrate briefly how byzantine the issues can get, consider a few of the questions arising in connection just with the evidence for responsive xenoglossy (speaking responsively in an unlearned language). I can't go into detail here, but the relevance of the questions should be obvious:

1. To what extent can we develop skills unconsciously or through non-normal means (say, in altered states)?

2. Are we entitled (in this context) to talk of *acquiring* skills rather than simply *manifesting* them?

3. To what extent is practice essential for manifesting skills (the relevance again of prodigies and savants, and the linguistically gifted)?

4. To what extent can we generalize over skills or abilities (e.g., can we legitimately compare mastering a language to mastering other skills, such as bicycle riding or playing bridge)?

5. What counts as language-mastery (e.g., how fluent must one be, and are standards of fluency context-dependent)?

6. Which conditions facilitate, or impede, the mastery of a second language (e.g., when the second language is similar to, or quite different from, one's native tongue)?

The Importance of Ideal Cases

I realize that many interpret my arguments as a defense of the LAP hypothesis. But that's not quite right. Granted, I defended the LAP hypothesis against some lame survivalist strategies, but I wasn't arguing that the LAP hypothesis ultimately triumphs over the survival hypothesis. Rather, I was making a plea for careful and empirically informed reasoning, and for not setting up a straw man by presenting the non-survivalist alternatives in implausible or oversimplified forms. That happens all too frequently in the survival literature, which (as a result) sometimes appears to honestly inquisitive outsiders as being dominated by the psychologically ignorant or naive, or else the inferentially challenged.

So perhaps it will clarify both my position and the issues generally if we approach things from a different angle. Let's consider what we'd say if we were confronted with a slam-dunk, ideal case suggesting survival, and what impact such a case would have on our thinking about survival and personal identity.

Presumably, such an ideal survival case would be one for which appeals to the Usual and Unusual Suspects have no plausibility whatever. It would also be one that, while perhaps not conclusively ruling out appeals to psychic functioning among the living, nevertheless strains that hypothesis to the breaking point—that is, a case where even people sympathetic to such paranormal conjectures would be inclined to throw in the towel. In *Immortal Remains*, I offered a list of desirable features of a survival case, the most important of which are as follows (I state these in terms of a psychic *subject*—not just the medium—in order to make the features applicable as well to reincarnation cases):

1. The case would be etiologically distinct from cases of DID or other psychological disorders. For example, mediums should not have a documented history of psychopathology. And in a reincarnation case the phenomena should not manifest after the subject experiences a traumatic childhood incident.

2. The manifestations of the deceased (previous personality or discarnate communicator) should not, in the light of competent depth-psychological probing, serve any discernible psychological needs of the living.

3. Those manifestations should make most sense (or better, only make sense) in terms of agendas or interests reasonably attributable to the deceased.

4. The manifestations should begin, and should be documented, before the subject (or anyone in the subject's circle of acquaintances) has identified or researched the life of the deceased.

5. The subject should supply verifiable, intimate facts about the deceased's life.

6. The history and behavior of the deceased (as revealed through the subject) should be recognizable, in intimate detail, to several individuals, preferably on separate occasions.

7. The subject should also display some of the deceased's idiosyncratic skills or traits.

8. These skills or traits should be as foreign to the subject as possi-

ble—for example, from a significantly different culture.

9. Skills associated with the deceased should be of a kind or of a degree that generally require practice, and which are seldom (if ever) found in prodigies or savants.

10. In order for investigators to verify information communicated about the deceased's life, it should be necessary to access multiple physically, culturally, and geographically remote sources.

Now it's one thing to consider the issues here purely in the abstract, and another to imagine in more detail what an overwhelmingly impressive case would look like. But I think the latter is precisely what we need to do, not simply to appreciate how the evidence might challenge us conceptually, but to show how in practice concerns about bodily continuity may play no role whatever. So consider what we'd do if confronted with the following case of ostensible mediumship:

Mrs. B is a gifted medium. As far as her education is concerned, she never completed primary school, and as a result she has only an average fourth-grader's level of literacy. Moreover, Mrs. B's exposure to the world has been confined exclusively to her immediate small-town environment in the American Midwest. She's never traveled beyond her hometown, or expressed any interest in books, magazines, or TV shows about other locales. Similarly, she's had no exposure to the world of ideas, to literature (even in cinematic form), or to the arts. In fact, when she's not channeling communications or caring for her home and family, she devotes her time to prayer and developing her psychic sensitivity.

One day Mrs. B gives a sitting for Mr. X, who lives in Helsinki. The sitting is what's known as a *proxy* sitting, because the person interacting with the medium is substituting for someone who wants information from the medium. In the most interesting cases, proxy sitters have little or no information about the person they represent, and they know nothing about the individual the medium is supposed to contact. Clearly, then, good proxy cases help rule out some Usual Suspects because we can't plausibly assert that the medium is simply extracting information from the sitter by means of leading questions, subtle bodily cues, etc. In the present case, Mr. X (using a pseudonym) sends a watch, once owned by a dear friend, to the Rhine Research Center (RRC) in North Carolina, requesting that someone there present it to Mrs. B on his behalf. So no one at the RRC knew (at least by normal means) the identity either of Mr. X or the original owner of the watch.

When Mrs. B handles the watch, she goes into trance and, speaking English as if it weren't her native tongue and with a clear Scandinavian accent, purports to be the surviving personality of the Finnish composer Joonas Kokkonen. She also speaks a language unknown to anyone at the séance, which the sitters record and which experts later identify as fluent Finnish. At subsequent sittings, native speakers of Finnish attend, along with the proxy, and converse with Mrs. B in their language. All the while, she continues to speak Finnish fluently, demonstrating an ability not only to utter, but also to understand, sentences in Finnish. In both Finnish and in accented English, Mrs. B provides detailed information about Kokkonen's life and his music, demonstrating in the process an intimate acquaintance with Finnish culture, a professional command of music generally, and a knowledge of Kokkonen's music in particular. For example, on one occasion she writes out the final bars to an uncompleted piano quintet and requests that they be given to Kokkonen's former colleague, Aulis Sallinen, who she claims correctly had possession of the original score, so that the quintet could be assembled into a performing edition. Investigation then reveals that Sallinen does in fact have the original score, in the condition described by the Kokkonen communicator.

These sittings cause a minor sensation in Finland and elsewhere, and before long many of Kokkonen's friends travel to America for anonymous sittings with Mrs. B. Because Kokkonen was a major international musical figure, and had friends and colleagues throughout the world, many of those friends were not Scandinavian. So at least those sitters provided no immediate linguistic clue as to whom they wished to contact. But in every case, Mrs. B's Kokkonen-persona recognizes the sitters and demonstrates an intimate knowledge of details specific to Kokkonen's friendship with them. When speaking to Kokkonen's musician friends, the Kokkonen-persona discusses particular compositions, performances, or matters of professional musical gossip. For example, with one sitter, the Kokkonen-persona discusses the relative merits of the Finlandia and BIS recordings of his cello concerto (neither of which the sitter had heard), and then complains about the recording quality of the old Fuga recording of his third string quartet. With another sitter, the Kokkonen-persona gossips enthusiastically and knowledgeably about a famous conductor's body odor. When speaking to non-musician friends, the trance-persona speaks in similar detail about matters of personal interest to the sitter. Some of these later sittings are themselves proxy sittings. For example, the composer Pehr Nordgren[22] arranges, anonymously, to be represented by a Midwestern wheat farmer, who takes with him to the séance a personal item of Nordgren's. Mrs. B goes into trance immediately, mentions a term of endearment by which Kokkonen used to address Nordgren, and begins relating a discussion the two composers once had about Nordgren's violin concerto. Communications of this quality continue, consistently, for more than a year.

I submit that if we actually encountered a case of this quality, we'd have to agree with philosopher Robert Almeder[23] that it would be irrational (in some sense) not to regard it as good (if not compelling) evidence of survival, even if we didn't know how to make sense of it theoretically, and (in the most extreme scenario) even if our preferred metaphysics was clearly uncongenial to the idea of postmortem survival. Moreover, if several cases of (or near) that quality appeared, they would have a cumulative force. They would obviously comprise precisely the kind of evidence that could lead us to revise, abandon, or at least seriously reconsider a conventionally materialist worldview. Philosophical intransigence in the face of such cases would not demonstrate admirable tough-mindedness. Instead, it would betray indefensible intellectual rigidity.

Unfortunately, we don't encounter cases of this quality; even the best of them disappoint in some respects. Nevertheless, the very best cases are rich enough to give us pause—at least if we don't have a metaphysical axe to grind. So one virtue of looking at hypothetically ideal cases is that they remind us that it's not an idle enterprise to consider less-than-ideal cases, even if the evidence is consistently frustrating in one way or another. The quest isn't futile; the evidence *can* point persuasively (if mysteriously) to postmortem survival, at least in principle.

Apparently, then, we should be able to apply to postmortem cases the same psychological criteria of identity that we apply, usually unproblematically, in our everyday dealings with others. Granted, we might still feel puzzled by the postmortem cases, and we may be unable to explain (or say anything interesting about) how survival could occur following bodily death. We may simply be at a loss philosophically and scientifically. But as I noted earlier, that's hardly unique to postmortem cases. Besides, it's pretty much irrelevant—although it may still be annoying— that hypothetically ideal postmortem cases challenge us conceptually and even violate some people's physicalist assumptions. Although philosophers are often reluctant to admit this, practical considerations trump abstract philosophy every time, and if we really encountered a case as good as the ideal cases we can construct, and especially if the case mattered to us personally, our reflective metaphysical scruples would count for nothing. We wouldn't hedge our bets and say (as some philosophers have proposed) that what the evidence points to is not really personal survival, but only the persistence of what matters to us in survival.[24] We'd say that the deceased individual had actually (if mysteriously) survived bodily death.

Dueling Analogies and Assumptions

Even if we were fortunate enough to encounter one or more cases close to the ideal, many would still find it difficult to dispel the lure of physicalism. And it's easy to see why. No matter how persuasive survival cases may be, there remains an extensive body of evidence indicating an intimate connection of some kind between brain states and mental states. So the question naturally arises: If our mental states—indeed, characteristic dispositions and large chunks of personal psychology—can persist after bodily dissolution, why do they at least *seem* to be so bodily dependent? Traditionally, survivalists deal with this question by claiming that the deceased's brain is merely one kind of *instrument* for expressing mental states. After death (they'd say), either the deceased uses some other instrument (e.g., the medium's brain or an astral or secondary body), or else the deceased uses no physical or quasi-physical instrument at all (e.g., if mediumistic interaction is telepathic).

Now you needn't be a hard-core physicalist to wonder about that gambit. But as the history of philosophy (and of rationalist philosophies in particular) has demonstrated, philosophical intuitions are all over the conceptual map, and what's intuitively clear and distinct to one person may not be to another. I suggest we heed the words of philosopher Trenton Merricks, who, despite his commitment to a physicalist conception of persons, warns sagely (in a slightly different context) against placing too much faith in our intuitions concerning the limits of the possible. He writes that

The dogmatic insistence on ... outright impossibility ... betrays ... an exaggerated and overweening confidence in one's modal intuition, in one's ability to peer into the space of possibility with a clear and unfaltering gaze and to see that what seems to be possible, in some sense and to at least some of us, is not really so. Modesty is more becoming.[25]

So suppose we agree to aim for a kind of temporary metaphysical agnosticism. If we then find ourselves instinctively rejecting the survivalist's move, we could at least try to proceed as though our reaction is unwarranted. But that leaves us with another problem: How do we tell the difference between (a) being presented with a genuinely implausible survivalist re-framing of the data and (b) *our* being caught in the grip of a seductively familiar and generally comfortable physicalist picture, one whose time has passed and whose limitations we're inclined to minimize or dismiss? For many at least, this may be the central conceptual dilemma in grappling with the survival data. Although I don't know how to resolve this dilemma, either generally or in this particular case, perhaps the following considerations will help.

First, the evidence suggesting postmortem survival is evidence counting *prima facie* against monistic physicalist theories (both reductive and non-reductive). Granted, some have tried to demonstrate the compatibility of physicalism and postmortem survival, usually by proposing resurrectionist theories.[26] But these proposals can't accommodate the more interesting case-types studied by psychical researchers. For example, good mediumship cases suggest that postmortem communicators continue to exist—presumably in a disembodied state—during periods of mediumistic inactivity (e.g., when the séance is over). At any rate, it's fair to say that the evidence suggesting survival (however mysterious it may be, at least right now) calls into question familiar forms of physicalism. But in that case, it's unclear to what extent physicalists can cite neurophysiological data in support of their objections to postmortem survival. After all, if we're entitled to entertain seriously the survival hypothesis in light of evidence initially in its favor, then we'd be entitled to question whether our mental states are dependent on our brain states in the ways many suppose. In fact, we'd be entitled to wonder whether much or at least some of the allegedly relevant neurophysiological data has been widely misinterpreted all along.

We need to remember, first, that scientific data don't come pre-interpreted, and second (as I mentioned earlier) that there's no such thing as a purely empirical science. Moreover, even though a background theory or cherished and formerly successful assumptions may be well-entrenched, they're always up for grabs, especially in the light of new data. In fact, apparently obvious interpretations of novel data may reveal more about our unexamined theoretical presuppositions (or lack of imagination) than they do about the phenomena in question. One of my favorite episodes from the history of psychology illustrates the point nicely.

In the 1920s, the psychologist and behaviorist Karl Lashley thought he could determine the location of a rat's memory in its brain. He trained rats to run a maze, and then he excised the portion of the brain where he believed the acquired memory to be. To his surprise, the rats continued to run the maze. So Lashley cut out even more of the brain, but the rats still navigated the maze (though with a bit less panache). This surprising result persisted as Lashley continued excising portions of the rats' brains. Only when a small fraction of the brain remained were the rats unable to run the maze. Unfortunately, at that point they also could do little else.[27] Later, others looked at these results and concluded that the rats' memories must have been localized in the brain in the way information is distributed diffusely in a hologram. In fact, the neuroscientist Karl Pribram has been mistakenly heralded as a pundit for that questionable inference and his resulting holographic theory of memory traces.[28]

In my view, however, Pribram's apparently easy recourse to a holographic model indicates that he was merely in the grip of a standard mechanistic and physicalistic picture or set of presuppositions. To those not antecedently committed to mechanistic analyses of the mental, Lashley's data take on a different kind of significance. In fact, they can easily be taken to support the view—held in some quarters—that the *container metaphor* (i.e., that mental states are *in* the brain) was wrong from the start and that memories are not localized *anywhere* or *in any form* in the brain. Moreover, that anti-mechanistic position can be supplemented by deep and apparently fatal objections to trace theories of memory generally.[29]

The evidence suggesting postmortem survival invites similar displays of metaphysical myopia. For example, David Bishai[30] challenged the familiar anti-survivalist argument (expressed, for example, by philosopher Paul Edwards) that reincarnation appears to be refuted by population statistics.[31] Bishai showed how various assumptions about the dwell time between incarnations yield different predictions about the peak of human population growth, and he sketched a simple circular migration model that does, in fact, account for the data from a reincarnationist perspective. He also showed that the alleged incompatibility between the reincarnation hypothesis, and the facts of population growth, rest on a very controversial assumption: namely, that the mean duration of stay in the afterlife has been constant throughout human history.[32] Apparently, Edwards didn't realize that his condescending and allegedly hard-nosed attack on reincarnationists was as deeply (and inevitably) metaphysical as the view he opposed. And no doubt he would have been hard-pressed to defend his required assumption about dwell time against alternative reincarnationist assumptions. At any rate, the major lesson of Bishai's study is that metaphysical assumptions are unavoidable no matter where one stands on the issue of reincarnation and population growth. Similarly, the debate about survival evidence generally is saturated with—usually hidden—metaphysical assumptions.

This situation is unavoidable and no cause for alarm. But it's a useful reminder that, for both survival evidence and the evidence for mind-brain correlations, we need to be circumspect about what the data shows. Nevertheless, survivalists still need to address the more obvious cases suggesting at least the causal dependency of the mental on the physical. For example, it's undeniable that changes in or damage to the brain can affect (and sometimes seem to obliterate) memory. Even if we grant that the brain is an instrument that needs to be intact in order to respond properly, we might still be reluctant to assert further (as survivalists do) that memory and other cognitive functions don't require that instrument. As the French physiologist and Nobel laureate Charles Richet put it,

> It is as if I were to say that in an electric lamp the passage of the current and the integrity of the mechanism of the lamp are not necessary for the production of its light.[33]

This analogy, and others like it, are initially seductive. But their appeal may reflect little more than our familiarity with a certain conventional picture of how the world works generally and of what the mind is in particular. If we're really engaged in an open-minded appraisal of exotic and challenging bodies of evidence, then we must be ready to entertain alternative pictures and alternative analogies. And in fact, other analogies, much more congenial to the survivalist, are not that difficult to find, as philosopher J. M. E. McTaggart demonstrated some time ago.[34] Many philosophers today would consider (and probably reflexively dismiss) McTaggart's discussion as old-fashioned. Nevertheless, it's an exemplar of admirably cautious metaphysics and deserves serious consideration.

To appreciate McTaggart's contribution to this debate, we should note first that survivalists are likely to express their position in terms that some will find unfamiliar or quaint, if not a bit peculiar. Because they reject reductive physicalism, survivalists claim that the self (whatever, exactly, it is) is not something identical with one's physical body or a body part (e.g., the brain). And because they reject epiphenomenalism, they must claim that the self is also not merely a byproduct of bodily activity, or something totally causally dependent (or supervening) on (part of) one's physical body. So survivalists must say something like the following: that the self (whatever, exactly, it is), as we know it introspectively and through our earthly commerce with others, is the kind of thing that can be said to *have* a body.

Anti-survivalists might object that it's question-begging to say that the self has a body because it presupposes precisely what's at issue: namely, that the self might not be embodied. But that would be a mistake. Granted, the claim that the self has a body may be *compatible* with the claim that the self can be disembodied. But it's also compatible with the more modest, and survival-neutral, claim that the self might not have *its current body*. Thus, the locution might seem unobjectionable even to hard-core physicalists who take seriously sci-fi scenarios about, say, computer-assisted body swapping or brain transplants. In any case, so long as we're taking the survivalist position seriously enough to evaluate its merits impartially, survivalists beg no questions by proposing that the self is the kind of thing that has a body. Until the survival debate is resolved, an anti-survivalist refusal to say that the self has a body is neither more nor less legitimate than the survivalist endorsement of that locution. Both positions are up for grabs. And of course, if (say, in the light of fabulous new cases) we accept the reality of postmortem survival, the survivalist's way of speaking will have been vindicated.

To be sure, some physiological evidence apparently casts doubt on the survivalist position. It's precisely what draws many people to some form of the identity theory or epiphenomenalism. In fact, McTaggart and survivalists would even concede that certain physiological discoveries can appear, at least initially, to challenge their position. That's why Richet's analogy seems compelling. But good survival evidence has a theoretical pull in the opposite direction and poses an apparently comparable *prima facie* challenge to the anti-survivalist. Moreover, McTaggart believed that survivalists can appeal to analogies of their own, and he believed that they're at least as weighty as analogies more congenial to physicalists.

McTaggart's discussion merits a close study, but for present purposes the following paraphrase will suffice. What McTaggart wanted to do was to expose several inferential leaps that many make all too unreflectively. We can grant, he argued, that our sensations and our mental life *seem* invariably linked to bodily processes of some kind. But no matter how intimate the mind-body connection seems to be, the data would show, at most, that *some* body was necessary to my self, and not that its present body was necessary.[35] And even that may be going too far; strictly speaking, the data show us only what *is* the case, not what *must be* the case. If our evaluation of the evidence for postmortem survival is to be genuinely open-minded, then we need to suspend (if only temporarily) our familiar physicalistic or reductionistic assumptions or biases. But in that case, it's clear that the data don't establish limits on the *possible* manifestations of selfhood. In particular, nothing *in the data* compels us to conclude that a self must be linked to a physical body. As we saw in the case of Lashley's experimental results, data will suggest certain specific interpretations only from specific philosophical vantage points. So on a more circumspect, theory neutral, or less assumption-laden appraisal of the data, we might conclude simply that *while a self has a body*, that body is essentially connected with the self's mental life.[36] McTaggart argued,

> ...it does not follow, because a self which has a body cannot get its data except in connexion with that body, that it would be impossible for a self without a body to get data in some other way. It may be just the existence of the body which makes these other ways impossible at present. If a man is shut up in a house, the transparency of the windows is an essential condition of his seeing the sky. But it would not be prudent to infer that, if he walked out of the house, he could not see the sky because there was no longer any glass through which he might see it.[37]

McTaggart makes a similar point with regard to the more specific, and apparently intimate, relation between brain states and mental states:

> Even if the brain is essential to thought while we have bodies, it would not follow that when we ceased to have brains we could not think without them.... It might be that the present inability of the self to think except in connexion with the body was a limitation which was imposed by the presence of the body, and which vanished with it.[38]

Perhaps we can supplement McTaggart's point with a contemporary analogy to counter that of Richet. Consider the case of portable electronic devices that can operate either on internal battery power or through a connection to AC lines, docking stations, or some other component to which they can be joined and through which they can draw power. In many cases, the latter connections allow a portable device to perform functions it might not be able to perform on its own, or to perform functions better than it can perform on its own. For example, docking stations can enhance the functionality of laptop computers, mobile phones, or tablets, and AC connections often permit them to display brighter screen images (or to do so for longer periods). Moreover (and perhaps more important), the connections bypassing the unit's battery power also impose *constraints* on the portable device's function, constraints from which it was free while operating as a stand-alone device. Of course, the external connections make the device less portable. But they also render the portable device vulnerable to processes (e.g., power surges or fluctuations) which can alter or impair its performance and even disable it. In fact, many audiophiles claim that their playback systems sound better on battery power than when connected to "dirty" AC lines.

Now I don't think it's plausible or helpful to push the admittedly mechanistic analogy between electronic devices and the self (or personalities). But if we ignore that for the moment, the connection between the portable device and an AC source seems to parallel the familiar dependence of thought processes on brain functioning, and the analogy captures an important feature of McTaggart's survivalist position. Like the connection to a wall outlet or docking station (which can both expand and constrain the device's functions), physical embodiment would simply be one possible medium for cognitive expression. And like running on battery power, disembodied existence or possession of a secondary (or astral) body might be others.

I consider McTaggart's view to be important and insightful. Strictly speaking, the physiological evidence doesn't show that selfhood or consciousness is *exclusively* linked to bodily processes, much less the processes of any particular physical body or body part. Perhaps anti-survivalist interpretations of the data seem initially compelling because physicalistic presuppositions are widespread and deeply rooted. And if so, it may be a useful intellectual exercise to try to divest ourselves of those presuppositions and then take a fresh look at the data. We might find in that case that McTaggart's (or the survivalist's) interpretation seems more immediately appealing. At the very least, McTaggart's discussion provides a useful introductory glimpse of how the empirical landscape would look, if we manage to shed our conventionally physicalist conceptual grid and internalize in its place a sophisticated survivalist point of view.

Conclusion

I think it's clear, then, that we have (or can have) at least *prima facie* evidence for postmortem survival, however mysterious that evidence may be to us, both scientifically and philosophically. Hypothetically ideal cases illustrate how compelling the evidence *could* be, and the best actual cases illustrate further that thinking about postmortem survival isn't just idle speculation. Moreover, I think it's clear that, if the evidence is compelling enough, our ignorance about how such survival could occur is simply an annoyance we'd have to accept but which we can hope to dispel.

It's clear also that philosophical issues—including very abstract metaphysical assumptions—greet us at every turn in evaluating survival cases. These may be precisely the matters about which we need to be most aware, and to which we should also be the least attached as we interpret the evidence. Once we grant that sufficiently powerful cases *could* persuade us—despite our philosophical predispositions or cherished scientific theories—that personal consciousness can survive bodily death and dissolution, the only relevant question then is whether the actual evidence pulls us sufficiently in that direction. Indeed, it's intellectually shameful, and obviously so, to take the position that evidence could *never* get us to change our mind on mere matters of theory.

Still, because we have nothing close to an ideal case at our disposal, we're faced with a difficult situation epistemically. As it stands empirically now, the LAP hypothesis remains a formidable obstacle to accepting the survival hypothesis as the best rational explanation of the data from mediumship. That leaves many students of the survival literature caught in a tug-of-war between the visceral pull of the best survival cases (such as they are) and a comparably powerful rational commitment to the empirical thoroughness and theoretical balance of robust forms of a motivated LAP hypothesis. Probably the only way to break that stalemate, at least for those of us still living, is to continue looking for better survival cases, or perhaps to keep accumulating evidence that raises the problem for LAP that I described (in *Immortal Remains*) as *crippling complexity*. And if those efforts fail to convince us of the reality of survival, we might as well be patient. Each of us will have the opportunity to resolve the matter sooner or later.

8. Can the Deceased Have a Perceptual Point of View?

Sketch of the Problem

Critics of survival research often claim that the survival hypothesis is conceptually problematic at best, and literally incoherent at worst. And many of them say that because they believe there's an essential link between the concept of a person (or personality or experience) and physical embodiment. For example, they argue that there's something wrong with the very idea of a postmortem person or personality (such as a mediumistic communicator) because *by hypothesis* postmortem individuals have no physical body. Consider, for example, the following representative passage from philosopher A.R. Miller.

> I find the very notion of *disembodied personality* logically inconceivable. A "person" is, essentially, a being which, among other things, perceives, acts, and thinks. Normally, perception requires sense organs, action requires limbs, and thinking (in the broadest, Cartesian sense) requires a brain; I cannot *see* and read the billboard unless my eyes are open, I cannot *kick* the football without a leg, I cannot *imagine* Santa Claus without a cerebral cortex, and so on. In the total absence of such physical accoutrements, I cannot see how any of the sorts of activities constitutive or personhood are or could be possible.[1]

Although this line of thought is hardly outlandish, some versions of it are admittedly disappointingly glib. For example, philosopher Antony Flew's variant turns on the methodologically naive assumption that something is logically impossible if we can't form a mental image of it.[2] But clearly, there are many things I can't imagine (much less produce a mental image of), some of which are impossible (such as square circles) and others of which are not (38-million-sided polygons). Similarly, of the many things that seem easy to imagine, some are possible and others appear not to be (e.g., time travel, singing swords, cartoon characters existing offscreen).

Fortunately, other accounts are more serious and raise genuine puzzles about postmortem existence–specifically, concerning the possibility and apparently *perspectival* nature of postmortem awareness of the physical world. In fact (and to his credit), Miller is one of those who recognizes that both advocates and critics of survival must address some interesting and complex issues here. Critics can't simply beg the question and say that physical embodiment is essential to personhood, personality, or experience, because the evidence suggesting survival is a *prima facie* challenge to the contrary. On the other hand, proponents of survival (hereafter, *survivalists*) need to grapple with puzzles arising especially from cases of apparent mediumship. That's because mediumistic communicators often respond appropriately to and describe correctly–and in fact, claim to experience–what's currently going on in the physical world. Of course, survivalists must endorse at least some of these occurrences in order to legitimate mediumistic communication as a source of evidence for their position. So they need to explain how postmortem awareness and knowledge of the current physical world can occur without a physical body that experiences the world and represents it accurately enough to ground veridical postmortem reports.

It may be surprising, then, that proponents of survival often have little to say about the relevance of physical embodiment to the manifestations of personhood and experience, apart from their efforts to deflect the more superficial and question-begging versions of the anti-survivalist critique. For example, readers will look in vain for a discussion or even acknowledgment of the issues in psychologist and former SPR President David Fontana's 2005 treatise on survival, widely (but incorrectly) regarded as a respectable defense of the survival hypothesis.[3] And in philosopher Robert Almeder's more conceptually sophisticated work,[4] the instructive problems about perspective (discussed below) are missed entirely, although Almeder correctly targets some related issues (including the superficiality of Flew's position).

In this chapter, I want first to consider carefully why survivalists face potentially serious, vexing, and largely unheralded problems in trying to make sense of apparent postmortem perception. Next, I want to consider a plausible—and arguably the only—way to deal with the issues. And finally, I want to show why that explanatory strategy is double-edged. Ironically, the best way to deal with the problem of perspectival postmortem awareness may render the survival hypothesis gratuitous.

The Perplexing Problem of Perspectival Postmortem Perception[5]
Let's now consider the matter in more detail. We begin with a seemingly seri-

ous, substantive problem:[6] Our everyday visual and auditory sense perceptions are perspectival–that is, they present themselves to us relative to and from the specific perspective of our location in space. That's why our experiences of seeing and hearing are always from a point of view. We see and hear things to the right, left, or straight ahead, and at a certain distance. Of course, we explain the perspectival nature of these experiences with reference to the fact that our sensory receptors occupy specific positions in space.

Now suppose it's true, as survivalists maintain, that after death we may continue having such perspectival experiences in the absence of a body. And suppose further that some of those experiences are veridical—that is, that they provide accurate information about states of the physical world. How are survivalists supposed to make sense of that? Can they satisfactorily explain how postmortem communicators know what things look like in the physical world, or what the living are doing? After all, some things can be observed or experienced only from certain points of view in space. For example, that a mirror or door is rectangular but not square can't be observed from the side, and the apparent color of an object is something that can vary with the observer's spatial orientation. So the survivalist's problem is to explain how there can be an analogous kind of spatially oriented awareness when the observer's body has decomposed (or at least ceased all organic functioning),

Initially, it might seem as if survivalists have a way to avoid this apparent problem. Perhaps they need only say that discarnate communicators experience physical states of affairs *as if* they're perceived from a spatial position. After all, by hypothesis these postmortem individuals no longer have (functioning) sensory organs to mediate sensory experiences. So perhaps survivalists should say that perspectival postmortem experiences are at best only *ostensibly* sensory, not genuinely sensory. But what does that mean? Under one reasonable interpretation, it even seems to undercut the survivalist position. For without sensory information arriving at spatially oriented sensory organs, why should we say that with these experiences mediumistic communicators are actually *gaining information* about a certain location? They seem, rather, merely to be *imagining* what's going on at a location.

Some of the more astute writers on mediumship have, in fact, taken this position, or at least come very close to it. For instance, Una Lady Troubridge[7] offered the following in connection with Mrs. Leonard's mediumship.

...Feda employs a vocabulary of very limited extent wherein erudite psychological terms have no place. Beyond the occasional emergence of such non-committal spiritualistic terms as "I sense" or "I get an impression of," Feda is content to tell the sitter that she "sees," "hears," "feels," or "smells," as the case may be, though the medium's eyes are invariably closed and neither the sights, sounds, sensations nor smells described are perceptible to the sitter.[8]

...there are certain aspects of the Feda phenomena which leave me very doubtful as to whether these simple sensory terms convey any accurate analogy with the processes really involved.[9]

For example, Lady Troubridge reports that on one occasion Feda described "to Miss Radclyffe-Hall with accuracy and in great detail a portrait of Miss Radclyffe-Hall herself." Feda correctly noted the coloring of the picture, the pose of the figure and hands, and the seriousness of the figure's expression. According to Feda's own statements, she

...*sees* this picture and is able to describe it at such length, [but] never apparently for a moment grasps the fact that the picture being described by her is a portrait, and a striking resemblance at that, of the very familiar sitter to whom she is speaking.[10]

Similarly, Lady Troubridge writes:

It is surely incredible that Feda or anyone else should *see* a person minus their most striking peculiarity of features or colouring, and yet this must frequently be presumed to be the case if Feda's seeing is to be accepted at face value. I have myself known her purport to see clearly a communicator whose appearance she minutely described, giving a perfectly accurate account of his features, complexion, expression, including the fact that he was remarkably handsome and struck her as having what she most evidentially described as "a clear look," but she remained to all appearance in ignorance that the most distinguishing features of his appearance were prematurely snow-white hair of remarkable abundance, and eyes of a peculiarly vivid blue.[11]

Parenthetically, I have to note that I'm unsure just how revealing this incident really is. Don't many or most people attend selectively to those things that matter to them, and don't the things that matter vary widely from one person to the next? I know many people, myself included, who routinely miss the color of someone's eyes in favor of other traits that they feel are more out-standing or meaningful.

But survivalists won't want to treat *all* mediumistic perception reports as nonveridical in that sense. That is, they can't treat communicators' ostensible perceptions *generally* as corresponding only fortuitously to the states of affairs in question because those experiences are supposed to undergird some of the true statements communicators make about the physical world. And those true claims comprise most, if not all, of the empirical support from medium-ship for the survival hypothesis.

Let's look at this more closely. The reason many consider mediumistic communicators' statements to provide evidence of survival is precisely because those statements suggest the postmortem, disembodied, existence of a former-ly living personality and that personality's *continuing awareness of and interaction with the physical world*. So when communicators respond appropriately to spoken sentences, or correctly describe what's currently going on either with the medium, sitters, or with more remote states of affairs, survivalists interpret that as evidence that a deceased person somehow survives bodily death and continues to be in touch with what's happening in the world of the living. In fact, the deceased's awareness of and interaction with the living is a *necessary condition* for mediumistic communication, at least of the sort documented since the early days of the Society for Psychical Research.

But that means survivalists must interpret *in causal terms* the ability of communicators to respond appropriately to interlocutors and make true claims about the current physical world. For example, they'd say that when deceased communicator "Uncle Harry" correctly describes the current location of an object in a sitter's house, what enables him to make that claim is his aware-ness of the actual state of the sitter's house. In that respect, at least, survival-ists understand some ostensible postmortem cognitive states to be analogous to ante-mortem perception. Ordinarily we'd say that I perceive—rather than merely imagine or hallucinate—the table before me because my experience results in part from my interaction with the object I perceive.

And not only that. Ordinarily we suppose that my ability to *correctly describe* the objects I perceive is not random or accidental. In fact, we suppose it needs to be explained in terms of lawlike *causal regularities* having to do both with properties of the objects perceived and the physical properties of my sen-sory system. For example, it's in virtue of those regularities that I'm generally able to describe green objects as green or rectangular objects as rectangular. Granted, if I instead hallucinate or imagine the table, my inner episode might be qualitatively identical to a genuine perception of the table. But if the experience isn't caused by the table before me, it's not a postmortem analogue to perception. Indeed, in the absence of relevant causal regularities between the object's properties and my own, it would seem to be a matter of sheer serendipity that I manage to describe the object correctly. So if postmortem communicators merely imagine or hallucinate things in the world, their alleged experiences would—at best—correspond only fortuitously to the states of the world they ostensibly represent. But that undercuts the principal basis for taking mediumship seriously.

So if survivalists know what's good for them, they *must* claim that mediumistic communicators can interact causally with states of the physical world in a way that results in their having non-hallucinatory (or non-imaginary), nonbodily, and perhaps quasi-sensory awareness of those states. And then we're back where we started; the question remains: In the absence of physical sensory receptors, how would a disembodied communicator be able to correctly describe current physical states of affairs? What enables that individual to detect the causally relevant features of the object(s) correctly described? And what supplies the perspective from which the information is apparently received and from which veridical mediumistic claims seem to be made?

Several potential survivalist maneuvers clearly won't work here. For example, survivalists can't claim that the medium's body temporarily supplies the physical basis for a communicator's sensory perspective, and that this enables communicators to perceive what's happening in the physical world. For one thing, communicators report that they're still aware of events in the physical world even when they aren't interacting with a medium. And for another, communicators often report physical states of affairs at locations perceptually remote from the medium. Moreover, survivalists can't maintain that a secondary or astral body supplies the needed perspective because in some survival cases information is provided about matters that can't be perceived from *any* position in space—for example, the contents of a page in a closed book. Must we conclude, then, that survivalists are committed to a process (postmortem awareness, with perspectival features analogous to those in ordinary sight and hearing) that, given the hypothesis of disembodied survival, seems to be incomprehensible or impossible?

One proposed strategy for preserving both logical coherence and veridicality is to posit telepathic causal chains between sitters (or remote others) and mediumistic communicators. For example, Lady Troubridge says she suspects

...that in many instances where Feda describes persons and objects, she uses the term "seeing" merely as a habit of speech, and that the process involved may be more likely a series of impressions received by her telepathically one at a time, or collected by her telepathically one by one from some mind incarnate or discarnate as the case may be.[12]

Although this strategy seems intelligible, it too can't be generalized to cover all communicators' reports of apparent sensory experiences. That's because communicators sometimes accurately report physical states of affairs unknown at the time to any living person and which are subsequently verified. Mrs. Leonard's book tests offer prime examples.

Philosophers Weigh In

Because only a handful of philosophers have taken both a serious and well-informed interest in the conceptual problems of survival research,[13] it would be odd to speak of a philosophical consensus about the issues. Nevertheless, it's interesting that two sophisticated philosophers have tried to make sense of ostensible perspectival postmortem experiences in purely subjective terms.

In his well-known essay, "Survival and the Idea of 'Another World,'" H.H. Price argued—contrary to the usual skeptical dismissals of survivalist claims—that the concept of a disembodied life subjectively similar to our own is at least intelligible.[14] He described how a dreamlike world of images could provide a discarnate postmortem individual with a first-person analogue to our subjective ante-mortem existence. And he suggested, further, that telepathic interactions between the deceased (including the telepathic production of apparitions) might furnish an analogue to objective relations and interactions between individuals in this world.

Now whether or not Price successfully demonstrates the intelligibility of a disembodied life in a next world, his conjectures are of no help to the survivalist in the present context. That's because Price doesn't explain how discarnate individuals in the next world manage to acquire veridical and apparently perspectival awareness of *this* world. In fact, Price makes no effort to explain how the deceased, locked into their own exclusively postmortem nexus of paranormal causality, interact with the living to produce *evidence* of their survival. Evidence of survival produced from a Pricean next world requires empirically discernable manifestations of postmortem existence—in particular, the deceased's continuing psychology (intentions, concerns, etc.). But that, in turn, requires some chain of causality *running in both directions* between the living and the deceased, allowing for mutual awareness and communication. But that's precisely what Price fails to posit, and without it anti-survivalist interpretations of survival cases (including those positing nothing but living-agent or so-called "super" psi) seem to have a clear explanatory edge.[15] Price even appears to grant as much when he considers the super-ESP hypothesis in another paper, "The Problem of Life After Death."[16]

Consider next philosopher Terence Penelhum's proposal to make sense of apparently perspectival postmortem experience.[17] At first, Penelhum seems to agree with Price that disembodied communicators enjoy an inner life of dreamlike images. But then he suggests, further, that we can construe these merely *seeing as if* (that is, only apparently sensory) experiences as cases of *genuine* seeing. Unfortunately, however, that approach seems to suffer from problems analogous to those afflicting the claim (provisionally attributed to Lady Troubridge) that all communicators' apparently sensory experiences are hallucinatory.
Penelhum writes:

> ...there seems no difficulty in saying of a disembodied person that it might look to him as though there were objects before him which looked to him as they would to a normal observer under optimal circumstances from a certain position in space. I feel obliged to start from some such account as this because I can attach no sense to the notion of seeing from no point of view, or seeing non-perspectivally. Given the intelligibility of this story, and given that there *are* objects in space arranged as stated, it seems quite pedantic to deny...that our disembodied person *sees* them[.] So let us say he does.[18]

There are several issues here. First, Penelhum may be right that the notion of *seeing* from no point of view is unintelligible or empty. However, he may also have overlooked a viable option. As I've already noted, the evidence for relatively humdrum clairvoyance indicates that subjects can be *aware* in some sense of physical states of affairs (such as targets sealed in envelopes) whose sensory perception ordinarily requires being suitably situated in space but which at the time couldn't be perceived from any position in space. Thus, some evidence of clairvoyance can be taken to show that veridical awareness of physical states of affairs is possible even when there's no actual point of view from which the states of affairs can be accessed by sensory means. So even if non-perspectival *perception* is unintelligible, non-perspectival *awareness* seems to be a genuine option in both logical and empirical space. I'll return to this point shortly.

Moreover, it seems easy to demonstrate the implausibility of Penelhum's suggestion that a disembodied person really sees objects under the conditions he describes—that is, conditions we might have described instead as being merely of the *seeing as if* variety. Consider the following situation. Suppose an embodied person S hallucinates an object X as being before him. Furthermore, since every hallucination (even the most fantastic or seemingly arbitrary) has some cause or other, let's suppose that S's experience occurs as the result of a hallucinogen mischievously added to his breakfast cereal. But suppose further that X is really before S, so that S would have had a qualitatively identical visual experience had he *seen* rather than hallucinated X. Now, because S's experience of X is caused by his spiked cereal rather than by X, the experience's phenomenal content corresponds only fortuitously to what is actually in S's perceptual field. That's why we wouldn't say that S saw or perceived X in this case. But then why attribute genuine seeing to a disembodied person S_d whose visual experience merely happens to be that which an embodied person would have from a certain position in space? Contrary to what Penelhum claims, it doesn't seem at all pedantic to say that S_d fails to really see the object.

Indeed, as I noted earlier, whether or not S sees X is something that needs to be cashed out in terms of an appropriate causal story. In particular, the existence, veridicality, and perhaps also the phenomenal (perspectival) quality of S's experience must be explainable, in part at least, as the *result* of lawlike causal relations obtaining between X and S. But on Penelhum's proposal, a sufficient condition for S's genuinely seeing a person wearing a pink shirt is the mere fact that the person is wearing a pink shirt. Incredibly, it wouldn't matter whether the content of S's experience is causally related to the state of the world it ostensibly represents. Thus, for Penelhum, genuine seeing (or sensing) gets robbed of its essential nomological character.

Interestingly, Penelhum seems to recognize this. At one point he considers whether to assign the disembodied observer a location in space—that is, a position from which X would look to a normal observer the way it does to the disembodied S. And he writes,

> ...we have to say that the disembodied person is at the place from which, when a normal observer sees the objects which our survivor now sees, they look to that observer the way they look to our survivor.

Roughly, he has to be at the centre of his visual field.[19]

But then Penelhum notes,

…the first thing that seems to follow is that his seeing things the way he does cannot be construed as a [causal] *consequence* of his being where he is, for his being where he is *consists in* his seeing things the way he does."[20]

And once again, the example about hallucinating X shows why this won't work. We must still be able to differentiate hallucinating or imagining X from seeing (or otherwise being genuinely aware of) X, whether or not S is embodied. But we can't do that unless we can tell some causal story about how the existence and nature of S's experience results (in part at least) from the presence of X in the world and also lawlike causal regularities obtaining between S and X.

Now there's a notorious philosophical position, *phenomenalism*, according to which physical objects—although real—are nothing more than logical constructs out of more primitive sense-data (that is, raw ingredients of perception, such as patches of color, shapes, textures, odors, etc.). So, for example, phenomenalists would say that the table before me isn't really a lump of mind-independent matter affecting my equally material, mind-independent, and lumpy sense organs. Rather, the table is nothing more than a construct out of the sense-data I do in fact currently experience and also the sense-data I and others *would* experience under an indefinitely large array of possible (counterfactual) circumstances. And those possible circumstances would likewise be analyzed in purely subjective sensory terms—for example, having the experience of seeing the table through tinted glasses, or having the experience of lying beneath the table, or of seeing the table from a great distance.

So, in the spirit of phenomenalism, some might think we can salvage the hallucination/perception distinction by claiming that only in the case of perception can we tell an appropriately robust counterfactual story. What we'd need to say would be something like the following: When a person genuinely perceives an object X, others, also having the experience of being suitably situated with respect to X, would also have experiences of X from corresponding points of view. However, if S merely hallucinated X, there would be no such correlations between what S experiences and what others do or *would* experience. For example, if I hallucinate (rather than perceive) a hippo in the corner, we wouldn't expect others having the experience of looking in that direction also to have visual hippo-in-the-corner inner episodes.

Of course, ordinary folk would explain this difference between hallucination and perception with respect to actual or possible relationships between observers and mind-independent physical objects. They'd say that in the case of genuine perception there really *is* some lump of matter that affects S's sense organs in accordance with various causal laws, and which does or would likewise affect the sense organs of suitably situated others. But that avenue isn't open to someone who construes physical objects as *constructs* out of actual and possible sense experiences, or as J.S. Mill put it, "permanent possibilities of sensation." So unfortunately for the phenomenalist, there seems to be no comparable causal story, since on that view there are no mind-independent lumps of matter to interact causally with a perceiver's sense organs. And that renders the difference between hallucination and perception completely mysterious. Unless one is prepared to abandon strict phenomenalism and posit a deity behind the scenes, either arranging things in advance (á la Leibniz) or holding models (archetypes) of objects in mind (á la Berkeley), phenomenalists have no explanation of why suitably situated possible observers *would* have the experience of perceiving a physical object. Of course, if survivalists were to adopt this phenomenalist strategy, that might be the least of their problems. They would also inherit *all* the famous problems afflicting the phenomenalist program, including having to defend themselves against the charge of solipsism and explain how—on their idiosyncratically empiricist grounds—they can justify reference to other minds and what others would experience. But that's another story.[21]

A Philosophical Digression
At this point, it might be useful to take a slight detour from the topic of postmortem survival. That's because key features of the debate we're considering about perspectival experiences may have a counterpart in traditional epistemology. If so, there's reason to think that errors in that arena may prove instructive for the topic at hand.

A well-known position in the philosophy of perception is *causal realism*. Roughly, the causal realist maintains that what we perceive directly are private internal states or mental images (such as Humean impressions and ideas), and that in at least many cases these subjective inner episodes are caused in us by mind-independent external objects and events. (A subset of causal realists maintain—arguably incoherently or at least gratuitously—that these inner states tend to resemble or represent their external causes. That view is usually called *representational realism*.) Following Hume, some have argued for causal realism along the following lines:

(1) When we look at a table and then back away from it, what we perceive gets smaller.

(2) But the table presumably doesn't change size as we back away from it.

(3) *Ergo*, what we perceive is not the table, but a private mental image caused in us by the table.

So causal realists maintain that we're not in direct perceptual contact with the physical world. Rather, a veil of ideas (or mental images) stands between us and the external things that produce many of those inner states. In effect, these mental images are *intermediate objects of perception*. Moreover, since we don't directly perceive tables and other external objects, the best we can do epistemologically is to infer that these things exist. Thus, the causal realist position very quickly raises the specter of solipsism. If what we know immediately are only private, inner episodes, and if we have to infer the existence of their causes in an external physical world, how do we know there's anything out there at all?

Beginning in the mid-twentieth century, many philosophers launched what they considered to be a kind of common-sense reaction against causal realism and (they hoped) its egocentric descent into the black hole of solipsism. Common sense seems to tell us that we are, in fact, directly in touch with the things around us—a view often disparagingly called *naive realism*. But the twentieth-century resurgence of that position (which I like to call *born-again naive realism*) offered an interesting argument strategy in its defense.

Born-again naive realists argued that traditional causal realism was misled (or seduced) by a too-easy adoption of perception language when describing the relationship we have to our impressions and ideas. They claimed that by carefully re-describing situations like backing away from a perceived table, we can undermine the temptation to posit intermediate objects of perception and thereby restore to respectability the view that we're in direct contact with the world around us.

The proposed re-description would go something like this. When we back away from the table, we continue to perceive the table all the while, but the table merely *seems* or *looks* smaller. In this way, we avoid positing an epistemological gap between the table and ourselves; the only object of perception is the table. The point of this re-description is not to deny the existence of inner experiences (sense impressions) such as mental images. It's merely to deny that perception of external things is *mediated* by a more basic perception of internal things (such as sense-data), so that we're inevitably separated from a world of things-in-themselves by a veil of ideas or sensuous curtain.[22]

A related strategy works even for hallucinations and dreams. For example, when I hallucinate a hippo in the corner, typical causal realists might say I perceive the hallucinated hippo (a collection of sense data), and that this intermediate and inner object of perception has no external counterpart as its cause. The born-again naive realist would counter that even here there's no need to say that I'm seeing a special, private mental object. Rather, in this case I *perceive* nothing at all. I merely *seem* to perceive a hippo. Again, no need to posit a perceptual relationship between me and a mental image.

Now, we needn't worry about whether or not this strategy succeeds in undermining Humean skepticism about the physical world. In fact, some would argue that so long as perceptual error is possible, skepticism can successfully drive a wedge between us and knowledge of the external world. Although I would dispute that dialectical strategy, we can nevertheless treat the debate between causal and born-again naive realists as a kind of philosophical cautionary tale. Even if skepticism about the physical world is a legitimate philosophical problem, it's far from obvious that Hume (or causal realists generally) have set up the problem correctly. At least one form of that problem may result from an inappropriate adoption of perception language and an unjustified positing of special, private objects of perception. Similarly, in the debate about perspectival postmortem awareness, both survivalists and anti-survivalists may have hastily adopted perception talk when describing how discarnate communicators respond to physical states of affairs.

The Solution That Isn't

We're now in a position to consider how survivalists might best respond to the puzzles about perspectival postmortem awareness. In my view, a promising strategy—arguably, the only one—is to focus on humdrum clairvoyance–and in particular, to note that living persons can have a kind of non-perceptual awareness of remote physical states (such as targets in sealed envelopes) whose perception ordinarily requires being suitably situated at a location, but which at the time couldn't be perceived from any position in space. Because that form of awareness apparently doesn't rely on ordinary (or, quite possibly, any) spatial cues, survivalists might therefore argue that postmortem awareness of the physical world is "merely" clairvoyance, and that the only difference between ante-mortem and postmortem clairvoyance is the ontological status of the subject. Survivalists can thereby deflect concerns about perspectival perception; they would be positing no form of perception at all. On this view, mediumistic communicators (like successful clairvoyant subjects) can enjoy either perspectival or non-perspectival awareness (not perception) of physical states in the absence of suitably positioned sensory organs.

This strategy has several virtues. First, it connects the survival hypothesis to a large body of both experimental and anecdotal evidence for clairvoyance. So even though some aspects of the survival hypothesis strike many as wildly conjectural, this way of interpreting the hypothesis at least gives it a kind of empirical footing, albeit partial and still somewhat controversial. Second, it preserves the pre-theoretically useful distinction between (on the one hand) hallucinating, imagining, or dreaming of an object and (on the other) having a veridical awareness of it causally mediated by that object.

After all, however unusual it may be in other respects, clairvoyance is still a fundamentally causal concept. When we posit clairvoyant awareness we posit a causal link between the subject and the (usually remote) state of affairs with which the subject is interacting and of which the subject is aware. Granted, the mechanisms of clairvoyance, if there are any,[23] may be mysterious. But if clairvoyance really occurs (as various converging strands of evidence indicate strongly), and especially if it ranges over objects not currently perceivable from any position in space, then we may need to regard it as a form of veridical awareness that differs profoundly from paradigmatically emanative or transmissive forms of perception such as seeing and hearing.[24]

And if we're willing to take that step, we might find it tempting to make a further bold move. We could entertain seriously the intriguing possibility that ordinary sensory (embodied) perception is merely a special case of a more primitive form of clairvoyant awareness.[25] That is, we could regard ESP (both telepathy and clairvoyance) as basic—and typically unconscious or subconscious—ways in which at least some complex organisms acquire information about mental and physical states of the world, and then we could take ordinary conscious and discursive forms of awareness to be subsets of those interactions not only mediated by, but also constrained by the organism's needs and psychological or physical limitations.

This would not be a new point. In fact, H.H. Price once cautiously advanced a similar suggestion and linked it to Leibniz's monadic theory.[26] For Leibniz, each monad (mental unit) represents or expresses the entire universe from a point of view, and that process of representing or expressing the universe is what Leibniz termed "perception." Price controversially interprets that claim as meaning that perception for Leibniz is always both telepathic and clairvoyant. I doubt whether that reading of Leibniz is justified, but in any case there are more serious obstacles to resolving the present problems in terms of Leibniz's monadology. For one thing, I'm not sure it's a good idea to dissolve the distinction between perceptual (causal) and non-perceptual awareness. As I hope this discussion has illustrated, that distinction has considerable utility. Second, Leibniz's metaphysics works only through the grace of a benevolent deity arranging all perception according to a principle of pre-established harmony. And third, even if we manage to purge this view of its theological trappings, we'd still need to explain "why there *seems* to be so little clairvoyance, and why the vast bulk of our perceptions or representations remain unconscious."[27] At any rate, important as this thread may be, it's an avenue of speculation that must be reserved for another time.[28]

A third virtue of the approach I've been suggesting concerns the fact that much of the evidence for clairvoyance points to a form of awareness not necessarily accompanied by rich mental imagery, or in fact any imagery at all. For example, in classic card-guessing experiments, many anecdotal reports, and even some successful remote-viewing trials, subjects may report nothing outstanding in the way of internal imagery, although they often have hunches and impulses to act. In that respect, clairvoyance would resemble subliminal perception, which also occurs in the absence of reportable phenomenal correlates. However, it differs from subliminal perception in that the latter relies on familiar causal links to objects in one's vicinity, the same kind that account also for the perspectival nature of ordinary, non-subliminal perception. By contrast, in clairvoyance the spatial location of a person's sensory receptors presumably plays no causal role.

The reason all this is important is that it offers a precedent for those survivalists willing to claim that discarnate communicators can have veridical awareness of physical states in the absence of mental imagery caused by those states. Granted, communicators often use perception terms to describe their states of awareness, but as Una Lady Troubridge suggested, that may indicate nothing more than our limited linguistic options for reporting those states. We needn't suppose that the awareness is actually accompanied by vivid, ordinary, or any mental imagery—the kind that has traditionally generated the puzzles we've been considering. So by modeling postmortem awareness after "ordinary" clairvoyance, survivalists can posit a process of postmortem awareness differing from both hallucination and subliminal perception with respect to the existence or nature of its causal links to the physical world, but which resembles subliminal perception in lacking the familiar phenomenal features of ordinary sensory perception.

So I think it would be prudent for survivalists to adopt a threefold strategy: first, to claim that discarnate communicators can be clairvoyantly (not perceptually) aware of physical states; second, to claim that this type of awareness may or may not be accompanied by internal imagery; and third, to claim that when there is imagery it's explainable either in terms of causal properties of the objects of which the subject is aware or else by the subject's own creative and idiosyncratic tendencies to generate internal imagery—just as seems to be the case with living subjects in successful clairvoyance experiments.[29]

Of course, many survivalists will probably be reluctant to pursue this strategy because then they'd clearly need to abandon an argument they unwisely use against the rival "super-psi" or living-agent psi (LAP) hypothesis–namely, that the nagging alternative of living-agent psi posits a kind and degree of psychic functioning that's antecedently implausible, or at least far in excess of any that's been demonstrated experimentally. Whether they like it or not, nonbodily postmortem awareness of the physical world would be a paradigm instance of clairvoyance. It would be an awareness of physical states unmediated by the physical and sensory mechanisms leading to ordinary perception. Moreover, in scope, consistency, or refinement it wouldn't differ significantly (if at all) from the clairvoyance living-agent psi proponents attribute to mediums or sitters instead. On the contrary, every exchange of information between a discarnate communicator and the mind of a living person, and every apprehension by a communicator of a physical state of affairs would be an instance of ESP. And of course, the mediumistic evidence for survival consists in a great many of these purported events, many of them quite startling in the specificity and obscurity of the information they provide.

So ironically, the best defense against the arguments noted earlier might be one that undercuts a survivalist standard attack against their chief parapsychological rival. It would require an explicit and serious concession to psi-sympathetic anti-survivalists: an endorsement of the view that the survival hypothesis presupposes the operation of refined or frequent clairvoyance and telepathy between the deceased and the physical world.

It seems to me, then, that survivalists are faced with the following challenge. First, they must learn to embrace the possibility of refined psi if they plan to count mediumship as a source of evidence for survival and if they hope to counter the puzzles we've considered about perspectival postmortem experiences. That's the only way survivalists can satisfactorily explain discarnate postmortem awareness of both physical states of affairs and also thoughts of the living. So not only is the appeal to postmortem ESP mandated by the survival hypothesis, it also offers significant explanatory benefits.

But in that case, if survivalists hope to argue effectively against living-agent psi as a general alternative to the survival hypothesis, they must rely on some strategy other than asserting the implausibility of so-called "super psi." My suspicion is that survivalists can escape this dilemma only by claiming—without any clear justification—that the anti-survivalist appeal to living-agent psi posits, not simply the unfortunately labeled super-psi, but something much grander and considerably more implausible. Let's call it (with tongue firmly and appropriately in cheek) *supercalifragilisticexpialidocious psi*.

I should emphasize that I'm not arguing against the survival hypothesis, even though I've appealed to clairvoyance to solve the more thoughtful puzzles raised about ostensible postmortem awareness. If my approach has any merit, it merely demonstrates again, and from another angle, why survivalists should abandon their insistence on the implausibility of anti-survivalist appeals to psi among the living. Granted, it also reinforces a conclusion I've defended elsewhere at length: that it's exceedingly difficult (if not impossible) to defend the survival hypothesis against the hypothesis of living-agent psi.[30] Nevertheless, it demonstrates how survivalists can deflect the usual concerns about the intelligibility of the survival hypothesis without severing needed causal links between the worlds of the living and the deceased.[31]

9. A Grumpy Guide to Parapsychology's Terminological Blunders

How the Conceptual Mess Began

Parapsychologists have never been entirely satisfied with their technical vocabulary, and occasionally their discontent leads to attempts at terminological reform. Not surprisingly, those suggestions have also failed to gain universal approval. For example, despite the widespread adoption of Robert Thouless and Bertold Wiesner's term *"psi,"* parapsychologists displayed little interest in their proposed "psi-gamma" and "psi-kappa (ostensibly synonymous with "ESP" and "PK")."[1] And John Palmer's term "omega" seemed to attract no adherents other than its author.[2]

More recently, a number of prominent parapsychologists, led by physicist Ed May, have regularly abandoned some of parapsychology's traditional and central categories in favor of novel alternatives.[3] They recommend replacing the term "ESP" with "anomalous cognition" (or AC) and "psychokinesis (PK)" with "anomalous perturbation" (or AP). Advocates of these new terms also propose replacing the term "psi" or "psi-phenomena" with "anomalous mental phenomena." Superficially at least, these proposals seem merely to be modest extensions of parapsychology's increasingly frequent use of the term "anomalous" as a substitute for "paranormal," a practice which (although controversial) isn't without merit, and which Palmer has vigorously defended.[4] But in my view, the proposed new terminology creates more problems than it solves.

Generally speaking, there's no justification for changing an established technical or professional vocabulary unless the proposed innovations offer an advantage of some kind. For example, the new terms might be more theoretically neutral, or make significantly fewer assumptions, than their predecessors. But the introduction of new terms might also be defended on pragmatic or political, rather than philosophical or theoretical, grounds. For example, in a controversial field such as parapsychology, one could argue that the changes promote more widespread understanding or acceptance of one's research and perhaps increase the probability of receiving funding. In that case, the new terms needn't introduce a substantive conceptual change. They might simply be synonymous with, but more practically or psychologically agreeable than, the older terms.

But the proposed new parapsychological vocabulary apparently has none of these virtues. For one thing, advocates of the new terminology don't specify clearly how the new terms relate semantically to the old. There are two main options. The new terms could be *synonyms* for (that is, have the same meaning as) their predecessors, or they could simply be *coextensive* with those expressions, that is, the old and new terms might merely pick out, or apply to, the same range of objects or events. For example, the terms "triangular" and "trilateral" are coextensive; they both apply to the class of triangles. But they clearly differ in meaning and therefore are not synonymous. But as we'll see, the new parapsychological terms are neither synonymous nor coextensive with the old. Of course, these differences in meaning or extension would be tolerable or desirable if the new terms offered a correspondingly tolerable or desirable conceptual advantage. But we'll also see that the new expressions are no more theoretically neutral and are demonstrably less useful theoretically than the terms they replace.

The Sordid Details

In one of their two papers, Ed May, statistician Jessica Utts, and parapsychologist James Spottiswoode offer a justification of the new terminology, which (despite the magnitude of the proposed change) is surprisingly terse and relegated to a footnote. The authors write:

> The Cognitive Sciences Laboratory has adopted the term *anomalous mental phenomena* instead of the more widely known *psi*. Likewise, we use the terms *anomalous cognition* and *anomalous perturbation* for ESP and PK, respectively. We have done so because we believe that these terms are more naturally descriptive of the observables and are neutral with regard to mechanisms.[5]

But (to put it mildly) this favorable assessment of the merits of the new terms seems unwarranted. To see why, let's begin by considering the most general of the terms, "anomalous mental phenomena." And for dialectical simplicity, I'll direct most of my criticisms toward Ed May, the apparent originator and leading proponent of the new terminology, although he's certainly not its only advocate.

First of all, the expression "anomalous mental phenomena" seems far too inclusive. On any reasonable and familiar construal of the term "anomalous," all sorts of occurrences count as anomalous mental phenomena that would not have been classified as ostensible cases of *psi*—for example, various types of psychopathology, as well as many non-pathological, but highly unusual, desires, thoughts, or volitions that may occur only once in a person's life (e.g., wanting to sit in the oven and pretend to be a loaf of bread, or wanting to have sex while covered in chutney). In fact, even more mundane examples of unusual behavior would arguably qualify as anomalous mental phenomena— for example, an ordinarily timid and mild-mannered person's sole outburst of uncontrollable anger.

Obviously, similar problems afflict the terms "anomalous cognition" and "anomalous perturbation." They will likewise easily pick out phenomena falling outside the domain of parapsychology. For example, the ability of calendar savants to identify the day of the week for any date, or a husband's only instance of experiencing sensitivity to his wife's emotional needs, would count as instances of the former. And object movements caused by unusual and unexpected tectonic shifts, or by the simultaneous jumping up and down of the entire population of New Orleans, would count as instances of the latter.

These awkward results are fairly obvious. So one would think that the originators of the expression "anomalous mental phenomena" would take steps to avoid them by explaining clearly how we're to understand the term "anomalous." But the only explanation I've seen is as follows (and which, for convenience, I'll dub criterion Ψ).

Ψ: In the crassest of terms, anomalous mental phenomena are what happens when nothing else should, at least as nature is currently understood.[6]

But clearly, that's not helpful. Scientists are hardly unified about what *should* occur in nature, and if those disagreements are taken seriously, all sorts of phenomena would count as anomalous mental phenomena that would never have been considered ostensible instances of psi—for example, every surprising discovery in astronomy, physics, or biology whose reality is initially questioned by the scientific community.

Even worse, criterion Ψ would countenance phenomena that are in no respect *mental*. According to Ψ, an example of an anomalous mental phenomenon (or at least an *ostensibly* anomalous mental phenomenon) would be the discovery that galaxies lying along a specific direction in space show significantly greater polarization of their radio waves than do galaxies in any other direction. On the surface, at least, that seems to challenge the prevailing belief that the universe has no preferred direction (e.g., no up or down).

Furthermore, as nature is currently understood, science is almost entirely mute on which mental phenomena should occur. Physics clearly has nothing to say on the matter, and there's hardly any general agreement within the behavioral sciences about what sorts of mental phenomena should occur. Besides, it's arguably not the business of science to dictate what should or should not occur in nature. Granted, science can appropriately make predictions, but its essential task is descriptive, not prescriptive.

Moreover, it's simply unclear how to interpret the force of "should" in criterion Ψ. If that criterion is supposed to pick out only those phenomena that most scientists consider highly improbable, then (again), too many things would count as anomalous mental phenomena—clearly far more than had ever been considered examples of psi. Most scientists would assign a very low probability to the appearance of a calendar savant, or a savant whose debilitating spasticity disappears only when playing the piano, or a mnemonist of the sort described by Luria[7]—or, for that matter, an instance of *situs inversus* (a highly abnormal condition in which the position of internal bodily organs is laterally transposed).

These considerations highlight another, and perhaps deeper, difference between "anomalous mental phenomena" and "psi." The latter term is not clearly relational, whereas the former term unquestionably has an underlying relational semantic structure. Something is an anomalous mental phenomenon only in relation to a person or theory (or some other standard) relative to which it counts as sufficiently unusual. In other words, objects or events are not anomalous *simpliciter*. They're always anomalous relative to a standard of normality. That's why frequent dissociative episodes might be anomalous in our culture but not in others. Similarly, wanting to have chutney-covered sex, or wanting to play loaf of bread in the oven, or wanting to read the complete philosophical works of Stephen Braude might be anomalous for some people but not others, or for some people only at certain times in their lives. By contrast, an event is a psi occurrence (or instance of ESP or PK) independently of these sorts of considerations.

Granted, what counts as PK (say) may be relativized to the current state of scientific knowledge, and in that respect the terms "psi," "ESP," and "PK" would also be relational. But "anomalous" is a relational term in quite a different way. In fact, unlike "psi," "ESP," and "PK," one could consider it to be a *normative* expression. Even against the same (admittedly shifting or variable) background of scientific knowledge or presuppositions, an event may be anomalous in one situation or for one person, but not for another.

So even if the familiar trio of traditional parapsychological terms counts as relational, we'd still want to distinguish those terms from "anomalous mental phenomena." We could say that "psi," "ESP," and "PK" pick out a *dyadic* relation between an event and a background theory (e.g., the current state of scientific knowledge), whereas "anomalous mental phenomena" picks out a *triadic* relation between an event, a background theory, and a standard of normality. Therefore, quite apart from the fact that the use of "anomalous" in "anomalous mental phenomena" encompasses phenomena that fall outside the domain of parapsychology, the terms "psi" and "anomalous mental phenomena" have different logical structures. Therefore, those terms seem to be neither synonymous nor coextensive. In fact, because the relational structure of the latter is more complex than that of the former, proponents of the term "anomalous mental phenomena" can't defend it on grounds of its greater simplicity.

Moreover, an additional set of problems emerges from May's 1996 definition of "anomalous cognition. According to May,

> Anomalous cognition is defined as a form of information transfer in which all known sensorial stimuli are absent. This is also known as Remote Viewing (RV) and Clairvoyance.[8]

The first problem rests with the second sentence in this passage, and it's easily avoidable. If, as May claims, "AC" is synonymous with "remote viewing" or "clairvoyance," then it's not a synonym for "ESP," as May has alleged previously because it explicitly omits all phenomena that would have properly counted as telepathic. Thus, it ignores the valuable distinction between ESP of an individual's mental states and ESP of purely physical states (such as a house on fire). And in that case, "AC" is obviously a less useful term than the one it's intended to replace. Utts 1996 is more circumspect on this matter, noting that "anomalous cognition is further divided into categories based on the apparent source of the information."[9]

I suppose one could try to defend the proposed synonymy of "AC" with "RV" and "clairvoyance" by rejecting the distinction between telepathy and clairvoyance. And in fact, it seems clear that this is what May, at least, really had in mind. May could argue that his definition of "AC" presupposes a commendably austere physicalistic ontology according to which mental states are less real (in some sense) than physical states, and in light of which cases of telepathy *reduce* to cases of clairvoyance (i.e., information transfer from physical—presumably, brain—states).

But that strategy would be uncompelling, quite apart from the notorious failure of attempts to reduce the mental to the physical. The problem is, again, one of conceptual and linguistic impoverishment. The distinction between telepathy and clairvoyance has considerable utility no matter *what* one's underlying metaphysics is. No matter how we analyze minds (or mental states) and physical objects (or physical states), it's still, and quite obviously, useful to distinguish mental→mental ESP from physical→mental ESP. For example, the distinction is presupposed in all discussions of the utility or eliminability of an agent (or "sender") in ESP tests. Besides (and perhaps more important), the demands of scientific taxonomy don't—and shouldn't--have to wait for solutions to long-standing metaphysical puzzles.

It Gets Worse

So perhaps the second sentence in May's definition of "AC" was an innocent slip, and perhaps May wouldn't insist on the synonymy of "AC" with "RV" or "clairvoyance." But even if May dropped that claim or in some other way amended the definition of "AC" so that it encompassed both telepathic and clairvoyant phenomena, the term would still suffer from a deeper and fatal defect. In this case, the source of the problem is the term "cognition," rather than "anomalous," and it demonstrates that "anomalous cognition" is not conspicuously "more neutral with regard to mechanisms" than the term it's intended to replace.

This lack of neutrality emerges clearly in the separate accounts provided by May and Utts. May claims that "anomalous cognition is *defined* as a form of *information transfer* in which all known sensorial stimuli are absent" (emphasis added). Utts makes it clear that "AC" is intended to be a synonym for "ESP," and she describes ESP as an ability "in which one *acquires information* through unexplainable means."[10] There are several problems here. First of all, the accounts of "AC" proposed by May and Utts seem to ignore the valuable distinction (first mentioned by C.D. Broad)[11] between telepathic (or clairvoyant) *cognition* and telepathic (or clairvoyant) *interaction*.

But why would it seem plausible or desirable from the outset to ignore the cognition/interaction distinction? After all, the distinction is both obvious and easy to understand. Every instance of ESP cognition would also be an instance of ESP interaction, but the converse doesn't hold—that is, interaction obviously may occur without cognition. And one reason this distinction matters is that it bears on a venerable worry many have about ESP—namely, that the reality of telepathic cognition would pose a threat to mental privacy. That would indeed seem to be a legitimate concern if others could come to know telepathically what we're thinking or feeling. Among other disquieting prospects, that would mean that our sins of the heart and most repulsive or embarrassing fleeting thoughts would potentially be available for public inspection.[12]

Now if telepathic cognition occurs at all, it would presumably be a form of non-sensorial *knowledge* about another individual's state of mind. More specifically, it would be a state of affairs in which so-called "percipient" *A* comes to know something about a telepathic interaction *A* has with another individual *B*. And what kind of things might *A* come to know? Well, presumably, in its most robust (and most intrusively intimidating) form, *A* would learn what's going on in *B*'s mind—that is, that *B* is having certain thoughts, perceptions, or emotions. But it would still be an instance of telepathic cognition—admittedly, less intimidating or threatening to one's mental privacy—if *A* learned merely that *B* was the telepathic cause of *A*'s current thought or experience—that is, that *B* was directly influencing or interfering with *A*'s stream of consciousness, whether or not *A*'s resulting thoughts or experiences were those of *B* or known to be those of *B*.

However, Philosopher C.D. Broad shrewdly recognized that the evidence for telepathy was seldom (if ever) evidence of these kinds of knowledge. On the contrary, what we usually find is evidence suggesting only telepathic interaction. In what is probably telepathy's most commonly reported form, person *B*'s mental state *merely influences* that of *A*, and *A* learns nothing from the process about *B*'s causal role, much less details of what *B* is thinking or feeling. For example, it would be telepathic interaction (not cognition) if my thought of the Eiffel Tower directly (that is, without sensory mediation) caused a remote person simply to think about the Eiffel Tower (or about towers generally, or about the Tower of London)—that is, without that person realizing that I played a causal role in that event, much less that I was thinking about the Eiffel Tower. Similarly, it would be a case of clairvoyant interaction (not cognition) if a burning house was the direct cause of someone at a remote location simply thinking about fire (or heat), or feeling a need to apply aloe to one's skin, or having the urge to watch *Blazing Inferno*. There's no need (and arguably not even a temptation) in these cases to insist that the percipient knows (presumably subconsciously) what caused the experience in question. The telepathic and clairvoyant scenarios would simply be paranormal analogues to the way our bombardment with environmental information can trigger various thoughts and associations, and perhaps distant or idiosyncratic associations at that. In both the paranormal and normal cases, we may be oblivious to the causal processes that led to our thoughts.

As it happens, when we look closely at the evidence for apparent telepathy, it does indeed seem as if it's largely (though perhaps not entirely) evidence merely of telepathic interaction. But even before we look at the evidence, we have to admit that, as far as we know, telepathy could occur between strangers or only very casual acquaintances, with the percipients never learning why, or even *that*, they had experienced telepathically-influenced (or tainted) mental states. We have no grounds at present for denying this possibility, and if that sort of telepathy occurs, we have no idea whether those moments of telepathic interaction are frequent or rare.

Granted, percipients in spontaneous cases (such as crisis cases) sometimes seem to know (or at least infer or suspect) who caused the surprising or anomalous thought they just had. And that's to be expected. After all, if I have an intrusive thought that my friend Jones had an accident and is in pain, it's a natural (though rationally risky) next move to infer that I'd been in touch psychically and momentarily with Jones. Nevertheless, it's often (if not usually) the case that percipients only learn *some time after their experience*, and through normal channels of information, that their anomalous mental states corresponded to the roughly contemporaneous thoughts or experiences of a remote individual in crisis. So in those cases at least, knowledge of that correspondence doesn't seem to be *telepathic* cognition.

In the interest of full disclosure, I must report that one could attempt here a theoretical maneuver that perhaps only a philosopher could love. The point of the maneuver is to argue that even in cases where there seems to be only mere telepathic interaction, what we find instead is a cornucopia of cognition. One could argue that the percipient's original telepathically-caused mental state was indeed telepathic cognition—presumably subconscious. And then one could claim that the percipient's subsequent knowledge of the correspondence between the earlier telepathic experience and the agent's crisis is a form of *second-order knowledge*—that is, non-telepathic knowledge that the earlier mental state was an instance of telepathic knowledge. So one could claim that at the time of the original telepathic interaction, the percipient knows that Jones is (or was) in crisis but doesn't know that (s)he knows this.[13]

However, if the appeal to second-order knowledge is viable at all, it may be applicable only to crisis cases. More typically, correspondences between the thoughts of agent and percipient are less clear-cut, and don't seem at all to refer or point to a presumptive agent. So they don't require positing any telepathic awareness or cognition of the agent's causal role, much less what the agent's mental state is. For example, in one well-known experiment in ostensible dream telepathy, the agent was concentrating on a target-print of Bichitir's *Man with Arrows and Companion*, which portrays three men in India sitting outdoors. One holds a musical stringed instrument; the most prominent of the three holds a bow and arrows. The third man has a stick over his shoulder that looks like a rifle muzzle. One minor detail of the painting is a stake with a rope tied around it, and the dreamer seemed to pick up on that small detail and incorporate images of rope prominently in his dreams. He had five dreams that night, and three of them contained rope (or coiled rope) as a prominent feature. Moreover, in another dream the subject saw a "hammock in which there was an awful lot of suspended strings."[14]

In another study, the agent (an orthodox Jew) concentrated on a print of Chagall's *The Yellow Rabbi*, in which an old rabbi sits at a table with a book in front of him. The subject of the experiment was a Protestant. In one dream, he saw a man in his 60s riding in a car. In another he reported "a feeling of older people. The name of Saint Paul came into my mind." In another, he dreamt of a professor of humanities and philosophy reading a book. In the summary of his dreams the next morning, the subject reported, "So far, all I can say is that there is a feeling of older people...The professor is an old man. He smoked a pipe, taught humanities as well as philosophy. He was Anglican minister or priest."[15]

So when people participate in informal experiments with friends or more formal experiments (like the Ganzfeld), it may not be outrageous to say that they can know whose mental state affected their own. But if so, it's only because the subjects understand from the start, *and through normal channels of information*, that there's a designated agent (or "sender") and that the goal of the experiment is to find significant correspondences between the mental states of the agent and subject. There doesn't seem to be even a superficial basis for saying that the subjects had telepathic knowledge all along, but didn't know that they know.

In any case, there's another reason to question whether a person's conjectures in these situations are types of knowledge. Perhaps the following analogy will make this clear. Suppose an unidentified person surreptitiously deposits a message with my signature or photo on your doorstep. Obviously, the deposited object doesn't indicate unambiguously who put it there. After all, it could be left there mischievously by someone other than me. But then knowledge of the object's source can't be derived simply from the object's presence on your doorstep. Similarly, a person's telepathically-induced state won't point unambiguously to its source, even if it contains features that seem to "refer" or point to a source.

Besides, and as the dream-telepathy examples illustrate, a telepathically-induced state needn't contain *any* such clues or pointers, and the vast majority of ostensible telepathic interactions lack those features. So there's no reason to think that paranormal experiences must include (or be preceded by) a warning or marker—something analogous to a flourish of trumpets, announcing that the experience is paranormal. Therefore, as long as people lack additional, normally-acquired contextual information about the presumed origin of their ESP-induced mental state, that state might seem to be a merely random intrusive thought—that is, one of the occasional incongruous or unexpected, and easily ignored, mental states probably all of us have during the course of the day.

We should now see clearly one reason why the ESP cognition/interaction distinction matters. If (as it seems) our evidence for telepathy overwhelmingly suggests telepathic interaction but not telepathic cognition, then we may have no grounds for worrying about an ongoing (or at least significant) loss of mental privacy. But whether or not we're really off the hook and can gratefully shield our most reprehensible or embarrassing thoughts from prying minds, it's still unacceptable to substitute "AC" for the entire and more familiar arsenal of ESP-related terms. By ignoring the useful cognition/interaction distinction, that strategy fails to supply the terminological resources even for beginning to describe adequately the relevant, interesting, and empirically unresolved issues discussed here. So irrespective of whether it can be defended on grounds of theoretical neutrality, the term "AC" can hardly be defended on grounds of empirical adequacy (i.e., being "naturally descriptive of the observables").

Perhaps the clearest examples of telepathic interaction (not cognition) are those in which a person's mental states seem to be the direct cause of a remote individual's *actions*. As psychiatrist Jule Eisenbud noted,

That a person can mentally influence not just the thoughts of other persons extrasensorially at a distance but also their decisions and actions must be one of the oldest facts of nature known to man. It has been woven into the core of every primitive culture described by anthropologists.[16]

But the evidence for this isn't simply anecdotal. In relatively modern times, the phenomenon has been investigated systematically and experimentally, and the best-documented cases concern the induction of hypnotic states at a distance. For example, hypnosis at a distance was reported in the eighteenth century by the early mesmerists, including Marquis de Puységur, and then, in the mid to late nineteenth century, in studies by Pierre Janet and Charles Richet.[17] Perhaps defenders of the new terminology forgot about this body of evidence, or more likely didn't know about it at all. Too often, psi researchers enter the field with—at best—only a very superficial knowledge of the rich history of relevant empirical and theoretical work that preceded them.[18] Nevertheless, it seems indefensible for partisans of the new terminology to exclude the phenomenon from their terminological considerations.

Interestingly, though, when it comes to the studies of apparent telepathic mind-control, even those familiar with the evidence do their best to avoid the subject. For example—and despite their successes—Janet and Richet abandoned the study of hypnosis shortly after completing their experiments and retreated to less momentously intriguing lines of investigation. Moreover, when Soviet physiologist L.L. Vasiliev demonstrated hypnosis at a distance once again in the mid-twentieth century, the community of psi researchers (and of course the rest of the academy) failed to pursue the matter further.[19] In fact, and contrary to what usually happens when parapsychologists report much less dramatic and noteworthy effects, there was no flurry of replication attempts—actually, no attempts at all. It's not that Vasiliev's work (or that of his precursors) was poorly done. Rather, it seems clear that the phenomenon was simply terrifying in its implications and thus too easily ignored.

I suppose May and Utts might have claimed that the expression "cognition" was merely a terminological infelicity, suggesting (admittedly misleadingly) that every instance of AC is a kind of knowing or cognition. What matters, May might have argued, is that AC is merely a kind of anomalous "information transfer." Similarly, Utts could claim that what matters is the "acquisition of information." And one could argue that some sort of information is acquired or transferred even when a thought about the Eiffel Tower causes someone to think about the Tower of London, or when a burning house causes someone to think about matches, or when someone remotely responds to my hypnotic command to fall asleep. But even if that terminological maneuver works for some instances of ESP interaction, other ostensibly telepathic and clairvoyant interactions more clearly resist definition or analysis in terms of information transfer.

Total Telepathic Control

At stake here is another intimidating issue, a modest extension of what we considered in connection with hypnosis at a distance—namely, that telepathic influence could—at least theoretically—be used for *total* control of another person's mind and body. Now presumably we wouldn't want to say that telepathic dominion over my thoughts and actions can be understood in terms of transfer or acquisition of information. After all, we wouldn't invoke information transfer to explain extreme, but normal, forms of forcing another to act. Whatever exactly the process might be, it's not analogous (say) to understanding and responding to a command.

The clearest examples are probably ordinary cases of behavioral coercion. It's not information transfer, in any helpful *epistemic* sense of the term "information," if I physically overpower you and compel you to pull the trigger of a gun, and we similarly wouldn't consider it to be information transfer if my willing alone both prevented you from exercising your volition and also compelled you to fire the gun. Perhaps we should describe that telepathic version of coercion as a form of *possession*. But what matters is that the degree of control posited in these coercion scenarios resembles the control of a puppet, and it's thoroughly unilluminating to describe the puppeteer as transferring information to the puppet. Likewise, we wouldn't consider it to be information transfer if I telepathically seized control of your mental life, blocking your access to your own stream of consciousness, and forcing you to have thoughts that are not your own. Victims of such telepathic influence would have no awareness at all—much less knowledge—of the interaction. And that's one reason why we wouldn't hold them morally responsible for their thoughts and actions at the time.

Actually, conflating telepathic influence and PK will probably appeal only to physicalists who would interpret the latter as a purely physical process and the former as a kind of physical influence on the percipient's brain. But if (as it seems) reductive physicalism is generally untenable, it again seems wise (for now at least) to entertain the possibility that telepathic influence and PK are distinct phenomena.

Before you dismiss these proposed scenarios as mere fantasy, we should note that there's actually an empirical basis for concern about this issue. It's not simply an abstract, theoretical matter we can acknowledge and then conveniently put out of mind. Total telepathic control of a human organism is ostensibly what happens during *mediumistic trance-impersonation*, a relatively common mediumistic occurrence in which the medium's body (and presumably, brain) are controlled by a deceased communicator who also apparently displaces the medium's waking consciousness. This is the process F.W.H. Myers called "telergy," and it remains an open question whether discarnate telepathic control is what really happens during mediumistic trance impersonations or whether (say) it's the medium's dissociative dramatic personation instead, with occasional verifiable mediumistic ESP thrown in for good measure.[20] At any rate, if there's a bright side to the possibility of telergy, it's that the process doesn't seem to require or involve some dreaded form of "mind-reading," on the part of either agent or percipient. Rather, it would be a situation in which one individual's mental states *displace* another individual's ordinary stream of consciousness.

Partisans of "anomalous cognition" might be tempted to reply that telergy should properly be called "anomalous perturbation" (AP), or (in more virtuous language) "PK". But that would blur the admittedly somewhat fuzzy, but at least apparently useful, distinction between telepathic influence and PK. For all we know at our still very preliminary level of understanding, the paradigmatic PK events of levitating a table, materializing a human figure, or biasing a random event generator, may be significantly different processes, *not only from each other*, but also from directly influencing a person's thoughts or actions. So until we have good reason for claiming that all these phenomena can be similarly explained, it seems unwise at the very least to embrace terminology that prevents us from tentatively classifying the latter only as a distinct, telepathic process.

We're fortunate to have developed the linguistic resources for making fine distinctions between classes of phenomena whose differences certainly make sense in theory, and which also seem to have empirical warrant. If later empirical or theoretical advances show that our distinctions have no basis in fact and only apparent theoretical utility, we can then comfortably simplify our arsenal of parapsychological categories. But we're a long way from that point. In the meantime, then, the taxonomical reform proposed by May, et al is unacceptably coarse, quite apart from the other shortcomings I've already enumerated.

Diehard proponents of the new terminology might still argue that the old terms "ESP," "telepathy," and "clairvoyance" suggest (at least superficially) that the phenomena in question are perceptual, and if so, those terms could be criticized for their theoretical bias in favor of a perceptual model of the phenomena in question. But that position would be untenable for at least two reasons. First, it's been clear for many years that the forms of ESP are unlike the perceptual processes occurring in sight and hearing,[21] and parapsychological theorizing has generally ignored perceptual models. So if the familiar terminology is biased in favor of perceptual models, that bias seems negligible. Second, as we've seen, the term "AC" commits a different sort of superficial sin, suggesting that the phenomena in question are all cognitions. So on that score, the old and new terms seem to be equally guilty of theoretical biases. Moreover, we've seen that "AC" also countenances phenomena falling outside the domain of parapsychology, and blocks a series of useful theoretical distinctions accommodated by the old terminology. Therefore, on grounds of theoretical utility (if not theoretical neutrality), the new term would seem to be a poor substitute for its predecessors.

As we've seen, advocates of the terms "AC" and "AP" claim that those expressions are, unlike their traditional predecessors, "neutral with regard to mechanisms." But as we've also seen, that doesn't mean the terms are free of theoretical biases or presuppositions. (In fact, no terms are presupposition-free.) It means only that the terms don't presuppose an underlying process or structure for the two classes of phenomena. It's odd, then, that some would consider the new terms to have the edge here over "ESP" and "PK" because those older terms likewise rest on no specific presuppositions regarding mechanisms. Indeed, the variety of theoretical proposals throughout the last century to explain both ESP and PK (under their traditional designations) demonstrates that no such presuppositions attach to the use of those terms. In fact, I've proposed that we understand the forms of psi to be *primitive* phenomena, not analyzable in terms of *any* subsidiary processes or mechanisms.[22]

Nonlocal Objections

Before turning to more practical or political issues, I should register my objection to two more fairly widespread modern terminological conventions favored by some psi researchers. I'm not sure how the first of these unsatisfactory conventions got started, but it's been embraced most conspicuously by parapsychologist Stephan Schwartz. Its ignominious basis is a careless, if not incoherent, appropriation of a term—"nonlocal"—borrowed from physics. The strategy, then, is to replace the venerable arsenal of ESP-terms with a single expression—either "nonlocal awareness" or "nonlocal consciousness."

I'll leave it to others to demonstrate how this deployment of "nonlocal" differs radically from its accepted and widely understood use in physics. For our purposes, we need only observe that, as with the terminological proposals of May, Utts and others, these allegedly all-purpose expressions ignore the critical cognition/interaction distinction. So once again, the interesting issues about mental privacy can't even be discussed without reverting to the old, allegedly superfluous old terms. Moreover, "nonlocal awareness" or "nonlocal consciousness" provide no replacement for "PK." The primary virtue of this terminological strategy is that, by borrowing a term deemed useful in much of contemporary physics, the sloppy thinking behind this strategy appears to be cutting-edge.

Besides, many apparent examples of both ESP and PK would seem to be flagrantly local. If psychic healers can diagnose subtle medical conditions of the client seated before them, that would presumably be an instance of ESP confined to that small region of space. Similarly, a successful Ganzfeld experiment must be explained in terms of events occurring within the confines of the lab. And we know exactly *where* telepathic influence is occurring when an experimenter's hypnotic command to fall asleep causes the person in the next room to suddenly fall asleep, or where causal influence is occurring when a medium levitates a table. Dubbing such interactions nonlocal serves no useful—or for that matter, intelligible—purpose here.

Finally, what used to be considered a subset of PK phenomena, sometimes called "bio-PK" (i.e., PK on living things), many now call "DMILS" (for "direct [or distant] mental influence on living systems"). This development strikes me as less significant (and probably less pernicious) than the proposals criticized earlier, but it suffers from similar flaws. "DMILS" can't be regarded as synonymous or coextensive with "PK" or even "bio-PK" because those terms, in principle at least, allow for the possibility of non-distant influence on one's own body. Some have suggested that ordinary volition, for example, involves the psychokinetic action of one's mind on one's brain, and others have proposed that (for all we know) PK might be operative in placebo effects, self-healing, and more familiar hypnotic effects on one's own body (e.g., raising welts on one's skin). My guess is that those who use the expression "DMILS" haven't worried about whether that term is coextensive or synonymous with older terms and haven't expected them to offer any *conceptual* advantage over their predecessors. Rather, they've been more concerned to describe their research in ways that sound more like mainstream science than parapsychology. But that raises a different set of issues to which we must now turn.

The Appeal to Political Expediency

A predictable reply at this point would be to argue for the new terminology on practical rather than theoretical grounds. One could say that adoption of the new vocabulary is pragmatically shrewd considering the prevailing intellectual climate, and especially when dealing with government agencies and other sources of potential funding. After all, some people's minds and wallets will close as soon as such terms as "ESP" and "parapsychology" are mentioned. So one could argue that it would be in the best interest of psi researchers to describe their work in familiar and accepted terms, or at least in terms similar to those used within conventional science, and which (for many) are less likely to raise the red flag of pseudoscience.

Now I don't deny the potential utility of this sort of strategy, at least in principle. But it's doubtful that promoters of the new terminology can expect their creations to offer this hoped-for advantage. Consider: Most of the previous research by May and others, as well as their attempts to change parapsychology's central terms, have appeared either in flagrantly parapsychological journals or in non-mainstream journals, such as the *Journal of Scientific Exploration*, that regularly publish papers explicitly about parapsychology. So those works couldn't be cited—much less circulated—to the funding bodies resistant to parapsychological research and for which the mere use of the old terms is toxic. One would have to apply for funds as if these articles never existed and as if the authors had no prior history of research related to the current proposal.

In fact, research proposals submitted to mainstream funding sources couldn't include in their lists of references *any* works or journals whose titles or text contain the dreaded terms. For at least a long while (until a body of research accumulates that's reported using only the new terminology), researchers would have to pretend that their work had virtually no historical antecedents, much less the history of replication and meta-analyses to which parapsychologists are so fond of referring, and which they recognize is often important to cite when applying for funding.

Moreover, it would be naive to think that skeptics, critical of the work described using the old terminology, will suddenly stop protesting once the work gets described in the new terms. Indeed, it would be naive to think that funding agencies and critics will be oblivious to the fact that the authors of the proposals have previously been engaged in parapsychological research. Some, if not most, will know (or discover on the internet) who the researchers are, and they'll recognize that the proposals are continuous (if not identical) with those they previously dismissed in virtue of being parapsychological. So one might even expect them to object that the work in question is still voodoo science parading as respectable research.

Like it or not, the truth is that parapsychologists are doing parapsychological research, no matter how it's described. It fools virtually nobody (at least not for very long) to pretend otherwise. A more honest and intellectually courageous course of action would be to take pride in the work and also in its—often quite distinguished—conceptual and empirical lineage. By attempting to disguise what they're doing and by disowning the historical roots of their research, parapsychologists would inevitably appear as if they really have something to be ashamed of. And of course, that's not an attitude likely to find approval and attract funding from within the mainstream scientific community.

10. A Peircing Examination of the Paranormal

I imagine that many readers will know who the philosopher and psychologist William James was, and that his influence on the development of psychology in the United States led him to be known as the "Father of American psychology." But I suspect only a few readers are familiar with Charles Sanders Peirce (pronounced *purse*). And if so, then it's a damn shame. Peirce was the founder of the philosophical view called American Pragmatism—not (as is often claimed) his good friend James or his student John Dewey. The latter two are often lumped together with Peirce, and in fact each member of that philosophical triumvirate made genuine contributions to the development of pragmatism. But Peirce was annoyed by the variations on his philosophical themes introduced by James and Dewey, and so he eventually renamed his view *pragmaticism* in order to make it clear he didn't accept their formulations of his original position.

But simply to label Peirce as a philosopher is to do him a great injustice. To show clearly and concisely how exceptional Peirce was, I can do no better than to quote Thomas A. Sebeok's description:

> Who is the most original and the most versatile intellect that the Americas have so far produced? The answer "Charles S. Peirce" is uncontested, because any second would be so far behind as not to be worth nominating. Mathematician, astronomer, chemist, geodesist, surveyor, cartographer, metrologist, spectroscopist, engineer, inventor; psychologist, philologist, lexicographer, historian of science, mathematical economist, lifelong student of medicine; book reviewer, dramatist, actor, short story writer; phenomenologist, semiotician, logician, rhetorician, metaphysician...He was, for a few examples, the first modern experimental psychologist in the Americas, the first metrologist to use a wave-length of light as a unit of measure, the inventor of the quincuncial projection of the sphere, the first known conceiver of the design and theory of an electric switching-circuit

computer, and the founder of "the economy of research." He is the only system-building philosopher in the Americas who has been both competent and productive in logic, in mathematics, and in a wide range of the sciences. If he has had any equals in that respect in the entire history of philosophy, they do not number more than two.[1]

So why is Peirce not known at least as well as James and Dewey? It may have something to do with his prose style, which at its worst can be as turgid and pedantic as that of Kant. However, Dewey was hardly a graceful or clear writer. So another reason may be that Peirce had a highly cultivated knack for rubbing people the wrong way—a personality characteristic that often stood in the way of his receiving opportunities for advancement and prominence. But however interesting that issue might be, we must turn our attention elsewhere, to matters parapsychological.

It's at least somewhat surprising, and maybe even scandalous, that relatively few philosophers acknowledge (or simply know about) William James's interest in psychical research. That interest consumed James throughout his career; it was the topic of a substantial portion of his written work; and it was part of a broader interest in unusual or extreme types of human behavior, an aspect of James's thinking that we ignore only at the risk of misunderstanding what James was all about.

However, it's less surprising that few philosophers acknowledge or know about Peirce's interest in psychical research. And the philosophers who do know this usually ignore the matter, or else dismiss it as an aberration having little relationship to Peirce's work as a whole. However, Peirce had things to say throughout his career on telepathy (he commented less frequently on Spiritualism and postmortem survival). Granted, although Peirce's interest in these topics was considerable, his interests (or at least his active areas of investigation) were more diverse than those of James. James wrote often and at length about topics in parapsychology, and he was also an active researcher in the field. He conducted frequent investigations of spiritist mediums—most notably the famous American trance medium, Leonora Piper, the woman who was his "white crow." It was Mrs. Piper who convinced James of the reality of supernormal (that is, psychic) mental powers, although her ostensible spirit communications didn't persuade him of the reality of personal survival beyond bodily death. James also lobbied actively for psychical research. He was one of the founders of the American Society for Psychical Research (ASPR) and he served two years as president of the parent British SPR.

By contrast, Peirce was something of an outsider. (For that matter, he was something of an outsider in life generally.) He seems never to have engaged regularly in either rigorous psi experiments or case investigations, although one autobiographical remark indicates he attended the occasional séance and witnessed ostensibly psychokinetic phenomena. And some of his critical comments suggest that he hadn't thought as carefully and deeply about the topic as he had about others perhaps closer to his heart. But unlike many who voice confident opinions about parapsychology despite knowing virtually nothing about the data and the complex theoretical issues surrounding them, Peirce had actually taken the time to absorb some of the more important research conducted at the end of the nineteenth and the beginning of the twentieth centuries. So his opinions weren't simply those of a dilettante; nor were they instances of the sort of ignorant posturing about parapsychology academics indulge in all too frequently. Moreover, given the enormous breadth and depth of Peirce's overall expertise in philosophy, science, mathematics, and logic, it should be of interest both to parapsychologists and philosophers to see what his thoughtful opinions were about psi research. For the former, Peirce introduced some novel twists on venerable parapsychological themes. And the latter should be interested to learn that Peirce's parapsychological views are consistent with the rest of his philosophy, an insight that can only enhance our appreciation of Peirce's intellectual integrity generally and (more specifically) the depth of his fallibilism--roughly, the view that knowledge claims can never be absolutely certain, but only provisional.[2]

Peirce's parapsychological writings are scattered throughout his career. Although it's not his most substantial or theoretically penetrating work in the area, the longest of Peirce's contributions to parapsychology was his extended dialogue with psychologist Edmund Gurney.[3] Gurney was one of the founders of the British SPR, and his untimely death undoubtedly robbed psychology of one of its most fertile and adventurous minds. Today he's remembered primarily for having conducted a series of exceptionally interesting and creative experiments in hypnosis (a topic discussed often in the SPR's *Journal* and *Proceedings*).[4]

Gurney, along with two other founders of the SPR, F.W.H. Myers and Frank Podmore, produced a massive two-volume work entitled *Phantasms of the Living*. Its fourteen hundred pages offered detailed presentations and discussions of approximately 700 cases of apparitional experiences that corresponded (sometimes closely, sometimes only vaguely) to a distant and roughly contemporaneous event. After evaluating different explanations of the phenomena, Gurney and his collaborators settled on telepathy as the most plausible hypothesis. Peirce took issue with this, and in 1887 he published a detailed criticism. Curiously, James (in the same year) had written, when reviewing *Phantasms*, "The book hardly admits of detailed criticism, so much depends on the minutiae of the special cases reported."[5] But Peirce, who had evidently read *Phantasms* very closely, headed directly for the minutiae, in order to challenge the authors' claim that the veridical apparitional experiences cited in *Phantasms* couldn't be attributed to chance.

Peirce's initial criticism occupied seven pages of small print in the *Proceedings of the American Society for Psychical Research,* and it was followed by a 22-page rejoinder by Gurney. But Peirce had the last word (at least in the first round), replying to Gurney in 36 pages. In a subsequent issue of the *Proceedings,* Gurney responded again in 14 pages, but since he died before making his final revisions, Myers appended a 2-page postscript to that reply. Although the tone of the exchange between Peirce and Gurney isn't always pleasant (Peirce is often characteristically condescending, and Gurney makes little effort to conceal his annoyance with some of Peirce's charges), Peirce nevertheless thought highly of Gurney. In an unpublished paper written in 1903, and which Arthur Burks later titled "Telepathy and Perception," Peirce wrote, "I had a somewhat prolonged controversy with Edmund Gurney which was only interrupted by his death; and this brought me into fine touch with the spirit of the man. I was most strongly impressed with the purity of his devotion to the truth."[6]

Apart from Peirce's exchange with Gurney, the two most extensive pieces Peirce wrote on parapsychology are, first, the aforementioned unpublished paper, "Telepathy and Perception" (7.597-7.688),[7] and another unpublished paper called "Logic and Spiritualism" (6.557-6.587), written in 1905 and intended for *The Forum.* Peirce also wrote a small piece called "Science and Immortality" (6.548-6.556) in 1887, published in the *Christian Register* and also a 1901 article called "Hume on Miracles" (6.522-6.547), which, although it doesn't deal directly with psychical research, connects clearly to later comments on miracles and parapsychology Peirce made in 1906, in a work entitled "Answers to Questions Concerning My Belief in God" (6.494-6.521). The remainder of Peirce's comments on parapsychology can be found in brief remarks scattered throughout other works.

Peirce on Telepathy
After his debate with Gurney, Peirce's next published comment on parapsychology appeared in 1894, in a work co-authored with psychologist Joseph

Jastrow, called "Small Differences in Sensation." The paper deals with the experimental investigation of a psychological problem—namely, whether subjects could identify when they'd been presented with slight variations in stimuli. Peirce and Jastrow found that even when subjects claimed to detect no difference between two sensations of pressure, they correctly guessed which of the two was greater in three cases out of five. Peirce claimed that this result had "highly important practical bearings" (7.35), because it suggested that our ability to extract information from our environment is subtler and more extensive than we might have supposed. Peirce wrote,

> ...it gives new reason for believing that we gather what is passing in one another's minds in large measure from sensations so faint that we are not fairly aware of having them, and can give no account of how we reach our conclusions about such matters. The insight of females as well as certain "telepathic" phenomena may be explained in this way.[8]

It's unclear if Peirce's use of scare quotes around "telepathic" indicated a general skepticism regarding telepathy. He may simply have wanted to refer to phenomena that were merely ostensibly (rather than genuinely) telepathic. What is clear, however, is that in his earlier exchange with Gurney, Peirce had already acknowledged both a general skepticism as well as some ambivalence regarding telepathy, while also demonstrating that he both knew the evidence and took it seriously. In the discussion of *Phantasms*, Peirce admits that "The degree of my disbelief in telepathy in general is such that I might say that I think the odds against it are thousands to one."[9] He also says, "I certainly profess a legitimate and well-founded prejudice against the supernatural."[10] But Peirce considers that bias to be little more than a prudent "conservative caution,"[11] probably for the sorts of reasons he articulated almost 20 years later in "Answers to Questions Concerning My Belief in God." So it's intriguing that, despite his avowed skepticism, Peirce concedes that "there is a considerable body of respectable evidence in favor of telepathy, in general."[12]

For the most part, Peirce's early problems with the telepathic hypothesis seem rather superficial. He makes the familiar claim that telepathy, if occurred, would be "contrary to the main principles of science." But as I and others have argued,[13] there are good reasons for regarding that view as confused. Peirce also makes the more original, and odd, claim that

…every force or other cause we know works almost everywhere and at all times. But telepathy, as the evidence stands at present, if it acts at all, does so with the extremest infrequency.[14]

However, that argument is also suspect, and for at least three reasons. First, in the realm of human psychology, it's simply false that every cause works almost everywhere and at all times. In fact, most psychological capacities are highly situation-sensitive.[15] Second, one could argue plausibly that the evidence for telepathy demonstrates, at most, only conscious or overt manifestations of the phenomenon. For all we know, telepathy could occur below the threshold of conscious awareness with great frequency, and only occasionally bubble up to the surface in ways that command attention. And third, we're likely to detect telepathic experiences only when they occur between acquaintances (and possibly only between people who know each other well). Telepathy between strangers or casual acquaintances is unlikely to be discovered. At any rate, Peirce's experiments with Jastrow were still a few years in the future. So perhaps by that time Peirce's skepticism had become less extreme or at least more sophisticated.

Furthermore, there's simply no basis for determining how common a phenomenon telepathy is likely to be, as long as we're ignorant of how situation-sensitive the phenomenon is. Despite what Peirce might have thought, he had no reliable evidence on that matter. In fact, we're not much better off today. And to make matters worse, because of the methodological obstacles to carrying out any controlled experiment in parapsychology,[16] and also for carrying out experiments that test only for telepathy,[17] whatever data we collect will inevitably be ambiguous.

Let me explain that last pair of problems in a bit more detail. Once we take psychic phenomena seriously enough to test for them, then it seems impossible to conduct a controlled experiment. For example, if ESP occurs, then strictly speaking there's no way to ensure that our experiment is double-blind. We know only how to shield participants from normal forms of information-acquisition—not from sneaky or naughty ESP snooping. And if psychokinesis occurs, there's no way to ensure that only the official subject (rather than the experimenter or some onlooker) uses that ability, and there's no way to guarantee that the phenomenon occurs only at the time expected or prescribed (that is, when the experimental trial officially begins). But that means that we can never be certain why the results of a parapsychology experiment

turn out as they do. We can do little more than note that something anomalous (and in the case of a successful experiment, seemingly highly improbable)
occurred.

Moreover, it's difficult, if not impossible, to conduct a pure telepathy experiment (that is, one that tests only for telepathy). This issue was already
known during the time Peirce was writing, thanks to some revelations arising
out of late nineteenth- and early twentieth-century experiments in thought
transference. In these early tests, one person (the *agent*) would concentrate on
a drawing or a card, and another (the *percipient*), separated by some means
from the agent, would try at a specific time to reproduce the drawing or identify the card. Some of those tests yielded seemingly impressive results and were
initially interpreted as providing evidence of mental suggestion (telepathy)–
that is, until researchers discovered that equally impressive results could be
obtained without an agent. They realized, then, that the earlier experiments
in thought-transference had been ambiguous. If they indicated the existence
of a paranormal phenomenon, it might have been clairvoyance rather than telepathy.[18] In fact, even the later experiments—those appearing to test only for
clairvoyance—were plagued by a related ambiguity. In principle, the impressive results of those tests could be explained as due to *precognitive* knowledge
of the *subsequent* recording of the order of the cards in the unexamined deck,
or of the subsequent examination of the sealed envelope containing the target
drawing. That meant that experimenters couldn't be certain whether, in a successful test of clairvoyance (or telepathy), ESP was operating in a real-time or
precognitive mode.

How, then, can one conduct a pure telepathy experiment while at the same
time satisfying the canons of scientific research? The main stumbling block
is that in order to have adequate experimental controls, crucial information
about the experiment must be *public* in nature, allowing for objective evaluation. However, if experimenters want to conduct a pure telepathy experiment
and ensure that it was only the agent's mental state that influenced the mind of
the percipient, they must avoid recording the target objects or the score of hits
and misses. As long as there exists a physical record (say, in writing or spoken
communication) of what the target objects were, or which trials were successful, impressive test results can easily be attributed to a phenomenon other than
telepathy—for instance, precognitive clairvoyance of the test scores. It was
this apparently ineliminable ambiguity that led J.B. Rhine, widely credited as
establishing parapsychology as a branch of experimental psychology, to coin
the expression "GESP" for "general ESP," thereby acknowledging that we can't

operationally distinguish between the two forms of ESP.

At any rate, no matter how difficult it may be to distinguish actual occurrences of telepathy from those of clairvoyance, it's not difficult to distinguish them in principle, and it's also not difficult to imagine that telepathy could be as fragile and situation-dependent as many other forms of human interaction, such as the ability to show compassion, make someone laugh, sing in front of an audience, or comfort another's grief. It's particularly surprising that Peirce didn't consider this last response to his objection. For one thing, the response is fairly obvious. And for another, a few years later Peirce adopted a similar strategy against an equally superficial attempt to reject the evidence for psychokinesis on the basis of its relative infrequency.

At any rate, Peirce was both clear and firm about the defects of the case for telepathy presented by Gurney, Myers and Podmore. Using a tone that was perhaps needlessly contemptuous and supercilious, he claimed that their statistical arguments for ruling out the hypothesis of chance were deeply confused. Although Gurney and his collaborators were not as naive about such arguments as Peirce alleged, Peirce nevertheless remarks,

> The continuance of the order of nature, the reality of the external world, my own existence, are not as probable as the telepathic theory of ghosts would be if Mr. Gurney's figures had any real significance.[19]

Peirce also offered detailed criticisms of the case descriptions provided by Gurney, Myers, and Podmore, arguing that many of the cases were not as evidential as those writers had claimed. It's unclear whether a careful re-reading of *Phantasms* would reveal Peirce's criticisms to be as petty, irrelevant, or confused, as Gurney seemed to think. But one could probably make a decent case for saying that Peirce (perhaps due to his admitted bias against telepathy) was one of those who lacked what James (in his review of *Phantasms)* dubbed "an investigator's instinct, or *nose*, as one might call it, for good and bad evidence."[20]

Approximately nine years after his exchange with Gurney and two years after his experiments with Jastrow, in a manuscript called "Lessons from the History of Science," Peirce commented briefly, and perhaps more thoughtfully, on the evidence for telepathy. In a section entitled "Some a priori dicta,"[21] Peirce illustrates and defends the claim that

> The last fifty years have taught the lesson of not trifling with facts

and not trusting to principles and methods which are not logically founded upon facts and which serve only to exclude testimony from consideration."[22]

As an example, he cites the French physician Claude Bernard's dictum that a disease is not an entity, which Peirce rightly notes is a metaphysical doctrine that's been refuted by the observation of many facts.

In the same spirit, Peirce then decries a relatively familiar, dismissive attitude about the reliability of human testimony (especially from the distant past). And although he doesn't consider explicitly how one should then evaluate the older historical evidence in parapsychology, what he does say seems to support a tolerant approach to anecdotal evidence in parapsychology—certainly more than that body of data usually receives. Peirce criticizes the

...dicta by means of which the internal criticism of historical documents was carried to such a height that it often amounted to the rejection of all the testimony that has come down to us, and the substitution for it of a dream spun out of the critic's brain.[23]

He argues that "ancient testimony ought to be trusted in the main, with a small allowance for the changes in the meanings of words."[24] It would have been interesting, then, to see how Peirce would have evaluated the abundant and exceptionally impressive seventeenth-century testimony for the levitations of St. Joseph of Copertino.[25]

Then[26] Peirce concludes this section by mentioning certain types of observed or putative mental phenomena, including telepathy. He criticizes the:

...dicta by which everything of the nature of extraordinary powers connected with psychological states of which the hypnotic trance is an example were set down to tricks. At present, while the existence of telepathy cannot be said to be established, all scientific men are obliged by observed facts to admit that it presents at least a very serious problem requiring respectful treatment.

This is followed by a discussion of the current and foreseeable limitations and fragmentary nature of scientific knowledge.

By far, Peirce's most extensive and subtle treatment of the topic of telepathy is the discussion in his unpublished "Telepathy and Perception." That paper weaves together various themes—for example, concerning the nature of perception generally, the differences between the raw ingredients of perception and perceptual judgments, the nature of time (and in particular, an argument, similar to that of St. Augustine, about the nature of the present), and finally, a recurring Peircean theme about the tendency of the human mind to have an instinct for the truth. It would take another entire paper to begin to do justice to the overall argument in Peirce's paper; so a brief sketch of his position will have to suffice.

Peirce begins by expressing his continued reservations about the evidence for telepathy, and also for telepathy as an explanatory hypothesis. If, by proving the existence of telepathy, we prove only that "very rarely mind acts upon mind in a way utterly unlike the normal way,"[27] then this is no contribution to science. It declares telepathy to be a mystery for which we can establish no exact connections with other phenomena. Peirce cautions that this isn't to say that telepathy is unreal, because "Science no more denies that there are miracles and mysteries than it asserts them."[28] It's merely a concession that science can have nothing fruitful to say about telepathy.

Peirce also speculates about whether Gurney and other investigators from the SPR had been more dominated by a desire to believe in telepathy than to seek the truth, wherever it may lie. He concludes that these investigators were genuine truth-seekers, although they might have been unprepared for the critical thinking their inquiries demanded. And he notes that there's nothing particularly comforting about a belief in telepathy, or at least nothing so comforting that it would divert one's attention from seeking the truth. In fact, Peirce argues that belief in telepathy tends to weaken the belief in a hypothesis that most would consider to be more comforting than that of telepathy— namely, the hypothesis of postmortem personal survival. That's because much of the apparent evidence for survival can be reinterpreted as evidence for telepathy (and clairvoyance) among the living. Of course, some would contend that Peirce has overestimated how easily the best evidence for survival can be explained in terms of ante-mortem telepathy. But that's another, and very complex, story.[29]

Peirce then embarks on a discussion about perception, in which he concludes (among many other things) that "there is no difference between a real perception and a hallucination, taken in themselves."[30] The difference is "in respect to the relations of the two cases to other perceptions."[31] This is followed by a discussion of time and its relation to perception. Peirce argues that "in the present moment we are directly aware of the flow of time, or in other words that things can change."[32] But he cautions that "there is no such thing as an absolute instant, there is nothing *absolutely present* either temporarily or in the sense of confrontation."[33] According to Peirce, the present moment always contains a bit of the past and a bit of the future, and our experience of it always has in it something of the nature of memory and also of anticipation. That is true no matter how narrowly we focus our attention on the present moment. So "there is nothing at all that is absolutely confrontitial [i.e., confrontational], although the confrontitial is continually flowing in upon us."[34]

Now Peirce had already made the Kantian move of distinguishing a *percept* (a sense-datum or ingredient of perception) from "the percept as it is immediately interpreted in the perceptual judgment,"[35] which he calls the "percipuum." So after making some familiar Peircean observations about the real being what it is independently of how we think it must be, Peirce argues that:

> ...the percipuum is not an absolute event. There is no span of present time so short as not to contain something remembered, that is, taken as a reasonable conjecture, not without containing something expected for the confirmation which we are waiting. The peculiar element of the present, that it confronts us with ideas which it forces upon us without reason, is something which accumulates in wholes in time and dissipates the more minutely the course of time is scrutinized.[36]

What this means is that there's no clear distinction between a percipuum and either memory or anticipation, and it reveals an inherent difficulty in saying to what extent a percipuum accords with the facts. It also means that "there is no percipuum so absolute as not to be subject to possible error."[37]

At this point, the discussion takes an interesting turn back in the direction of telepathy. Peirce begins by reviewing some of his best-known and most characteristic philosophical positions—for example, about how we tend to see connections between things and thereby systematize our observations. Peirce says that's one reason science grows. In fact, Peirce claims that scientific growth would be impossible if human beings lacked "a tendency to conjecture rightly."[38] Accordingly, he argues that our ability to guess right as often as we do can't be explained on the hypothesis of chance.[39] For any observed fact, there are simply too many hypotheses one *could* come up with to account for it. As Peirce puts it, "The truth is that very few [of these possible] hypotheses will appear...to be reasonable; and the one true hypothesis is usually of this small number."[40] Why is that, he asks? It's because, from primitive humans to the present, we've had "some decided tendency toward preferring truthful hypotheses." So Peirce concludes that "it is absolutely necessary to admit some original connection between human ideas, and the events that the future was destined to unfold."[41]

But then, he argues, "that is something very like telepathy."[42] And that's because if telepathy were an established fact, "it would then be proved that people not very infrequently have hallucinations [which Peirce has already argued don't differ intrinsically from genuine or veridical perceptions], and that one hallucination out of a great number (but more frequently than chance coincidence could account for) coincides with subsequent experience to such a degree as to attract attention."[43] Peirce notes that even if telepathy occurs, human nature is such as to exaggerate just how closely these hallucinations accord with the truth. But then Peirce says that telepathy, in that case, would be a phenomenon that differs only slightly from phenomena whose existence we already accept. Telepathy would be "somewhat more remote from perception than the conjectures by which physicists so often hit upon the truth."[44] Telepathy, in other words, may simply be continuous with the power of conjecture that distinguishes human beings from creatures of other sorts.

Some might find it odd that Peirce would try to link the power of conjecture to telepathy rather than precognition. Granted, many parapsychologists maintain that precognition isn't a phenomenon distinct from ESP (telepathy or clairvoyance). They'd say it's merely one form or mode or ESP—a time-displaced mode. Perhaps it never occurred to Peirce to make any such distinction. In fact, in light of his earlier remarks about the nature of the present, he might have thought that there was no genuine distinction to make between ESP of contemporaneous as opposed to future events, or between real-time and precognitive forms of telepathy. Nevertheless, it will undoubtedly frustrate some readers that Peirce's discussion at this point isn't fleshed out further.

At any rate, Peirce seemed clearly to want to take some of the mystery out of telepathy by linking it to more familiar cognitive capacities. Now, Peirce evidently didn't recognize some of the profound methodological problems inherent in investigations of psychic functioning generally and telepathy in particular (especially the apparent impossibility of conducting controlled parapsychology experiments, and the obstacles to designing pure psi experiments). Parapsychologists themselves have been slow to appreciate these difficulties.[45] So his concluding remark is perhaps unjustifiably optimistic or hopeful. According to Peirce, whether or not the human power of conjecture exists in such a way that "one mind can know what passes in another at a distance," that is "a question to be investigated as soon as we can see our way to doing so intelligently."[46]

Peirce on Spiritualism and Psychokinesis

Peirce's views on parapsychology extended beyond the topic of telepathy. In particular, he commented several times on Spiritualism and the belief in survival of bodily death, and he also had things to say about the evidence for psychokinesis. It's not surprising that he sometimes discussed these two topics together because many considered the phenomena of physical mediumship (especially table turning) to be types of evidence for postmortem survival. But Peirce knew the evidence well enough to know that the physical phenomena of mediumship might instead be evidence of antemortem psychokinesis—that is, the direct (unmediated) causal influence of a living agent's intention on the physical world.

It's hard to determine how thoroughly Peirce had studied the evidence for both physical and mental mediumship. But it's clear that he'd read some of the more important case investigations of the day. For example, in his 1906 "Answers to Questions Concerning My Belief in God," Peirce notes, apparently approvingly, the evidence concerning James's star subject, Mrs. Piper. He also remarks that the researches of William Crookes, Lord Rayleigh, and Richard Hodgson make for a "very strong" case for mediumistic phenomena.[47] And earlier, in "Telepathy and Perception," he again expresses his admiration for William Crookes, who conducted a series of ingenious, pioneering, and (in my view) compelling experiments with the medium D.D. Home.[48] Moreover, in his "Logic and Spiritualism," he comments in some detail on German astrophysicist J.C.F. Zöllner's experiments with the medium Henry Slade. In my opinion, most discussions of Slade and Zöllner have been foolish and ignorant. Zöllner's work, like that of Crookes, was creative, careful, and important. To his credit, Peirce recognized this, describing Zöllner as "eminent astronomer and mathematical physicist, man of true genius, keen and subtle."[49]

Peirce commented on one of the many experiments with Slade that, according to Zöllner, suggested the existence of a fourth spatial dimension. This discussion occurs after some typically Peircean remarks about the value and general rightness of common sense, and how difficult it is for special experience to overthrow common sense, especially when common sense is "in harmony with individual good judgment from general experience."[50] The experiment Peirce discusses is one in which Slade seemed to make a knot appear in a string whose ends Zöllner had tied together and sealed. Zöllner attempted to explain this in terms of the existence of a fourth dimension. And Peirce considers what sort of impact this experiment might have on the dictates of common sense.

He notes, first, that "no experiences, familiar or otherwise, are absolutely inconsistent with space having four dimensions."[51] And then he considers the argument that all experience counts against the hypothesis of a fourth dimension because if it were true, phenomena similar to the anomalous tying of a knot would be more common. But Peirce counters by arguing, "If space has fourth dimension there is no determining *a priori* how often it would happen that something would project into it; experience seems to show it happens so rarely that Mr. Slade furnishes the first conclusive instance of it."[52] He then adds, "no experience whatever can furnish the slightest reason for thinking that an event of any conceivable kind will *absolutely never* happen."[53] In fact, even if accumulated experience suggested that bodies never jutted out into a fourth dimension, one could reasonably hold that this occurs somewhere, "since every rule has exceptions."[54] Still, he says, common sense compels us to hold that this jutting is so infrequent that the probability of its occurring "in any particular case, as in the person of Mr. Slade, is beyond all compare smaller than the probability of trick, even were we at a loss to conceive how trick could be."[55]

The upshot of Peirce's discussion is that Slade's phenomena, and (more generally) the phenomena offered as evidence for postmortem survival, are likely to be regarded as evidential only to those who are already predisposed to reject the dictates of common sense. However, Peirce's attitude toward the investigation of ostensibly paranormal phenomena is clearly respectful, just as it was (at least most of the time) in his earlier dialogue with Gurney. Here, as before, he balances his avowed open-minded skepticism with a respect (and sometimes an admiration) for parapsychological research, and he recognizes the tension between these attitudes. He writes that even though the results of parapsychological investigations will encounter a great, and reasonable, obstacle from common sense, "those who are engaged in psychical research should receive every encouragement ... scientific men, working in something like scientific ways, must ultimately reach scientific results."[56]

Peirce comments again on psychokinetic phenomena in his earlier work, "Lessons from the History of Science." This passage occurs in a section dealing with the classification of sciences. Peirce is discussing the legitimacy of distinguishing physical from psychical sciences, and he appears to be arguing for their relative autonomy and appropriateness in different contexts. For example, he says, "There can be no objection to a man's engaging at one time in tracing out final, or mental, causation, and at another time in tracing out material, or efficient, causation. But to confound these two things together is fatal."[57] He then makes a claim that might have pleased Spinoza: "To ask whether a given fact is due to psychical or physical causes is absurd. Every fact has a physical side; perhaps every fact has a psychical side."[58] Then he applies this conclusion to some of the phenomena of parapsychology.

> ...Its physical aspect—as a mere motion—is due exclusively to physical causes; its psychical aspect—as a deed—is due exclusively to psychical causes. This remains true, though you accept every doctrine of telepathy, table-turning, or what you will. If I can turn a table by the force of my will, this will simply establish the fact that something between me and the table acts just as a stick with which I should poke the table would act. It would be a physical connection purely and simply, however interesting it might be to a psychologist. But on the other hand, as my hand obeys, in a general way, my commands, clutching what I tell it to clutch..., so the table turning experiment would, I suppose, show that I could give similar general orders to the untouched table. That would be purely psychical, or final, causation, in which particulars are disregarded."[59]

Later, in Book III of *The Principles of Philosophy*, when discussing "Polar Distinctions and Volition" (1.330-1.331), Peirce once again takes up the topic of table turning. Here, the interest of the passage doesn't so much concern any theoretical or empirical claims Peirce makes about the phenomena. Rather, it's interesting because it seems autobiographical. It indicates that Peirce had some apparently successful experiences trying to influence tables at a distance. Peirce suggests that volition (or willing)

> ...is not perfected, and perhaps does not take place at all, until something is actually effected. Trying to shove something too heavy for the man to stir nevertheless accomplishes, in considerable measure, the only thing he directly willed to do—namely, to contract certain muscles.[60]

At this point, Peirce seems to wax autobiographical.

In the days of table-turning we used to be commanded to sit quite away from a table, and *"with all our might"* to will that the table should move; and...while we were possessed of no other "might" over the table than through our muscles, we used to be speedily rewarded, by a direct consciousness of willing that the table move, accompanied by the vision of its wondrous obedience.[61]

It's worth mentioning an interesting comment Peirce makes in a long footnote to his "Lectures on Pragmatism" (1902). In 5.47, Peirce reasserts his familiar endorsement of the spontaneous conjectures of instinctive reason, which in this passage he dubs "anthropomorphic." He writes,

Every single truth of science is due to the affinity of the human soul to the soul of the universe, imperfect as that affinity no doubt is. To say, therefore, that a conception is one natural to man...is as high a recommendation as one could give to it in the eyes of an Exact Logician.

Then, in a footnote appended to that passage, Peirce applies this view to what is by now a venerable dispute in parapsychology—namely, whether the evidence for postmortem survival might be explained instead in terms of telepathy (or psychic functioning generally) among the living. Peirce writes,

...other things being equal, an anthropomorphic conception, whether it makes the best nucleus for a scientific working hypothesis or not, is far more likely to be approximately true than one that is not anthropomorphic.[62]

He then considers how we might decide between the hypothesis of telepathy and the hypothesis of Spiritualism. Telepathy, he suggests, is the better working hypothesis "because it can be more readily subjected to experimental investigation." Here, I believe Peirce is simply mistaken because (as I noted earlier) he doesn't appreciate the methodological problems of studying telepathy experimentally, ruling out clairvoyance and determining the actual source of psi. Nevertheless, he argues that as long as the only evidence for telepathy is evidence that Spiritualism is "equally competent to explain," then "Spiritualism is much more likely to be approximately true, as being the more anthropomorphic and natural idea." He then adds that he similarly would choose believing in an anthropomorphic "old-fashioned God" rather than a "modern patent Absolute...if it is a question of which is the more likely to be about the truth."

Clearly, an important feature of Peirce's reasoning here is his distinctive and long-held respect for common sense and human instincts when it comes to choosing among rival hypotheses. It's quite unusual to approach the survival question from that angle, and so Peirce's view perhaps deserves a few more comments. As I mentioned previously, Peirce argued correctly that for any data we want to explain, there will always be many more hypotheses fitting the data than we can ever evaluate individually. But despite that obstacle, humans have a good track record of initially limiting the number of serious hypothesis-candidates and then choosing those that advance the course of science. As Peirce often maintained, the best explanation of that state of affairs is that we have a native ability to get at the truth, and it's in virtue of that ability that science has managed to progress.

Furthermore, Peirce offers an interesting supplementary argument in defense of that view. First, he claims that animals of all kinds exceed the general level of their intelligence when they exercise certain peculiar abilities. In fact (and sounding surprisingly like Plato), he claims that all animals have proper functions, or activities to which they're especially well-suited. For example, birds are expert aviators, navigators, and nest-builders, and beavers are also accomplished nest-builders and engineers. So why shouldn't humans also have a proper function and distinctive abilities at which they excel? But what might those be? Peirce says it's our ability to use general or abstract ideas in art, the useful crafts, and especially in theoretical reasoning.[63] One reason this position is intriguing is that the more typical approach to arguing that humans are uniquely rational stresses the *difference* between humans and what Descartes labeled "brutes." Peirce, on the other hand, focuses on our *continuity* with the rest of the animal kingdom.

Peirce often warned that saying we have a faculty for *understanding* things is not to say that we're always right in settling on our instinctive preferences. But he believed we should take seriously the fact that we've increased our understanding of nature over the years, as should be obvious by the success of science in various domains. Indeed, science has advanced steadily, and Peirce claimed the most natural hypothesis to explain that progress is that the human mind is attuned to the truth, that we *do* have an ability to understand the world around us, and that our instincts do lead us (at least eventually) in the right direction.

But is Peirce justified in claiming that a spiritist explanation of survival evidence is a more natural conjecture than positing living-agent psi? And how would one evaluate that claim? I doubt we'd find much guidance on the matter by polling the human race to see, overall, in which direction human instincts are leaning. After all, instincts seem to vary widely on several crucial issues—first, about whether some kind of postmortem existence is possible at all, and if so, then whether identity is preserved there. And those beliefs are further divided according to different conceptions of the afterlife.

Of course, not all opinions or instincts are created equal. So perhaps we should simply consider only instincts of those who know something about the evidence. But I doubt that will help; instinct-diversity reigns there as well. More generally, many people from diverse walks of life, enjoying varying degrees of familiarity with the evidence suggesting survival, believe strongly in personal persistence after bodily death. But many others, equally informed (or uninformed) disagree. And to make matters worse, both groups tend to rely on abysmal reasoning to reach their final judgment on survival.[64] So for now at least we seem to have good reason to question whether appealing to human instincts helps resolve the long-standing debate about survival.

In any case, Peirce makes some additional tantalizing comments on the topic of postmortem survival, many of which anticipate contemporary philosophical discussions about survival and identity. For example, in his "Answers to Questions Concerning My Belief in God," he writes, "If I am in another life it is sure going to be most interesting; but I cannot imagine how it is going to be *me*."[65] In fact, Peirce abruptly ends this manuscript with a thought experiment about identity and memory similar to those raised prominently toward the end of the last century, as philosophers flirted with the view that identity isn't what matters in survival.[66] He asks us to suppose that in our postmortem life we lose all recollection of our earthly existence; and then he considers whether that would matter to our anticipation of our postmortem future. Similarly, he imagines a case of administering a drug prior to surgery that wipes out memory, and he wonders whether this would make us lose interest in the suffering we can expect.[67]

An earlier work, "Science and Immortality," written at about the same time as his exchange with Gurney, is less impressive. Peirce voices the relatively familiar complaint about the banality of most ostensible spirit communications. He also questions the peculiar solemnity of most of those communications (as well as the behavior attributed to ghostly apparitions), arguing that one would instead have expected liberated spirits to regard their situation as a "stupendous frolic."[68] Of course, it's not clear why that's the only (or even primary) postmortem mental state or attitude one would expect. Alternatives come readily to mind, including remorse or grief due to intense attachments with the living or with vital unfinished business, and (as we hear from many near-death accounts) the blissful experience of being drenched in feelings of love and oneness. Interestingly, Peirce's explanation (such as it is) seems to offer a glimpse into Peirce's own state of mind at the time. He says,

> I fancy that, were I suddenly to find myself liberated from all the trials and responsibilities of this life, my probation over, and my destiny put beyond marring or making, I should feel as I do when I find myself on an ocean steamer, and know that for ten days no business can turn up, and nothing can happen. I should regard the situation as a stupendous frolic, should be at the summit of gayety, and should only be too glad to leave the vale of tears behind. Instead of that, these starveling souls come mooning back to their former haunts, to cry over spilled milk.[69]

Then, in a somewhat more unusual and original passage, Peirce alludes to the phenomenon of multiple personality, suggesting that it might pose a problem for a spiritist conception of the afterlife. He writes,

> Under the head of positive evidence apparently unfavorable to the doctrine [of spiritualism], we may reckon ordinary observations of the dependence of healthy mind-action upon the state of the body. There are, also, those rare cases of double consciousness where personal identity is utterly destroyed or changed, even in this life. If a man or woman, who is one day one person, another day another, is to live hereafter, pray tell me which of the two persons that inhabit the one body is destined to survive?[70]

Because these remarks from "Science and Immortality" were written relatively early in Peirce's career, it's perhaps not surprising that they betray the sort of superficiality that tarnished Peirce's exchange with Gurney. The issues regarding ostensible mediumistic communications, and also multiple personality and the concept of a person, are much subtler than Peirce seemed to realize (at least at that early stage of his career).[71] And indeed, his later comments on parapsychology show that he subsequently began to appreciate at least some of those complexities.

Peirce also argues, in that early work, that spiritistic theories and the possibility of another life will seem more credible as people recognize the "palpable falsity"[72] of mechanistic views of nature. He argues that the universe is not governed by blind law, and that necessitarian (strictly deterministic) metaphysics must give way to more spiritistic views that may in fact establish the reality of a future life.[73]

Later, in "Logic and Spiritualism," Peirce reveals his familiarity and frustration with an attitude encountered also by many psi researchers (myself included) trying to study the evidence for survival. Peirce writes,

> I run up my colors and confess myself scientific specialist. Spiritualists do not take kindly to scientific men, and never forego opportunities of instancing scientific follies. Though eminent scientists be their allies, they would not have spiritualism judged by the scientific kind of intelligence, surely anticipating disfavor from such judgment. For scientific men, we may well acknowledge it, are, as such, mere specialists. That stigma! We are blind to our own blindnesses; but the world seems to declare us simply incapable of rising from narrowness and specialism to take broad view of any facts whatsoever.[74]

Peirce on Miracles

Peirce was quite clear on what he took to be the errors in Hume's discussion of miracles. Writing in about 1901, in a paper called "Hume on Miracles," Peirce argued that an assessment of the evidence for miracles should focus on *objective probabilities,* rather than *mere likelihoods.* The former express real facts (for example, that in a fair dice the probability is one in six that any particular face will turn up). The latter are merely expressions of our preconceived ideas.[75] So according to Peirce, the problem with Hume's argument against miracles is that it's "based on the assumption that we ought to judge of testimony by balancing the likelihood that the witnesses tell the truth against the likelihood that no such event as that to which they testify ever took place."[76] And "no regard at all, or very little indeed, ought to be paid to subjective likelihoods in abduction."[77] Peirce concludes that Hume "has completely mistaken of the true logic of abduction."[78]

But quite apart from his specific objections to Hume, Peirce was unsympathetic to any attempt to legislate generally against anomalous occurrences. The line Peirce took in 1906, in "Answers to Questions Concerning My Belief in God," is (first) that there is no way to "ascertain *a priori* whether *miracles* (be they violations of the laws of nature or not) and special providences take place or not."[79] He notes that if there are no miracles nowadays, that tends to count against claims of miracles having occurred in the past. But, he asks "are there no miracles nowadays? I do not feel so sure of it."[80] Peirce then mentions Mrs. Piper and the investigations conducted by Crookes and others. That evidence, he says, is so strong, that "but for one circumstance I should unhesitatingly accept it. That circumstance is that every surprising discovery of science...is soon followed by others closely connected with it." What happens then is that the originally anomalous phenomenon is no longer anomalous. But miracles, Peirce claims, "are always *sui generis.*" Nevertheless (echoing a point we encountered earlier), he cautions, "The isolatedness of the miracle is really no argument against its reality." However, "it effectively prevents our ever having sufficient evidence of them."[81]

In his earlier paper on Hume, Peirce also focused on the meaning of the term "miracle" and whether it should be regarded as a violation of a law of nature. He ends that paper with a comment about the 18th-century philosopher, Bishop Joseph Butler, approvingly citing Butler's argument (in his *Analogy of Religion*)[82] that if we regard the universe as lawlike, then this actually *requires* miracles to occur. Regrettably, Peirce doesn't go into detail here, but he notes in conclusion that Butler's argument contains, deep within it, "an idea which has only to be developed to refute all such reasonings as that of Hume about miracles."[83]

A Parapsychologist By Default

In light of his more general philosophical positions, Peirce's views on the paranormal aren't especially surprising. His comments on miracles, and on the generation and assessment of novel hypotheses, fall squarely within his familiar and long-held views on the nature of science and the growth of knowledge. They're also not surprising in light of his clear cynicism regarding the attitudes of many scientists. In "Telepathy and Perception" he notes that

> ...the general public is no fool in judging of human nature; and the general public is decidedly of the opinion that there is such a thing as a scientific pedantry that swells with complaisance when it can sneer at popular observations, not always wisely.[84]

Even if the philosophical and scientific communities have failed to acknowledge the depth of Peirce's interest in the paranormal, one might have expected more from Peirce's biographer.[85] However, Joseph Brent raises the subject only twice, almost in passing. He observes that Peirce had a "strong interest in the occult"[86] and the bearing of spiritistic phenomena on our views of mind and body. But he apparently dismisses those concerns as less important than Peirce's "far more serious cosmological speculations."[87] And later, he offers a brief paragraph in which Peirce's interest in psychical research generally and the topic of postmortem survival in particular are simply and inadequately characterized as "skeptical."[88]

I suppose some might find it surprising that Peirce gave as much attention as he did to the data of parapsychology. But I can't see how one could have expected anything else without dismissing, implausibly, Peirce's fallibilist epistemology, his avowed and clearly serious dedication to the truth, and his respect for novel hypotheses arising from the spontaneous conjectures of instinctive reason.

11. Multiple Personality and the Structure of the Self

How it All Began

The phenomenon previously labeled "multiple personality disorder" (MPD) and now called "dissociative identity disorder" (DID) offers an irresistible opportunity to theorize about the nature of mind, or the self. And it's easy to see why. On the surface at least, it looks as if one body houses more than one psychologically—and sometimes physically—distinct identity, or center of self-awareness. A multiple's alter-identities (alters) can have their own characteristic sets of beliefs, attitudes, agendas, skills, facial expressions, speech patterns, posture, bodily movements, handedness, allergies, drug sensitivities, and voice quality (most dramatically between alters of different ages or sex). It's no surprise, then, that many have tackled the related issues of what a person is, whether there can be more than one person to a body, and whether our apparent unity of consciousness is a mere illusion. So it should likewise come as no surprise to learn that in this thorny philosophical terrain, confusions abound.

I've taken a lengthy stab, elsewhere, at sorting through those confusions.[1] And I've argued that, despite the impressive distinctness and semi-autonomy of alters, multiplicity presupposes a deeper underlying unity and continuity of consciousness. I contend that this is the best way to explain how multiples erect adaptationally-appropriate alters in the first place, and then later make the kinds of adjustments necessary to maintain alter-integrity in the face of unpredictable environmental pressures.[2] But it's a big job to explain how I arrived at that position; I needed an entire book to do it properly. My goal here is more modest. I want to expose a tangled thread that has run through the theoretical and clinical literature since dramatic dissociative phenomena were first identified. It concerns a suspicious principle that's apparently guided both clinical practice and theorizing about multiplicity, and which has led more broadly to a distorted picture of the importance of dissociation for our understanding of the mind. I call it the *Principle of Compositional Reversibility* (or *CR-principle*), and I'll try to show that it commits what I call the *Humpty-Dumpty Fallacy*. The underlying, and I'd say mistaken, idea behind the

CR-principle is that the divisions we find in dissociative identity disorder are clues as to how the self is composed right from the beginning. But the correct view, I'll argue, is that those divisions are instead creative and discretionary adaptations to contingent environmental stresses.

Now if I'm correct that the CR-principle is flawed, it's not because it's foolish. On the contrary, it's easy to see how some fell under its spell. It probably all began in the eighteenth century, when the Marquis de Puységur, a disciple of Franz Anton Mesmer, discovered a sleeplike hypnotic trance state which he called "magnetic sleep," and which appeared to reveal the existence of a normally hidden second self with its own memories and dispositions.[3] Since that time, dissociative phenomena generally—but especially the dramatic cases of dissociative identity disorder—have inspired a great deal of theorizing over the structure of the mind and the nature of mental unity and disunity. However, because that theorizing inevitably rests on various abstract presuppositions, it's all too easy to make deep mistakes.

It's important to understand that when Puységur and his successors observed apparent forms of dual or multiple personality, they believed their magnetic (hypnotic) techniques had *uncovered* an otherwise hidden aspect of mental functioning generally. That is, they didn't see themselves as having hypnotically *created* or invited the intriguing phenomena they observed. From their perspective, the therapeutic techniques of animal magnetism disclosed a doubling (or multiplying) of consciousness that existed already within the patient. Thus, the early mesmerists clearly supposed they were evoking phenomena that revealed something about the underlying structure or operation of the self or personality. And in making that assumption, they were relying on a form of the CR-principle.

However, the pioneers of hypnosis never managed (or attempted) to formulate that assumption clearly. And that's usually a good indication that trouble awaits. The most prominent overt proponents of some kind of CR-principle were late nineteenth- and early twentieth-century advocates of the colonial view of the self—that is, the view that a person is a kind of colony of lower-order selves or homunculi. For example, classical scholar, poet, and early Society for Psychical Research stalwart F.W.H. Myers wrote that

> ...observation of the ways in which the personality tends to disintegrate may suggest methods which may tend on the other hand to its more complete integration.[4]

And later, he says (less tentatively),

> Subjected continually to both internal and external stress and strain, its [i.e., the personality's] ways of yielding indicate the grain of its texture.[5]

Similarly, a few years earlier psychologist Théodule Ribot had stated, even more boldly and explicitly, "Seeing how the Self is broken up, we can understand how it comes to be."[6]

Fifty years later, psychologist William McDougall argued along the same lines. He claimed, first, that

> ...we cannot hope for clear and adequate understanding of the various ways in which the mind falls into disorder unless and until we have adequate insight into the conditions of its orderly and harmonious functioning and development.[7]

Then, after asserting that the *historical* structure or aspect of the mind "is the product of, is built up by...associative links or bonds," he claimed that dissociation is

> ...a weakening, or an undoing, or a failing of the work or product of the associative processes, the links of association.[8]

I'd understand if you're wondering already just what these early proponents of the CR-principle are asserting. What, *exactly*, are the components of the pre-dissociative self supposed to be? In my view, the best way to shed light on the subject is to examine the CR-principle in a variety of substantively different formulations to see the distinctive weaknesses of each version. In that way we'll be able to see that embracing any kind of CR-principle— any attempt to infer pre-dissociative divisions of the self from the presence of post-dissociative divisions— was a bad move, right from the start.

Varieties of Reversibility

Although their assertions are far from clear, Myers, Ribot, and McDougall all seem to be making a kind of historical or developmental claim—namely, (and very roughly) that splitting of the personality (or self) into parts reveals *an underlying pre-dissociative structure of the self that made those post-dissociative divisions possible.* In its strongest form the principle claims that dissociation *reverses* earlier processes leading to pre-dissociative functional organization or unity. So, from the phenomena of dissociation, we should be able to reason backwards (as it were) and infer the elements or organizing principles underlying prior functional unity or integrity. Stated in these general ways, however, the CR-principle is ambiguous. In order to appreciate its weaknesses, we must first consider it in two major distinct forms.

The first, and stronger, version of the CR-principle holds that there's a correlation (or perhaps even an identity) between the *particular* clinical entities produced in dissociation and the components of the predissociative self. And allegedly that's why, from our discovery of the former, we can infer the existence of the latter. Let's call this the *Token* CR-principle; it's the view to which nineteenthcentury writers came perilously close. The weaker version of the CR-principle asserts a correlation merely between the *kinds* of clinical entities produced dissociatively and the kinds of elements composing the predissociative self. Let's call this the *Type* CR-principle.[9]

The Type CR-principle is weaker in the following sense. According to the Type CR-principle, the post-dissociative existence of a sexual (aggressive, angry) alter requires the pre-dissociative existence of a sexual (aggressive, angry) component of the personality. But it needn't be that the *particular* sexual (aggressive, angry) identity that we call Dorothy existed pre-dissociatively, or that some specific Dorothy personality ancestor or germ existed prior to dissociation. Furthermore, in polyfragmented cases in which multiples have a great many alter identities, the Type CR-principle needs to posit only one sexual (aggressive, angry) predissociative personality component for all postdissociative identities of that type. But the Token CR-principle requires a distinct predissociative component for each distinct postdissociative entity.

It's easy to demonstrate that both versions of the CR-principle are fatally flawed. Let's begin with the Token CR-principle. First, it's not a *general* truth that things always divide or split along some preexisting grain, or that objects divide only into their historically original components. For example, Humpty Dumpty may have been reduced to forty pieces of shell after his fall. But it would be a mistake to infer that he'd previously been assembled and united out of forty parts, much less those forty parts. Similarly, I can break a table (or a board) in half with an axe. But it would be a mistake to conclude that the object resulted initially from the uniting of those two halves. Furthermore, some cases of splitting are clearly *evolutionary*. For example, the familiar process of cell division *creates* entities that didn't exist previously. So if the Token

CR-principle is true, it's not because it's an instance of a more general truth about the way things divide or break up. Presumably, it would be true—at best—in virtue of the special way the self breaks up.

But there's no reason to think that the self always breaks neatly, or along the grain, especially under extreme trauma—or stress—for example, of the sort that apparently leads to dissociative identity disorder. For one thing, a multiple's total number of alters (fullblown or fragmentary identities or personalities) can, in polyfragmented cases, apparently range into the hundreds.[10] Even if we grant the difficulty of taking a precise inventory of the number of distinct alters, must we suppose, on the Token CR-principle, that the predissociative self consisted of *so many* distinct protopersonalities?

But more important, it's preposterous to suppose that the historically original components of personality are those (or correspond to those) that seem clearly to be *adaptational*—indeed, trauma- or situation-specific. Most alters appear to be formed in response to *contingent* (and often quite uncommon) stressful situations, and they appear to be similarly contingent *products* of creative adaptation or defense.[11] For example, I knew a multiple who apparently developed several animal alters to deal with the incomprehensibility of parental abuse. The abuse occurred during early childhood, and at that time the only way she could grasp the acts into which she was coerced was by relating them to things she'd seen dogs and horses do.[12] Psychiatrist Eugene Bliss reports another sort of clearly adaptational alter, who

> is blind, or virtually so, because her field of vision is fragmented into pieces, representing an intolerable event the patient witnessed at age six, when the patient's mother cut her live puppy into pieces as part of a voodoo ritual.[13]

Bliss (like many others) also reports that he's encountered alters who seem to have no physical sensations, apparently in order to cope with repeated sexual and physical assaults by a parent.

Moreover, many multiples eventually begin to dissociate habitually, after finding it to be an effective (or at least easily-mastered) technique for coping with virtually any kind of stress, traumatic or otherwise. But at that point highly specialized alters (really, personality-fragments) begin to appear, some created to deal merely with inconveniences or relatively minor unpleasant situations. For example, some alters may deal exclusively (or at least principally) with such circumscribed activities as eating, baking muffins, handling domestic finances, cleaning the toilet, participating in oral sex (but sex of no other kind), receiving enemas, and interacting with inlaws. Granted, they might engage in other identifiable types of activities in the process of executing these general functions. But it's nevertheless clear that certain functions rather than others make sense of the alter's role within the total alter-system. These, we could say, are an alter's *centrally defining* functions, and there's no reason to suppose that they played any part in the original organization of the predissociative self. On the contrary, it's antecedently implausible to suppose that an earlier united or integrated self consisted in part of components identical to (or correlated with) exactly these contingent postdissociative entities. But then it's highly implausible to insist that the self always breaks along the grain, or even that it *has* a grain corresponding to contingent situation or trauma-specific alter identities.

Furthermore, a multiple's inventory of alters often evolves over time in response either to therapeutic intervention or to day-to-day difficulties in life. The problem for the Token CR-principle isn't simply that the inventory may continue to enlarge; hardcore advocates of that principle could always argue that additional alters reveal the finer structure of the predissociative self. Rather, the problem is that the alter-system might undergo *fundamental functional reorganization* into a different number of identities. Multiples might (indeed, often seem to) integrate (perhaps only partially) and then split again, but along *new functional lines*. So not only might the multiple create different alters (and a different number of alters) to deal with the same problems, but also the problems themselves might change and accordingly elicit a substantially different set of alters. But then it becomes arbitrary to choose one temporal slice of an evolving system of alters and claim that it reveals the grain (or fundamental structure) of the predissociative self. It's far more reasonable to maintain that a multiple's array of alters *at any time* represents merely one of many possible dissociative solutions to contingent problems in living.

Obviously, this point also works against the Type CR-principle. Since a multiple's system of alters at different times may divide along significantly different functional lines, it becomes arbitrary to select one set of alter-*types* as representing the deep functional divisions of the predissociative self. Those functional divisions are clearly as contingent as the situations in response to which the alters were formed.

In other respects, however, the problems with the Type CR-principle differ somewhat from those afflicting the Token CR-principle. For one thing, it's very difficult to know what the principle means. In particular, to *which* types of postdissociative entities is it supposed to apply? Presumably not *every* type—for example, alters that hate Stephen Braude, drink only Starbucks coffee, refuse to do business with Uber, or believe that Elvis still lives, or alters that are addicted to their smart phones, enjoy video games, or prefer streaming over cable television. For one thing, that would imply that the historically original predissociative components of the self can have functions specific to things that didn't exist at the time of birth or during early childhood. And for another, if postdissociative kinds are identified too specifically—for example, the type that has *exactly* the characteristics of the alter called Dorothy—then the Type CR-principle is indistinguishable from the Token CR-principle.

Furthermore, even if we were to identify types less specifically, the Type CR-principle would still seem committed to an absurdly inflated inventory of original component parts. Suppose an alter emerged to handle witnessing the murder of one's parents. Does that mean there had already existed a pre-dissociative component of the type suited specifically to dealing with the murder of one's parents? And if so, must we posit a distinct component waiting in the wings (so to speak) to deal specifically with the murder of siblings, and another for inlaws, or nextdoor neighbors, or friends in St. Louis, and another for total strangers? Moreover, if the parents' murder was committed with a gun, was the original pre-dissociative component designed only to deal with the murder of parents with firearms? Would another component already exist just in case the subject needed to deal with murder by chainsaw, or by poison? Even if there needed only to be a pre-dissociative component for dealing with murder, *of some kind or other*, of one's parent's (or of any loved one), would we then need to posit a component that could have been dissociated just in case the victims had been tortured instead, and another just in case they'd been relentlessly harassed?

An Appeal to Psychological Primitives

Partisans of the Type CR-principle might protest that we need to identify postdissociative entities very broadly. They might claim that the relevant types are those having to do only with the most *basic* general personality traits or functions—perhaps such as anger, fear, sexuality, helpfulness, compassion, and so on. Presumably, these traits would transcend the familial, cultural, and social influences that help shape the more specific personality types found in dissociative identity disorder. For example, it may not matter that the alter claims to be a possessing spirit of the sort appropriate to a specific cultural milieu or the more local belief system of a family or religious cult, or that it displays the stereotypic traits of a Southern belle, 1960s hippie, or a streetwise tough from the Bronx. Similarly, it may not matter that an alter's centrally defining function is to repair plumbing, write term papers, or deal with telephone solicitations. What would matter is whether the alter's basic function is to be generally angry, helpful, sexual, and so on. Thus, some might argue for a correlation between only between very general dissociated personality traits or functions and the comparably general and basic component functions that formed the predissociative self.

We may call this variant of the CR-principle the *Minimal* Type CR-principle. Like the other versions of the CR-principle, it's committed to the existence of distinct personality components around which the predissociative self is formed and organized, and which can correspond to—and probably guide the development of—whatever postdissociative functions happen to be revealed. But this view differs from its brethren in maintaining that the original components of the self express or exemplify only the most general—and probably very few—psychological or behavioral functions. Undoubtedly, the Minimal Type CR-principle will strike some as commendably conservative. But it's still thoroughly unsatisfactory, for two reasons.

First and foremost, there's no justification for claiming that *any* set of general personality functions is absolutely primitive, either pre or postdissociatively. For example, our descriptive categories of anger, helpfulness, sexuality, and so on, are hardly the only plausible ways of slicing up behavior into a set of putatively basic regularities or functions. Alternatively, one might prefer the inventory of functions proposed in Transactional Analysis (into parent, child, etc.), while another might defend a Platonic division into reason, appetite, and emotion, and another might prefer a division along the lines of 5-element (or 8-official) diagnosis in Chinese medicine, or perhaps even Jungian archetypes or the Freudian triumvirate of id, ego and superego. In fact, many different sets of categories can lay equal claim to dividing the self into basic functions. And they might all be able to countenance, in their distinctive ways, exactly the same particular behaviors. The different category-sets would simply take those behaviors to be instances of different regularities.

The moral, of course, is that these sets of personality functions, like descriptive categories of every sort, are no more than perspective or context-appropriate divisions of nature into kinds. There's no reason to think that one of our categorizations is inherently preferable to another, or that it captures a privileged, built-in parsing of the self into discrete functions. On the contrary, it's only relative to a perspective or point of view, or against a background of continually shifting needs and interests (both local and global), that certain categories rather than others will be appropriate. None are intrinsically appropriate or perspective-independent. Thus, it's only relative to a context, perspective, or background that we divide nature in one way rather than another and determine which descriptive categories and which level of specificity are appropriate. To take a familiar kind of example, that's why there's no privileged answer to the questions, "How many things are in this room?", "How many events were there in World War II?", and "How many slices are there in this (unsliced) pie"?

It might help to think of sets of descriptive categories as conceptual *grids* through which we view the world around us. Because there's not one and only one way to parse reality into objects or events and relations between those things, we use different grids for different purposes. Thus, different conceptual grids will divide reality differently, accommodating certain types of things rather than others (namely, those that fit into the spaces in the grid), and also certain types of lawlike connections or natural regularities (namely, the sort that obtain between those kinds of things). And although some grids may bear lawlike relations to others, some may parse reality in mutually incommensurable ways. That is, a conceptual grid may countenance or reveal objects, properties, and relations that have few (if any), or perhaps only fortuitous, connections to alternative grids.

Moreover, because our deployment of descriptive categories can be justified only with respect to a guiding background of interests or purposes—that is, some *perspective* relative to which those categories (rather than others) are appropriate, the claim that some set of psychological categories is inherently basic rests on the presupposition that some associated perspective on nature (some set of interests or purposes) is inherently fundamental, or more concerned with basic questions than other perspectives. But that presupposition is simply preposterous. It's no more than a thinly disguised and thoroughly indefensible chauvinism for merely one of many ways of looking at the world.

In some ways, then, the self is like the unsliced pie I mentioned above. We can slice a pie any number of ways—for example, along the radius, diameter, or by means of a vast array of conceivable grids or templates. And even if we select a general method of slicing the pie—say, along the radius, we still have to decide how large to make the slices. The self, too, can be divided functionally in a vast number of ways. Any method we choose, however, represents only one way of understanding, one sort of conceptual map we may trace over the surface of our subject. Moreover, like maps of any sort, our descriptive categories can't be evaluated apart from a background of needs and interests or in isolation from an actual context of inquiry. And clearly, there's no reason to suppose that our conceptual maps, tailored to context-specific needs to understand, must describe actual or natural partitions of the domain under investigation, any more than state or county borders on a map of the United States must correspond to actual or natural features of the topography.[14]

Similarly, there's no reason to think that regional divisions on a map must correspond to features of the terrain that are inherently basic (it's not even clear what that could mean). Granted, we might regard certain cartographic divisions as more important or useful than others. But if so, that's only because we've stipulated that they have that status. Both our parsings and our rankings of them are subject to revision and reordering. More generally, when we divide a region or domain of investigation in certain ways (rather than others) and consider some divisions to be more important or fundamental than others, that reflects, not only a network of widely shared assumptions and predispositions, but also a range of specific and perhaps more ephemeral interests and concerns. In that respect, our choice and ranking (or hierarchical arrangement) of conceptual categories tells us at least as much about us as it does about the region or domain in question.

Apparently, then, the Minimal Type CR-principle suffers from two related, and very deep, conceptual flaws. First, it presupposes that in the classification of psychological functions some set of descriptive categories is absolutely basic. And second, it mistakes the merely pragmatically justifiable outlines of those categories for inherent divisions in nature. Thus, the Minimal Type CR-principle fails to transform the Type CR-principle into a viable theoretical claim.

Anomalous Multiplicity
Nevertheless, the foregoing arguments may still not be enough to subvert the CR-principle altogether. Many writers seem to subscribe to a kind of CR-principle but refrain from endorsing any one version in particular. Perhaps that's because they don't realize they even have a choice. But whatever the reason, they betray their allegiance to the CR-principle by means of an apparently modest claim. They argue that the self *can't* be unitary because if it were, dissociative identity disorder (and other dissociative phenomena) would be impossible. The underlying and muddled intuition behind this seems to be what psychologist Alfred Binet had in mind when he wrote, "What is capable of division must be made up of parts."[15] However, that assertion is so obvi-

ously false, it's astonishing that Binet (and others) didn't see it. In any case, it expresses the core of an idea that also undergirds the work of contemporary mental health professionals such as John Beahrs, Ernest Hilgard, John and Helen Watkins, and many others.[16] We may call this the *noncommittal CR-principle*. And to state it more carefully, the principle is that *predissociative functional divisions of the self are necessary for the occurrence of post-dissociative functional divisions*.

Some might protest that, because these writers take no stand on the nature of the correlation between pre and postdissociative entities, it's unclear whether they subscribe to a *reversibility* principle at all. Theoretically, at least, they have the option of affirming the existence of predissociative divisions of the self while denying that postdissociative divisions correlate with them in *any* meaningful or interesting way. (Borrowing another bit of terminology from contemporary work in the philosophy of mind, we could call this the *anomalous multiplicity principle*, since the correlations between pre and postdissociative divisions of the self would be nonlawlike.)

I suspect, however, that few (if any) researchers into dissociative identity disorder would be attracted to that rather skeptical position. If they believed that postdissociative divisions afforded *no* clue as to the nature of predissociative divisions—that is, if there were no lawlike connections between the two—then the entire enterprise of examining dissociative phenomena in detail would have had a markedly different and presumably less abstract cast.

Now granted, it may be that in order to φ postdissociatively, one must already have had a predissociative capacity for φing. But if *that's* all that partisans of the noncommittal CR-principle are willing to claim, then the principle is theoretically vacuous. For one thing, it's *trivially* true that for one to have φd, one must already have had a capacity for φing. And for another, dissociative phenomena would then be no more revealing than nondissociative phenomena. After all, in order to manifest *any* trait or ability, the agent must already have had the capacity for it. Furthermore, the noncommittal CR-principle would in that case not support inferences about the development or formation of the predissociative self—for example, about the nature of the elements or processes out of which the self was originally composed. But Binet and most other major figures in the history of the field have considered dissociative phenomena to be of enormous theoretical interest and not merely of relevance (say) to therapy. They believed that dissociation promised great and *distinctive* insights into the structure and function of the mind, insights presumably not forthcoming from the study of nondissociative phenomena. It's extremely unlikely, then, that in articulating the CR-principle, they were asserting no more than anomalous multiplicity.

To put the point somewhat less abstractly, consider why partisans of a Type CR-principle would ever consider the functional type of a dissociative entity or phenomenon to be of theoretical interest. We obviously don't need angry or sexually promiscuous alters (say) to demonstrate that people have a predissociative capacity for anger or sexual promiscuity. So what is theoretically distinctive about the dissociation of anger (or any other trait or ability)? For example, what special sort of fact might advocates of a Type CR-principle hope to learn about the predissociative self from the existence of an angry alter? The answer, presumably, is that an alter of that type would reveal something about how the predissociative self *came to be*—that is, it would tell us something about the self's processes of organization and formation, or about the historically original components of the predissociative self. If that were not the case, dissociated anger would apparently be no more theoretically illuminating, at least as a developmental principle, than any other sort of anger or angry behavior.

More generally, it seems that researchers have expected dissociative phenomena to illuminate the predissociative features of the self that make *those* phenomena possible. They seem to be searching for a certain kind of nontrivial lawlike connection between pre and postdissociative divisions. But that means they have to decide between the Token, Type, or Minimal Type CR-principles, all of which are fatally flawed. Thus, proponents of the noncommittal CR-principle are impaled on the horns of a dilemma. On the one hand, they could decide that there are no—or only trivial—lawlike correlations between pre and postdissociative divisions of the self, in which case they would have to concede that dissociative identity disorder, hypnosis, and other dissociative conditions tell us virtually nothing (or at least nothing distinctive) about the nature or development of the predissociative self. And on the other, they could assert the existence of nontrivial lawlike connections, which would require subscribing to one of the three views I've shown to be defective.

Interestingly, the noncommittal CR-principle is widely used in physics, where it has contributed to the almost comical proliferation of "fundamental" particles. Actually, physicists tend to endorse the Token CR-principle, and its weaknesses undermine the familiar argument that atomic collisions reveal deeper preexisting structures and components of the atom. Of course, many physicists realize that they may be creating, rather than discovering, new particles. I'm merely calling attention to the flawed principle underlying the standard argument in favor of the latter alternative. Even if physicists *are* discovering more fundamental units of matter, they won't establish it by appealing to the Token CR-principle, or even the noncommittal CR-principle. So perhaps now you see more clearly why I call this defective general argument-form the *Humpty Dumpty Fallacy*.

The Significance of Dissociation

A few might still protest that *some* kind of CR-principle is required simply to explain (or at least clarify) the theoretical relevance of dissociative phenomena. After all, they might say, if that principle were false, how could dissociative phenomena ever teach us anything about the self? But it's important to understand that we can abandon the CR-principle and still maintain it's possible to learn something distinctive about the self or the mind from the study of dissociation.

For example, it's clear that we couldn't dissociate at all, or in certain ways, unless we already had a capacity for it. Thus, dissociative phenomena promise to enhance our understanding of the limits and varieties of cognitive functioning. But of course, one couldn't be *nondissociatively* timid, witty, longwinded, or anything else unless one already had the corresponding capacity. So (as we've seen) dissociative phenomena are no more distinctively illuminating in that respect than nondissociative phenomena. Naturally, one would hope to discover a range of unusual or enhanced capacities that occur rarely (if at all) outside of dissociative contexts—for example, hypnotic anesthesia, negative hallucinations, and the astonishing intelligence and literary talents of Patience Worth.[17] Indeed, one might *expect* dissociation to elicit infrequently used or displayed human capacities and yield insights into the conditions conducive to their manifestation. But the discovery of capacities unique to dissociation is of no greater *developmental* significance than the discovery that people are nondissociatively capable of anger, sarcasm, or compassion. In discovering the existence of the capacity, we don't discover anything in particular about its role in the original formation or basic structure of the self. But it's only that latter sort of developmental claim that we reject when we abandon the CR-principle.

To avoid another possible misunderstanding, I should also emphasize that my criticisms of the CR-principle are not arguments against the view that the self has parts. (I've noted, though, that no set of descriptive categories—including psychological predicates—is inherently fundamental, and thus that no parsing of the self into functional units is inherently basic.) Nor are my criticisms arguments against the view that the predissociative self is (in some sense) a colony of lowerorder selves. As I noted briefly at the beginning of this essay, that's a claim I've examined critically elsewhere, and rejected.[18] Granted, the etiological data weighs heavily against the view that the predissociative self consists of multiple self-aware identities (which in *First Person Plural* I've dubbed *apperceptive centers*). From what we know of the life histories of multiples, it appears that new apperceptive centers *develop* in response to contingent events in the subject's life, and that their development and maintenance is a creative, adaptive strategy for handling trauma, one which perhaps only hypnotically endowed individuals are capable of exploiting.[19]

Of course, *how* additional centers of self-awareness develop is still a mystery—perhaps the central mystery of dissociative identity disorder. But *when* they develop seems fairly clear. In any case, my arguments against the CR-principle are rather limited in scope. Their main purpose is to show that the principle fails to *establish* the colonial, or even the nonunitary, view of the pre-dissociative self. The problem with the principle (in all of its versions) is that it infers the existence of predissociative divisions of the self from the existence of postdissociative divisions. But that strategy was doomed from the start. In order to argue successfully for the predissociative complexity of the self, one must show—say, via Freudian or Platonic arguments based on ordinary internal conflicts (for example, simultaneously wanting and not wanting to eat a rich dessert)—that it's required to handle *nondissociative* phenomena.[20] Otherwise, one can always maintain plausibly that alter identities and the like are simply products (rather than prerequisites) of dissociation.

Postscript: Commissurotomy

Certain phenomena associated with brain bisection are nearly as striking as those found in cases of dissociative identity disorder, and they likewise suggest a profound form of mental disunity. Moreover, as in the case of dramatic dissociative phenomena, many researchers interpret the behavior of split-brain patients as demonstrating the existence, *prior to surgery*, of two distinct minds or selves, corresponding in this case to the two hemispheres of the brain. Of course, this position has been extremely influential, especially outside the academic community. Indeed, many seem to regard as dogma the idea that every person is a compound of two subsidiary selves, the left-brain self and the right-brain self. But not surprisingly, it seems as if the inference leading to that conclusion rests on a tacit application of the CR-principle, and if so, it would be no more legitimate than it was in connection with dissociative identity disorder. Therefore, a few remarks about this relatively common use of the CR-principle seem in order.

As readers may realize, the apparently disunified behavior of split-brain patients occurs only under highly artificial or otherwise exceptional conditions. In the majority of everyday situations their behavior seems as unified as that of most ordinary, nondissociated individuals. Nevertheless, on rare occasions in daytoday life, a patient's left and right hands might seem to exhibit distinct and conflicting tendencies (although this generally occurs only in the few months following surgery). For example, the patient might embrace and push away his wife with different hands, or with different hands select different clothes to wear for the day.

However, these spontaneous and quite uncommon displays of disunity are perhaps less impressive than others. In particular, under conditions in which input to the two hemispheres is carefully segregated, subjects will tend to behave in some *predictably* curious ways. For example, suppose that we show subjects two words—say, "house boat," in such a way that the left visual field (going to the right hemisphere) contains only "house" and the right visual field (going to the left hemisphere) contains only "boat." If we ask the subjects what they saw, they'll respond verbally by saying that they saw "boat." Moreover, if we ask the subjects what kind of boat it is, they'll not necessarily say "house boat." Apparently, they're as likely to name some other sort of boat—say, row boat or steam boat. But if we ask subjects to point with the left hand to a picture of what they saw from a display of several pictures (including pictures of a house, boat, and a house boat), they'll probably point to the picture of a house. In general, when the subjects' response is controlled by the left hemisphere, they'll indicate that they were aware of "boat" and not "house." Similarly, responses controlled by the right hemisphere will indicate that they were aware of "house" and not "boat." One can perhaps understand, then, why some conclude that a split-brain patient has two minds, or that the patient is two persons (even if one disagrees with that position).

However, this isn't the place to discuss the topic of commissurotomy in detail. Although that topic is unquestionably very interesting, in order to do it justice we'd have to address complex issues that would carry us far afield. I also can't consider here whether or in what respect we might sensibly regard a human being as more than one person or whether the split-brain patient has two minds (or even just apperceptive centers). Instead, I want merely to examine the claim, made by philosopher Roland Puccetti, that

...even in the normal, cerebrally intact human being there must be two persons, though before the era of commissurotomy experiments we had no way of knowing this.[21]

And even then, I wish only to make a rather limited point—namely, that this inference seems to rest on the fallacious CR-principle.

From our earlier examination of the CR-principle, it should be clear by now that the apparent disunities exhibited by split-brain patients show *at most* that a person *can be made to have* two minds or that a person can be made to be two persons. Puccetti, however, in his influential 1973 paper, seemed quite oblivious to this. He said it's a mystery how brain bisection could *create* two minds when there was only one before. The reason, he claimed, is that we'd then have to choose *which* of the postoperative minds is new. Therefore (he argued), there must have been two minds all along.

But that argument is clearly unconvincing. Assuming it makes sense to attribute two minds to one person, why *not* say that both postoperative minds are new? Analogously, in cell division (or in slicing a flatworm), one gets two new cells (or worms), *neither* of which existed as such before. There's simply no problem of having to decide which of the two worms (or cells) is new. Puccetti quite obviously committed the same error as those who argued from the complexity of the postdissociative self to the complexity of the predissociative self. Indeed, the trauma of surgery is the clear analogue of the trauma leading to the development of alter identities. In order to show that cerebrally intact individuals have two minds, one must argue that two minds are required to explain the apparent disunities of *normal* mental phenomena. Otherwise, it will always be more plausible to maintain that commissurotomy *causes* split-brain patients to have two minds.

In any case, the view that commissurotomy either causes or reveals two minds in patients is not dogma among researchers in that field, however popular (or at least tempting) that view might have been at one time. In fact, I find it somewhat encouraging that this view has been challenged by recent research.[22] So it seems as if the deployment of the CR-principle in that field is far less problematic than it is in the study of dissociation.

12. The Language of Jazz Improvisation

Prelude

Non-musicians are frequently puzzled or amused when they see how members of a jazz group react to one another during a performance. For example, they often find it inscrutable or comical when players laugh, smile knowingly, or nod approvingly at something another has played. Laughter, in fact seems to occasion the most surprise; one non-musician once said to me, "I feel like I'm being left out of a private joke." Of course, jazz players themselves rarely think twice about such matters. From their perspective, these reactions are totally routine. And that's probably because they tacitly (or at least casually) accept a certain view of their musical activity without fully appreciating its scope and implications. According to that view, jazz improvisation in a group setting is similar in many ways to an ordinary conversation, and the individual contributions to that conversation are subject to many of the constraints and criteria of evaluation that apply to everyday verbal exchanges.

Of course, like all analogies, the match between jazz-improvisational interactions and verbal communication is imperfect. But the fit is extensive enough to justify pursuing the matter further. As we'll see, the analogy affords a way of clarifying for non-musicians some otherwise enigmatic behaviors of performing jazz musicians. What many jazz players readily understand in technical musical terms—and what they'd probably explain by appealing to matters of harmony, rhythm, and melody—can be explained easily to laypersons in terms of conversational dynamics. And perhaps most surprising, there's even a connection here to the paranormal topics covered throughout this book.

Development

The analogy between musical and verbal communication operates on a number of different levels. For example, a musician's improvisational and conversational *styles* can be noticeably similar. That is, a soloist's verbal and musical utterances might both be laconic and careful, whereas other soloists might consistently express themselves in a more flashy, prolix, or nervously energetic

273

manner. Similarly, a musician's sense of humor or lightness of spirit (or the relative lack of those qualities) might be apparent in both modes of expression. I think many would agree that, quite apart from purely musical disparities, the styles of trumpeter Dizzy Gillespie and (at least pre-fusion) Miles Davis consistently reflect such differences in their personalities. Along the same lines, many have noted that alto saxophonist Paul Desmond's musical and verbal styles tended to be understated and witty, and that those of pianist Bill Evans were analogously thoughtful and introverted.

Not surprisingly, there's no simple correlation between conversational and improvisational styles, or (for that matter) musical and verbal "eloquence." Whereas some musicians display conspicuous stylistic regularities between the two forms of expression, others do not. In fact, their musical and verbal "selves" might seem to be alter egos. In some cases, social extroverts become musical introverts, their verbal glibness or volubility replaced by a pensive and more deliberate form of musical expressivity. However, it seems that in most cases in which musical and verbal selves differ, musicians who are socially awkward or reserved find their "voice," so to speak, in more dramatic, emotional, and confident forms of musical expression. It seems as if music frees them from the presumably self-imposed constraints that limit or inhibit their verbal behavior, allowing them to display a greatly expanded range of ideas and feelings.

But these sorts of connections between musical and verbal expression exist in many musical forms—not just jazz. Therefore, they don't reveal features of self-expression in jazz that are idiosyncratic to that musical idiom and arguably to some other improvising idioms as well, such as traditional Indian music. More important, however, they're not at the heart of the interactions between performing jazz musicians that laypersons (and perhaps also non-jazz musicians) often find so inscrutable. To understand those interactions, we can note, first, that the change from one soloist to another resembles the thread of a conversation passed from one speaker to another. For example, in some cases a soloist may continue to develop the ideas of the preceding solo, whereas in others the thread of a musical "conversation" may get lost in the transition, and sometimes the new "speaker" (soloist) takes the topic in an unexpected direction. Moreover, as in verbal communication, those changes can spark a variety of reactions from the other soloists, ranging from discomfort and uncertainty to excitement, surprise, laughter, and annoyance.

Of course, sometimes a series of solos (like a conversation) consists of people more or less automatically covering territory they know all too well, or which otherwise holds little interest for them, or to which they're paying little attention. In those cases, and in both musical and verbal dialogues, people can be easily tempted to behave like expressive automata and fall back on stock phrases or remarks, or other personal clichés. For example, in verbal communication, people may rely too easily on their routine—and perhaps context-inappropriate—repertoire of observations, anecdotes, or jokes. Similarly, jazz solos (like verbal statements) may be glib, irrelevant, boring, repetitious, or simply out of place. On the other hand, during jazz improvisations (especially, perhaps, when the musicians are trading fours or eights)[1] some statements seem analogous to wry comments and clever retorts, and the entire dialogue might resemble witty repartee.

In fact, jazz improvisation reveals and duplicates a wide variety of conversational dynamics. Consider, for example, "cutting sessions," contexts in which soloists competitively try to outdo one another in (say) virtuosity or cleverness. These situations often display the sort of competitiveness and one-upmanship that pervades many conversations. And occasionally, something analogous to conversational tensions emerges in soloists' improvisations. Perhaps the most dramatic example of that phenomenon is the musical "argument" between bassist Charles Mingus and multi-reed player Eric Dolphy in their recording of "What Love," on the album *Charles Mingus Presents Charles Mingus*. Here, the musicians' improvisations mimic the sound and inflection of increasingly angry verbal exchanges. And indeed, the musical dialogue seems to have reenacted an earlier argument between the two musicians, in which Dolphy had announced his intention to leave Mingus's group.

A related but subtler phenomenon concerns the level of intimacy or familiarity of the musicians in a group. In conversations, how much of ourselves we reveal to others usually depends on how comfortable we feel. For example, most people will sing, tell certain kinds of jokes, discuss certain subjects, or disclose certain sides of their character (such as their sensuality or emotional vulnerability) only with those in whose company they're sufficiently comfortable and with whom they don't need to fear reproach. For example, in the company of some people I might joke in the manner of a raunchy nightclub comedian, and I might not worry about whether my attempts at humor fall flat. With others, however, I might tailor my humor to their distinctive preferences by joking more in the style of Oscar Wilde. Moreover, with that circle of friends I might be more reluctant to tell a joke I think might fall flat or offend. Something similar occurs within the context of a jazz group. For instance, whether or not a soloist is willing to take chances rather than rely on old "licks" (clichés), or whether or not a soloist is willing to be musically assertive and take the dialogue in new directions (rather than those of the nominal leader of the group) will depend on the sorts of dynamics that undergird ordinary verbal communication. It will be a complex function of how confident the soloist is generally, how well the musicians know one another, and how judgmental or critical the other musicians tend to be.

Group dynamics affect the nature of a jazz improvisational "conversation" in yet another way. In ordinary verbal communication, people with powerful personalities and strong points of view often draw others into their orbit. They raise the overall level of conversation, and sometimes they intentionally or unintentionally impose their assumptions and vocabulary on the other speakers. However, once outside this conversational orbit or atmosphere, the others might drift back to their usual level and style of discourse (although occasionally traces remain of their 'brush with greatness"). The analogue to this phenomenon in jazz concerns the influence of a handful of very powerful musical personalities on the musicians they've hired for their bands. For example, many would argue that most of the musicians who worked for Miles Davis, Charles Mingus, and John Coltrane (and possibly also Thelonious Monk) played the best music of their careers with those leaders, and that when they led their own groups or worked for other—less dynamic, inspiring, or demanding—leaders, the level of their performance declined accordingly.

Other similarities between improvisation and verbal conversation reveal that certain behavioral norms are common to both forms of communication. For one thing, conversations usually occur against a background of unstated assumptions about protocol and etiquette. For example, we usually expect participants in a conversation to listen to each other, and when that doesn't happen, we often express our annoyance. A similar phenomenon occurs (all too frequently) on the bandstand. Moreover, in ordinary conversation, we typically expect participants to make distinctive sorts of contributions and thereby demonstrate the individuality of their "voice." Usually, these participants would do this by saying something the others haven't yet said. But they might instead find an idiosyncratic or alternative way of making a point already made by another speaker—hopefully one whose novelties complement or justify duplicating the content already expressed. Jazz soloists tend to operate under an analogous constraint. They expect each other to make a genuine contribution to the musical dialogue, and success in that endeavor depends in part on the distinctiveness of a solo's substance and style.

Along the same lines, we expect people not to participate in a discussion for which they're unqualified. At the very least, we usually expect people to recognize that some individuals speak with more authority than others, and that in many cases it's proper to defer to them. It appears that a similar assumption underlies the scorn, derision, or condescension shown toward musicians who try to sit in but who can't "cut it." Those players are like people who try to participate in a technical discussion without the requisite background knowledge. Probably every academic discipline has a version of that phenomenon. More than once I've seen presumptuous undergraduates (say, at a conference) try to enter into an intricate discussion among professional philosophers, unaware that they were unprepared for participating at a professional level and that they were in fact both lowering that level and retarding the flow of the conversation.

The fact that some people may be unqualified to participate in a musical or verbal dialogue connects to another similarity between improvisation and conversation. The number of people who want to communicate on a topic and who feel they have something to say probably far exceeds the number the people who actually have something to say, much less something really novel, interesting, or substantive to say. Whether we like it or not, some people have more ideas, or better ideas, than others. My suspicion is that many musicians are reluctant to acknowledge this fact openly (even if they accept it privately). Rather than criticize their peers, they'd prefer to say that different musicians simply exhibit different styles (or dialects), and that we should be reluctant to make normative judgments about such differences. Now to be sure, jazz musicians' stylistic accents and dialects do vary. But so does the quality of their musical thought. That's why listening to a series of solos is usually no more uniformly interesting than listening to a sequence of speakers. And that's why members of a jazz group listening to a solo often exhibit a range of reactions similar to those found among participants in a conversation. They might exhibit surprise, boredom, delight, admiration, impatience, puzzlement, and many other reactions.

Of course, it's not always easy to distinguish the substance of a musical thought from the style in which it's expressed. In fact, in the case of some jazz musicians and classical composers, distinctive stylistic gestures *comprise* (at least a major part of) the substance of the music. Some have made that charge in connection with Debussy and Varèse, and in the jazz world it's been leveled at a broad spectrum of musicians, from avant-garde players such as pianist Sun Ra to neo-conservatives such as trumpeter Wynton Marsalis. Whether or not one agrees with this assessment of particular musicians, most recognize that for some musicians, style is the point of their music and not simply an idiom in which musical ideas are manipulated or developed. Moreover, the parallel here with certain types of verbal communication is striking. The success of a debate team, for example, is usually a triumph of style over substance (if substance matters at all). And the effectiveness of charismatic speakers, or the charm of some celebrities, often depends less on what they say than on how they say it.

In any case, we shouldn't underestimate the importance of stylistic considerations to understanding the conversational dynamics of a musical dialogue between improvising jazz musicians. Jazz players improvise within broad constraints imposed by the jazz idiom generally and also by the more or less specific style they adopt within that idiom. Analogously, our verbal utterances are shaped by general constraints of grammar and vocabulary, and also by more specific sets of constraints provided by shared assumptions, needs, and interests. Failures to communicate verbally often occur because of radical differences in vocabulary or because speakers operate from conflicting sets of assumptions or constraints. We see this, for example, in quarrels between spouses, or between religious or political adversaries, or when one person speaks largely in a vernacular or jargon unknown to another. And apparently, something similar happens when, say, a soloist and rhythm section are stylistically disparate or incompatible—for example, when a pianist or guitar player lays down an inappropriate harmonic or rhythmic foundation behind a soloist.

A clear example of this phenomenon can be found on a recording saxophonist John Coltrane made with pianist Cecil Taylor, called *Coltrane Time*. This recording is one of the more egregious (but interesting) failures in Coltrane's discography. No doubt some would say that the failure reflects the disparity in the quality of the two musicians' ideas or abilities. They'd contend either that Taylor was inept or that he simply had less to say musically than Coltrane. But quite apart from that issue, perhaps the most striking feature of the recording date is the awkward mismatch between the "languages," "dialects," or styles of the two musicians. Although it sounds as if Taylor attempted to modify his playing somewhat to fit Coltrane's solos and the generally boppish nature of the recording date, he nevertheless seemed uncomfortable or unfamiliar with that musical idiom.

So, even if Taylor had the ability to play bebop competently (a matter perhaps worth pursuing on another occasion), or maybe just the ability to transcend his own harmonic and rhythmic gestures for the sake of overall musical coherence, the vestiges of his style clash and interfere with the efforts of his partners. The failure to communicate here resembles difficulties encountered by speakers of dramatically different regional dialects or local idioms or slang, or (perhaps more appropriately) between speakers of widely divergent political, religious, or other theoretical persuasions. In fact, many academic disciplines offer similar opportunities for awkward communication or outright miscommunication. The musical dialogue between Coltrane and Taylor was perhaps as inevitably unsuccessful as a conversation between a Freudian and behaviorist, or analytic and continental philosopher, or communist and capitalist.

The flip side of this phenomenon, of course, occurs when musicians share a musical vocabulary or dialect. In verbal communication, speakers sometimes find conversation unusually easy or natural, even from the beginning, because of pervasive similarities in their assumptions, interests, goals, and style of talking. In the same way, apparently, certain combinations of musicians have been uncommonly successful. In fact, in some of these cases, it almost seems as if the different members of the group are all parts of the same musical "voice." Many would argue that Coltrane enjoyed this sort of relationship with pianist McCoy Tyner and drummer Elvin Jones, as did saxophonist Gerry Mulligan and trumpeter Chet Baker, or saxophonist Stan Getz and trombonist Bob Brookmeyer, or pianist Thelonious Monk and saxophonist Charlie Rouse, and that Miles's quintet with saxophonist Wayne Shorter, pianist Herbie Hancock, bassist Ron Carter and drummer Tony Williams displayed a similar singularity of purpose and unity of expression.

However, I should add that when stylistic disparities occur, they don't always frustrate musical interaction as they did in the case of Coltrane and Cecil Taylor. They might even elicit gratifyingly distinctive and novel sorts of responses from other musicians. Monk once recorded some tunes with clarinetist Pee Wee Russell that demonstrate this possibility. Another example would be saxophonist Ben Webster's contributions to saxophonist Oliver Nelson's *More Blues and the Abstract Truth*. It's easy to find conversational analogues to these successes. For example, clinical and experimental psychologists often engage in fruitful professional discussions, as do philosophers of different specialties, or philosophers and scientists, or (for that matter) theoretical physicists and truck drivers.

In certain respects, the stylistic conflicts and compatibilities considered here play a role in a rather different sort of musical phenomenon, one that also has a counterpart in verbal communication. Sometimes, the success or failure of a conversation has to do with how familiar the speakers are with each other's histories, personalities, and interests. Such knowledge about one's conversational partners helps a speaker to know what kinds of references, allusions, jokes, or choice of vocabulary will be appropriate or effective. Like the broader sets of similarities between speakers noted earlier (e.g., speaking the same language and regional dialect, and sharing numerous underlying general assumptions), these relatively fine-grained variations between speakers might also be considered differences in their styles or conversational "dialects." But because they tend to exhibit numerous personality-specific features, it might be more instructive to think of them as analogous to character traits.

For example, some speakers won't understand or appreciate conversational references to art history (or simply French Impressionism), or television shows from the 1950s, just as some people will be singularly amused (or offended) by scatological or ethnic humor. Similarly, speakers sometimes differ primarily with respect to syntactical idiosyncrasies or "verbal rhythm." That is, some might speak at great length, in long sentences, and in convoluted phrases, whereas, others might adopt a simpler syntactical style and confine themselves to brief comments rather than oratory. Knowledge of these sorts of idiosyncrasies helps one to anticipate when a speaker will pause, or know when a speaker has completed a thought. So it enables one to know when to begin speaking and how to interject comments without interrupting.

In jazz, familiarity with a soloist's syntactical idiosyncrasies helps a pianist or guitarist know when to place a chord behind a solo, and familiarity with subtleties of musical vocabulary helps in the selection of particular voicings. Moreover, knowledge of a soloist's history, interests, sense of humor, etc., helps others in the group to collaborate successfully. For example, just as speakers who know each other well often volunteer the same or similar joke or comment at the same time, jazz musicians might also spontaneously make a similar musical joke, play a similar phrase, or complete another's thought.

The disanalogies between verbal and jazz-improvisational dialogue also merit some comment. Perhaps most notably, in a typical jazz performance, the soloist doesn't function as independently as a speaker in a conversation. The latter is relatively autonomous and may hold the floor while the others simply listen. Of course, that can also happen in a jazz performance. But usually a soloist is constantly interacting with others in the group, at least (in a conventional jazz setting) with members of the rhythm section. For example, the piano, bass, or guitar feed chord changes and also provide rhythmic support to the soloist. And assuming those musicians are listening to the soloist, how they fulfill these tasks will depend on what the soloist has just played or suggested would be appropriate. So their supporting role is based in part on reactions to the soloist, and (ideally, at least) the soloist will respond to the aptness or stimulation of that support.

You might think, then, that the analogy between verbal and jazz-improvisational dialogue fails here, not only because soloists are seldom as autonomous as participants in a conversation, but also because unlike soloist and supporting rhythm section, participants in a conversation seldom talk at the same time. However, I suspect the analogy may hold after all, at the very least for situations in which soloist and rhythm section have a relatively egalitarian relationship, and where members of the rhythm section don't simply supply a rhythmic or harmonic foundation for the soloist. In those cases, their musical interaction resembles a conversation in which people *collaboratively* exchange ideas that both support and overlap the "statements" of the other speakers. For example, some "brainstorming" sessions seem quite similar to the musical dialogues between Bill Evans and bassist Scott La Faro, or the interplay between the members of Mingus's quartet with Eric Dolphy, trumpeter Ted Curson, and drummer Danny Richmond (e.g., "Folk Forms No. 1" on Charles *Mingus Presents Charles Mingus*).

But I think there's even a conversational analogue to the more conventionally supportive role of a player in a rhythm section. Many conversations are indeed one-sided, with a single person doing most of the talking. And in those conversations, others often do little more than interject appropriate expressions of understanding or support, or questions that provide a basis for additional comments by the dominant speaker. The secondary conversational role here is to provide a nurturing and stimulating background for the central speaker.

Scherzo from the Far Side

Something else of interest and relevance occasionally happens on the bandstand—something linking jazz improvisation to the more exotic topics tackled in the rest of this book. Often enough to be really interesting, jazz players will suddenly and simultaneously hit upon the same unusual or unexpected musical idea. For instance, a horn player might suddenly depart radically from the expected chord changes at the same time the pianist makes the same (or at least an equally radical and complementary) harmonic detour. Or, when two soloists are improvising together, they might play the same dramatic or surprising phrase.

Now of course, some might say this is merely a reflection of the familiarity between particular musicians, or at least a predictable and mundane consequence of sharing a common musical idiom. So perhaps many (or most) of these happy correspondences are the kinds of random "hits" that are bound to occur no matter what. After all, the musicians usually *do* share a common musical idiom, and there are only so many notes available (or appropriate) to play. But especially when the common phrases or harmonic detours are unprecedented or at least very unusual—not the sort of thing the players have done before (or regularly)—the players themselves may feel as if they had experienced something *telepathic*. For example, when two horn players are soloing together, they might simultaneously take a dramatic and unprecedented pause in playing, creating a rhythmic "hiccup" at a point in the tune where they'd never done that before. Or two or more members of the group might simultaneously decide to play a tune's bridge very softly, even though that had never happened in the many times they'd played the tune before.

Along the same lines, sometimes two soloists improvise simultaneously, hoping to produce a musically satisfying duet. Famous examples of such efforts would be the many recorded joint improvisations of Paul Desmond with Gerry Mulligan, Chet Baker with Gerry Mulligan, and Stan Getz with Bob Brookmeyer. A lot can go wrong during these duo improvisations because the individual solo lines can easily clash if the two players don't listen carefully to each other. But sometimes a duet of this sort works splendidly, and for more than just a few bars, with the individual lines complementing each other remarkably well, both melodically and harmonically. Many listeners feel that Desmond and Mulligan's aptly titled album *Two of a Mind* contains quite a few of these delightful moments. Once again, it's probable that most of them can be attributed to the musician's shared idiom and familiarity with each other's stylistic idiosyncrasies. But there's still a small residue of times when something—seemingly spookier or magical—happens, and the two solo lines weave together in a spectacularly successful way. Here, too, the players might feel that they were peculiarly *connected* to each other.

I've experienced some of these moments. And because they've occurred most frequently with musicians with whom I've worked closely for a while, I understand the temptation to regard the moments as quite ordinary and what we'd expect—merely inevitable expressions of sharing a common idiom and knowing each other's musical habits. But again, and especially in those cases where the correspondences are between musical gestures that *aren't* habitual—and indeed, when they're very unusual—I also understand why some might be drawn to parapsychological conjectures. The same is true for occasions when a successful duo improvisation seems inspired or "in the zone" for an extended period, almost as if the two complementary solo lines were composed ahead of time. These surprising musical experiences make it easy to understand why some consider *rapport* between agent and percipient to be particularly conducive to telepathic interaction, even if it's not a necessary condition for telepathy to occur.

But although it's easy enough to see why some make that inferential leap, the relationship between telepathy and rapport is actually far from clear. In fact, the importance or irrelevance of pre-existing rapport for psychic connectivity has been debated since the early days (in the late nineteenth century) of the Society for Psychical Research. Granted, there seems to be plenty of anecdotal evidence suggesting that rapport (or at least familiarity or comfort) is psi-conducive or psi-favorable. But there are also intriguing cases where it seems clear that strangers have connected telepathically—for example, apparition cases in which it may even have been in the agent's interest for the apparition to occur to a stranger.[2] Those cases remind us that we actually have no idea how much telepathic or other psychic interaction occurs between strangers, or simply between people who are unlikely to have a conversation intimate enough for the relevant correspondences to emerge.

At any rate, whether the musical incidents we're considering are really telepathic and as magical as they might feel to the players themselves (and maybe also to their colleagues on the bandstand), the relevant point for this essay is that even here, there's an analogue to ordinary conversational dynamics. As I noted earlier, we've all had experiences in which conversation flows unusually easily, either momentarily or for longer stretches, with participants thinking along the same lines. And I imagine that many of us—probably less frequently—have had the experience of simultaneously hitting upon the same conversational detour as another participant in the conversation—for example, a surprising or superficially incongruous change of subject, or the same, uncharacteristic and unexpected comment or reaction. These happy "hits" can feel as spooky and special to the conversationalists as their musical counterparts feel to musicians, and they can occasion the same kinds of reactions among those involved. Moreover, the phenomenon of an unusually successful joint improvisation likewise has a conversational analogue. It resembles a rapid-fire brainstorming session in which participants exchange and expand upon each other's ideas. And sometimes during particularly fruitful and smooth brainstorming the conversationalists might feel as though their time "in the zone" was a brush with the paranormal. So even in these ostensibly telepathic moments we see another way in which conversational dynamics parallels and illuminates the dynamics of jazz-improvisation.

Coda

So what should one say to the layperson who's mystified by the way jazz musicians react to each other on the stand? At least one can note that the musicians are engaged in something very much like an ordinary verbal conversation. We've probably all had the experience of overhearing a conversation between people speaking a language we don't know. We may not understand what they're saying, but their reactions are often quite clear and familiar. Moreover, in some cases the reactions afford clues to the content of the remarks. Similarly, listeners who don't understand the language of jazz may nevertheless grasp the reactions of the musicians on the stand. And those gestures of approval, indifference, perplexity, and so on, might likewise provide some insight into the substance of the musical utterances. In that respect, appreciating the social components of the language of jazz may enhance the non-musician's understanding of jazz itself.

Endnotes & References

1. THE FEAR OF PSI

Endnotes

1   As it happens, that freedom isn't all it's cracked up to be. For readers interested in some of the sordid details, I recommend the Preface to Braude, 2007.

2   See, e.g., Braude, 1997, 2003, 2007; Eisenbud, 1970, 1982, 1992; also Tart, 1986; Tart & Labore, 1986, for a somewhat different but complementary view of the matter.

3   Eisenbud, 1992.

4   Eisenbud, 1992, p. 153.

5   Janet, 1885, 1886; Myers, 1903; Richet, 1885, 1888; Vasiliev, 1976.

6   For more on this topic see Chapter 9, and Eisenbud, 1992.

7   For a more complete discussion, see Braude, 1997, 2007.

8   Braude, 1997, 2007; Crookes, 1874; Medhurst, Goldney, & Barrington, 1972.

9   Lamont, 2005.

10   Braude, 1997, 2007.

11   Honorton, 1974; Keil, Hermelin, Ullman, & Pratt, 1976; Pilkington, 2015; Ullman, 1974; Watkins & Watkins, 1974.

12   Brandon, 1983; Hall, 1984. For a good criticism of Brandon, see Inglis, 1983.

References

Brandon, R. (1983). *The Spiritualists*. New York: Alfred A. Knopf.

Braude, S.E. (1997). *The Limits of Influence: Psychokinesis and the Philosophy of Science, Revised Edition*. Lanham, MD: University Press of America.

Braude, S.E. (2003). *Immortal Remains: The Evidence for Life after Death*. Lanham, MD: Rowman & Littlefield.

Braude, S.E. (2007). *The Gold Leaf Lady and Other Parapsychological Investigations*. Chicago: University of Chicago Press.

Crookes, W. (1874). *Researches in the Phenomena of Spiritualism*. London: J. Burns.

Eisenbud, J. (1970). *Psi and Psychoanalysis*. New York: Grune & Stratton.

Eisenbud, J. (1982). *Paranormal Foreknowledge: Problems and Perplexities.* New York: Human Sciences Press.

Eisenbud, J. (1992). *Parapsychology and the Unconscious.* Berkeley, California: North Atlantic Books.

Hall, T.H. (1984). *The Enigma of Daniel Home.* Buffalo: Prometheus.

Honorton, C. (1974). "Apparent Psychokinesis on Static Objects by a 'Gifted' Subject." In W.G. Roll, R.L. Morris & J.D. Morris (Eds.), *Research in Parapsychology 1973* (pp. 128-131). Metuchen, NJ: Scarecrow Press.

Inglis, B. (1983). "Review of R. Brandon, *The Spiritualists." Journal of the Society for Psychical Research,* 52: 209-212.

Janet, P. (1885). "Note sur quelques phenomènes de somnambulisme." *Revue Philosophique de la France et de l'Etrangere,* 21: 190-198. Trans. "Report on Some Phenomena of Somnambulism." *Journal of the History of the Behavioral Sciences* 4(2): 124-131, 1968.

Janet, P. (1886). "Deuxième note sur le sommeil provoqué à distance et la suggestion mentale pendant l'état somnambulique." *Revue Philosophique de la France et de l'Etrangere,* 22: 212-223. Trans. "Second observation on sleep provoked from a distance and mental suggestion during the somnambulistic state." *Journal of the History of the Behavioral Sciences* 4(3): 258-267, 1968.

Keil, H.H.J., Hermelin, B., Ullman, M., et al. (1976). "Directly Observable Voluntary PK Effects: A Survey and Tentative Interpretation of Findings from Nina Kulagina and Other Known Related Cases of Recent Date." *Proceedings of the Society for Psychical Research,* 56: 197-235.

Lamont, P. (2005). *The First Psychic: The Peculiar Mystery of a Notorious Victorian Wizard.* London: Little, Brown.

Medhurst, R.G., Goldney, K.M., & Barrington, M.R. (Eds.). (1972). *Crookes and the Spirit World.* New York: Taplinger.

Myers, F.W.H. (1903). *Human Personality and its Survival of Bodily Death.* London: Longmans, Green, & Co.

Pilkington, R. (2015). "Interview with Felicia Parise, August 6, 2013." *Journal of Scientific Exploration,* 29 (1): 75-108.

Richet, C. (1885). "Un fait de somnabulisme à distance." *Revue Philosophique de la France et de l'Etrangere,* 21: 199-200.

Richet, C. (1888). "Expériences sur le sommeil à distance." *Revue de l'hypnotisme,* 2: 225-240.

Tart, C.T. (1986). "Psychics' Fears of Psychic Powers." *Journal of the American Society for Psychical Research,* 80: 279–292.

Tart, C.T., & Labore, C.M. (1986). "Attitudes Toward Strongly Functioning Psi: A Preliminary Survey." *Journal of the American Society for Psychical Research,* 80: 163–173.

Ullman, M. (1974). "PK in the Soviet Union." In W.G. Roll, R.L. Morris & J.D. Morris (Eds.), *Research in Parapsychology 1973* (pp. 121-125). Metuchen, NJ: Scarecrow Press.

Vasiliev, L.L. (1976). *Experiments in Distant Influence*. New York: Dutton. (Reprinted as *Experiments in Mental Suggestion* (2002), Charlottesville: Hampton Roads.)

Watkins, G., & Watkins, A. (1974). "Apparent Psychokinesis on Static Objects by a 'Gifted Subject': A Laboratory Demonstration." In W.G. Roll, R.L. Morris & J.D. Morris (Eds.), *Research in Parapsychology 1973* (pp. 132-134). Metuchen, NJ: Scarecrow Press.

2. INVESTIGATIONS OF THE FELIX EXPERIMENTAL GROUP

Endnotes

1   Barham, 1988; Batcheldor, 1984; Isaacs, 1984.

2   By this time, relations had soured between Kai and Peter Mulacz. Kai was upset over Peter's failure to adhere to some of his specified séance conditions. However, I believe that only some of those failures were intentional. But in any case, Peter and Kai were clearly incompatible personalities, and so Peter rather quickly became persona non grata.

3   Braude, 2003.

4   Braude, 1997.

5   In a private meeting with noted magician Jeff McBride, Jeff claimed that table levitations can be simulated with a four-legged table by using only two thumbs. Jeff tried demonstrating this to me with one of his own tables. He was indeed able to raise that table, but its movement was not nearly as smooth or level as those I've experienced with the FEG. Now admittedly this was a different and heavier table, and Jeff claimed that one only needed more practice to simulate smoother levitations. However, although I have great admiration for Jeff's expertise and knowledge of mediumistic tricks, I think one needs to take this assurance with a grain of salt. Although Jeff is not biased against the possibility of psi phenomena generally, he's clearly and antecedently convinced that all *mediumistic* phenomena are fraudulent (he does apparently accept the reality of PK in what he deems to be less suspicious contexts). So it's difficult to say to what extent Jeff's confidence on this matter resembles the empty assurances concerning mediumistic fraud often expressed by magicians. It remains true that I and others have been unable to raise Kai's table (or that in the Austrian sessions described below) using only our thumbs, and in any case I doubt that this explanation would suffice for the many accounts (from other FEG séances) of the table rising to the ceiling and remaining there for several seconds. That explanation also fails for the infrared-documented levitation described below, occurring in our last séance, where Kai waved one of his hands above the table as it rose, imitating one of Palladino's familiar gestures.

6   For more details on the arrangement of the room during an FEG cabinet séance, see Nahm, 2014.

7   See Nahm, 2014 for a detailed description of the Hanau cellar séance room.

8   See, e.g., Bottazzi's descriptions in his studies of Palladino--Bottazzi, 1907, 2011; Giuditta, 2010.

9   See Braude, 1997, p. 65; Podmore, 1902, 1910/1975.

10   Nahm, 2014

11   Lodge, 1894.

12   See Nahm, 2014, which accompanied the present report in the *Journal of Scientific Exploration*, and which offers a valuable second perspective as well as additional details.

13   Braude, 2007.

14   The video of this and the extruding ectoplasm will be unavailable for public viewing until the release of Robert's documentary, "Finding PK." However, frames from the video may be viewed on the SSE website, in my 2013 SSE conference presentation.

15   Michael also installed the temperature gauge in the vicinity of Kai during two of the table sittings. There, too, no temperature shift was recorded.

16   Dingwall, 1924, p. 332, italics added.

17   The outward flapping of the cabinet curtain has been a frequently-reported feature of carefully investigated spiritist séances—for example, in the Palladino case. See, e.g., Bottazzi, 1907, 2011; Giuditta, 2010, and Feilding, 1963. But in the Palladino case, the medium sat outside the curtain when this occurred.

18   I'm grateful to Jeff McBride for pointing this out to me. But I should note that dhauti practitioners are warned against using synthetic material for this procedure, and arguably anything that looks like the material Kai displays as ectoplasm. A quick web search on dhauti will show clear images of the kind of material recommended for the cleansing. Practitioners are also warned against swallowing large quantities of liquid during this procedure, which of course Kai did when he polished off his bottle of ice tea before the séance. Moreover, dhauti practitioners are instructed to leave the material in their stomach for from five to no more than twenty minutes, a much smaller interval than the time that elapsed between my strip search of Kai and the actual production of ectoplasm.

19   For more on Kluski, see Geley, 1927/1975; Richet, 1923/1975; Barrington, 1994a, 1994b; Weaver, 1992.

20   At the risk of becoming obnoxiously graphic, I should also add that even if Kai had placed the material in a condom or plastic bag which he hid in his rectum, he would still have had to remove it and its contents without transferring some odor to his hands, clothes, or a paper towel. But neither Jochen nor I detected an odor when the medium's hands were brought within an inch or two of our faces, and I detected no odor from anything in the cabinet immediately after the séance ended.

21   Feilding, 1963; Feilding, Baggally, & Carrington, 1909; Braude, 1997, 2007.

22   The resolute skeptic can always claim that shining the flashlight into Kai's mouth was simply misdirection.

23   Cleverly and ironically, Jeff produced an apport of fool's gold.

24   I should note that this paper "ectoplasm" looked nothing like what emerges from Kai's mouth. The paper emerged from Jeff as a bunch of thin streamers, all of which had many small accordion-like folds, indicating that they'd previously been tightly compressed into those folds.

25   Personal communication, November 21, 2013.

26   In a subsequent email exchange with me, Kai defended this falsehood on the grounds that it would only have further fueled Nahm's suspicion to have admitted to purchasing the cobweb. However, it seems to me that the best—and obvious—way to have countered Michael's suspicion would have been to speak openly and honestly when the opportunity arose.

27   Personal communication, April 12, 2014.

28   Kai has recently told me that he does in fact have uneventful séances, witnessed by many people. Lucius Werthmüller, President of the Basel Psi Association, confirms this to some extent. Werthmüller has attended more than 50 FEG séances and reports that, although he never experienced a completely blank sitting, he's seen a great difference in the strength of séances from one occasion to another—greater, in fact, than he's experienced with other mediums. Of course, that doesn't exactly neutralize the skeptical concern about Kai's mediumistic consistency. It could be explained not only in terms of variations in Kai's mediumistic powers, but also variations in opportunities for successfully executing a trick.

29   However, one intriguing incident deserves mention. The first time Kai and Jochen met Lucius Werthmüller, during dinner Lucius mentioned his close relationship to the discoverer of LSD, Albert Hofmann. Two hours later, in a séance, a wax ball appeared containing inside a message on a piece of paper, ostensibly from Hofmann, and apparently in Hofmann's handwriting. That indeed seems impressive, except for the fact that Werthmüller's association with Hofmann is very well known (in fact Werthmüller wrote an award-winning book about Hofmann). So although Kai considers this incident one of the major successes of the FEG, some might suggest that Kai didn't first learn about the Werthmüller/Hofmann connection only two hours before the séance and that he had both time and information to prepare an astonishing apport. On the other hand, Werthmüller reports:

> Before his death Albert Hofmann promised me to give me a message from the other side. I know for sure that I had not told that to Kai before. Regarding the handwriting his two living children (in their seventies now) spontaneously said "this is the handwriting of our daddy." Also regarding the wording of the apport I can assure you that every word has a meaning for me of which Kai could not know." (Personal communication April 30, 2014)

One particularly puzzling feature of this incident is how the apport got into Werthmüller's hand. Kai claims that the apported wax ball appeared inside his closed hand. Perhaps it did. But Werthmüller's account is unclear on the matter. On his website in 2009 he wrote,

> We all had put our hands again on the table when we heard a noise and I felt an object that touched my hand and then fell on the floor. We turned on the lights and Ines, my young neighbor-sitter said that she had felt the object on her thigh. She was convinced that it had fallen on the floor and began to search for it. It took a few long seconds until I realized that it was in my hand, I then remembered a touch at the side of my hand and that I had just closed it around the object. (Translated by Lucius Werthmüller, personal communication April 30, 2014)

Moreover, Jochen, who attended that séance, confirms that all present heard the dropping of the apport, and that it landed on the leg of Lucius's neighbor at the table before falling to the floor. He then writes, "While Lucius also started immediately to search for it, he noticed it in his hand, though he wasn't aware how it came into it." (Personal communication, April 29, 2014).

30   Braude, 2007; Eisenbud, 1967, 1989.

31   Irwin, 1987.

32   For a good example of that phenomenon, see Richet, 1899, p. 157.

33   See, e.g., Barham, 1988; Batcheldor, 1966, 1984; Brookes-Smith, 1973; Brookes-Smith & Hunt, 1970; Isaacs, 1984.

34   Feilding, 1963, p. 107; Feilding et al., 1909, p. 397.

35   Lodge, 1894, p. 324.

36   E.g., Braude, 1997, 2014.

References

Barham, A. (1988). "The Crawford Legacy Part II: Recent Research in Macro-PK with Special Reference to the Work of Batcheldor and Brookes-Smith." *Journal of the Society for Psychical Research,* 55 (813): 196-207.

Barrington, M.R. (1994a). "Kluski and Geley: Further Case for the Defence." *Journal of the Society for Psychical Research,* 60: 104–106.

Barrington, M.R. (1994b). "The Kluski Hands." *Journal of the Society for Psychical Research,* 59: 347–351.

Batcheldor, K.J. (1966). "Report on a Case of Table Levitation and Associated Phenomena." *Journal of the Society for Psychical Research,* 43: 339-356.

Batcheldor, K.J. (1984). "Contributions to the Theory of PK Induction from Sitter-Group Work." *Journal of the American Society for Psychical Research,* 78: 105–122.

Bottazzi, F. (1907). "The Unexplored Regions of Human Biology: Observations and Experiments with Eusapia Paladino." *Annals of Psychic Science,* 6: 149-156, 260-290, 377-422.

Bottazzi, F. (2011). *Mediumistic Phenomena Observed in a Series of Sessions with Eusapia Palladino* (I. Routti & A. Giuditta, Trans.). Princeton: ICRL Press.

Braude, S.E. (1997). *The Limits of Influence: Psychokinesis and the Philosophy of Science, Revised Edition.* Lanham, MD: University Press of America.

Braude, S.E. (2003). *Immortal Remains: The Evidence for Life after Death.* Lanham, MD: Rowman & Littlefield.

Braude, S.E. (2007). *The Gold Leaf Lady and Other Parapsychological Investigations.* Chicago: University of Chicago Press.

Braude, S.E. (2014). *Crimes of Reason: On Mind, Nature & the Paranormal.* Lanham, MD: Rowman & Littlefield.

Brookes-Smith, C. (1973). "Data Tape Recorded Experimental PK Phenomena." *Journal of the Society for Psychical Research,* 47: 69-89.

Brookes-Smith, C., & Hunt, D.W. (1970). "Some Experiments in Psychokinesis." *Journal of the Society for Psychical Research,* 45: 265-281.

Dingwall, E.J. (1924). "Telekinetic and Teleplastic Mediumship." *Proceedings of the Society for Psychical Research,* 34 (Part 92): 324-332.

Eisenbud, J. (1967). *The World of Ted Serios.* New York: William Morrow & Co.

Eisenbud, J. (1989). *The World of Ted Serios (2nd edition).* Jefferson, NC: McFarland & Co.

Feilding, E. (1963). *Sittings with Eusapia Palladino and Other Studies.* New Hyde Park, NY: University Books.

Feilding, E., Baggally, W.W., & Carrington, H. (1909). "Report on a Series of Sittings with Eusapia Palladino." *Proceedings of the Society for Psychical Research,* 23: 309-569. Reprinted in Feilding, 1963.

Geley, G. (1927/1975). *Clairvoyance and Materialization: A Record of Experiments* (S. De Brath, Trans.). London: T. Fisher Unwin. (Reprinted: New York: Arno Press).

Giuditta, A. (2010). "The 1907 Psychokinetic Experiments of Professor Filippo Bottazzi." *Journal of Scientific Exploration,* 24 (3): 495-507.

Irwin, H.J. (1987). "Charles Bailey: A Biographical Study of the Australian Apport Medium." *Journal of the Society for Psychical Research,* 54 (807): 97-118.

Isaacs, J. (1984). "The Batcheldor Approach: Some Strengths and Weaknesses." *Journal of the American Society for Psychical Research,* 78: 123–132.

Lodge, O. (1894). "Experience of Unusual Physical Phenomena Occurring in the Presence of an Entranced Person (Eusapia Paladino), with discussion." *Journal of the Society for Psychical Research,* 6: 306-360.

Nahm, M. (2014). "The Development and Phenomena of a Circle for Physical Mediumship." *Journal of Scientific Exploration,* 28 (2): 229–283.

Podmore, F. (1902). *Mediums of the Nineteenth Century, 2 vols.* New Hyde Park, NY: University Books. (Reprint of *Modern Spiritualism,* 1902)

Podmore, F. (1910/1975). *The Newer Spiritualism.* New York: Arno Press.

Richet, C. (1899). "On the Conditions of Certainty." *Proceedings of the Society for Psychical Research,* 6: 66-83.

Richet, C. (1923/1975). *Thirty Years of Psychical Research.* New York: Macmillan/Arno Press.

Weaver, Z. (1992). "The Enigma of Franek Kluski." *Journal of the Society for Psychical Research,* 58 (828): 289-301.

3. A FOLLOW-UP INVESTIGATION OF THE FELIX CIRCLE

Endnotes

1   And published originally as Braude, 2014.

2   Braude, 2014; Nahm, 2014.

3   However, after the revelations of Kai's clear cheating, Nahm came to feel nearly all Kai's phenomena had been faked.

4   For more on Nahm's change of attitude, see Nahm, 2016.

5   Mulacz, 2015; Nahm, 2015.

6   Kean, 2010, 2017.

7   Nahm, 2016.

8   Of course, I can't say that Julia had no access to an LED device. But I make no claims for the authenticity of this or any of the other observed lights. I merely note that they were observed, and neither Kai nor Julia seemed particularly concerned about them either. They certainly made no effort to call our attention to them. I can add that throughout the series of séances, Julia's behavior seemed exemplary, especially during the last two sittings where her neighbors remained in bodily contact with her while phenomena occurred.

9   And even admitted it in Mulacz, 2015.

10   Batcheldor, 1984; Isaacs, 1984.

11   See Braude, 2007, chapter 7.

12   Colvin, 2010.

13   See, e.g., my editorials in Volumes 23:3 and 27:2 of the *Journal of Scientific Exploration*.

14   Mulacz, 2015. See my letter in *Paranormal Review* 75 (Summer, 2015), p. 36.

15   This research was supported by a generous grant from the Parapsychological Association's Gilbert Roller fund. I'm grateful also to Robert Narholz, Leslie Kean, Loyd Auerbach, and Michael Nahm for helpful comments on ancestors of this report.

References

Batcheldor, K.J. (1984). "Contributions to the Theory of PK Induction from Sitter-Group Work." *Journal of the American Society for Psychical Research*, 78: 105–122.

Braude, S.E. (2007). *The Gold Leaf Lady and Other Parapsychological Investigations*. Chicago: University of Chicago Press.

Braude, S.E. (2014). "Investigations of the Felix Experimental Group: 2010-2013." *Journal of Scientific Exploration*, 28 (2): 285–343.

Colvin, B.G. (2010). "The Acoustic Properties of Unexplained Rapping Sounds." *Journal of the Society for Psychical Research*, 73 (2): 65-93.

Isaacs, J. (1984). "The Batcheldor Approach: Some Strengths and Weaknesses." *Journal of the American Society for Psychical Research*, 78: 123–132.

Kean, L. (2010). *UFOs: Generals, Pilots, and Government Officials Go On the Record*. New York: Three Rivers Press.

Kean, L. (2017). *Surviving Death: A Journalist Investigates Evidence for an Afterlife*. New York: Crown Archetype.

Mulacz, P. (2015). "Fall of the House of Felix?". *Paranormal Review*, 74 (Spring): 16-22.

Nahm, M. (2014). "The Development and Phenomena of a Circle for Physical Mediumship." *Journal of Scientific Exploration,* 28 (2): 229–283.

Nahm, M. (2015). "Promissory Mediumship." *Paranormal Review,* 74 (Spring): 15.

Nahm, M. (2016). "Further Comments about Kai Mügge's Alleged Mediumship and Recent Developments." *Journal of Scientific Exploration,* 30 (1): 56-62.

4. THE MEDIUMSHIP OF CARLOS MIRABELLI

Endnotes

1   Mirabelli changed his name when he was young, concerned over the similarity between his name and the woman's name Carmen.

2   Dingwall, 1930, p. 296.

3   Playfair, 2011, p. 23.

4   For example, the dog whose photo appears in the paper by Medeiros, 1935.

5   Inglis, 1984, pp. 221ff.

6   Braude, 1997; Dingwall, 1962; Inglis, 1977.

7   Playfair, 1992, 2011.

8   Moreover, because most of the primary material in this case is written in Portuguese, which I do not know (but for which online translation programs provided some help), this report inevitably focuses on the accounts written in English.

9   Playfair, 2011, p. 25.

10   Inglis, 1984, p. 222; Playfair, 2011, p. 25.

11   Dingwall, 1930, p. 297.

12   Besterman, 1935.

13   Ibid, p. 298.

14   Besterman, 1935.

15   Dingwall, 1930, p. 298, emphasis in original.

16   Playfair, 2011, p. 31.

17   Dingwall, 1930, p. 298.

18   Dingwall, 1930, p. 304.

19   Playfair, 2011, pp. 32-33.

20   Dingwall, 1930, p. 304.

21   Inglis, 1984, p. 224.

22   Dingwall, 1930, p. 299. See Fig. 1 for a photo of a materialized poet.

23   Dingwall, 1961, p. 81.

24   Inglis, 1984, p. 226.

25 Mentioned several times in de Goes, 1937, and also in Dingwall, 1930, Inglis, 1984 and Playfair, 2011.

26 Imbassahy, 1935.

27 Playfair, 2011, p. 47.

28 Quoted in Playfair, 2011, p. 47, from Imbassahy, 1935.

29 Playfair, 2011, p. 47.

30 Quoted in and translated by Playfair, 2011, p. 47.

31 Playfair, 2011, p. 33.

32 Ibid., p. 34.

33 Ibid.

34 Ibid, pp. 34-35.

35 Dingwall, 1930, p. 298.

36 Driesch, 1930.

37 Ibid, p. 486.

38 Ibid, p. 487.

39 Ibid.

40 Ibid.

41 Ibid.

42 Walker, 1934.

43 Walker, 1934, pp. 75-76.

44 Ibid, p. 76.

45 Ibid.

46 Ibid, p. 77.

47 Ibid, p. 78.

48 Besterman, 1932b.

49 Besterman, 1932a.

50 Besterman, 1930.

51 Playfair, 2011, p. 24.

52 Ibid, p. 27.

53 Ibid.

54 Besterman, 1935, p. 144.

55 Ibid, p, 145.

56 Besterman, 1935, p. 147.

57   Ibid.

58   Ibid, p. 148.

59   Dingwall, 1936.

60   Ibid, p. 169.

61   Ibid, pp. 169-70.

62   Besterman, 1936, p. 236.

63   Playfair, 2011.

64   Ibid, p. 44.

65   See, for example, Feilding, 1963; Feilding, Baggally, & Carrington, 1909.

66   See the discussion of Palladino in Braude, 1997.

67   de Goes, 1937, p. 125.

68   Playfair, 2011, p. 45.

69   de Goes, 1937, p. 105.

70   Playfair, 2011, p. 45.

71   Stein, 1991.

72   Playfair, 1992, 2011.

73   Feilding, 1963; Feilding et al., 1909. This series of sittings was criticized toothlessly—in fact, absurdly—by Richard Wiseman. For an analysis of his critique, see Braude, 1997, Chapter 2.

74   Playfair, 2011, p. 26.

75   Besterman, 1935, p. 142.

76   Ibid, p. 143.

77   Braude, 1997, 2007.

78   Dingwall, 1930, pp. 301-02.

79   See, e.g., Braude, 1997; Inglis, 1977; Weaver, 2015.

80   Richet, 1923/1975, p. 491.

81   I'm very grateful to Carlos Alvarado, Leslie Kean, Michael Nahm, and Guy Playfair for helpful comments on several ancestors of this essay. Any remaining defects are entirely their responsibility.

References

Besterman, T. (1930). "Review of *Mensagens do Além obtidas e controladas pela Academia de Estudios Psychicos "Cesar Lombroso" atravez do celebre Medium Mirabelli.".* *Journal of the Society for Psychical Research*, 26: 142-144.

Besterman, T. (1932a). "The Mediumship of Rudi Schneider." *Proceedings of the Society for Psychical Research*, 40: 428-436.

Besterman, T. (1932b). "The Psychology of Testimony in Relation to Paraphysical Phenomena." *Proceedings of the Society for Psychical Research*, 40: 363-387.

Besterman, T. (1935). "The Mediumship of Carlos Mirabelli." *Journal of the Society for Psychical Research*, 29: 141-153.

Besterman, T. (1936). "Letter to the *Journal.*" *Journal of the Society for Psychical Research*, 29: 235-236.

Braude, S.E. (1997). *The Limits of Influence: Psychokinesis and the Philosophy of Science, Revised Edition*. Lanham, MD: University Press of America.

de Goes, E. (1937). *Prodígios da Biopsychica Obtidos com o Médium Mirabelli*. São Paulo: Typographia Cupolo. (Reprinted: In *Coleção Mirabelli vol. 2*, ed. M. Bellini. São Paulo: Centro Espírita Casa do Caminho Santana, 2016.).

Dingwall, E.J. (1930). "An Amazing Case: The Mediumship of Carlos Mirabelli." *Psychic Research*, 34: 296-306.

Dingwall, E.J. (1936). "Letter to the *Journal.*" *Journal of the Society for Psychical Research*, 29: 169-170.

Dingwall, E.J. (1961). "Review of H. Gerloff, *Das Medium Carlos Mirabelli: Eine Kritische Untersuchung.*" *Journal of the Society for Psychical Research*, 41 (708): 80-82.

Dingwall, E.J. (1962). *Very Peculiar People*. New Hyde Park, NY: University Books.

Driesch, H. (1930). "The Mediumship of Mirabelli." *Journal of the American Society for Psychical Research*, 24: 486-487.

Feilding, E. (1963). *Sittings with Eusapia Palladino and Other Studies*. New Hyde Park, NY: University Books.

Feilding, E., Baggally, W.W., & Carrington, H. (1909). "Report on a Series of Sittings with Eusapia Palladino." *Proceedings of the Society for Psychical Research*, 23: 309-569.

Imbassahy, C. (1935). *O Espiritismo à Luz dos Fatos*. Rio de Janeiro: FEB.

Inglis, B. (1977). *Natural and Supernatural*. London: Hodder & Stoughton.

Inglis, B. (1984). *Science and Parascience: A History of the Paranormal 1914-1939*. London: Hodder & Stoughton.

Medeiros, T.d.A. (1935). "The Mediumship of Carlos Mirabelli." *Journal of the American Society for Psychical Research*, 29: 15-18.

Playfair, G.L. (1992). "Mirabelli and the Phantom Ladder." *Journal of the Society for Psychical Research*, 58: 201-203.

Playfair, G.L. (2011). *The Flying Cow*. Guildford: White Crow Books.

Richet, C. (1923/1975). *Thirty Years of Psychical Research*. New York: Macmillan/Arno Press.

Stein, G. (1991). "The Amazing Medium Mirabelli." *FATE Magazine*, 44 (3 (March)): 86-95.

Walker, M.C. (1934). "Psychic Research in Brazil." *Journal of the American Society for Psychical*

Research, 28: 74-78.

Weaver, Z. (2015). *Other Realities? The Enigma of Franek Kluski's Mediumship.* Hove: White Crow Books.

5. A CASE STUDY IN SHODDY SKEPTICISM

Endnotes

1   See Chapter 6 for more on that topic.

2   Randi frequently boasted that he would explain away Home's phenomena as magic tricks. The boast was empty.

3   Hall, 1984.

4   Even as recently as an Amazon review published several weeks prior to the writing of this chapter.

5   Best-known (to me, at any rate) as the inventor of stereo (3D) photography.

6   For details concerning Brewster's behavior, see, e.g., Gordon, 1869; Inglis, 1977; Jenkins, 1982; and Braude, 1997.

7   D. D. Home, 1863/1972, p. 241.

8   A relatively accessible source for the correspondence is Home, 1863/1972, pp. 237-261.

9   Home 1863/1972, p. 247, italics in original.

10   Gordon, 1869, pp. 257-58.

11   See D. D. Home, 1863/1972, pp. 22-23; M. D. D. Home, 1888/1976, pp. 14-15; Braude, 1997, pp. 67-68.

12   This was Home's famous "earthquake effect," in which the séance room and its contents would shake violently, even though things apparently remained calm outside the room.

13   See Besterman, 1932; Hodgson, 1892; Hodgson & Davey, 1887.

14   Readers unfamiliar with the evidence are directed to Medhurst & Goldney, 1964; Medhurst, Goldney, & Barrington, 1972.

15   Perovsky Petrovo Solovovo, 1909.

16   See Braude, 1997, 2007, for extended discussions of the Argument from Human Bias.

17   Zorab, 1971, 1975.

18   Perovsky Petrovo Solovovo, 1912, p. 228.

19   M. D. D. Home, 1888/1976, p. 259.

20   But see the accounts in D. D. Home, 1863/1972; M. D. D. Home, 1888/1976.

21   Jenkins, 1982.

22   Adare, 1871/1976.

23   M. D. D. Home, 1888/1976.

24   Barrett & Myers, 1889, pp. 127-128.

25   Ibid. 129-130.

26   Ibid. 133-134.

References

Adare, V. (1871/1976). *Experiences in Spiritualism with D.D. Home.* New York: Arno Press.

Barrett, W.F., & Myers, F.W.H. (1889). "Review of *D.D. Home, His Life and Mission.*" *Journal of the Society for Psychical Research,* 4: 101-136.

Besterman, T. (1932). "The Psychology of Testimony in Relation to Paraphysical Phenomena." *Proceedings of the Society for Psychical Research,* 40: 363-387.

Braude, S.E. (1997). *The Limits of Influence: Psychokinesis and the Philosophy of Science, Revised Edition.* Lanham, MD: University Press of America.

Braude, S.E. (2007). *The Gold Leaf Lady and Other Parapsychological Investigations.* Chicago: University of Chicago Press.

Gordon, M. (1869). *The Home Life of Sir David Brewster.* Edinburgh: Edmonston & Douglas.

Hall, T.H. (1984). *The Enigma of Daniel Home.* Buffalo: Prometheus.

Hodgson, R. (1892). "Mr. Davey's Imitation by Conjuring of Phenomena Sometimes Attributed to Spirit Agency." *Proceedings of the Society for Psychical Research,* 8: 253-310.

Hodgson, R., & Davey, S.J. (1887). "The Possibilities of Mal-Observation and Lapse of Memory from a Practical Point of View." *Proceedings of the Society for Psychical Research,* 4: 381-495.

Home, D.D. (1863/1972). *Incidents in My Life.* Secaucus, N.J.: University Books.

Home, M.D.D. (1888/1976). *D.D. Home, His Life and Mission.* London: Trübner & Co. (Reprinted: New York: Arno Press). (Reprinted, New York: Arno Press)

Inglis, B. (1977). *Natural and Supernatural.* London: Hodder & Stoughton.

Jenkins, E. (1982). *The Shadow and the Light: A Defence of Daniel Dunglas Home, the Medium.* London: Hamish Hamilton.

Medhurst, R.G., & Goldney, K.M. (1964). "William Crookes and the Physical Phenomena of Mediumship." *Proceedings of the Society for Psychical Research,* 54: 25-157.

Medhurst, R.G., Goldney, K.M., & Barrington, M.R. (Eds.). (1972). *Crookes and the Spirit World.* New York: Taplinger.

Perovsky Petrovo Solovovo, M. (1909). "The Hallucination Theory as Applied to Certain Cases of Physical Phenomena." *Proceedings of the Society for Psychical Research,* 21: 436-482.

Perovsky Petrovo Solovovo, M. (1912). "On the Alleged Exposure of D.D. Home in France." *Journal of the Society for Psychical Research,* 15: 274-288.

Zorab, G. (1971). "Were D.D. Home's 'Spirit Hands' Ever Fraudulently Produced?". *Journal of the Society for Psychical Research,* 46: 228-235.

Zorab, G. (1975). *D.D. Home the Medium: A Biography and a Vindication* ((Unpublished in English; published in Italian as *D.D. Home, il Medium* [Milano: Armenia Editore, 1976]; revised and published in Dutch as *D.D. Home, het krachtigste medium aller tijden...* [Den Haag: Uitgeverij Leopold, 1980].)

6. REFLECTIONS ON SUPER PSI

Endnotes

1   For my attack on memory trace theory, see Braude, 2014, Chapter 1.

2   In Braude, 2003 I call these alternatives the "Usual Suspects."

3   See Braude, 1997, Chapter 6 for more on that topic, and also Eisenbud, 1982.

4   For example, if causation is transitive, then if *A causes B and B causes C, we may say that A causes C.*

5   For more on psi and the nature of abilities, see Braude, 2014.

6   See Braude, 1997 for details.

7   Braude, 1997; Eisenbud, 1982.

8   Braude, 1997, Chapter 1.

9   And as I discuss in much greater detail in Braude, 2003.

10   Murphy & White, 1978.

11   Sturrock, 1987, p. 93.

12   Anderson, 1987, p. 10.

13   But see Eisenbud, 1992, Chapter 14, for a possible example of experimenter influence on the content and presentation of mediumistic communications.

14   See Braude, 1997 for details.

15   For more on St. Joseph, see Braude, 1997; Grosso, 2016.

16   Richet, 1923/1975, p. 491.

17   Beloff, 1985, p. 114.

18   Braude, 2003.

19   See, e.g., Schmidt, 1976, 1981, 1985 and also Braude, 2002.

20   Schmidt, 1974; And see Braude, 2002 for a discussion of task complexity.

21   Braude, 2003; Eisenbud, 1970, 1982, 1992.

22   Basmajian, 1963, 1972; Crabtree, 1993; Frank & Frank, 1991; Gauld, 1992.

23   In Braude, 2003.

24   And for more on the subject, see Braude, 2003.

References

Anderson, R.I. (1987). "Review of S.E. Braude, *The Limits of Influence*." *Parapsychology Review* (Nov.-Dec.): 9-11.

Basmajian, J. (1963). "Control and Training of Individual Motor Units." *Science,* 141: 440–441.

Basmajian, J. (1972). "Electromyography Comes of Age." *Science,* 176: 603–609.

Beloff, J. (1985). "Review of J. Eisenbud, *Parapsychology and the Unconscious*." *Journal of the Society for Psychical Research,* 53: 111-114.

Braude, S.E. (1997). *The Limits of Influence: Psychokinesis and the Philosophy of Science, Revised Edition*. Lanham, MD: University Press of America.

Braude, S.E. (2002). *ESP and Psychokinesis: A Philosophical Examination (Revised Edition)*. Parkland, FL: Brown Walker Press.

Braude, S.E. (2003). *Immortal Remains: The Evidence for Life after Death*. Lanham, MD: Rowman & Littlefield.

Braude, S.E. (2014). *Crimes of Reason: On Mind, Nature & the Paranormal*. Lanham, MD: Rowman & Littlefield.

Crabtree, A. (1993). *From Mesmer to Freud: Magnetic Sleep and the Roots of Psychological Healing*. New Haven: Yale University Press.

Eisenbud, J. (1970). *Psi and Psychoanalysis*. New York: Grune & Stratton.

Eisenbud, J. (1982). *Paranormal Foreknowledge: Problems and Perplexities*. New York: Human Sciences Press.

Eisenbud, J. (1992). *Parapsychology and the Unconscious*. Berkeley, California: North Atlantic Books.

Frank, J.D., & Frank, J.B. (1991). *Persuasion & Healing: A Comparative Study of Psychotherapy*. Baltimore and London: Johns Hopkins University Press.

Gauld, A. (1992). *A History of Hypnotism*. Cambridge: Cambridge University Press.

Grosso, M. (2016). *The Man Who Could Fly: St. Joseph of Copertino and the Mystery of Levitation*. Lanham, MD: Rowman & Littlefield.

Murphy, M., & White, R.A. (1978). *The Psychic Side of Sports*. Reading, MA: Addison-Wesley.

Richet, C. (1923/1975). *Thirty Years of Psychical Research*. New York: Macmillan/Arno Press.

Schmidt, H. (1974). "A Comparison of PK Action on Two Different Random Number Generators." *Journal of Parapsychology,* 38: 47-55.

Schmidt, H. (1976). "PK Effect on Pre-Recorded Targets." *Journal of the American Society for Psychical Research,* 70: 267–291.

Schmidt, H. (1981). "PK tests with pre-recorded and pre-inspected seed numbers.". *Journal of Parapsychology,* 45: 87-98.

Schmidt, H. (1985). "Addition effect for PK on prerecorded targets.". *Journal of Parapsychology,* 49: 229-244.

Sturrock, P.A. (1987). "An Analysis of the Condon Report on the Colorado UFO Project." *Journal of Scientific Exploration,* 1: 75-100.

7. MAKING SENSE OF MENTAL MEDIUMSHIP

Endnotes

1   Readers versed in philosophy might recognize that these assumptions are all challenged by the so-called *new riddle of induction* (sometimes called the "grue paradox").

2   To see how some of the issues are relevant to the problem of survival, see Sudduth, 2016.

3   For a fuller treatment, see Braude, 2005a, 2005b.

4   We'd say that a person's mental properties supervene on the person's physical properties if there can't be a difference in the former without there also being a difference in the latter.

5   See Braude, 1995. Also, Gowler, 1972.

6   For a discussion of the slippery concept of a natural kind, see Stroud, 1996.

7   See, e.g., https://www.radio.com/blogs/alt-producer/orangutan-considered-non-human-person-now-living-florida.

8   Quinton, 1975.

9   See Braude, 2003 for a considerably expanded treatment of the issues.

10   For examples of how anti-survivalists would frame counter-explanations in terms of these abnormal or unusual capacities of the living, see Braude, 2003.

11   Sudduth, 2009, 2014, 2016.

12   See, e.g., Almeder, 1992; Fontana, 2005; Lund, 2009.

13   Eisenbeiss & Hassler, 2006.

14   Neppe, 2007.

15   Ibid., p. 147.

16   See, e.g., Braude, 1997, 2007; Grosso, 2016.

17   Sudduth, 2016.

18   Thomas, 1932, p. 156.

19   Ibid., pp. 157-158.

20   For some detailed examples, see Braude, 2003.

21   But see Braude, 2003.

22   Now in fact deceased.

23   Almeder, 1992.

24   Martin, 1998; Parfit, 1984.

25   Merricks, 2001, p. 197.

26   Corcoran, 2001; Merricks, 2001.

27   Beach, Hebb, Morgan, & Nissen, 1960; Lashley, 1929, 1950.

28   Pribram, 1971, 1977; Pribram, Nuwer, & Baron, 1974.

29   Bennett & Hacker, 2003; Braude, 2014; Bursen, 1978; Heil, 1978; Malcolm, 1977.

30   Bishai, 2000.

31   See, e.g., Edwards, 1996, p. 227.

32   Op. cit., p. 419.

33   Richet, 1924, p. 109.

34   McTaggart, 1930.

35   Ibid., p. 104.

36   Ibid., p. 103.

37   Ibid., p. 105.

38   Ibid., p. 106.

References

Almeder, R. (1992). *Death and Personal Survival*. Lanham, MD: Rowman & Littlefield.

Beach, F.A., Hebb, D.O., Morgan, C.T., et al. (Eds.). (1960). *The Neuropsychology of Lashley: Selected Papers of K. S. Lashley*. New York: McGraw-Hill.

Bennett, M.R., & Hacker, P.M.S. (2003). *Philosophical Foundations of Neuroscience*. Oxford: Blackwell.

Bishai, D. (2000). "Can Population Growth Rule Out Reincarnation? A Model of Circular Migration." *Journal of Scientific Exploration*, 14: 411–420.

Braude, S.E. (1995). *First Person Plural: Multiple Personality and the Philosophy of Mind* (Rev. ed.). Lanham, MD: Rowman & Littlefield.

Braude, S.E. (1997). *The Limits of Influence: Psychokinesis and the Philosophy of Science, Revised Edition*. Lanham, MD: University Press of America.

Braude, S.E. (2003). *Immortal Remains: The Evidence for Life after Death*. Lanham, MD: Rowman & Littlefield.

Braude, S.E. (2005a). "Personal Identity and Postmortem Survival." *Social Philosophy and Policy*, 22 (2): 226-249. Reprinted in E.F. Paul, F.D. Miller, and J. Paul (eds), *Personal Identity*. Cambridge: Cambridge University Press: 226-249.

Braude, S.E. (2005b). "Personal Identity and Postmortem Survival." In E.F. Paul, F.D. Miller & J. Paul (Eds.), *Personal Identity* (22 ed., pp. 226-249). Cambridge: Cambridge University Press.

Braude, S.E. (2007). *The Gold Leaf Lady and Other Parapsychological Investigations*. Chicago: University of Chicago Press.

Braude, S.E. (2014). *Crimes of Reason: On Mind, Nature & the Paranormal*. Lanham, MD:

Rowman & Littlefield.

Bursen, H.A. (1978). *Dismantling the Memory Machine*. Dordrecht, Boston, London: D. Reidel. (Label: 69)

Corcoran, K. (2001). "Physical Persons and Postmortem Survival without Temporal Gaps." In K. Corcoran (Ed.), *Soul, Body, and Survival* (pp. 201–217). Ithaca & London: Cornell University Press.

Edwards, P. (1996). *Reincarnation: A Critical Examination*. Amherst, NY: Prometheus Books.

Eisenbeiss, W., & Hassler, D. (2006). "An Assessment of Ostensible Communications with a Deceased Grandmaster as Evidence for Survival." *Journal of the Society for Psychical Research,* 70: 65-97.

Fontana, D. (2005). *Is There an Afterlife?* Hampshire: O Books.

Gowler, D. (1972). "On the Concept of the Person: A Biosocial View." In R. Ruddock (Ed.), *Six Approaches to the Person* (pp. 37–69). London & Boston: Routledge & Kegan Paul.

Grosso, M. (2016). *The Man Who Could Fly: St. Joseph of Copertino and the Mystery of Levitation*. Lanham, MD: Rowman & Littlefield.

Heil, J. (1978). "Traces of Things Past." *Philosophy of Science,* 45: 60-72.

Lashley, K.S. (1929). *Brain Mechanisms and Intelligence*. Chicago: University of Chicago Press.

Lashley, K.S. (1950). "In Search of the Engram." *Symposia of the Society for Experimental Biology,* 4: 454–482.

Lund, D.H. (2009). *Persons, Souls, and Death: A Philosophical Investigation of an Afterlife*. Jefferson, NC: McFarland.

Malcolm, N. (1977). *Memory and Mind*. Ithaca: Cornell University Press.

Martin, R. (1998). *Self-Concern: An Experiential Approach to What Matters in Survival*. Cambridge: Cambridge University Press.

McTaggart, J.M.E. (1930). *Some Dogmas of Religion*. Bristol: Thoemmes Press.

Merricks, T. (2001). "How to Live Forever without Saving Your Soul: Physicalism and Immortality." In K. Corcoran (Ed.), *Soul, Body, and Survival* (pp. 183–200). Ithaca & London: Cornell University Press.

Neppe, V.M. (2007). "A Detailed Analysis of an Important Chess Game: Revisiting 'Maróczy versus Korchnoi'." *Journal of the Society for Psychical Research,* 71 (3): 129-147.

Parfit, D. (1984). *Reasons and Persons*. Oxford: Oxford University Press.

Pribram, K.H. (1971). *Languages of the Brain*. Englewood Cliffs, N.J.: Prentice Hall.

Pribram, K.H. (1977). "Holonomy and Structure in the Organization of Perception." In U.M. Nicholas (Ed.), *Images, Perception and Knowledge* (pp. 155-185). Dordrecht: Reidel.

Pribram, K.H., Nuwer, M., & Baron, R.U. (1974). "The Holographic Hypothesis of Memory Structure in Brain Function and Perception." In D.H. Krantz, R.C. Luce & P. Suppes (Eds.), *Contemporary Developments in Mathematical Psychology, vol. 2* (pp. 416-467). San Francisco: Freeman.

Quinton, A. (1975). "The Soul." In J. Perry (Ed.), *Personal Identity* (pp. 53–72). Berkeley: University of California Press.

Richet, C. (1924). "The Difficulty of Survival from the Scientific Point of View." *Proceedings of the Society for Psychical Research,* 34: 107–113.

Stroud, B. (1996). "The Charm of Naturalism." *Proceedings and Addresses of the American Philosophical Association,* 70 (2): 43-55.

Sudduth, M. (2009). "Super-Psi and the Survivalist Interpretation of Mediumship." *Journal of Scientific Exploration,* 23 (2): 167-193.

Sudduth, M. (2014). "Is Postmortem Survival the Best Explanation of the Data of Mediumship?" In A.J. Rock (Ed.), *The Survival Hypothesis: Essays on Mediumship* (pp. 40-64). Jefferson, NC: McFarland.

Sudduth, M. (2016). *A Philosophical Critique of Empirical Arguments for Postmortem Survival.* New York and London: Palgrave Macmillan.

Thomas, C.D. (1932). "A Consideration of a Series of Proxy Sittings." *Proceedings of the Society for Psychical Research,* 41: 139–185.

8. CAN THE DECEASED HAVE A PERCEPTUAL POINT OF VIEW?

Endnotes

1   Miller, 1998, p. 480.

2   See Flew, 1976, 1987, and the discussions in Braude, 1993, 2003. Also Almeder, 1992.

3   Fontana, 2005. See Kelly, 2005 for a critical review.

4   Almeder, 1992.

5   Sorry, but the temptation for excessive alliteration was irresistible.

6   See Penelhum, 1970 and Sorabji, 2006 for presentations of the relevant arguments.

7   Sculptor, writer, and keen observer and student of mental mediumship.

8   Troubridge, 1922, p. 369.

9   Ibid.

10   Ibid., pp. 370-371.

11   Ibid., pp. 371-372.

12   Troubridge, 1922, p. 371. See also Salter, 1921, pp. 87ff.

13   On the other hand, philosophers have had plenty to say—both pro and con—about the intelligibility and possibility of disembodied existence. Typically, though, these works proceed without any consideration of the evidence suggesting survival, and sometimes they're adorned with the usual ignorant disparaging references to that material. For example, Blose says that the survival hypothesis "is supported by meager evidence and that from the most disreputable of sources," none of which he bothers to cite (Blose, 1981). At any rate, the philosophical literature on disembodied existence, while extensive, is singularly unhelpful in the present

context. Nevertheless, intrepid readers might wish to investigate, e.g., Everitt, 2000; Gillett, 1986; Hocutt, 1974; Long, 1977; Smart, 1971; Steinberg & Steinberg, 2007; Taliaferro, 1997; Tye, 1983.

14   Price, 1953.

15   "Super psi" is a very unfortunate term which by now may be too well-entrenched to abandon. For a discussion of the problems with that clearly loaded expression, see Chapter 9 and also Braude, 2003. I prefer to follow Michael Sudduth in replacing the term "super psi" with the less prejudicial and clearer "living-agent psi." See Sudduth, 2014, 2016.

16   Price, 1968.

17   Penelhum, 1970.

18   Ibid., p. 25.

19   Ibid., p. 25.

20   Ibid., pp. 25-26.

21   See Aune, 1985 for a nice summary.

22   The debate here also concerns other related issues—for example, whether inner experiences can be known with certainty, or whether they can be described in a way not parasitic on a more fundamental level of description applicable to outer things. But those issues needn't concern us here.

23   For comments on the possibly irreducible nature of paranormal causal connections, see Braude, 1997, 2003.

24   See also Broad, 1953.

25   I'm grateful to Andreas Sommer for reminding me of this.

26   Price, 1940.

27   Ibid., p. 57.

28   Ed Kelly has pointed out to me another intriguing possibility considered by some psychologists—namely, that "ordinary perception is oneiric activity constrained by sensory input" (personal communication, 7/9/2008). This, too, is a topic which, although clearly relevant—and perhaps also happily compatible with Price's suggestion (noted earlier) that mediums dream aloud—goes beyond the scope of the present discussion.

29   For more on the idiosyncratic and highly variable experiences of clairvoyant subjects, see Braude, 2003, Chapter 8.

30   See Braude, 2003.

31   Research for this essay was supported by a grant from the Helen Reeder Foundation. Thanks also to Michael Sudduth, for helpful comments on several of the paper's ancestors.

References

Almeder, R. (1992). *Death and Personal Survival.* Lanham, MD: Rowman & Littlefield.

Aune, B. (1985). *Metaphysics: The Elements.* Minneapolis: University of Minnesota Press.

Blose, B.L. (1981). "Materialism and Disembodied Minds." *Philosophy and Phenomenological Research,* 42 (1): 59-74.

Braude, S.E. (1993). "Review of A. Flew, *The Logic of Mortality.*" *Journal of the American Society for Psychical Research,* 87: 114–117.

Braude, S.E. (1997). *The Limits of Influence: Psychokinesis and the Philosophy of Science, Revised Edition.* Lanham, MD: University Press of America.

Braude, S.E. (2003). *Immortal Remains: The Evidence for Life after Death.* Lanham, MD: Rowman & Littlefield.

Broad, C.D. (1953). *Religion, Philosophy and Psychical Research.* London: Routledge & Kegan Paul. (Originally published in *Philosophy* 24 (1949):, pp. 291-309)

Everitt, N. (2000). "Dualism and Disembodied Existence." *Faith and Philosophy,* 17: 333-347.

Flew, A. (1976). *The Presumption of Atheism.* London: Elek/Pemberton.

Flew, A. (1987). *The Logic of Mortality.* Oxford: Blackwell.

Fontana, D. (2005). *Is There an Afterlife?* Hampshire: O Books.

Gillett, G. (1986). "Disembodied Persons." *Philosophy,* 61 (237): 377-386.

Hocutt, M. (1974). "Armstrong and Strawson on 'Disembodied Existence'." *Philosophy and Phenomenological Research,* 35 (1): 46-59.

Kelly, E.W. (2005). "Review of D. Fontana, *Is There an Afterlife?*". *Journal of Parapsychology,* 69 (2): 390-395.

Long, D.C. (1977). "Disembodied Existence, Physicalism and the Mind-Body Problem." *Philosophical Studies,* 31: 307-316.

Miller, A.R. (1998). "Survival and Diminished Consciousness." *Journal of Philosophical Research,* 223: 479-496.

Penelhum, T. (1970). *Survival and Disembodied Existence.* London: Routledge & Kegan Paul.

Price, H.H. (1940). "Some Philosophical Questions about Telepathy and Clairvoyance." *Philosophy,* 15 (60): 363-385. Reprinted in F.B. Dilley (Ed.), *Philosophical Interactions with Parapsychology.* New York: St. Martin's Press (1995): 35-60.

Price, H.H. (1953). "Survival and the Idea of 'Another World'." *Proceedings of the Society for Psychical Research,* 50: 1–25. Reprinted in J. Donnelly (Ed.), *Language, Metaphysics, and Death.* New York: Fordham University Press: 176-195.

Price, H.H. (1968). "The Problem of Life After Death." *Religious Studies,* 3 (2): 447-459. Reprinted in F.B. Dilley (Ed.), *Philosophical Interactions with Parapsychology.* New York: St. Martin's Press (1995): 221-236.

Salter, M.W.H. (1921). "A Further Report on Sittings with Mrs. Leonard." *Proceedings of the Society for Psychical Research,* 32: 1–143.

Smart, B. (1971). "Can Disembodied Persons Be Spatially Located?". *Analysis,* 31 (4): 133-138.

Sorabji, R. (2006). *Self: Ancient and Modern Insights about Individuality, Life, and Death.*

Chicago: University of Chicago Press.

Steinberg, J.R., & Steinberg, A.M. (2007). "Disembodied Minds and the Problem of Identification and Individuation." *Philosophia*, 35: 75-93.

Sudduth, M. (2014). "Is Postmortem Survival the Best Explanation of the Data of Mediumship?" In A.J. Rock (Ed.), *The Survival Hypothesis: Essays on Mediumship* (pp. 40-64). Jefferson, NC: McFarland.

Sudduth, M. (2016). *A Philosophical Critique of Empirical Arguments for Postmortem Survival.* New York and London: Palgrave Macmillan.

Taliaferro, C. (1997). "Possibilities in Philosophy of Mind." *Philosophy and Phenomenological Research,* 57 (1): 127-137.

Troubridge, U., Lady. (1922). "The Modus Operandi in So-Called Mediumistic Trance." *Proceedings of the Society for Psychical Research,* 32: 344–378.

Tye, M. (1983). "On the Possibility of Disembodied Existence." *Australasian Journal of Philosophy,* 61 (3): 275-282.

9. A GRUMPY GUIDE TO PARAPSYCHOLOGY'S TERMINOLOGICAL BLUNDERS

Endnotes

1   Thouless & Wiesner, 1946, 1948.

2   Palmer, 1988.

3   May, Spottiswoode, Utts, & James, 1995; May, Utts, & Spottiswoode, 1995a, 1995b.

4   Palmer, 1986, 1987, 1992.

5   May, Utts, et al., 1995a, p. 454. In May, Lantz, & Piantineda, 1996, this last phrase is changed to "neutral in that they do not imply mechanisms" (p. 211). Utts, 1996 is more laconic, noting that the terms "extrasensory perception" and "psychokinesis" are to be replaced by "the more neutral terminology" (p. 5) "AC" and "AP." However, she never explains in what respects the newer terms are more neutral.

6   May, Utts, et al., 1995a, p. 454; May, Utts, et al., 1995b, p. 195.

7   Luria, 1987.

8   May, 1996, p. 89.

9   Utts, 1996, p. 5.

10   Ibid., emphasis added.

11   Broad, 1953, 1962.

12   For more on that topic, see Braude, 2014, Chapter 7.

13   We also can't rule out that the percipient's telepathically-influenced experience occurs simultaneously with clairvoyant awareness of the crisis occurring to the agent. In that case, we should be reluctant to consider the incident a case purely of *telepathic* cognition—perhaps GESP [general ESP] cognition instead.

14   Ullman, Krippner, & Vaughan, 2002, p. 125.

15   Ullman et al., 2002, pp. 91ff.

16   Eisenbud, 1992, p. 87.

17   Janet, 1885, 1886; Richet, 1885, 1888. For more details, see Eisenbud, 1992.

18   This is not entirely their fault. Parapsychology, unlike mainstream disciplines, offers very few opportunities to undertake a systematic and comprehensive study of the psi domain before embarking on one's own research.

19   Vasiliev, 1976. For a good discussion of telepathy at a distance, see Eisenbud, 1970, Chapter 5, and Eisenbud, 1992, Chapter 6.

20   See Braude, 2003, for a discussion of these issues.

21   See, e.g., Broad, 1935.

22   Braude, 1997, 2002.

References

Braude, S.E. (1997). *The Limits of Influence: Psychokinesis and the Philosophy of Science, Revised Edition*. Lanham, MD: University Press of America.

Braude, S.E. (2002). *ESP and Psychokinesis: A Philosophical Examination (Revised Edition)*. Parkland, FL: Brown Walker Press.

Braude, S.E. (2003). *Immortal Remains: The Evidence for Life after Death*. Lanham, MD: Rowman & Littlefield.

Braude, S.E. (2014). *Crimes of Reason: On Mind, Nature & the Paranormal*. Lanham, MD: Rowman & Littlefield.

Broad, C.D. (1935). "Normal Cognition, Clairvoyance, and Telepathy." *Proceedings of the Society for Psychical Research*, 43: 397-438. Republished in Broad, C. D. (1953), *Religion, Philosophy and Psychical Research*, London: Routledge & Kegan Paul, pp. 27-67.

Broad, C.D. (1953). *Religion, Philosophy and Psychical Research*. London: Routledge & Kegan Paul. (Originally published in *Philosophy* 24 (1949): pp. 291-309).

Broad, C.D. (1962). *Lectures on Psychical Research*. London: Routledge & Kegan Paul. (Reprinted by Routledge, 2011.)

Eisenbud, J. (1970). *Psi and Psychoanalysis*. New York: Grune & Stratton.

Eisenbud, J. (1992). *Parapsychology and the Unconscious*. Berkeley, California: North Atlantic Books.

Janet, P. (1885). "Note sur quelques phenomènes de somnambulisme." *Revue Philosophique de la France et de l'Etrangere*, 21: 190-198. Trans. "Report on Some Phenomena of Somnambulism." *Journal of the History of the Behavioral Sciences* 4(2): 124-131, 1968.

Janet, P. (1886). "Deuxième note sur le sommeil provoqué à distance et la suggestion mentale pendant l'état somnambulique." *Revue Philosophique de la France et de l'Etrangere*, 22: 212-223. Trans. "Second observation on sleep provoked from a distance and mental suggestion during the somnambulistic state." *Journal of the History of the Behavioral Sciences* 4(3): 258-267, 1968.

Luria, A.R. (1987). *The Mind of a Mnemonist.* Cambridge: Harvard University Press.

May, E.C. (1996). "The American Institutes for Research Review of the Department of Defense's STAR GATE Program: A Commentary." *Journal of Scientific Exploration,* 10: 89–107.

May, E.C., Lantz, N.D., & Piantineda, T. (1996). "Feedback Considerations in Anomalous Cognition Experiments." *Journal of Parapsychology,* 60: 211-226.

May, E.C., Spottiswoode, S.J.P., Utts, J., et al. (1995). "Applications of Decision Augmentation Theory." *Journal of Parapsychology,* 59: 221-250.

May, E.C., Utts, J., & Spottiswoode, S.J.P. (1995a). "Decision Augmentation Theory: Applications to the Random Number Generator Database." *Journal of Scientific Exploration,* 9: 453-488.

May, E.C., Utts, J., & Spottiswoode, S.J.P. (1995b). "Decision Augmentation Theory: Toward a Model of Anomalous Mental Phenomena." *Journal of Parapsychology,* 59: 195-220.

Palmer, J. (1986). "Progressive Skepticism: A Critical Approach to the *Psi* Controversy." *Journal of Parapsychology,* 50 (1): 29-42.

Palmer, J. (1987). "Have We Established *Psi?*". *Journal of the American Society for Psychical Research,* 81 (2): 111-123.

Palmer, J. (1988). "Conceptualizing the Psi Controversy." *Parapsychology Review,* 19 (1): 1-5.

Palmer, J. (1992). "From Survival to Transcendence: Reflections on Psi as Anomalous.". *Journal of Parapsychology,* 56 (3): 229-254.

Richet, C. (1885). "Un fait de somnabulisme à distance." *Revue Philosophique de la France et de l'Etrangere,* 21: 199-200.

Richet, C. (1888). "Expériences sur le sommeil à distance." *Revue de l'hypnotisme,* 2: 225-240.

Thouless, R.H., & Wiesner, B.P. (1946). "On the Nature of Psi Phenomena." *Journal of Parapsychology,* 10: 107-119.

Thouless, R.H., & Wiesner, B.P. (1948). "The Psi Processes in Normal and "Paranormal" Psychology." *Proceedings of the Society for Psychical Research,* 48: 177-196.

Ullman, M., Krippner, S., & Vaughan, A. (2002). *Dream Telepathy: Experiments in Nocturnal Extrasensory Perception.* Charlottesville: Hampton Roads.

Utts, J. (1996). "An Assessment of the Evidence for Psychic Functioning." *Journal of Scientific Exploration,* 10 (1): 3-30.

Vasiliev, L.L. (1976). *Experiments in Distant Influence.* New York: Dutton. (Reprinted as *Experiments in Mental Suggestion* (2002), Charlottesville: Hampton Roads.)

10. A PEIRCING EXAMINATION OF THE PARANORMAL

Endnotes

1   Sebeok, 1981, p. 17.

2   So fallibilists maintain that scientific theories will never be categorically certain; at best they will have some probability of being true. Fallibilism is therefore opposed to *foundationalism*—the view that some domain(s) of inquiry rest on a bedrock of absolute certainty—for example, mathematics, metaphysics, or natural science. Thus, both fallibilism and foundationalism can be held in varying degrees of comprehensiveness. Peirce's fallibilism seemed to extend to every area of inquiry.

3   Gurney, 1887a, 1887b; Myers, 1887; Peirce, 1887a, 1887b.

4   For a description of some of these experiments, see Braude, 1995 and especially Gauld, 1992.

5   James, 1887/1986, p.24.

6   7.612.

7   Throughout this chapter I will follow the standard procedure of citing references from *The Collected Papers of Charles Sanders Peirce,* volumes 1-6 edited by C. Hartshornc and P. Weiss (1931-1935) and volumes 7 and 8 edited by A.W Burks (1958)(Cambridge, Mass: Belknap Press). For example, vol. 7, para. 597 would be 7.597.

8   7.35.

9   Peirce, 1887b, p. 188.

10   Ibid., p. 189.

11   Ibid.

12   Ibid., p. 187.

13   Braude, 1997. And see the Editorial and replies to Reber and Alcock in the *Journal of Scientific Exploration,* vol. 33/4 (2019).

14   Peirce, 1887b, p. 188.

15   See "Psi and the Nature of Abilities" in Braude, 2014a.

16   Braude, 1997.

17   Braude, 2002.

18   Very roughly, the distinction between telepathy and clairvoyance is that the former is extrasensory interaction between two minds, while the latter is extrasensory influence on one's mind of an objective physical state of affairs.

19   Peirce, 1887b, p. 182.

20   James, 1887, p. 26).

21   1.110-1.115.

22   1.110.

23   1.113.

24   Ibid.

25   See Braude, 1997; Grosso, 2016.

26   In 1.115.

27   7.601.

28   Ibid.

29   For careful overviews of the issues, see Braude, 2003; Sudduth, 2016.

30   7.644.

31   Ibid.

32   7.649.

33   7.653.

34   Ibid.

35   7.643.

36   7.675.

37   7.676.

38   7.679.

39   7.680.

40   Ibid.

41   Ibid.

42   7.681.

43   Ibid.

44   Ibid.

45   Braude, 1997.

46   7.687.

47   6.514.

48   See 7.685.

49   6.574 . For a detailed presentation and discussion of Crookes, Slade, and other cases of physical mediumship, see Braude, 1997.

50   6.574.

51   6.575.

52   Ibid.

53   Ibid.

54   Ibid.

55   Ibid.

56   6.587.

57   1.265.

58   Ibid.

59   Ibid.

60   1.331.

61   Ibid.

62   Ibid.

63   6.476

64   Braude, 2003; Sudduth, 2016.

65   6.519.

66   See, e.g., Martin, 1998; Parfit, 1984.

67   6.521.

68   6.550.

69   Ibid.

70   6.551. And see Braude, 1995, for an extended discussion of the concept of a person in connection with multiple personality.

71   See, e.g., Braude, 2003, 2014b; Broad, 1962; Gauld, 1982; Sudduth, 2014, 2016. Also, Chapters 6 and 7 in this volume.

72   6.553.

73   6.555.

74   6.560.

75   6.535.

76   6.537.

77   6.536.

78   For those readers who don't know what abduction is, it's a form of argument sometimes called "inference to the best explanation," and Peirce considered it to be a fundamental feature of pragmatism. Roughly, the form of an abductive argument is as follows:

> Surprising fact C is observed.
> If hypothesis A were true, C would be a matter of course.
> *Therefore*, there is reason to believe that A is true.

79   6.514.

80   Ibid.

81   Ibid.

82   Butler, 1878, Part II, Chapter IV.

83   6.547.

84   7.685.

85   Brent, 1993.

86   Ibid., p. 205.

87   Ibid.

88   Ibid., p. 311.

References

Braude, S.E. (1995). *First Person Plural: Multiple Personality and the Philosophy of Mind* (Rev. ed.). Lanham, MD: Rowman & Littlefield.

Braude, S.E. (1997). *The Limits of Influence: Psychokinesis and the Philosophy of Science, Revised Edition*. Lanham, MD: University Press of America.

Braude, S.E. (2002). *ESP and Psychokinesis: A Philosophical Examination (Revised Edition)*. Parkland, FL: Brown Walker Press.

Braude, S.E. (2003). *Immortal Remains: The Evidence for Life after Death*. Lanham, MD: Rowman & Littlefield.

Braude, S.E. (2014a). *Crimes of Reason: On Mind, Nature & the Paranormal*. Lanham, MD: Rowman & Littlefield.

Braude, S.E. (2014b). "The Possibility of Mediumship: Philosophical Considerations." In A.J. Rock (Ed.), *The Survival Hypothesis: Essays on Mediumship* (pp. 21-39). Jefferson, NC: McFarland.

Brent, J. (1993). *Charles Sanders Peirce: A Life*. Bloomington & Indianapolis: Indiana University Press.

Broad, C.D. (1962). *Lectures on Psychical Research*. London: Routledge & Kegan Paul. (Reprinted by Routledge, 2011.)

Butler, J. (1878). *The Analogy of Religion, Natural and Revealed*. London: George Bell & Sons.

Gauld, A. (1982). *Mediumship and Survival*. London: Heinemann.

Gauld, A. (1992). *A History of Hypnotism*. Cambridge: Cambridge University Press.

Grosso, M. (2016). *The Man Who Could Fly: St. Joseph of Copertino and the Mystery of Levitation*. Lanham, MD: Rowman & Littlefield.

Gurney, E. (1887a). "Remarks on Professor Peirce's Paper." *Proceedings of the American Society for Psychical Research*, 1: 157-180.

Gurney, E. (1887b). "Remarks on Professor Peirce's Rejoinder." *Proceedings of the American Society for Psychical Research*, 1: 286-300.

James, W. (1887). "Review of *Phantasms of the Living*." *Science*, 9 (Jan. 7): 18-20. Reprinted in *The Works of William James: Essays on Psychical Research*. Cambridge: Harvard University Press.

Martin, R. (1998). *Self-Concern: An Experiential Approach to What Matters in Survival.* Cambridge: Cambridge University Press.

Myers, F.W.H. (1887). "Postcript to Mr. Gurney's Reply to Professor Peirce." *Proceedings of the American Society for Psychical Research,* 1: 300-301.

Parfit, D. (1984). *Reasons and Persons.* Oxford: Oxford University Press.

Peirce, C.S. (1887a). "Criticism on 'Phantasms of the Living'." *Proceedings of the American Society for Psychical Research,* 1: 150-157.

Peirce, C.S. (1887b). "Mr. Peirce's Rejoinder." *Proceedings of the American Society for Psychical Research,* 1: 180-215.

Sebeok, T.A. (1981). *The Play of Musement.* Bloomington: Indiana University Press.

Sudduth, M. (2014). "Is Postmortem Survival the Best Explanation of the Data of Mediumship?" In A.J. Rock (Ed.), *The Survival Hypothesis: Essays on Mediumship* (pp. 40-64). Jefferson, NC: McFarland.

Sudduth, M. (2016). *A Philosophical Critique of Empirical Arguments for Postmortem Survival.* New York and London: Palgrave Macmillan.

11. MULTIPLE PERSONALITY AND THE STRUCTURE OF THE SELF

Endnotes

1   Braude, 1995.

2   See also Braude, 2014, Chapter 4.

3   See Crabtree, 1985; Gauld, 1992; Laurence & Perry, 1988.

4   Myers, 1903, p. 3.

5   Ibid., p. 39.

6   Ribot, 1887, p. 20.

7   McDougall, 1938, p. 143.

8   Ibid., p. 144.

9   See Beahrs, 1982, and Watkins & Watkins, 1979, for perhaps the most explicit recent versions of this view.

10   See Braude, 1995.

11   For more on the creativity of dissociative adaptations, see Braude, 2014.

12   For more on the significance and prevalence of animal personalities, see Hendrickson, McCarty, & Goodwin; Smith, 1989.

13   Bliss, 1986, p. 144.

14   See Heil, 1983 for an illuminating discussion of the map analogy.

15   Binet, 1896, pp. 348f.

16   Beahrs, 1983; Hilgard, 1986; Watkins & Watkins, 1979.

17   See Braude, 2003.

18   Braude, 1995, Chapter 7.

19   See Bliss, 1986; Braude, 1995; Putnam, 1989; Ross, 1989, 1997.

20   I consider that position in Braude, 1995, Chapter 6.

21   Puccetti, 1973, p. 351.

22   See, e.g., Pinto et al., 2017

References

Beahrs, J.O. (1982). *Unity and Multiplicity: Multilevel Consciousness of Self in Hypnosis, Psychiatric Disorder and Mental Health.* New York: Brunner/Mazel.

Beahrs, J.O. (1983). "Co-Consciousness: A Common Denominator in Hypnosis, Multiple Personality, and Normalcy." *American Journal of Clinical Hypnosis,* 26: 100–113.

Binet, A. (1896). *Alterations of Personality.* New York: D. Appleton & Co. (Reprinted: University Publications of America/ Washington, DC, 1977).

Bliss, E.L. (1986). *Multiple Personality, Allied Disorders, and Hypnosis.* New York & Oxford: Oxford University Press.

Braude, S.E. (1995). *First Person Plural: Multiple Personality and the Philosophy of Mind* (Rev. ed.). Lanham, MD: Rowman & Littlefield.

Braude, S.E. (2003). *Immortal Remains: The Evidence for Life after Death.* Lanham, MD: Rowman & Littlefield.

Braude, S.E. (2014). *Crimes of Reason: On Mind, Nature & the Paranormal.* Lanham, MD: Rowman & Littlefield.

Crabtree, A. (1985). "Mesmerism, Divided Consciousness, and Multiple Personality." In N.M. Schott (Ed.), *Franz Anton Mesmer und die Geschichte des Mesmerismus* (pp. 133–143). Stuttgart: Franz Steiner.

Gauld, A. (1992). *A History of Hypnotism.* Cambridge: Cambridge University Press.

Heil, J. (1983). *Perception and Cognition.* Berkeley & Los Angeles: University of California Press.

Hendrickson, K.M., McCarty, T., & Goodwin, J.M. *Edgar Allen Poe and the Animal Alters.*

Hilgard, E.R. (1986). *Divided Consciousness: Multiple Controls in Human Thought and Action (expanded edition).* New York: Wiley-Interscience.

Laurence, J.-R., & Perry, C. (1988). *Hypnosis, Will, and Memory: A Psycho-legal History.* New York & London: The Guilford Press.

McDougall, W. (1938). "The Relation Between Dissociation and Repression." *British Journal of Medical Psychology,* 17: 141–157.

Myers, F.W.H. (1903). *Human Personality and its Survival of Bodily Death.* London: Longmans, Green, & Co.

Pinto, Y., Neville, D.A., Otten, M., et al. (2017). "Split brain: divided perception but undivided consciousness." *Brain,* 140 (5): 1231-1237. doi: 10.1093/brain/aww358

Puccetti, R. (1973). "Brain Bisection and Personal Identity." *British Journal for the Philosophy of Science,* 24: 339–355.

Putnam, F.W. (1989). *Diagnosis and Treatment of Multiple Personality Disorder.* New York: Guilford.

Ribot, T. (1887). *Diseases of Personality.* New York: Fitzgerald.

Ross, C.A. (1989). *Multiple Personality Disorder: Diagnosis, Clinical Features, and Treatment.* New York: Wiley.

Ross, C.A. (1997). *Dissociative Identity Disorder: Diagnosis, Clinical Features, and Treatment of Multiple Personality.* New York: John Wiley & Sons.

Smith, S.G. (1989). "Multiple Personality Disorder with Human and Non-Human Subpersonality Components." *Dissociation,* 2: 52–57.

Watkins, J.G., & Watkins, H.H. (1979). "Ego States and Hidden Observers." *Journal of Altered States of Consciousness,* 5: 3–18.

12. THE LANGUAGE OF JAZZ IMPROVISATION

Endnotes

1   That is, alternately improvising in 4- or 8-bar units, typically following the music's chord changes.

2   See the discussion of dramatic appropriateness in Braude, 1997, Chapter 4.

References

Braude, S.E. (1997). *The Limits of Influence: Psychokinesis and the Philosophy of Science, Revised Edition.* Lanham, MD: University Press of America.

Index

CPSIA information can be obtained
at www.ICGtesting.com
Printed in the USA
LVHW021529061120
670969LV00009B/768